EDITED BY ALVERA MICKELSEN

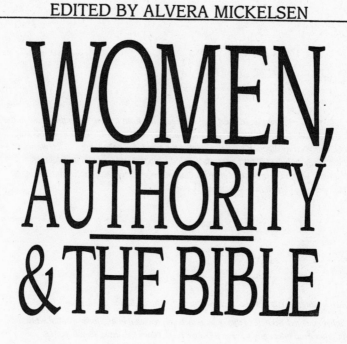

WOMEN, AUTHORITY & THE BIBLE

InterVarsity Press
DOWNERS GROVE, ILLINOIS 60515

The essays and responses contained here were selected from among those presented at the Evangelical Colloquium on Women and the Bible held October 9-11, 1984, in Oak Brook, Illinois. Thirty-six evangelical leaders attended the three-day colloquium, which was open by invitation only, in hopes of furthering dialog on the biblical and hermeneutical issues surrounding women in ministry. Catherine Clark Kroeger, David M. Scholer and Stanley N. Gundry were the conference conveners.

InterVarsity Press is the book-publishing division of InterVarsity Christian Fellowship, a student movement active on campus at hundreds of universities, colleges and schools of nursing. For information about local and regional activities, write Public Relations Dept., InterVarsity Christian Fellowship, 6400 Schroeder Rd., P.O. Box 7895, Madison, WI 53707-7895.

Distributed in Canada through InterVarsity Press, 860 Denison St., Unit 3, Markham, Ontario L3R 4H1, Canada.

Philip Barton Payne's response in chapter 6 is © *P. B. Payne 1984 and used by permission.*

Cover illustration: Roberta Polfus

ISBN 0-87784-608-1

Printed in the United States of America

Library of Congress Cataloging in Publication Data

Women, authority & the Bible.
    Includes bibliographical references.
      1. Women—Biblical teaching—Congresses. 2. Bible—
Evidences, authority, etc.—Congresses. I. Mickelsen,
Alvera. II. Title: Women, authority, and the Bible.
BS680.W7W55   1986   261.8'344   86-7158
ISBN 0-87784-608-1 (pbk.)

17   16   15   14   13   12   11   10   9   8   7   6   5   4   3
99   98   97   96   95   94   93   92   91   90

In memory of
Frank E. Gaebelein

Another piece of unfinished business relates . . . to the place of women in our society. . .   There are areas in which they need greater freedom and more support and recognition. An attitude of male domination rather than mutual submission in Christ still persists among us, and we need to do more about it.—
Frank E. Gaebelein, "Evangelicals & Social Concern," ETS Annual Meeting, December 29, 1981

WHY ARE WE HERE?

I

1

WHY WE'RE HERE

Patricia Gundry

I WOULD LIKE to tell you a story; it's two stories, actually. You people are scholars. Most people don't tell you stories anymore. They just tell you facts. And arguments. Neat and crisp, or fuzzy and half-formed, but almost always the kind of thing you can file in orderly piles in your head, or quickly put in your mental wastebasket.

And that is why I am going to tell you a story instead. Maybe because I know you need to hear stories, and not just arguable facts. When you were little boys and girls you loved stories. You could see the soldiers as you heard the words marching along. You could feel the fear and the relief. Stories bring us to experience and to life.

Once upon a time there was a little boy. He was smart in school. People praised him for being quick to figure things out and remember facts. Most of those people were grown-ups—people with authority. Some people did not like him because they suspected he was smarter than they were. They threw rocks at him sometimes as he walked the path on the way home enjoying the flowers and listening to all the human and animal sounds, and the earth sounds like wind, and feeling the rain.

He found he enjoyed learning more than playing with people who threw rocks. And so more and more he studied and less and less he played with others who could throw rocks.

When this little boy grew bigger he went to a big building where there were lots of books. He stayed there many years. More and more people praised him for his learning. Less and less people carrying rocks could reach him. He forgot about them eventually, and—spending so much time in the big building, where there were no flowers or wind or rain or other children—he forgot them too, almost. In fact, ideas and facts became more important to him than people. He loved ideas like *truth* and *justice,* but when he thought about them they often had no real people in them.

Near the little boy lived a little girl. She also was smart. People praised her, too, for this. A few rocks came her way. But usually, rather than throw rocks, those who did not like her smartness laughed at her, or stranger still, they pretended that she was not there.

When it came time to go from her small school to the large building where the little boy went, the big people did not even see her hand raised asking to go. They did not call her. Finally she went away and did not ask anymore. But she still wanted to learn. So she learned without the help of the big building filled with books and authorities to tell you which ones to read.

She read books she chose for herself. As she walked outdoors, feeling the rain and looking at the flowers, she thought about what she had read and she wondered about things no one had ever told her. She thought of questions and went searching for answers. Where she went to find them was to people she thought might know or have clues that she could trace. And to history books full of stories about people who had wrestled with ideas and questions and had lived and died in the midst of struggling with them or for them.

As she walked and thought and made the beds and stirred the contents of pots and pans on the stove, she would remember those people she had read about and feel surrounded by them. And eventually she wanted to speak for those who had died working for what she could now enjoy, reaching for what she could now grasp. They were ever with her, beseeching her with loving and longing eyes to speak for them, to enjoy for them, to make their efforts bear fruit. To reach for their still-longing hands.

When she did speak and write, others reached out to her and said, tell my story too, I don't have the words or the skill. So she stands before you with their words, words they cannot say because it is too hard to stand before people who have not seen your hand up for too long and cry as you search for words to say. So they told them to me and they wrote them to me, because they thought I would understand.

Some of you are that little boy. You have insulated yourself from the eyes of the people. And some of you are somewhere not far from that situation. It is not that you do not care; it is just that clean, dry, neatly folded facts are less messy and easier to fold up and put away at the end of the day.

But you need to know that facts are not really what this is all about. We use facts, yes, but only as a means to freedom for those who are bound. The facts are our weapons and our tools. The people are the real story, and must be our concern: the people, their pain, their need, and their loss.

I hate pain. So I fight it any way I can. I even know places you can press with your finger and make the pain of your headache go away. I do not like to talk about pain because it is abhorrent to me. I do not like to remind anyone of it who can escape it. But I will make an exception this time. I will talk about it. And I want you to feel it. The reason is that I want you to know it is real. And that you are the only people who can do what needs to be done at this moment to stop it. You have the ways, and fingers to press that I do not have.

In the sixteenth century in Scotland, Eufame MacLayne was pregnant. Most of you don't know what it's like to be pregnant. In the sixteenth century it was even less fun than now. Eufame was very big; she was carrying twins. When labor began, things got rough. Sometimes twins do not come the easy way. They can be in odd positions, causing long and difficult labors. Eufame, for whatever reason, requested a certain painkilling herb be given to her. I do not know how much it helped, but she survived and so did her babies.

However, someone found out what she had done. Painkillers were forbidden to women in childbirth. It was against God's law. He wanted women to suffer in labor. The Bible said so, their punishment for Eve's sin.

So Eufame was brought before those who decided punishment. And they could not of course let her go free (there was also the possibility of witchcraft, you see, because she had not relied solely on the grace of God for relief from her pain). So her babies were taken from her arms and given to someone else's care. Eufame was tied to a stake. Bundles of wood were laid at her feet. Then new mother Eufame was burned alive.[1]

Now that was a long time ago. And maybe you think things like that don't happen anymore. But I can still see Eufame there with tears running down her face, watching her babies leave. And I can hear her groaning in labor and begging for help. I can see the pity in some midwife's eyes as she gives it. I can see the heartless churchmen pronounce her doom in God's name. And *I* cannot forget her. They didn't think Eufame was fully human, because she was a woman. So it was all right to do that to her.

A few years ago I was at a large convention in Detroit. I was one of the token women speakers. (I don't resent that—you can ride the bus with the right token as well as with real money.) Just before I was to leave to go home and bake a birthday cake for one of my sons, a woman stopped me, very hesitantly. She wanted a couple of minutes, she said; something bothered her that I had said in a workshop. So I sat down and listened.

With the iron-controlled intensity of those who are near the breaking point, she told me how she resented my saying we must be gentle and understanding in making changes in the church, that we can open doors a crack in some hearts and that is enough for a beginning. She said she thought I didn't know how difficult it really was or what people like her were experiencing.

She told me of her superhuman attempts to maintain a large and successful youth ministry at her church while sitting under a scathingly antifemale pastor who did nothing but laugh at her honest and sincere questions. She was trying to hold on and wait for change but she was being literally eaten alive by the flames of inner conflict.

This was a twenty-four-carat woman. The kind of person you know right away is competent and good and absolutely reliable and level-headed. She would not exaggerate. If anything, she was unaware of how close she was to flying in a million pieces. She was being burned alive

---

[1]Bernard Seeman, *Man against Pain* (Philadelphia: Chilton, 1962), p. 96; see also A. D. White, *A History of the Warfare of Science with Theology in Christendom*, vol. 2 (New York: Dover Publications, 1960), p. 62.

because she was reaching out for help from those who should be giving it and they were putting her in an impossible position. She was sacrificial material to her church. I will never forget her and sometimes I wonder what has become of her.

Everywhere I go, women like her come to me and tell me their stories. I am quite sure that most of the people in their churches do not know how difficult things are for these women. They have no one to tell. They even suspect that something is wrong with *them*. Like the child who naively believes that his parent abuses him because he is bad, they suspect they are in the wrong somehow, even though all they know of themselves, the Bible and God as friend and Father tells them otherwise.

Their letters to me are poignantly revealing:

It wasn't too long ago that I cried myself to sleep because of an excess accumulation of church-dispensed propaganda on the inferiority of women (oppression in the name of Christ, I call it). I was so devastated that I was beginning to almost believe the Holy Spirit in me was somehow not the same Holy Spirit that indwelled "the brethren," or if otherwise, why am I to keep quiet in the church and not let that Holy Spirit speak through me, simply because I have a woman's body? God surely makes more sense than that. But they pointed to Holy Scripture for "proof" and I was about to sink under it. "Bring your pies, ladies, but leave your ideas at home." Our pastor, in addressing a group of young girls, our nine-year-old daughter among them, laid it on them that they could never be pastors but they could do other things—like bake a pie for a church supper. If I sound angry, I am, but it just seethes inside me. I don't say much here. This is a small town in rural _____, and to challenge the traditions of male dominance here is to rush in where angels fear to tread. But I'm gathering enough strength to question the things they are trying to tell me I must believe. "It will come," they tell me. "You'll understand someday." I think at last I'm beginning to!

It's finally dawned on me that it's not a sin or an act of rebellion for a woman to have a desire for success.

You spoke to that deep split in me that has almost torn me apart over the past few years. .... I have known that I cannot live with honesty or integrity if I refused my relationship with Christ. I also could not live with honesty or integrity within a context of continual putting-down, cutesy jokes about women, and the assumption that women really only live through their husbands and children.

A few months ago I attended an adult Sunday morning class at a large church near my home. They were going to discuss women's equal participation, and a friend who goes there told us we might find it interesting.

The room was completely filled with well-dressed adults from this prosperous, rather intellectual community of Christians. As the hour wore on, man after man spoke his opinions about the pros and cons of allowing women to participate in the higher echelons of leadership. Not one woman said a single word. Not one male commented on the women's silence or asked for their views. Though at least fifty per cent of the group consisted of intelligent female adults, they were as invisible beings to the participants.

I looked around me. The women's faces were drawn tight, their bodies held totally still. The atmosphere was electric with tension, yet they said nothing.

The time for the session was almost gone. I thought I would say something myself, something carefully thought out so as to not be intrusive (after all, I was an outsider), but at least *something*.

I was immediately seized with a terrible fear. I was terrified of speaking out in this group. On some level I knew that I was alien and unwelcome—not because I was a visitor but because I was female. Three years before, in that same building on the Calvin College campus, I had spoken to an audience of 1,200 people without a fraction of the fear I now felt.

Finally I managed, shaking, to choke out that I, as an outside observer, could not help noticing that not a woman there felt safe enough to speak on a subject that greatly affected them all. And that I thought their silence was a profound comment on the subject.

Then another woman, braver than I, spoke eloquently and openly of her concerns. She was interrupted, even as she spoke, by a derogatory comment from the moderator. Later, on the way out of the church, she and I happened to be at the door at the same time. She said to me, "I will never come back here again."

Why am I telling you all this? Do I just want to create some kind of emotional response in you, that dirty tactic of too many sermon preachers who substitute horror and pain for worthwhile content in their sermons to get a crowd response? No, I hope I would never do that.

I am telling you this because I want you to know how crucially important you are to freeing women here and now, women who are the successors to Eufame MacLayne and thousands, maybe millions, like her.

History progresses in stages. You can study it and find that ideas and changes develop in a predictable sequence. We have passed the stage of opening the door a crack, of introducing the subject and getting people to think about it and talk about it. People like me have written books, spoken and taken a few bricks on the chin to do that.

But we cannot do the next item of business on this issue. After the first wave of interest and discussion, people who have a certain credibility, people in intellectual authority, if you will, eventually validate the findings of the ground breakers and present them to their constituency. In any era, in any issue, this happens. And until it does, vulnerable people who have been sensitized to the issue by those who have cracked the door will be slaughtered by the powers that be wherever and whenever the times and conditions are right for it.

I cannot go out and do what only you can do. You are the people with credentials. You are the ones who will make this all respectable. You can do what only you can do.

I was very conscious of my silent sisters while I began my first book, and I remained conscious of them throughout its production. I knew there were thousands, probably millions, who wanted answers to the same questions I had. But they were afraid to ask, embarrassed to pursue the first rebuffs, or they didn't know whom to ask. But they wanted so much to know. Not just because they were curious, but because their whole lives are bounded and boxed in by these questions.

As I continued in my research I became aware of other silent ones who were even more needy and pitiful. I heard the voices of my sisters from the past, crying out to me from page after page of historical narrative and document, saying, speak for us, vindicate our loss and sorrow, we never had a chance to do so.

I want you to know that we are dealing here, now, not with ideas and facts, theories and proofs, but with people. Flesh-and-blood women's lives are being contorted and restricted here and now by a situation we have all inherited from the past.

And I believe that I owe something to those women from the past who were not only deprived of opportunity, enlightenment and joy in participation, but often deprived of their very lives.

If you men and women had been there with the information, the skill and power you now possess, Eufame MacLayne would not have died, nor would the thousands of others who were accused as witches. I owe Eufame something, and I think you do too.

But all we can do now, besides tell her story, is do what we can to make sure the same kinds of ignorance and error that tortured her do not bind and torture women any longer.

Since we are talking about women, and pain, and freedom from that pain, and most particularly about the tools and tool holders to gain that freedom, I would like to tell you one more story. This one is also from the annals of childbirth. I chose that area purposefully because it is uniquely woman's experience. Because it can either be an experience full of promise and joy, or one of pain, sorrow and tragedy. And because all too often *other* people have had the choice as to which it would be for the woman.

So many of the ironies of woman's condition hinge on her capacity to give birth. She presented the body and blood of the Savior to the world, yet she is prohibited from presenting the elements representing that body and blood at the Communion table.

Did the woman say,
When she held him for the first time in the dark dank of a stable,
After the pain and the bleeding and the crying,
    "This is my body; this is my blood"?

Did the woman say,
When she held him for the last time in the dark rain on a hilltop,
After the pain and the bleeding and the dying,
    "This is my body; this is my blood"?

Well that she said it to him then.
For dry old men,
Brocaded robes belying barrenness,
    Ordain that she not say it for him now.[2]

I recognize anger and anguish in that poem. Many people see the anger of women working for freedom and equal opportunity and do not see the anguish it represents. That anger is the only healthy way many women know to express their pain. And it *always* represents pain: personal, searing, emotional pain.

And now the story. In 1569 a French Huguenot physician, named William Chamberlen, landed at Southampton, in England. He proceeded to produce, with the help of his wife, a large family. Two sons—both named Peter, for some reason that escapes me, but called the elder and the younger to differentiate them—became physicians in their father's footsteps.

The two Peters settled in London and became particularly proficient in midwifery. "They then attempted to control the instruction of midwives, and to justify their pretensions, claimed that they could successfully deliver patients when all others failed."[3]

What we know now, but no one else knew then, is that they had good reason to make such claims. They had developed a tool, the obstetrical forceps, that revolutionized difficult deliveries. Forceps of the kind the Chamberlens had developed made it possible to save many mothers and babies who would otherwise have surely died.

But this is not the end of the story. This is only the beginning of the story, because the Chamberlens did not share their invention. No, they secreted it away and protected it for four generations.

The next generation of Chamberlens produced another physician, again, named Peter. This man was well educated, studying at "Cambridge, Heidelberg, and Padua. On his return to London he was elected a Fellow of the Royal College of Physicians."[4] He was very successful,

[2]A poem by Frances C. Frank, appearing in *Women's Network News*, no. 22 (February/March 1980), p. 2; reprinted from the *National Catholic Reporter*.
[3]Louis M. Hellman and Jack A. Pritchard, *Williams Obstetrics* (New York: Appleton-Century-Crofts, 1971), p. 1116.
[4]Ibid.

many of his clients being of the royal family and of the nobility. "Like his father and uncle, he attempted to monopolize control of the mid-wives, but his pretensions were set aside by the authorities. These attempts gave rise to much discussion, and many pamphlets were written about the mortality of women in labor attended by men. He answered them in a pamphlet entitled 'A Voice in Ramah, or the Cry of Women and Children as Echoed Forth in the Compassions of Peter Chamber-len.' "[5]

Did this compassionate, religious man share his lifesaving invention with others at this point? No, he did not.

He, like his grandfather, produced a large family, and three of his sons became physicians. And they (we know why) also specialized in mid-wifery. One of them, Hugh, when forced to leave England for a time because of his political views, attempted to sell the forceps to a French physician, making great claims for its effectiveness. The French physician produced a dwarf woman with a deformity who was in labor. After several hours of effort, Chamberlen admitted defeat, so no sale occurred.

But Hugh did translate this physician's book into English, and in the preface he refers to the secret forceps in this manner, "My father, brothers, and myself (though no one else in Europe as I know) have by God's blessings and our own industry attained to and long practiced a way to deliver women in this case without prejudice to them or their infants."

"Some years later he went to Holland and sold his secret to Roger Roonhuysen. Shortly afterward the Medico-Pharmaceutical College of Amsterdam was given the sole privilege of licensing physicians to practice in Holland, to each of whom, under the pledge of secrecy, was sold Chamberlen's invention for a large sum. The practice continued for a number of years until" two purchasers made the device public.[6] But what they revealed was only *one blade* of the forceps. Either Chamberlen had swindled the original purchaser, or the Medico-Pharmaceutical College had swindled all the rest.

The next generation of Chamberlen physicians consisted of another Hugh. This man was a well-respected, well-educated philanthropist, and a friend of the Duke of Buckingham (who had a statue of Chamberlen

[5]Ibid., pp. 1116–17.
[6]Ibid., p. 1117.

erected in Westminster Abbey). He too kept the forceps a secret, until, when an old man, he finally let the secret leak out.

Before this time, "in 1723, Palfyn, a physician of Ghent, exhibited before the Paris Academy of Medicine a forceps he designated *mains de fer* ["hands of iron"]. It was crudely shaped and impossible to artic-ulate [join the two halves]. In the discussion following its presentation, De La Motte stated that it would be impossible to apply it to the living woman, and added that if by chance anyone should happen to invent an instrument that could be so used, and kept it secret for his own profit, he deserved to be exposed upon a barren rock and have his vitals plucked out by vultures. He had little knowledge that at the time he spoke such an instrument had been in the possession of the Chamberlen family for nearly one hundred years."[7]

I said earlier that there is a historical progression to reforms. First there is need, producing pain. There is a cry for help, but no one comes. Then someone does come. The help that appears is opposed by the establishment and denounced by clerical institutions. Then, those with credentials begin to help also, and change accelerates. Eventually, over time, the changes become established.

Right now we are at the point at which those with credentials can accelerate changes begun already and bring lasting change into actu-ality. It is time for needed help. You are the helpers we need.

I am not asking you to defend, protect and free facts and ideas, but living, breathing women.

They are the sheep of your pasture. Help them be fed the truth.

They are your sisters. Help them to equal access to your joint inher-itance among the saints.

There is but one central and watershed question in this conflicted issue: Are women fully human? All other questions and issues are pe-ripheral to this question.

If the answer is yes, then say a clear yes, not yes, but. . . . Yes, but . . is not yes. It is closer to maybe, or not yet, or even no because yes, but . . . always carries restrictions and prohibitions that intrinsically deny that full humanity expression, opportunity or essence. Usually it denies all three.

---

[7]Ibid., p. 1118.

So if you can say yes, yes, women are fully human creatures, as fully human as men, then be about the business of dealing with those peripheral issues with that central truth in mind.

If women are fully human, then help distinguish between inspiration and interpretation, between cultural and temporal instruction and divine and eternal principle, between doctrinal and practical, between then and now.

If women are fully human, then Augustine was wrong,[8] but you can be right.

If women are fully human, then Aquinas was wrong,[9] but you can be right.

If women are fully human, then Tertullian was wrong,[10] but you can be right.

And you can right those wrongs, not just on paper, or in lectures and books, but in people's lives. Please do it.

Patricia Gundry is an author and lecturer.

---

[8]"The woman herself alone is not the image of God: whereas the man alone is the image of God as fully and completely as when the woman is joined with him." *On the Trinity* 7.7, 10.

[9]"As regards the individual nature, woman is defective and misbegotten, for the active force in the male seed tends to the production of a perfect likeness in the masculine sex, while the production of women comes from a defect in the active force or from some material indisposition, or even from some external influence, such as that of a south wind. . . ." As quoted by Susan G. Bell, *Women from the Greeks to the French Revolution* (Belmont, Calif.: Wadsworth Publishing Co., 1973), p. 122.

[10]"God's sentence hangs still over all your sex and His punishment weighs down upon you. You are the devil's gateway; you are she who first violated the forbidden tree and broke the law of God. It was you who coaxed your way around him whom the devil had not the force to attack. With what ease you shattered that image of God; man! Because of the death you merited, the Son of God had to die." As quoted by Julia O'Faolain and Lauro Martines, eds., *Not in God's Image* (New York: Harper & Row, 1973), p. 132.

RESPONSE
Gretchen Gaebelein Hull

As Patricia Gundry made her presentation, were any of you thinking, "Why the childbirth stories? We're here to discuss theology"? But how we treat people physically is the true measure of our evaluation of their worth. Inhumane treatment makes a statement that all the doctrinal formulations and pious platitudes in the world cannot change. The evils of slavery and apartheid confirm this truth. Any form of physical oppression says, "You don't matter to me."

Yes, But . . .
Patricia Gundry has gone to the core of the "women issue" by asking, "Are women fully human?" Most of my adult life I have been dealing with that "Yes, but . . ." answer. When I initially joined my sisters in asking, "As God calls us, may we too teach and preach and administer to help spread the good news?" the reply was "No." When we asked, as has Gundry, "Why not? Aren't we fully human?" the answer was always "Yes, but. . . ."

Thinking back over my life, I hear the way that answer was given. "Yes, you can aim for a graduate degree in philosophy, but not for one in theology." "Yes, you're an excellent and promising graduate student, but there's no point in continuing your education because Christian wives don't have independent careers." "Yes, you are as competent to teach and lead as any man in our church, but those areas of service are inappropriate for you because you are a woman."

As I yearned to serve alongside my Christian brothers, to stand up for Jesus as a fellow soldier of the cross, I finally became aware that "Yes, but . . ." is really "No." Reading a recent commercial advertisement, I saw confirmation that other people have the same perception. The ad said, "Yesbutters don't just kill ideas. They kill companies, even entire industries."[11] Well, "yesbutters" can also kill the human spirit. When they do, there is pain.

In the poem "Margaret Clitheroe," Gerard Manley Hopkins wrote,
She was a woman, upright, outright;
Her will was bent at God. For that
Word went she should be crushed out flat. . . .[12]
Do you know how it feels to be crushed out flat spiritually? Have advocates of rigid hierarchical roles and patriarchal clericalism considered the pain that women feel when told they cannot freely and fully answer God's call to them? The anguish when a woman is told that her husband can negate a vow she made to the Lord? The agony when she reads that Eve's frailty disqualifies all women for all time?

How many people are aware of the intense inner struggle a woman goes through after her spirit has been touched at a meeting or through a Bible passage, and she receives a call to ministry, only to be told, "You can't serve in that capacity because you are a woman"? There is guilt because she has suppressed her call. There is frustration, even anger, with those who have denied her call. There is deep sorrow at being considered forever barred from answering that call.

Traditionalists say of a woman's call to mutuality in ministry that she is deluded or disobedient, probably influenced by that current catch phrase, "secular humanism."[13] Since this woman may also have heard that "God will not frustrate desires of his making," she is left to agonize over the question "Is my call from God or from Satan?"

I know, because I had to search my soul for the answer to that. For my search, God blessed me with a father, Frank Gaebelein, who believed in mutual submission in marriage and who was open enough to rethink

---

[11]General Electric advertisement, *New York Times* (September 26, 1984).

[12]Gerard Manley Hopkins, *Poems and Prose* (Harmondsworth, Middlesex: Penguin Books, 1983), p. 79.

[13]A. Duane Litfin, "Do Biblical Feminists Have a Point?" *Moody Monthly* (December 1979), pp. 20-23. This position does not deal with a biblical feminist like me, who fully accepts the inspiration of all the Pauline passages and does not try to "erase" them but rather sees them as a "hard problem" yet to be resolved. As a conservative biblical feminist, I fully accept God's authority and therefore look to his atoning power to effect my complete redemption. I believe this power saves me "to the uttermost" (Heb 7:25) and assures my full standing with all the family privileges of an "heir of God and joint-heir with Christ" (Rom 8:16-17).

and then affirm women's ordination. How blessed I have been to have a husband who encourages me in ministry, and how fortunate I am to have a family who rejoiced when, at the age of 50, I was ordained an elder in the Presbyterian Church.

I now rejoice with other women whose hurts are being healed, as they too move out into freedom of ministry. Last year a woman seminarian under care of our presbytery was asked, "Why do you seek ordination to the pastorate?" Her reply warmed my heart. She had for years been a volunteer at the nearby Presbyterian Home for the Aged, then joined the paid staff and now—at about age forty—felt called to offer full pastoral care to the elderly. Who could question her proven love for those who are often so unlovely? In the light of Romans 14:4, who would dare deny her call to serve them as their ordained pastor? Who would dare to say she *could not* be in God's will?

But there are still many women being crushed flat by tradition, and I grieve for my sisters whose hurts are not yet healed. I grieve that today the unresolved "women question" is crippling the body of Christ.

Are Women Fully Redeemed?

As we explore the tension between the traditional and egalitarian approaches to this issue, we must remember that Christian discipleship is not a matter of role playing. We are either disciples of Christ or we are not. The enemy of the cross does not see the traditionalists' contrived distinction between status and role. From the day Saul imprisoned both female and male disciples, to the day when Betty as well as John Stam died for Christ, to the present day as women and men are persecuted equally for their faith, those outside the body have always seen its members as equal disciples.

How sad that *within* the body the inequity occurs. We have shared with you the pain that discrimination causes. Now we ask you to help relieve that pain as you examine the theological implications of the traditional answer, "Yes, but. . . ." So I suggest that we go further than Gundry did and ask this question: "Are women fully redeemed?"

Jesus himself said of his redemptive act, "It is finished." Yet the traditionalists qualify that by saying to women who desire full participation within the body of Christ, "Yes, but. . . ." The traditionalists' qualification is twofold: first, yes, you are redeemed, but you are permanently flawed because of Eve's frailty;[14] second, yes, you are redeemed, but because of your flaw you must work out your salvation through a certain role.[15]

How those two answers limit the substitutionary atonement of Christ! Whatever the Pauline references to Genesis 2 and 3 mean, those references cannot mean that women must remain permanently flawed, for

---

[14]In articles on 1 Timothy, the following commentators indicate this first qualification of women's redemption: (1) "Paul makes one further point. It was the woman who was deceived by Satan and who disobeyed God. . . . Since she was so easily deceived, she should not be trusted as a teacher"—Ralph Earle, in *The Expositor's Bible Commentary*, vol. 11 (Grand Rapids, Mich.: Zondervan, 1978), p. 362; (2) "The tragedy of the Fall established the general truth that a woman is more easily deceived than a man: so it is out of place for her to take the lead in settling either doctrine or practice for the Christian community"—A. M. Stibbs, in *The New Bible Commentary: Revised* (Grand Rapids, Mich.: Eerdmans, 1979), p. 1171; (3) "The woman in succumbing to deception revealed a tendency which disqualifies for leadership"—Alan G. Nute, in *The New Layman's Bible Commentary* (Grand Rapids, Mich.: Zondervan, 1979), p. 1556; (4) "It is difficult to avoid the conclusion that Paul cites Eve's failure as exemplary and perhaps causative of the nature of women in general and that this susceptability to deception bars them from engaging in public teaching"—Douglas J. Moo, "1 Timothy 2:11-15: Meaning and Significance," *Trinity Journal* (Spring 1981), p. 70. Since most of these writers also admit that Adam's disobedience made him as culpable as, or more so than, Eve, this begs the question: Why do they disqualify women forever from full ministry, and not men? Why does Christ's sacrifice fully restore the disobedient man but not the deceived woman?

[15]In comments on 1 Timothy 2:15, the following writers indicate this second qualification of women's redemption: "The wife may find both physical health and a higher spiritual state through the experience of bearing and rearing children" (Earle, p. 362). "The concluding sentence indicates that each particular woman must actively do in order to experience the blessings of salvation in relation to the discharge of her function of motherhood" (Stibbs, p. 1171). "The realization of (woman's) noblest instincts lies in the realm of motherhood (NEB), in which, provided 'she continues in faith and love and holiness, with modesty' she will know the salvation which is 'achievement' in its highest sense. Her greatest work will ever be in the home, and her profoundest influence in the moulding of the children she bears" (Nute, p. 1556). Of various options in interpreting 1 Timothy 2:15, Moo says this is to be preferred: "It is not through active teaching and ruling activities that Christian women will be saved, but through faithfulness to their proper role, exemplified in motherhood" (p. 71). "Maintaining their proper role will also, finally, insure [women's] participation in the eschatological salvation" (p. 73). "It is in devoting herself to such activities consonant with her created role that the Christian woman experiences the salvation to which she has been called" (p. 83). "Paul adds in verse 15 that [woman] is preserved for a contribution to the Christian cause through her divinely appointed function as child-bearer (and rearer), a function to be accompanied by a godly life"—Walter W. Wessel, "1 Timothy" in *The Biblical Expositor* (Philadelphia: A. J. Holman, 1973), p. 1139. These writers might ponder their insensitivity to both single and childless women, as well as their implication that a biological function is necessary to "complete" the salvation process.

that would mean that Christ's shed blood is not powerful enough to cleanse them and make them a new creation. Those passages cannot mean that women are forever restricted in role because then Christ does not want to make them full children of God.

Can Jesus fully restore me, a woman? Of course! Surely John 1:12-13, Romans 1:16-17; 5:12-21, along with 2 Corinthians 5:17 and Hebrews 7:25 apply to women as well as to men. Does Jesus *want* to restore me fully? Of course! To all who came to Jesus for healing, he said, "I will." As recorded in John 6:37, he said, "I won't turn away anyone who comes to me."

The Bible tells me that Jesus *can* save me and Jesus *wants* to save me. Therefore, redeemed women are heirs of God and joint-heirs with Christ. Sisters can enter into that inheritance equally with brothers and can share equally in its administration.

Yes, the Pauline "hard passages" *are* a genuine problem that needs our full attention. But those who affirm the efficacy of Christ's redemptive act must reject the traditionalist approach because it leaves *women only* on a works basis, salvation through role,[16] and creates for *women only* this dreadful uncertainty: "If I, a woman, am so flawed that Christ cannot or will not save me fully in this life, how can I be sure of my completed salvation in the next?".

So, please, think carefully about that answer, "Yes, but. . . ." I suggest that we go further than Gundry as we consider "Yes, but . . . what?" We can no longer ignore what seems to many to be the underlying problem. If we let the answer remain "Yes, woman is equal in the sight of God, but she is limited in the sight of man," we are really saying that it is not Christ who has the problem with woman, but her brother who does not want her fully restored, who does not want her joining hands with him in mutual ministry.

Consider the parable of the good Samaritan. "Do you love your Christian sister as yourself? She *is* your neighbor." So many sisters are spiritually wounded, lying by the roadside, robbed of their inheritance as children of God. Because they have desired to claim their full legacy, they have felt the pain of personal rejection, job insecurity, academic

---

[16]I keep returning to the question: if Christ can redeem the total depravity of humankind's sinful nature, can he not redeem any defect of my sex? If my salvation is "Christ *plus* working at a female role," then surely I join all women in being most miserable.

hostility or even theological ostracism.

Do you see their hurts? Will you help bind up their wounds? So many are passing by on the other side. Passing by is a way of saying, "You don't really matter. You aren't fully human."

In Jesus' parable, those who passed by were the professional clergy and theologians of their day. The one who stopped to care was someone whom those elite professionals considered a lesser human, but he stopped because an outcast knows what it is like to have hurts ignored.

I am grateful for people brave enough and open enough to come to a colloquium like this one. But if you stop to care, to listen to the hurt, to begin to bind up the wounds, you also risk becoming an outcast.

If you can affirm the full humanity and therefore the full redemption of women, if you can offer women the right hand of fellowship and accept women as equal children of God with equal inheritance rights, you must risk being "written off" by the traditionalists. But whatever the risk, your sisters lying there in pain *do* matter and, if you stop, you will find that their pain is your pain, because the whole body is hurting until this hard problem is resolved.

If you can affirm that within the body of Christ the position, the spiritual status, of men and women is equal, please help us stop this game of role playing. Christian brothers, let women—who are bone of your bones and flesh of your flesh—be welcomed to take their place as equal partners.

If you rejoice with us that the risen Savior can and does redeem sisters as equally and as fully as brothers, then—for Christ's sake—don't pass by on the other side any longer.

Gretchen Gaebelein Hull is a writer and conference speaker.

BIBLICAL AUTHORITY

II

2

BIBLICAL AUTHORITY & INTERPRETATION: THE TEST CASE OF WOMEN'S ROLE IN THE CHURCH & HOME UPDATED

Robert K. Johnston

IN 1979 I published a brief volume entitled *Evangelicals at an Impasse: Biblical Authority in Practice.*[1] One chapter was entitled "The Role of Women in the Church and Family: The Issue of Biblical Hermeneutics."[2] To this topic I want to return.

How Can Biblical Authority Be Maintained?

The question I addressed in 1979 was this: "How can evangelicals maintain their theoretical paradigm of biblical authority while subscribing to contradictory positions on a variety of significant theological issues," including the role of women?[3] The disparate positions within evangelicalism concerning women seemed to challenge the very nature and efficacy of biblical authority. I wrote: "If evangelicals are to move beyond their current impasse, a clarification concerning their method of understanding Scripture must be made. For behind the apparent differences in approach and opinion regarding the women's issue are opposing

---

[1] Robert K. Johnston, *Evangelicals at an Impasse: Biblical Authority in Practice* (Atlanta: John Knox Press, 1979).

[2] The chapter first appeared in slightly revised form as "The Role of Women in the Church and Home: An Evangelical Testcase in Hermeneutics," in *Scripture, Tradition, and Interpretation,* ed. W. Ward Gasque and William Sanford LaSor (Grand Rapids, Mich.: Eerdmans, 1978), pp. 234–59.

[3] Johnston, *Evangelicals at an Impasse,* p. 50.

principles for interpreting Scripture—i.e., different hermeneutics. Here is the real issue facing evangelical theology as it seeks to answer the women's question."[4]

I suggested eleven interpretive principles that could be used by those seeking biblical answers to such questions as women's place in marriage and in the church:[5]

1. A text must be treated within its full unit of meaning (e.g., the discussion of women in Eph 5 begins with v. 21).

2. Some translations must be corrected for their sexist bias (e.g., 1 Tim 3:1 KJV, "if a man . . .").

3. The literary form of a passage must be understood if it is to be adequately interpreted (e.g., 1 Tim is Paul's letter to Timothy as he is sent to Ephesus).

4. The historical context of a passage helps the interpreter understand both the function and the meaning a text had in its own day (e.g., texts such as Sirach 42:13-14 concerning a woman's shame help us understand the liberating force of Jesus' words and actions; the situation of women in Ephesus with regard both to schooling and the mystery cults sheds light on 1 Tim).

5. The immediate context of a passage should be considered before one looks at other parallel texts (e.g., 1 Cor 14:40 is more helpful in interpreting 1 Cor 14:34 than 1 Tim 2:11-14).

6. The author's explicit intention, methodology, theology and practice, as understood in other biblical texts, can provide helpful interpretive clues (e.g., Paul's specific advice concerning women needs to be understood in light of his larger oeuvre).

7. The Bible has an overarching consistency despite its multiple theological foci. Thus, all interpretations of given texts can be productively correlated with wider biblical attitudes, statements, themes and descriptions (e.g., Mt 20:25-28 provides insight into Jesus' attitude toward authority and is useful in understanding Eph 5:25-33).

8. Insight into texts that are obscure must be gained from those that are plain (e.g., the difficult text in 1 Tim 2 needs to be read in the light of both the Genesis creation texts and Gal 3:28, which describes rela-

---

[4]Ibid.
[5]Ibid., pp. 69-75.

tionships in the new creation).

9. Scripture should be read in faith for faith (i.e., a controlled subjectivity is our goal).

10. Interpreters of Scripture should seek the help of the Christian community, past and present, in order that insights can be shared, humility fostered, and biases of culture and theological tradition overcome (e.g., the history of biblical interpretation with regard to slavery—Eph 6:5-8, Col 3:22-25, 1 Pet 1:18-25—should suggest the continuing possibility of cultural and personal bias).

11. Scriptural interpretation must allow for continuing actualization as necessary implications are drawn out (cultural pressure can be the occasion for renewed biblical reflection and debate).

I still believe these principles to be useful within the discussion of women's rightful roles. Moreover, these principles are typical of those expressed more widely within evangelicalism. All who have recognized the need for more than a surface reading of the text have posited (or at least made use of) a similar set. I personally believe such guidelines lead the biblical interpreter to posit an egalitarian understanding of male and female relationships. Yet many evangelicals using these or similar exegetical guidelines come to differing conclusions.[6] Let me give two examples.

In the spring of 1980 Douglas Moo wrote an article in the *Trinity Journal* entitled "I Timothy 2:11-15: Meaning and Significance." Moo argued that, in all too many cases, a superficial and arbitrary exegesis of relevant New Testament passages was found in the contemporary discussion over the role of women in Christian ministry. He lamented the fact that even when the study was more thorough, there was a failure to come to agreement on both the meaning and the significance of the texts, even by those scholars who held a similar view of Scripture's authority and interpretive procedures. Moo, therefore, attempted a thorough interpretation of the 1 Timothy 2 text.[7] After a detailed

---

[6]See also A. Duane Litfin, "Evangelical Feminism: Why Traditionalists Reject It," *Bibliotheca Sacra* 136 (July-September 1979): 258-71; Douglas Moo, "I Timothy 2:11-15: Meaning and Significance," *Trinity Journal* I (Spring 1980): 62-83; James B. Hurley, *Man and Woman in Biblical Perspective* (Grand Rapids, Mich.: Zondervan, 1981); John R. W. Stott, *Culture and the Bible* (Downers Grove, Ill.: InterVarsity Press, 1979).

[7]Moo, "I Timothy 2:11-15," p. 62.

analysis of the text's meaning (for its own day), he summarized its significance (for our own day):[8] "The results of the exegetical investigation carried out in Part I must stand as valid for the church in every age and place: Women are not to teach men nor to have authority over men because such activity would violate the structure of created sexual relationships and would involve the woman in something for which she is not suited."[9]

Moo's conclusion failed to create consensus, producing in the pages of *Trinity Journal* itself a lengthy challenge by Philip B. Payne. Payne argued that 1 Timothy 2:11-15 "does not provide a solid basis for excluding women from positions of teaching or authority in the church." The situation in Ephesus demanded that Paul restrict the activity of women there, but Paul does not extrapolate to say that women should never teach or have authority.[10] Why this fundamental difference in perspective between these two evangelical interpreters? Is there a hermeneutical issue at stake, or merely a lack of clarity on one or the other's part?[11]

On a denominational level, the same contradictory conclusions based on similar commitments to biblical authority and hermeneutical rigor can be illustrated by position papers drawn by the Christian Reformed Church, on the one hand, and by the Evangelical Covenant Church, on the other. In 1981 the Synod of the Christian Reformed Church concluded that the question of women's rightful service in church office could not be answered without an understanding of the scriptural notion of headship in 1 Corinthians 11 and elsewhere. Thus a committee was appointed that brought back to the synod in 1984 a majority report

---

[8]See also Walter Kaiser, Jr., "Legitimate Hermeneutics," in *Inerrancy*, ed. Norman L. Geisler (Grand Rapids, Mich.: Zondervan, 1979), pp. 116-47. Kaiser seeks to maintain "the important distinction [adopted from E. D. Hirsch] between meaning (that *single* idea represented by the text *as meant by the human author* who received God's revelation) and significance (which represents a relationship that exists between that single meaning and the reader, a situation, or an idea)."

[9]Moo, "I Timothy 2:11-15," p. 82.

[10]Philip B. Payne, "Libertarian Women in Ephesus: A Response to Douglas J. Moo's article, 'I Timothy 2:1-15: Meaning and Significance,' " *Trinity Journal* 2 (Fall 1981): 169-97.

[11]For a similar impasse, see the series of dialogs between Alvera and Berkeley Mickelsen, who favor women in ministerial leadership, and John Piper, who opposes it, which appeared over several months in the winter and spring of 1984 in *The Standard,* the official magazine of the General Conference Baptist Church.

which declared "that 'the headship principle,' which means that the man should exercise primary leadership and direction-setting in the home, in the church, and in society in general, is a creational norm recognized in both the Old and the New Testament."[12] The conclusion, therefore, was that women may not be ordained as ministers, elders or evangelists, although they should be allowed to serve in a nonleadership capacity as deacon.

The Board of the Ministry of the Evangelical Covenant Church, on the other hand, affirmed the opposite conclusion at its June 1984 meeting, adopting as a working paper a report it commissioned, entitled "A Biblical and Theological Basis for Women in Ministry."[13] The report argued for a legitimate biblical and theological basis for women in ordained ministry (it discussed Genesis, Jesus' actions, the role of women in the early church, the teachings and descriptions of Paul, a biblical notion of authority, a theology of the priesthood of all believers, an understanding of ministry based on gifts and a recognition that Christian doctrine has always developed over time).

Why Are Evangelicals Divided?

Given this continuing debate over egalitarian and traditionalist positions, I would now formulate a different question concerning evangelical perspectives on women. Rather than question *how* evangelicals can maintain their (our) commitment to biblical authority, I would now ask *why* evangelicals cannot come to agreement on biblical interpretation, given their common commitment to the Bible's full authority. With a growing acceptance of the need for careful interpretation according to accepted hermeneutical procedures, why are evangelicals unable to adjudicate their differences concerning the role of women in the church and home? My question has moved from a primary focus on biblical authority (How can it be maintained?) to a focus on biblical interpretation (What is behind our continuing inability as evangelicals to agree?).

---

[12]Quoted by Nicholas Wolterstorff, "On Keeping Women Out of Office: The CRC Committee on Headship," *The Reformed Journal* 34 (May 1984): 8.

[13]"A Biblical and Theological Basis for Women in Ministry," a position paper of the Board of the Ministry, the Evangelical Covenant Church. This paper was drafted by Klyne Snodgrass, David Scholer, Robert K. Johnston and Jean Lambert.

A number of answers suggest themselves. Geoffrey Bromiley, in his article on biblical interpretation for *The Expositor's Bible Commentary*, enumerates residual problems that militate against a beneficial use of the norm of biblical authority, even by those subscribing to valid principles of interpretation.[14]

1. The incompleteness of any interpreter's knowledge makes all interpretations reformable.

2. The knowledge available suggests different but equally valid possibilities of understanding.

3. It is unavoidable that interpreters will draw the line differently between what has enduring validity and what has more limited applicability, and there is no evident basis for an irrefutable ruling between the options.

4. It is difficult to judge what needs cultural transplantation and what is transcultural, what is temporary or indifferent and what is essential.

5. Although Scripture must be interpreted in its unity, this can be viewed very differently by interpreters depending on their theological perspective.

6. There is the persistent personal problem of sin, which inclines the reader against a true objectivity, receptivity and reorientation.

All these limitations find ready illustration in the continuing spate of evangelical literature on women's role in the church and family. Basic to each, moreover, is the more central issue: *the role of the reader/ interpreter in the hermeneutical process*. It is the reader who uses incomplete knowledge as the basis of judgment. It is the reader who chooses between equally valid possibilities based on personal preference. It is the reader who develops criteria for what is universal and what is culturally specific, what is translatable and what is transcultural. It is the reader who brings to a text a specific understanding of Scripture's overarching unity. It is the reader who finds it difficult to remain vulnerable to the text as it confronts Christian and pagan alike.

Yet evangelicals, in their desire to escape the supposed relativity of such reader-oriented perspectives, have too often attempted to hide themselves behind the veneer of objectivity. They have failed to take

---

[14]Geoffrey W. Bromiley, "The Interpretation of the Bible," in *The Expositor's Bible Commentary*, vol. 1, ed. Frank E. Gaebelein (Grand Rapids, Mich.: Zondervan, 1979), pp. 78-79. (The list is a paraphrase of Bromiley's discussion.)

seriously biblical hermeneutics' "second horizon" (the phrase owes its origin to Gadamer and is used by Anthony Thiselton in his major work, *The Two Horizons*).[15] The horizon of the reader is as crucial as the horizon of the author, if an adequate biblical interpretation is to be forthcoming. Failing to recognize this, the evangelical has too seldom allowed the Word of God to come as an *adversarius noster*, our adversary, to use a concept from Martin Luther. Scripture "does not simply confirm and strengthen us in what we think we are and as what we wish to be taken for."[16] At least it should not! Unfortunately, we as evangelicals have learned how to read the Bible and interpret its texts in such a way as to remain complacent to God's Word as it challenges *our* particular human situation. A reader-sensitive hermeneutic is the first step in changing this.

A New Hermeneutic

A reader-sensitive hermeneutic remains a highly dubious procedure within evangelicalism. Clark Pinnock, for example, believes that the current trend in the wider church to relate theology to present-day concerns is a "recipe for Scripture twisting on a grand scale."[17] R. C. Sproul argues for "an objective understanding of Scripture" in which the biblical interpreter reads "without mixing in his own prejudices."[18]

Walter Kaiser, in his article "Legitimate Hermeneutics," is even more pointed. Following E. D. Hirsch, he distinguishes between *meaning* (going through the text to that single idea that was meant by the human author) and *significance* (the relationship between that single meaning and the reader). "To interpret, we must in every case reproduce the sense the Scriptural writer intended for his own words." To turn to the reader is to adopt neo-orthodox or liberal perspectives.[19]

Similarly, David Wells argues for theology's twin task of "decoding" (of discovering what God has said in and through Scripture) and of

[15]Anthony C. Thiselton, *The Two Horizons* (Grand Rapids, Mich.: Eerdmans, 1980).

[16]Gerhard Ebeling, *Introduction to a Theological Theory of Language* (London: Collins, 1973), p. 17; quoted by Thiselton, p. xx.

[17]Clark Pinnock, "How I Use the Bible in Doing Theology," in *The Use of the Bible in Theology: Evangelical Options*, ed. Robert K. Johnston (Atlanta: John Knox Press, 1985).

[18]R. C. Sproul, *Knowing Scripture* (Downers Grove, Ill.: InterVarsity Press, 1977), pp. 39, 105.

[19]Kaiser, "Legitimate Hermeneutics," pp. 118, 147.

"encoding" (of clothing that conceptuality in fabric native to our own age). Although theology must take both tasks seriously, our basic understanding of doctrine should be derived from Scripture without reference to contextualization. Context is what changes doctrine into theology; doctrine, on the other hand, is precontextual.[20] Or is it? Bromiley's cautions would have us think otherwise.

Can we neatly separate the two hermeneutical horizons and operate within them independently? For example, can we distinguish "meaning" and "significance" as Douglas Moo attempts in his article on 1 Timothy 2? By what criteria does he choose among competing options? How does he fill in matters of incomplete knowledge? Are his lines between the culturally specific and the universal derived solely from internal criteria? Evangelicals such as Anthony Thiselton, Harvie Conn, René Padilla, Charles Kraft and William Dyrness think not, and they argue instead for a hermeneutical circulation between text and reader.[21] Stephen C. Knapp recognizes in the "second horizon" a "needed corrective to traditional evangelical hermeneutics":

> Theology (and exegesis) is inevitably influenced by the ideological, cultural, and socio-political values and commitments of the interpreter/theologian. Standard evangelical textbooks on hermeneutics have been next to silent on this critical dimension of interpretation. The emergence of the "theology of liberation" and other distinctive theological and interpretative approaches from the Third World as well as from women, Blacks, and other oppressed groups in the U.S.

---

[20]David F. Wells, "The Nature and Function of Theology," in Johnston, ed.

[21]Thiselton, *The Two Horizons,* cf. Anthony C. Thiselton, "Understanding God's Work Today," in *The Lord Jesus Christ,* vol. 1, *Obeying Christ in a Changing World,* ed. John R. W. Stott (Glasgow: Collins/Fountain Books, 1977); Harvie M. Conn, "Contextualization: Where Do We Begin?" in *Evangelicals and Liberation,* ed. Carl E. Armerding (Grand Rapids, Mich.: Baker, 1977), pp. 90–119; cf. Harvie M. Conn, *Eternal Word and Changing Worlds: Theology, Anthropology, and Mission in Trialogue* (Grand Rapids, Mich.: Zondervan, 1984); C. René Padilla, "Hermeneutics and Culture—A Theological Perspective," in *Down to Earth: Studies in Christianity and Culture,* ed. John R. W. Stott and Robert Coote (Grand Rapids, Mich.: Eerdmans, 1980), pp. 63–78; cf. C. René Padilla, "Evangelism and the World," in *Let the Earth Hear His Voice,* ed. J. D. Douglas (Minneapolis: Worldwide Publications, 1975), pp. 116–46; Charles H. Kraft, *Christianity and Culture* (Maryknoll, N.Y.: Orbis, 1979), "Theology and Theologies," *Theology News and Notes* 18, nos. 2 and 3 (June and October 1972), "Christian Conversion or Cultural Conversion," *Practical Anthropology* 10 (1963): 179–87; William A. Dyrness, "How Does the Bible Function in the Christian Life," in *The Use of the Bible in Theology,* Johnston, ed.

forces, it seems to me, something approaching a major adjustment in standard hermeneutical approaches. It exposes the myth of objective exegesis and the tendency to equate any fruit of exegesis or any theological construction with revelation itself. For evangelicals, who have traditionally found in the doctrine of inerrancy a final refuge against theological relativism, this new development would appear to have significant implications and could signal the beginning of a new phase in the discussion of Scripture.[22]

In his Olivier Beguin Memorial Lectures in Australia, delivered during the spring of 1979, John Stott argued similarly to Knapp, even while illustrating his lecture with conclusions concerning women's roles that seem ironically wedded to traditional modes of interpretation and practice. For all of us, at one time or another, our theory is better than our practice. Stott recognized that an inspired text is of little value if we cannot understand it. To read it aright, Stott believed both "the Old Hermeneutic" (which focused on the first horizon) and "the New Hermeneutic" (which recognizes the need for a "fusion of horizons" between biblical times and our own) were necessary. To illustrate his point, he discussed the place and ministry of women in modern society. He bemoaned "the sad polarization in the Christian community on this issue." He continued, "Some, whenever they find biblical teaching couched in cultural terms other than their own, declare the teaching irrelevant because the culture is alien. Others make the opposite mistake and invest both the kernel of the teaching and the cultural shell with equal normative authority. The more judicious way, however, is to preserve the inner substance of what God is teaching or commanding, while claiming the liberty to reclothe it in modern dress." Stott thus argued it was wrong to deny God-given differences between men and women. It was equally wrong to require veils and silence of women in all churches. Instead we should affirm male and female equality, without confusing this with identity. In creation, God established the two equally in his image but gave to man a loving, caring headship that enables both men and women to fulfill themselves.[23]

John Stott writes out of an evangelical Anglican perspective that has

---

[22]Stephen C. Knapp, "A Preliminary Dialogue with Gutierrez: A Theology of Liberation," in *Evangelicals and Liberation,* Armerding, ed., p. 18.
[23]Stott, *Culture and the Bible,* pp. 19, 24-32.

traditionally opposed women's ordination. Although he personally supports women in ordained ministry, he would have them serve under male leadership so as to preserve the symbol of headship.[24] His position is similar to J. I. Packer's in his "Postscript: I Believe in Women's Ministry," which appeared in the late 1970s in *Why Not? Priesthood and the Ministry of Women.*

In a more recent essay, "In Quest of Canonical Interpretation," Packer returns to the issue of role-relationships between the sexes but is much less univocal. He writes, "For Christians the basic question is, whether the undisputed spiritual equality of the sexes before God and in Christ sanctions equality of function . . . or whether God has ordained a hierarchical pattern whereby . . . men are to lead. . . ." Packer goes on then to recognize the complexity of the hermeneutical task. He posits a helpful list of hermeneutical principles but concludes that certainty of interpretation is largely lacking. All one can claim is that (1) men and women are equal before God; (2) man is "the head" of woman (or at least of his wife), although the meaning of headship is unclear; and (3) Christian partners are to model the redeeming love/responsive love relationship of Christ and the church. All other interpretations are "a matter of rival possibilities." He writes, "It is the way of Evangelicals to expect absolute certainty from Scripture on everything and to admire firm stances on secondary and disputed matters as signs of moral courage. But in some areas such expectations are not warranted by the evidence, and such stances reveal only a mind insufficiently trained to distinguish certainties from uncertain possibilities."

Packer pleads that finally "the horizons of text and student must mesh." The inspired text, which we properly question concerning its cultural specificity, must ultimately question us and our cultural bondage until we are set free to relativize all cultural absolutes. Not spelling out what this might mean in concrete terms concerning the gender-roles he has been discussing, Packer concludes: "I take the discussion of role relationships no further."[25]

It is not my point to enter into debate concerning either Stott's or Packer's conclusions, although I disagree with both. What is crucial for

---

[24]John R. W. Stott, lecture at First Presbyterian Church, Berkeley, California, January 1981.
[25]James I. Packer, "In Quest of Canonical Interpretation," in *The Use of the Bible in Theology,* Johnston, ed., p. 54.

our discussion of biblical authority is the openness to a "new hermeneutic" that is evidenced by both Stott and Packer. The result seems to
be a moderation of former dogmatic viewpoints and a willingness to
have the Word of God address us as our "adversary."

Karl Olsson, in his discussion of relationally oriented Bible studies,
Find Yourself in the Bible, recalls the story of Søren Kierkegaard: "There
is a room with two doors. Over one there is a sign, 'Heaven.' On the other
a sign, 'Lecture on Heaven.' And people flock through the door to the
lecture. It is safer to keep the Bible an object. If I do, I can worship it,
attack it, or ignore it. But if I let the Bible become God's voice speaking
to me and working in me, there is no escape, not even if I stick my
fingers in my ears."[26] Such is the challenge facing all who would seek
to learn from the Bible concerning the role of women in the church and
home.

Conclusion

Stephen Knapp questions whether a shift to a recognition of the role of
the interpreter in evangelical hermeneutics might not allow for a "greater emphasis on the work of the Holy Spirit and the corrective influence
on interpretation of a multi-cultural Christian community." "Could the
charismatic movement," he writes, "with its emphasis on the former and
Anabaptism with its emphasis on the latter contribute to the development of an evangelical approach to hermeneutics able to find and keep
its bearings in the face of this new challenge?"[27] Knapp's observation
is astute. A reader-sensitive criticism has often proven too subjective,
revealing more about the interpreter than about the written text. One's
critical judgments can easily be biased by the end in mind, with the
result that the biblical text becomes a mere tool for some external
goal.[28]

To protect against a destructive subjectivism, a reader-sensitive criticism will need (1) the wider insights of the Christian community, past
and present; (2) the continuing canonical check of the whole of Scripture; (3) the recognition of the role of the Holy Spirit to energize and

---

[26]Karl A. Olsson, *Find Yourself in the Bible* (Minneapolis: Augsburg, 1974), p. 31.
[27]Knapp, *"Dialogue with Gutierrez,"* p. 38.
[28]See Robert K. Johnston, "Interpreting Scripture: Literary Criticism and Evangelical Hermeneutics," *Christianity and Literature* 32 (Fall 1982): 33-48.

enlighten, not only to restrain from sin; and (4) the witness of multiple cultures to their hearing of God's Spirit in the Word.[29] Even with such helps the hermeneutical task is full of risk. Yet that risk has positive potential (a life or culture transformed) as well as negative potential (a text misread).

The continuing discussion of women's rightful role(s) in the church and home can prove a test case for evangelical hermeneutics. Just as the Pharisees' challenge to Jesus concerning his understanding of divorce (Mk 10:2-12) became the occasion for him to argue for the linking of biblical authority and biblical interpretation, so the present discussion is forcing evangelicals to address more carefully and comprehensively the link between the full authority of Scripture and its conscientious interpretation. As John Stott has cautioned, we have too often been "better at defending biblical inspiration than at wrestling with biblical interpretation," at attempting to "affirm the authority of the Bible than to demonstrate its relevance."[30] The discussion by evangelicals of women's roles demands both.

Robert K. Johnston is dean of North Park Theological Seminary, Chicago, Illinois.

---

[29]Robert K. Johnston, "Pentecostalism and Theological Hermeneutics: Evangelical Options," *The Covenant Quarterly* 42 (May 1984): 3-16.
[30]John R. W. Stott, *Culture and the Bible* (Downers Grove, Ill.: InterVarsity Press, 1979), p. 20.

3

BIBLICAL AUTHORITY & FEMINIST ASPIRATIONS

Roger Nicole

IN FIVE WAYS, feminist aspirations are viewed as involving a repudiation of, or at the very least a challenge to, biblical authority. It is my purpose to argue that no such conflict need arise when a suitable understanding of Scripture prevails, as well as an appropriate outlook on the role of women in the home, in society and in the church.

I. Bible As Enemy

The most acute type of conflict is apparent when people understand the Bible as a sharply restrictive book, written in a patriarchal culture and projecting an image of women that is clearly unacceptable to those who espouse feminism. In this view, the Bible, as well as the church in most ecclesiastical traditions, is perceived as a grievous enemy that must be strenuously opposed. This position is marked by serious misapprehensions, with respect both to Scripture and to what is truly desirable for women.

Scripture is misrepresented in this view because it is understood as monolithic. No proper account is taken of the progressive character of revelation, and a misleading uniformity is projected on Scripture, and specifically on the practice of the Old and New Testaments. Furthermore, this view often fails to give appropriate recognition to the distinction between descriptive passages and mandates: what is portrayed as the position or the experience of women in biblical times is misapprehended as what Scripture enjoins.

This view ignores the fact that the Bible clearly stands for the improvement of the status of women as compared with the prevailing attitudes found in the surrounding social structures at the time of its writing. Specifically, the standing of women among the Jewish people was more favorable than in some other contemporary nations, and the *intimations* of the Old Testament rise well above the *practice* of the Jews. The rabbinic outlook, developed after the close of the canon, does not do justice to the ennobling elements presented in the Hebrew Scriptures. Furthermore, the New Testament—particularly the teaching and practice of Jesus—lifts womanhood to new heights. The practice of the Apostle Paul, often viewed as chauvinistic, does in fact militate strongly in favor of the aspirations of women.

Only by misunderstanding Scripture can the Bible be interpreted as inimical to the appropriate feminist cause. When this happens, a great harm is done to feminism and, in fact, to women themselves, for it mistakenly assesses one of women's best friends as an enemy and raises unnecessary friction where women could find effective support for their aspirations. No book more appropriately supports the dignity and worth of women than the Bible; no teacher of world repute proves himself more supportive and friendly than the Lord Jesus Christ. When the feminist movement ignores the norms and boundaries set by Scripture, it skews the truly helpful advocacy of women's rights, and it moves into a direction that deprives women of a sense of adequacy and fulfillment if they have chosen as their primary aim and career to be homebuilders and mothers. It would be difficult to steer a course more harmful than this.

II. Biblical Writers As Wrong

Another approach that sets certain feminist aspirations in conflict with Scripture is found among those who claim that certain writers of Scripture were wrong in what they taught or enjoined concerning women. Such people recognize that certain portions of Scripture are supportive, but they view other portions as conflicting with the former and believe that the Bible contradicts itself at times in this area. This results in choosing which teaching we should endorse, and it results in rejecting those Scriptures that are interpreted as being in conflict. This view restricts the authority of Scripture to those passages of which "we" approve. In doing so, it places the authority of the reader above the authority of Scripture.

It grieves me that Paul K. Jewett's *Male and Female* sets an opposition between Paul the Christian apostle and Paul the unreformed Jewish rabbi. The volume abounds with excellent insights, but this defect mars it. In addition to implying that we need another authority besides the Scripture to discern what is and what is not authoritative, it tends to accredit the interpretation that Paul does have a chauvinistic streak. If the Bible is not authoritative, women have lost one of their most effective courts of appeal, and if Paul is ambivalent, it would seem that one could repudiate the first part of his teaching as well as the second part. This surely is not an appropriate path to follow.

III. Pauline Authorship As Questionable
There are those who feel that the Pauline authorship of 1 Timothy, Ephesians and perhaps certain portions of 1 Corinthians may be denied. This method would explain the difference in the point of view taken by the true Paul (Gal 3:28) and passages that are thought spurious. While this position spares us from attributing instability to the mind of the great apostle, it sets one portion of canonical Scripture against another. Furthermore, it dismisses as false the traditional view of authorship of some books and raises questions about the appropriateness of their place in the canon. The view—represented, for instance, by Leonard Swidler in *Biblical Affirmations of Woman*—mars the basic unity of the biblical teaching and raises questions concerning the authority of the Bible. An evangelical can hardly look for dividends in this area.

IV. Scripture As Circumstantial or Cultural
The authority of the Bible may appear to be compromised if passages that are viewed by some as holding a perennially normative significance are interpreted as circumstantial or cultural. Proper hermeneutics here is very complex. Yet an interpretation that deems a certain mandate of Scripture as culturally oriented is not necessarily grounded in a desire

to evade the mandates of Scripture. The passages mainly in view are 1 Corinthians 11:3-16; 14:33-35; and 1 Timothy 2:9-15. To lump these three passages together and rule out their relevance to our present age and society appears to me arbitrary and likely to raise questions about the seriousness of one's commitment to biblical authority. On similar grounds, some people conclude that Scripture does not provide present mandates against homosexuality in spite of its resolute abhorrence for and condemnation of homosexual practices. The handling of the three passages above might be carried out as follows:

A. 1 Corinthians 11 has some cultural points of reference, for the meaning of having a woman's head covered is not the same in every culture. This particular form of recognizing God's order for the relation between male and female does not have a transcultural permanency. Specifically, the wearing of a hat or a veil in twentieth-century America does not connote any kind of recognition of headship. That aspect of the matter therefore impresses me as being culturally oriented.

In this same context, however, Paul also invokes the situation at creation and the relationship of the Christian to Jesus Christ as significant for an understanding of male and female roles. This may well have its point of reference in the situation in the home since Adam and Eve were husband and wife, and the relation of Christ to the church is the prototype for the conjugal union (Eph 5:22-23). These features are clearly transcultural, and it would not do to say that this passage does not provide principles of action that affect the relationship between men and women in the present context of the church.

It is important to recognize that in this context Paul does two things that are strongly supportive of the cause of women: (1) He emphasizes that there is a certain mutuality between male and female and that the priority of Adam (v. 8) should not be pressed without giving adequate recognition to the interdependence of the sexes (vv. 11-12). (2) This passage expressly asserts that a woman may participate in worship by public prayer and prophecy, so the injunction of 1 Corinthians 14:34 cannot be interpreted to mean that her voice should not be raised in public worship.

B. 1 Corinthians 14:33-35 would appear to me to be circumstantial. The passage relates to disruptions apparently occasioned by whisperings and questionings during the divine service that interfered with a proper worshipful atmosphere at Corinth. The reason women are mentioned rather than males in this passage appears to be that at Corinth they were the principal source of disruption of this type, perhaps because they were less carefully instructed than men and would be more likely to raise questions. Judging from the general tenor of 1 Corinthians, it appears that the new freedom that Christianity brought may at times have been abused, so that rules for a sober behavior had to be provided (see also 1 Cor 11:17-34). The impact of Paul's exhortation would therefore relate to anyone—man, woman or child—whose behavior disrupts the worship rather than to embody a restriction applicable to women alone.

C. 1 Timothy 2:8-15 includes some matters that are cultural, such as the posture in prayer and the meaning of feminine apparel. The injunction in verses 11 and 12, however, cannot readily bear this kind of limitation, in my judgment, although the context in 1 Timothy does suggest that circumstantial features may well have strengthened Paul's resolve to warn against heretical women who abused Christian freedom to promote disgraceful teaching and practices (see also 1 Tim 3:11; 4:7; 2 Tim 3:6-8; and the instruction for widows in 1 Tim 5). Yet in view of the appeal to the transcultural events of the creation and fall of Adam and Eve, it would appear that the Timothy passage constitutes a permanent mandate, and my mind does not find complete rest in the suggestion that the reference is restricted to the church in Ephesus in view of special abuses to be found there.

V. Scripture As Perennially and Transculturally Significant

Those who see a perennial and transcultural significance in 1 Timothy 2:8-15 may appear to set aside this passage of Scripture if they open the door to the exercise of preaching and the pastoral ministry to otherwise qualified women. At this point, the earnestness of the commitment to the authority of Scripture by biblical feminists is challenged. I do not believe, however, that there is a basic incompatibility between a recognition of the normative character of 1 Timothy 2 and an acceptance of the legitimacy of the exercise by a woman of ministerial service. The suggestion that the passage is perfectly plain and admits no other interpretation than that it disqualifies women for the office of elder or pastor is simply not acceptable. There are at least eight very puzzling features in this passage.[1] Patricia Gundry has shown that at least four alternative interpretations of it are possible.[2] Thus it cannot glibly be construed as a blanket disapproval of teaching or preaching by women. To do so would seem to put it in conflict with 1 Corinthians 11, where praying and prophesying in public are expressly allowed.

In view of these difficulties, it is important to consider carefully certain areas in which Paul can hardly be thought to have imposed a restriction. This can be done in the light of other Scriptures, of Paul's practice and

---

[1] These puzzling features may be listed as follows: (a) It is not clear whether Paul is speaking in 1 Tim 2:8-15 with respect to church activities (cf. 1 Cor 14:34-35) or to relationships within the home (cf. Eph 5:22-32). The former would fit well the total context of 1 Timothy and specifically the previous and following pericopes, dealing, respectively, with prayer, presumably public prayer, and with the office of the *episcopos*. There are elements in 2:8-15, however, that have hardly any bearing on church life, notably "child-bearing," and the whole passage could be understood as relating to the relationship between husbands *(andres)* and wives *(gynaikes)*. Adam and Eve, whose situation is adduced in support of Paul's injunction, can be viewed as the prototype of a married couple just as well as the archetypal male and female. (b) The word "likewise" *(ōsautōs)* that introduces v. 9 is puzzling, for it is not apparent in what way a suitable attitude for men in prayer is analogous to the manner in which Christian women adorn themselves. One way to construct the passage would indicate that, as men should pray with clean hands, women should pray in decent apparel. This, however, would leave the subsequent infinitive dangling, and a majority of commentators have construed it to depend directly from "I want" *(boulomai)*, but they do not show wherein the analogy between men and women resides. (c) It is puzzling that Paul enjoins upon males (or husbands, *andres*) a duty that is equally applicable to women (or wives). If it be thought that the reference is to public prayer, 1 Cor 11:5-13 shows us that this was a suitable activity for women. If the emphasis is placed on appropriate attitudes in prayer (cf. Mk 11:25; Mt 5:23-24), these are mandatory for praying women as well as for praying men. (d) There is a very puzzling shift in number in the sentences concerning women, vv. 9-15. Paul uses plurals in vv. 9-10. Then he shifts to the singular from vv. 11-15, only to revert to the plural in v. 15. It is difficult to determine whether this is merely an anacoluthon, or whether there is a particular design at the root of that shift. (e) The verb *authentein* (translated "have authority," NIV) is not only a *hapax legomenon* in the New Testament, it is an extremely rare word in Greek. One of the more extensive discussions of its meaning appears in Moulton and Milligan, followed in references and conclusions by Bauer-Arndt-Gingrich. A much fuller study by Catherine C. Kroeger ("Ancient Heresies and a Strange Greek Verb," *Reformed Journal* 29 [March 1979]: 12-15) makes a very interesting case to the effect that this root connotes improper sexual advances. This matter needs further study. See also George W. Knight III, "ΑΥΘΕΝΤΕΩ in Reference to Women in 1 Timothy 2:12," *New Testament Studies* 30 (January 1984): 143-57. (f) It is not clear how the chronological priority of Adam over Eve functions in this passage. The rights of primogeniture in Israel are well known, but it is also obvious from the text of Genesis 1 that the creation of animals antedated that of humanity, yet no similar excellence and dignity is ascribed to

of the experience of divine blessing bestowed by God on women's ministries as documented in church history. Here the dictum "Don't doubt in the dark what you have seen in the light," often used as a counsel for spiritual attitudes, can also be applied to the hermeneutical task. Here are seven areas in which Paul could scarcely be thought to have enjoined silence to women.

A. In the private training of her children, a mother is required by the Law to exercise a teaching ministry[3] (Prov 1:8; 6:20; 31:26; and implicitly

---

them on that account. One could argue, as Matthew Henry did in his own quaint way, that Eve, being last, represents the greatest masterpiece of the created order. (The text of Genesis 2 could not be properly invoked in conflict with Genesis 1 as reversing the order. A proper translation by a pluperfect, found in the Vulgate, Luther's Bible, the Douay version, the NIV and others, is appropriate and requisite to manifest the harmony of Holy Writ.) (g) A major difficulty arises when one considers whether the fact that Eve was deceived in the Fall while Adam was not disqualifies her (and other women) more than Adam (and other men) for the task of teaching. Obviously, someone who is gullible has a handicap that impairs the reliability of a teaching ministry, but someone who proceeds in a wrong direction knowingly is probably even more clearly disqualified. It is difficult to think that this would be Paul's point. A solution might be that the chronology of the Fall is the reverse of that of creation: Eve first and Adam next, and this might warrant a certain limitation in terms of teaching. This solution is not entirely acceptable in view of Paul's emphasis on the word *seduce* in v. 14. (h) The statement "She shall be saved through childbirth" is extremely puzzling. Surely Paul is not presenting here an alternative to salvation by grace through faith, an alternative that would be accessible only to fertile wives and misbehaving females! Nor is it appropriate to interpret the passage as indicating that God would protect Christian women at the time of delivery of babies, for experience has shown that their pain is not lighter than that of other women, and furthermore many have died in childbirth since the first century A.D. Perhaps Paul is indicating God's seal of approval on motherhood as a career for women. The use of the singular "she," however, may be intended to refer to that supreme case of childbearing mentioned already in Gen 3:15 and by which salvation has come into our race through the incarnation and priestly office of Jesus Christ. This would fit the context where Eve is mentioned and follows the pattern of 1 Cor 11:11-12, where Paul, after having said something that may appear to be injurious to the cause of women's equality, hastens to restore the equilibrium by providing a balancing statement.

[2]Patricia Gundry, *Women Be Free* (Grand Rapids, Mich.: Zondervan, 1977), pp. 75-77; summarized in *Heirs Together* (Grand Rapids, Mich.: Zondervan, 1982), pp. 68-69. Her four suggestions are: (a) "This portion may refer to women disrupting the public meetings." (b) "There may have been two kinds of services in the early church—one was public where unbelievers could observe, and another was private for believers only." Women would not be permitted to speak in the former because it might appear objectionable to unconverted Greeks. (c) "There may have been two kinds of teaching at that time." Women would be barred from argumentative teaching. (d) "This was a local situation in which Paul was limiting the participation of women for a time until they had learned Christian doctrine."

Deut 6:7; 21:18-20; see also the many passages where father and mother are used together or in parallelism). This is made even stronger by the fact that Timothy himself was instructed in the faith by his mother and grandmother (2 Tim 1:5).

B. In Titus 2:4, Paul enjoins older women to train younger women, so this kind of teaching could not be included in Paul's interdiction in 1 Timothy 2.

C. Aquila and Priscilla jointly instructed Apollos (Acts 18:26), and for this activity the name of Priscilla surprisingly is mentioned first, as is also the case in the greetings of Romans 16:3. Surely Paul would not forbid what Priscilla is commended for elsewhere.

D. Teaching in general and in a secular context can scarcely be in view in 1 Timothy 2, since in biblical times it did not connote a very special authority: often slaves were selected as the preceptors of children of noble birth. Furthermore, since the majority of teachers throughout the world are women, it would seem strange that God would here condemn this practice, and that in a context which surely has little to do with society in general.

E. The Sunday-school movement is now more than two hundred years old and has been used by God as a source of rich blessing for multitudes of pupils of all ages. The immense majority of teachers there have been women, and one may well wonder whether God would so signally bless what he expressly forbade in 1 Timothy 2:11-12.

F. The teaching ministry of women in missions has been greatly blessed over the last two hundred years. On the mission field, women have taught religious subjects to children and adults, male and female, in innumerable locations where men did not venture to go—at least in sufficient numbers. Can we imagine that God's blessing has rested to that extent on labors which were forbidden in principle in 1 Timothy 2?

G. Women have been notably blessed by God in writing hymns and other religious literature, which have been extremely useful for the development of spiritual life and for the worship of innumerable congregations. Surely this activity can hardly have been envisioned in Paul's prohibition.

What then does Paul forbid? This is difficult to determine, and we must be prepared to honor those whose conscience does not permit them to endorse certain forms of feminine ministry because they think that such might well fall within the area over which Paul sets restrictions.

I do not feel such uneasiness, since the seven areas listed above appear to be clearly outside that range. In any case, in the preaching of the Word or in pastoral counseling, the authority in view is not the personal authority of the preacher or pastor but rather the authority of God speaking through his written Word. The work therefore is ministerial (note the words *doulos* and *diakonos*) rather than magisterial. Since God was pleased to incorporate songs and statements by women in Holy Writ (Ex 15:21; Judg 5; Lk 1:42-45, 45-46; etc.), is it improper to think that he may use women in expounding and applying his word? Paul himself, in 2 Timothy, implies otherwise, for after asserting that "all Scripture is God-Breathed," he writes that it is "useful for teaching, rebuking, correcting and training in righteousness, so that the man of God may be thoroughly equipped for every good work" (3:16-17). Now the "man of God" who is to perform these tasks is not *anēr,* an adult male person, but rather *anthrōpos,* the generic term for a human being, male or female. If women were to be excluded, is it likely that Paul would have used this manifestly inclusive word?

Roger Nicole is professor of theology, Gordon-Conwell Theological Seminary, South Hamilton, Massachusetts.

4

BIBLICAL AUTHORITY
& THE ISSUES IN QUESTION

Clark H. Pinnock

BECAUSE OF A commitment to the authority of the Bible, there is a primary and fundamental issue for evangelicals in the matter of feminism: Does the Bible teach it?

Alongside this truth question stands another, more practical one: Are evangelicals at large likely to be persuaded that it does? It is this second question that gave rise to the present meeting. Biblical feminists are frustrated by their inability to convince other evangelicals.

The term *feminism* is relatively new coinage and is used to mean a lot of things. Therefore, let me begin by giving it specific content so that we can discuss it intelligently. Feminism is an advocacy of the rights of women based on a theory of the equality of the sexes. It is a belief in social role interchangeability, especially in regard to leadership roles in church and society. Feminism holds that it is bad that males dominate leadership roles in church and society, and biblical feminists deny that the Bible justifies such a situation. Biblical feminists want to prove that the Bible, fairly read, does not teach the subordination of women to men or a hierarchy of authority that places men above women.

Just how strongly some biblical feminists feel is indicated in a statement by Virginia Mollenkott in a letter to the *Christian Century*: "I am beginning to wonder whether indeed Christianity is patriarchal to its very core. If so, count me out. Some of us may be forced to leave Christianity in order to participate in Jesus' discipleship of equals."[1] Apparently her commitment to feminism transcends her commitment even to Christian faith.

---

[1] Virginia Mollenkott, *Christian Century*, March 7, 1984, p. 252.

The Great Difficulty

An enormous obstacle confronts biblical feminists in the area of herme-neutics. Some scholars, both on the feminist side and on the nonfeminist side, agree that the Bible as presently constituted does not teach a fem-inist position. To illustrate this, I shall review four volumes: two feminist books—Elisabeth Schüssler Fiorenza's *In Memory of Her,* and Rosemary Radford Ruether's *Sexism and God-Talk*—and two nonfeminist books— James B. Hurley's *Man and Woman in Biblical Perspective,* and Stephen B. Clark's *Man and Woman in Christ.*[2] These two women and these two men, though hardly on speaking terms, agree that the Bible, taken as a canonical whole and not subject to content-criticism, supports patriar-chal and not feminist assumptions about reality. All four writers say that it is hopeless to try to make the Bible teach feminism.

If this is a war of ideas, biblical feminists face not only traditionalist but also radical feminist exegetes on this crucial question. These four authors press the same point: unless the Bible is edited along feminist lines, it cannot be made to support feminism. The situation is not made easier by the apparent fact that biblical feminists have not yet produced many works that can stand on a level with these four books and show where they are mistaken. Biblical feminists say it can be done, but has it been done? When may we expect it to be done?

The Four Titles

1. *In Memory of Her* holds that the Bible as it stands is the enemy of feminism and a source of female oppression. Although termed "holy scripture," it was produced by the (literally) patristic church to keep women in their subordinate place. The starting point, therefore, is the modern experience of feminism itself. One starts from a commitment to feminism and proceeds from there to put the Bible in order. The one point at which the Bible is least subject to content criticism is the re-constructed Jesus story, where Schüssler Fiorenza finds a discipleship of equals that agrees with her feminist ideology. Even the Jesus tradition has

---

[2]Elisabeth Schüssler Fiorenza, *In Memory of Her: A Feminist Theological Reconstruction of Christian Origins* (New York: Crossroad, 1983), Rosemary Radford Ruether, *Sexism and God-Talk* (Boston: Beacon Press, 1983), James B. Hurley, *Man and Woman in Biblical Perspective* (Grand Rapids, Mich.: Zondervan, 1981), Stephen B. Clark, *Man and Woman in Christ* (Ann Arbor, Mich.: Servant Books, 1980).

been tampered with by the male sexists, but still the truth gets through if you work at it. The rest of the Bible does not fare so well. Colossians, Ephesians, 1 Peter and the Pastorals are all sexist compromises of feminist truth, and even the historical Paul has to be blamed for making some bad moves that aided and abetted the sexist developments that were to follow. This book is not calculated to convince evangelicals of the biblical truth of feminism. The author hands the canon over to the traditionalists.

2. *Sexism and God-Talk* is a book in the same genre. Ruether insists that the Bible is the product of a sexist church. The locus of revelation has to be our own experience. Guided by feminist experience, she goes to the text and looks for liberating insights. Fortunately, there is a "prophetic principle," which, while not explicitly feminist, calls for overcoming patterns of domination and subordination. Although the Bible as a whole cannot be appealed to by a feminist, an important trajectory in the Bible can be used to make feminist points. Chapter one of the book is a clear statement of Ruether's feminist theological method. Because the book is a systematic theology, it goes further than the previous book in indicating what a revolution in theology is being called for. The God in the Bible who is called Father and King had better be prepared to vacate his throne and accept banishment. "A new god is being born in our hearts to teach us to level the heavens and exalt the earth and create a new world without masters and slaves, rulers and subjects" (p. 11). Obviously, feminism in her eyes involves a great deal more than fairer translations and female ordinations. But my point is simply that this radical feminist scholar does not believe that biblical feminism will work.

3. Among evangelical feminists and nonfeminists alike there is widespread agreement that Hurley's book *Man and Woman in Biblical Perspective* is the best of its type. Like the first two books mentioned, the author contends that the Bible as a whole teaches role differentiation for males and females—husbands are to be head over their wives, and men are to be the leaders of the churches. To use Hurley's words, the Bible teaches "appointive male headship" (p. 237). He acknowledges the great liberation that Jesus introduced into human life by his accepting attitude toward women, but he does not see this as contradicting scriptural teaching elsewhere in the New Testament on questions of structure and polity. Nevertheless, in applying his belief in a hierarchy of authority, the author

comes close to the feminist ideal of mutuality. This makes the book something of a bridge over troubled water, building from the nonfeminist side.

4. *Man and Woman in Christ* is much disliked by all feminists, partly because it sets out to refute feminism on biblical, traditional and social grounds. Clark strongly contends that the Bible teaches the traditional view, not feminism. It has been said to have only an appearance of scholarship and not to be a book one needs to take very seriously. I think that it is certainly a scholarly work and that it is disliked so vehemently because, like Susan Foh's *Women and the Word of God,*[3] it is so negative toward feminism in general. Clark's book touches a sensitive nerve when it goes into feminist hermeneutics and lays the charge of Scripture twisting. No evangelical likes to be told that he or she is cheating in exegesis, even if one is. All four books, however, level that charge one way or another. They agree that one cannot make the Bible be feminist without either dropping some large chunks of it or explaining them away in a display of exegesis that is ultimately unsound.

The Big Question

Can biblical feminists succeed against this criticism and make the case for biblical feminism on the basis of belief in the infallibility of the Bible? All four of these books say that this cannot be done. Are they right or wrong? Let us refer to their arguments with this question in mind.

1. All evangelicals, whether feminist or not, ought to be united in deploring the blatant bias imposed on Scripture by *In Memory of Her.* The author says that the Bible teaches patriarchalism when read as a canonical whole, and therefore she denounces the Bible and proceeds to create a "women's Bible" by means of a feminist critical reconstruction. This is a clear denial of the Scripture principle, and no evangelical can have any part of it.

The problem arises when one asks what biblical feminists are going to do with the evidence the author adduces that such a reconstruction is necessary if one hopes to find feminism in the Bible. Evangelicals such as Jewett and Mollenkott, on a more modest scale, perform the same

---

[3]Susan T. Foh, *Women and the Word of God: A Response to Biblical Feminism* (Grand Rapids, Mich.: Baker, 1980).

kind of content criticism. Perhaps it *is* necessary to reject parts of the Bible in order to come up with the feminist belief. If it were not, why would these two engage in it?

The issue is not just whether there is a way to make verses such as "Wives, be subject to your husbands, as is fitting in the Lord" (Col 3:18) and similar texts say something other than they seem to say. It is the practical problem of getting people at large to believe that they do. The radical feminists and the traditionalists both argue that such texts are not feminist in content, and I suspect that their view, agreeing as it does with the "plain sense" reading so widely held, will prevail and not be success-fully refuted by biblical feminists. Of course, the biblical feminist inter-pretation is possible; the problem is that it does not strike many people, either scholarly or untutored, as plausible.

Without question, the strongest suit of the biblical feminist is the Jesus story, and this is where *In Memory of Her* places its own hopes for feminism. The difficulty here will be in convincing people that what Jesus says necessarily contradicts male headship thinking. It is more likely that Jesus' attitude to women will be integrated into traditionalist thinking than that it will lead people to accept implausible explanations of other texts such as Ephesians 5. Hurley's point is likely to carry the day when he says that Jesus does not comment on the relation of women and men in marriage or lay down authority structures for the life of the early church. Schüssler Fiorenza pushes even the Jesus tradition much further than it can be pushed. In my view, she damages the biblical feminist case by her content criticism and does not help it much in her appeal to Jesus.

2. The same points apply to *Sexism and God-Talk*. The writer insists that the Bible as presently constituted is the enemy of women's libera-tion. The only way to get feminism out of the Bible is to edit it according to a feminist criterion. This is not likely to attract many evangelicals to feminism.

As for Ruether's prophetic trajectory, which is supposed to yield fem-inist insights, even Schüssler Fiorenza questions its purity (p. 17), while Ruether herself admits it is not really feminist yet (p. 32). More serious still, why does it have to be read in such a way as to deny other passages of Scripture, when it can be read in congruence with them?

3. What makes *Man and Woman in Biblical Perspective* attractive to evangelicals is that the all-over biblical interpretation does not require

us to set the New Testament against itself. It appeals to the assumption that coherence can be expected from inspired Scripture. In any choice between Hurley and the two books just reviewed, Hurley would win.

But, you ask, what if it were a choice between Hurley and a biblical feministic hermeneutic that also strives for a unitive interpretation faithful to the whole Bible? Hurley has a certain advantage here also partly because of the down-field blocking and interference that these other two books do for him. They agree with him that if it is an interpretation of the whole Bible as it stands you want, then you may as well forget about feminism. Certain passages in the New Testament, to say nothing of the Old, cannot be feministically interpreted. Biblical feminists are not going to be able to overcome this widespread impression, even in feminist ranks, it would seem.

Nevertheless, among evangelicals there are some who do not believe that the Bible teaches appointive male leadership. They point to female leaders in Paul's own entourage, and they try to evade the traditional interpretation of various passages in the epistles. For example, they find mutual submission in Ephesians 5 and not female subordination. They seek to remove any sense of authority from the male headship to which Paul refers there. Of this line of argument, one must say that is possible and often productive of fresh insight; but in the last analysis for most people, it is unconvincing. Why? Not because the individual points made by the biblical feminists lack truth and relevance, and not (I hope) owing to sexism on the other side. Rather, the impression one gets is that Hurley has a simpler hypothesis to offer. He can accept the hierarchical texts and allow liberating insights from Jesus' attitude to modify it and does not find himself in as many awkward situations exegetically as biblical feminists seem to. This simplicity of hypothesis, coupled with the weight of traditional interpretation, gives Hurley quite an edge.

4. *Man and Woman in Christ* is more disliked by biblical feminists because Clark, like Schüssler Fiorenza and Ruether, is fiercely partisan. He resists the implementation of feminism in the modern world. Clark sees feminism as false ideology and goes after it with zeal. In the present climate of opinion, a book that says that patriarchalism is mandated by both the creation and the gospel is more than controversial.

Since Clark is a book of advocacy scholarship, the exegesis probably has been affected. Although the author follows much of Hurley's line, he is less inclined to grant the relevance of Jesus' liberating attitude to the hierarchy framework and more inclined to keep gender-roles clearly distinct. Whereas Hurley appears to have learned from what the feminists have been saying on exegetical grounds, Clark seems unwilling to do so. A polarization is evidently at work in this discussion and contaminates arguments on both sides.

Concluding Reflections

Based on my reading for this report, I have come to believe that a case for feminism that appeals to the canon of Scripture as it stands can only hesitantly be made and that a communication of it to evangelicals at large is unlikely to be very effective. Biblical feminism will have difficulty shaking off the impression of hermeneutical ventriloquism. It may have to be satisfied with the role of introducing into the traditional thinking some liberating insights. The effect of this can be seen plainly in Karl Barth's (and Donald Bloesch's) handling of the question. They have a theology that works with a category of male headship yet renders it practically acceptable to moderate feminists. Such a solution is plausible exegetically and intelligible to a large number of evangelicals in a way that biblical feminism is not and will not be in my opinion.

I would not expect my opinion to be welcomed in the circles of modern feminism. One feels considerable hatred (not too strong a word) for any suggestion that God might have created the sexes with an important role differentiation. If it were true that God intended men to predominate in roles of leadership, this is taken to mean that females are inferior to them and to imply the history of suffering and oppression that we have experienced. The world cannot be just unless distinctions between sexes are for the most part denied. In Ruether, this is part of a broader revolutionary rage against reality that leads her to link her feminism to her Marxism. I think Michael Novak is right to connect it with utopian thinking that is gnostic in origin (*Confessions of a Catholic,* Harper & Row, pp. 193–99).

So I would not expect the feminist ideologues to be warm toward my suggestion that we may have to content ourselves with a modified patriarchalism. But how do the biblical feminists react to it? What if it does appear that the more plausible interpretation of the Bible as a whole sustains the category of male headship? What if the majority of evangelicals continue to believe that it does, supported by the four books we have discussed? Will they begin to consider bolting Christianity? I certainly hope not.

I think that we could lessen the likelihood of such a tragedy if the following moves were made. Nonfeminist evangelicals should recognize good will on the part of the biblical feminists and give credit to the fresh exegetical insights that they have presented. It would also help if they would do more to express the positive side of their vision in this area. Due to polemics, it often sounds as if their delight is to keep women in their subordinate place, whereas in reality there is great beauty in the relationship between women and men that they describe. The delicate interplay, the give and the take between man and woman—a mirror of the redemptive relationship between Christ and the church—speaks nothing of superiority and inferiority, but only of a vastly fulfilling love that welcomes the differentiations God has assigned.

On the other side, the biblical feminists must stop depicting the traditional view in such dark colors. If it should turn out to be true that God did intend males to exhibit strength in leadership roles and females to excel more as the guardians of society's emotional resources, why would this be viewed ipso facto as an evil arrangement? I worry that the biblical feminists are painting themselves into a corner. It would be wiser for all concerned to be respectful of both the traditional and the biblical feminist models.

The topic of our panel is very much to the point. Feminism has a problem of biblical authority. In addition to its other difficulties (see Steven Goldberg, *The Inevitability of Patriarchy*, Temple Smith, 1977), the adjective *biblical* clashes with the noun *feminism* in the term *biblical feminism*. If it is the Bible you want, feminism is in trouble; if it is feminism you desire, the Bible stands in the way. My own experience in preparing for this panel has been a slight loss of confidence that biblical feminism can make its case or be able to sell it effectively among evangelicals.

Clark H. Pinnock is professor of theology, McMaster Divinity College, Hamilton, Ontario.

RESPONSE TO PINNOCK, NICOLE AND JOHNSTON

Stanley N. Gundry

Clark Pinnock poses two important questions regarding feminism. One is the truth question, "Does the Bible teach it?" Alongside it stands a more practical question, "Are evangelicals at large likely to be persuaded that it does?" Pinnock interweaves these questions in such a way that one is often not sure whether he is addressing the truth question or the practical question. But the bottom line for Pinnock is quite clear. I quote from his last paragraph: "Feminism has a problem of biblical authority. . . . The adjective *biblical* clashes with the noun *feminism* in the term *biblical feminism*. If it is the Bible you want, feminism is in trouble; if it is feminism you desire, the Bible stands in the way. My own experience in preparing for this panel has been a slight loss of confidence that biblical feminism can make its case or be able to sell it effectively among evangelicals."

An Inaccurate View of Biblical Feminism

There are several items in Pinnock's discussion that I will address briefly. I object to his definition of feminism as inaccurate and skewed. Feminists in general do not base their advocacy of the rights of women on a theory of the equality (or sameness or interchangeability) of the sexes. Feminists base their claims on the belief (not theory) in the full humanity of women. Biblical feminists in particular believe that the issue of the full humanity of women is the central issue and that the Bible supports this full humanity. They therefore argue for equal opportunity for both men and women in all fields and levels of service, ministry and leadership. This clarification eliminates a number of false issues.

In setting up his case that "biblical" and "feminism" are incompatible, Clark cites two rather radical nonbiblical feminists and extreme statements from two biblical feminists. I do not believe that the statements from Mollenkott and Jewett are typical of the mainstream of biblical feminists. (Taken in context, Mollenkott's statement does not seem to imply that she may leave Christian faith, but rather Christianity in its institutional expressions.) Pinnock ignores the fact that many biblical feminists have come to their position from traditionalism because they felt compelled to do so by Scripture itself. At least that was my experience. I have seen students make that same journey. I have seen professors of theology and biblical studies make that same journey. The truth question has made biblical feminists of us. That does not prove that so-called biblical feminism is in fact biblical, but it is simply incorrect to suggest that biblical feminists start with feminist presuppositions and make the Bible conform. Perhaps some do, but others do not. Granted, as interpreters we are all susceptible to this danger. But there is no reason to suspect that feminists are any more susceptible to the danger than traditionalists.

I also question Pinnock's conclusion that biblical feminists will have difficulty selling their case to evangelicals. If he wants to discuss the question in these pragmatic terms, he must reckon with the increasing interest and sensitivity of evangelical women to the issue and with the increasing number of women in evangelical seminaries preparing for the ministry or going on for doctorates in church history, theology and biblical studies. Some of these women are already teaching these same subjects in leading evangelical seminaries. This is having its impact on evangelical pastors, congregations and denominations.

But this is really peripheral to the fundamental problem that I have with Pinnock's paper. I refer to the route by which he reached his conclusion. Since two radical feminist books and two traditionalist books agree that certain passages of both testaments cannot be feministically interpreted, he has come to believe "that a case for feminism that appeals to the canon of Scripture as it stands can only hesitantly be made," and he has "a slight loss of confidence that biblical feminism can make its case." Although the evidence Pinnock adduces should be considered in analyzing the *practical* question he raises, surely this is not the way for anyone committed to biblical authority to settle the *truth* question. Yet that appears to have been his procedure.

But even if it were the way to settle the truth question, I believe that Pinnock has misread the significance of the fact that radical feminists and traditionalists agree that certain biblical passages cannot be made to teach feminism. The Bible does reflect the conditions of patriarchal societies and is addressed to people who lived in these societies. On the surface (the "plain sense" reading Pinnock refers to), some passages may seem to favor traditionalism. They describe patriarchal circumstances and at times even the instructions have patriarchal overtones. On the other hand, a host of other passages seem to favor feminism—the full humanity of women and the full opportunity and partnership of women with men in home, church and society, including any and all ministry and leadership positions. These two strands of biblical evidence *appear* to be in conflict. How shall they be resolved?

Radical feminists such as Ruether and Fiorenza have no particular reason to try to resolve them. They have long since given up on the authority of Scripture in any magisterial sense, so it poses no problem to them to dismiss the apparently patriarchal sections as sexist and to embrace those portions that are conducive to feminism.

The case of traditionalists is quite different. Because they accept the final authority of Scripture, they rightly want to see a harmony in Scripture. They interpret the patriarchal portions as prescriptive and harmonize those parts that teach the full humanity of women by saying, "yes, but." Yes, women are created in the image of God, but man is given appointive headship, and women are to be in subordination to men in a way that men are never to be to women. If some object that subordination is inconsistent with full humanity and equality, the answer is that no, it is not inconsistent because it is an economic subordination. If some object that in Christ there is neither male nor female, the traditionalists reply that this is spiritual. When examples of women in leadership over men are cited, the traditionalists either say that they are exceptions or insist that women ministered under the authority of men. Thus, the traditionalists conclude that the Bible does not teach feminism. They have accomplished the task of harmonization to their satisfaction. (I realize that I have oversimplified the complex exegetical arguments, but if one looks at the big picture, this is what happens.)

Surely, in light of these radically different views of and approaches to Scripture, there is no particularly compelling significance to the face that Ruether, Fiorenza, Stephen Clark and Hurley agree that the Bible as a unitive whole cannot be made to teach feminism.

Biblical feminists who respect the final authority of Scripture also must harmonize these apparently discrepant strands in the Bible. But they find phrases like "economic subordination" to be unbiblical and unpersuasive evasions. They are merely games played with words that still deny women the implications of their full humanity. To relegate Galatians 3:28 exclusively to the spiritual realm strikes them as an evasion of the full impact and implications of the passage. To say that biblical examples of women in leadership were exceptions strikes them as special pleading and inconsistent with the very verses to which traditionalists so commonly appeal. To say that biblical women in ministry must have been serving under men is to assume what is yet to be proved. In short, the biblical feminist cannot accept the radical feminist's rejection of Scripture and finds the traditionalist's harmonization lacking.

The biblical feminist approaches the matter of harmonization differently. The passages describing the patriarchalism of the cultures and the people in them are seen as just that—descriptive, not prescriptive. Rather than follow the "plain reading" of many passages, biblical feminists understand them as circumstantial and cultural, as Nicole points out so well. The "plain reading" is really a simplistic reading, universalizing what was intended as particular, descriptive and occasional. Indeed, feminists see a striking similarity between the manner in which traditionalists appeal to the cultural and circumstantial reflections of patriarchalism in the Bible and the manner in which some midnineteenth-century theologians and Bible scholars defended slavery by appealing to the cultural and circumstantial reflections of slavery in the Bible.

Instructions that have overtones of patriarchalism are understood by feminists as culturally oriented. They are realistic but temporary accommodations to those circumstances. Nevertheless, these teaching passages contain principles that transcend the circumstantial. Underlying this realistic accommodation to the circumstances of that time and place, biblical feminists see the Bible tied together by the creational themes of complementarity, full humanity and equal opportunity/accountability, with this triad thrown radically out of kilter by the Fall, but restored by redemption.

Now, this does not prove feminism to be true and traditionalism to be false. But it does show that biblical feminists and traditionalists are trying to do the same thing, albeit by different routes. Both are trying to harmonize two apparently discrepant strands in Scripture. They are equally concerned about the truth question.

Pinnock may have lost some confidence in the feminist case. I hope that my analysis and at least some of the papers to follow in this colloquium will restore his confidence that the case for biblical feminism can be made and be sold effectively among evangelicals.

Hanging in Midair

I turn now to Roger Nicole's paper. You will not be surprised to hear that I am in basic agreement with him. Although I suspect that I am not quite as tentative on some points as Nicole appears to be, I think he has analyzed the question of biblical authority and feminism accurately, and I agree with the approach he describes and models in his section IV.

However, at this very point I confess to some uneasiness. He admits that "the authority of the Bible may appear to be compromised if passages that are viewed by some as holding a perennial normative significance are interpreted as circumstantial or cultural. Proper hermeneutics here is very complex." Indeed it is. Although Nicole models how the approach may be wisely used in 1 Corinthians 11 and 14 and 1 Timothy 2, some people will nevertheless feel that they have been left hanging in midair. Although I would hope that Nicole's discussion would take some of the dogmatic wind out of the traditionalists' sails, experience has taught me that it will not.

Most knowledgeable evangelicals, including traditionalists, admit in principle the legitimacy of the general hermeneutical approach that Nicole uses. Then why do biblical feminists apply the method to these passages but traditionalists refuse to do so? Without an adequate rationale for why one should or should not follow the feminists or the traditionalists, it looks suspiciously like either biblical feminists or traditionalists, or perhaps both, are purely arbitrary in their application of the method. If this is true, traditionalists *and* biblical feminists are subject to the charge that they are sitting as loose to biblical authority as those who decide on their own authority which scriptural teachings they will endorse (see Nicole's section II). Obviously, neither group wants to be in this position.

Captives to Subjectivity

Robert Johnston's paper shows a clear understanding of this problem. Quoting from his 1979 book, *Evangelicals at an Impasse,* he identifies eleven interpretive guidelines that spell out in more detail the kind of hermeneutical approach Nicole advocates. But Johnston is also aware that many evangelicals use similar guidelines but come to differing conclusions on the question before us. He rightfully identifies the reader as the problem. In so doing he exposes the myth of reader objectivity.

But I am also uneasy with parts of Johnston's analysis and proposal. Perhaps Pinnock, Sproul, Kaiser and Wells are not sufficiently aware of the factors that make complete reader objectivity impossible. But is not their real point that the Bible is an objective word from God that in principle can be understood by the reader? Are not they saying that it should be the goal of every reader to understand the original author's intent? Johnston would not disagree with this, would he?

Johnston is correct in warning us against the danger of setting up the Bible and its teaching as an object that is never allowed to address readers and their predispositions subjectively. One sees this all too frequently in evangelical biblical-theological debate. We carry on our discussions as if they were wars to be won by one side or the other. Many of these discussions leave little room to step back and allow the living and powerful Word of God subjectively do its work within us or those who disagree with us.

If the idea of a reader-sensitive hermeneutic is intended to expose the myth of reader objectivity, and if it is intended to set the reader of the Bible free from his or her illusions of objectivity so that the objective Word of God can subjectively address, confront and change the reader, it is an idea whose time has come. But some discussions advocating a "circulation between text and reader" seem to embrace reader subjectivity in a way that makes readers as much a captive of their subjectivity as they once were of their imagined objectivity.

The ideal, it seems to me, is that we be aware of and freed from our subjective personal and cultural biases and predispositions so that we can be subjectively changed by God's Word. It is right and good that we have this colloquium and discuss the exegetical issues surrounding the biblical teaching about women. But the evangelical impasse will not be resolved by debate alone.

Stanley N. Gundry is Publisher, Academic and Professional Books, Zondervan Publishing House, Grand Rapids, Michigan.

BIBLICAL VIEWS OF AUTHORITY & HEADSHIP

III

5

AUTHORITY, HIERARCHY & LEADERSHIP PATTERNS IN THE BIBLE

Richard N. Longenecker

JEWISH SOCIETY has always been avowedly patriarchal. Yet the Jewish family, the basic unit of Jewish society, has been matriarchal in character. At times, Jewish women have had public leadership roles that theoretically were reserved for men—such as Deborah in antiquity and Golda Meir of this century.

Christianity, as the daughter of Judaism, has inherited many Jewish viewpoints. Yet Judaism and Christianity do not view matters pertaining to authority, hierarchy and leadership exactly alike. There are basic differences, and each has developed somewhat differently since their parting.

In what follows, I will sketch the patterns of authority, hierarchy and leadership in the Bible as they pertain to the status of women. Then I will survey some of the ways scholars have explained the data. Finally, I will propose what I believe to be a better understanding of the data—one that at the same time gives guidance as to how we as Christians should think, speak and act on this question today.

I. Women's Status in the Old Testament and Second-Temple Judaism

Genesis gives us two accounts of the creation of woman. In the first, women, as well as men, are created in the image of God and so are partners in working out God's purposes on earth. Genesis 1:26-27 reads:

Then God said, "Let us make man in our image, in our likeness, and let them rule over the fish of the sea and the birds of the air, over the livestock, over all the earth, and over all the creatures that move along the ground." So God created man in his own image, in the image of God he created him; male and female he created them.

The second account, in Genesis 2, however, makes a distinction between men and women. While Adam was formed "from the dust of the ground" and became "a living being" by receiving from God "the breath of life" (v. 7), Eve was created from the body of Adam (vv. 21-23).

The immediate implication drawn in Genesis 2 from the woman's being "taken out of man" (being, as Adam says, "bone of my bones and flesh of my flesh") has to do with a proper understanding of marriage: "For this reason a man will leave his father and mother and be united to his wife, and they will become one flesh" (v. 24). Also implied, it seems, are ideas of subordination and submission, even though equality and mutuality are also maintained because of being created in the image of God.

In working out the relations between equality and mutuality, on the one hand, and subordination and submission, on the other hand, a distinction seems to be made in the Old Testament between the public and the private spheres of life. The public sphere of life was considered the domain of a man and the private sphere the dominant area for a woman. The story of Abraham and Sarah was seen by Jewish tradition to illustrate this distinction. Although Abraham took the public role and Sarah was "in the tent" (Gen 18:9), in their private life together Sarah was often dominant—and once Abraham was explicitly told by God to "listen to whatever Sarah tells you" (Gen 21:12).[1] Psalm 45:13 has been seen by many Jews to epitomize the Jewish attitude toward the female role: "The entire glory of the princess lies on the inside."[2]

In ancient Israel, the status of a woman was directly related to her

---

[1]The comment of Rashi (Solomon ben Isaac, 1040-1105) on Gen 18:9 is: "Sarah is a private [צנוע, 'modest' or 'retiring'] person"; on Gen 21:12: "Hence we may learn that Abraham was secondary to Sarah in the gift of prophecy." In the classical tradition of Jewish education, the Pentateuch was always studied with the aid of Rashi's commentary.
[2]Ps 45:14 (MT): כָּל־כְּבוּדָּה בַת־מֶלֶךְ פְּנִימָה , which NIV translates "All glorious is the princess within her chamber." See also M. Meiselman, *Jewish Women in Jewish Law* (New York: KTAV, 1978), p. 14.

place in the family. The unmarried girl was under the authority and protection of her father, but it was a relationship of kinship and love, not ownership. She enjoyed a status considerably higher than that of a slave, but her position was lower than that of her brothers, particularly in respect to education, worship and inheritance. The marriage laws of Israel gave women an honorable and protected place, yet one that was circumscribed and subordinate to that of their husbands. A married woman's role was essentially that of a mother and homemaker, with her praise coming derivatively through the wisdom, influence and exploits of her husband and sons.

Deborah was an exception, for she was a prophetess who held public court as a judge over Israel's affairs in the hill country of Ephraim (Judg 4:4-5). She joined with Barak in directing the defeat of a Canaanite army led by the general Sisera (Judg 4:6—5:31). But though a prophetess and a judge, her status in Israelite society is stated as being that of "the wife of Lappidoth" (4:4). Although she had a major part in the defeat of Sisera's army, she acknowledged how unusual it was for a Jewish woman to so act, and she taunted Barak with the words, "The Lord will hand Sisera over to a woman" (4:9). Deborah was an exception in Jewish society, being not only a prophetess but also a judge and military leader.[3] But Jews have never been so rigid in their thinking as to prohibit "exceptions."[4] The heroines Esther and Judith, however, conform more typically to Jewish standards. Although their actions were important for the entire nation at two times of crisis, their activities were carried out in quite private circumstances, whether in a royal palace or in a general's tent.[5]

Sirach 44-50 assumes this understanding of the public sphere as the

---

[3]Miriam (Ex 15:20) and Huldah (2 Kings 22:14) were both prophetesses, whose status in Jewish society is given as being "Aaron's sister" and "the wife of Shallum son of Tikvah," respectively. But neither went public as a judge or military adviser, although, of course, Miriam led the women in praise (Ex 15:20-21), joined with Aaron in criticism of their brother Moses (Num 12:1-15) and was later extolled with her brothers as one of Israel's leaders (Mic 6:4).

[4]Salome Alexandra, the shrewd and ruthless Hasmonean queen who reigned during 76-67 B.C. after the death of her second husband, Alexander Jannaeus, was also an exception, although her rule, partially legitimized by association with the Pharisees, was contested by many in her day and thought best forgotten by most afterward.

[5]See the canonical book of Esther (10 chaps.) and the apocryphal book of Judith (16 chaps.). Jael's killing of Sisera (Judg 4:11, 17-22) was also a private act with public consequences, though, of course, she was a Kenite.

domain of the man and the private sphere as that of the woman when it praises the nation's heroes entirely in terms of "famous" or "pious" men, without mention of women (see also 1 Macc 2:51-60; 4 Macc 16:20-23). In the same vein, the most famous woman of early rabbinic lore, Rachel, Rabbi Akiba's wife, is praised in the Talmud for her private support of her husband. For, the story goes, the young wife Rachel recognized in Akiba—then only a poor, ignorant shepherd—a man of great potential and encouraged him to learn Torah and supported him in his studies through her self-sacrificing service.[6] Later, when wives of less distinguished rabbis asked their husbands why they were not as great as Akiba or why they had not given them gifts as fine as Akiba gave Rachel, the answer often came: "Because you are not as great as Rachel," thereby acknowledging a close relation between the public and private spheres of life, yet holding a distinction between the proper domains of men and women.

In the fourth or third centuries B.C., however, an ominous note arose within Judaism, which widened the traditional division between men and women and provided a twisted rationale for male chauvinistic attitudes. Based on a certain reading of Genesis 3, women were looked on as (1) chiefly responsible for God's curse on humanity because of Eve's part in the Fall and (2) temptresses to sin because of their sexuality.

The association of women with humanity's curse is not argued from Eve's derived creation, nor is it a feature in all Jewish treatments of the Fall (e.g., only Adam is in view in Sirach 15:14; 4 Ezra 3:7-8, 21-22; 7:116-26; 2 Baruch 23:4; 48:42-43; 54:15, 19; 56:5-6; Numbers Rabbah 13). The joining of sexuality with sin is not an Old Testament motif, but it was probably a Hellenistic intrusion into Jewish thought that appears first in 1 Enoch 6:1-8 (where Gen 6:1ff. is interpreted as an account of fallen angels having sexual intercourse with women, thereby bringing about great evil on the earth).

Sirach 25:24 states: "From a woman did sin originate, and because of her we all must die." This sentiment is dramatically expressed in The Life of Adam and Eve 3, where Eve is portrayed as saying to Adam: "My

---

[6] See L. Finkelstein, *Akiba: Scholar, Saint and Martyr* (New York: Covici-Friede, 1936), pp. 22-27, 79-80, 135.

lord, if you want, kill me. Perchance the Lord God will then lead you back into Paradise, for it was only through my fault that the anger of the Lord God was kindled against you."

The traditional Jewish understanding of public and private roles for men and women was not the only reason that the covenanters of Qumran shunned the company of women (though an early, separate section of graves for women at Qumran suggests that the first members of the community brought their wives with them). Rather, when ideas of curse and sinfulness met with those of subordination and submission, the Dead Sea sectarians renounced the company of women and asserted in their celibacy the supremacy of the male before God. Likewise, Philo of Alexandria, combining his Jewish theology with Grecian philosophy, was more chauvinistic than Judaism generally. Philo taught that since women are more able to be deceived than men, the proper relation of a wife to her husband is epitomized in the verb "to serve as a slave" and the only purpose in marriage is procreation (Questions on Genesis I.33).

Rabbinic Judaism was not as blatantly chauvinistic as Philo was. Nevertheless, ideas about women being primarily responsible for the curse and being temptresses to sin were carried on. The Talmud has numerous statements—even in its most noble tractates—that depreciate the place and worth of women: "He that talks much with women brings evil upon himself and neglects the study of the Law and at last will inherit Gehenna" (Mish Aboth 1:5); "Every man who teaches his daughter Torah is as if he taught her promiscuity" (Mish Sotah 3:4); "Let the words of Torah be burned up, but let them not be delivered to women" (Jer Sotah 19a); and "All we can expect of them [women] is that they bring up our children and keep us from sin" (Bab Yebamoth 63a).

Admittedly, women in ancient Jewry were often treated better than such statements suggest. Women, like men, were created in the image of God, with men and women ordained to be partners in the working out of God's purposes on earth (Gen 1:26-27). But a woman was not accepted as equal with a man in the public spheres of life, whether cultic, governmental or social. In public life she was expected to be subordinate; her proper domain was the private life of the home. So while the family may have been matriarchal because of the strong personality of the wife and mother, Jewish society as such was always patriarchal. In the synagogues women were separated from men and allowed to take no part in the services except, at most, on one annual occasion to read one of the lessons (see Tos Megilla 4:11; Bab Megilla 23a). In the home, the father instructed in Torah and led his family in worship.

II. Women's Status in the New Testament and Early Christianity

The data in the New Testament on the status of women appears to be diverse, even contradictory. Some statements and actions appear to promote equality and mutuality between the sexes; others speak of subordination and submission of women to men. Furthermore, in the New Testament the distinction between the private and public spheres of life seems blurred. The explicit statements about women, except for 1 Peter 3:1-6, are all in Paul's letters, though the Gospels and Acts reflect significant attitudes.

The attitude of Jesus toward women in our four canonical Gospels is different from that of his contemporaries, whether Greek or Jewish. As Charles Carlston notes, all of the ancients' "so-called wisdom [about women] is totally absent from the traditions about Jesus . . . Jesus was perfectly at ease in the company of women" since "for him equality between the sexes was not so much a distant legislative goal as a rather self-evident fact."[7] He had women followers who learned from him, traveled with him at times and supported him financially (Lk 8:2-3; see also Mk 15:41). He frequently ministered to women: he healed Peter's mother-in-law (Mk 1:29-31, par.); he exorcised a demon from the daughter of a Syrophoenician woman (Mk 7:24-30; Mt 15:21-30); he raised Jairus' daughter from the dead (Mk 9:18-19, 23-26); he healed the woman with a pernicious hemorrhage (Mk 9:20-22); he raised a widow's son at Nain (Lk 7:11-17); he taught Mary and Martha in their home at Bethany (Lk 10:38-42); and he healed a crippled woman in a synagogue (Lk 13:10-17).

Many rabbis of the day doubted the ability of women to learn Torah and depreciated their worth. Jesus' attitude was totally different. By granting women the right to learn the good news of the kingdom and

---

[7]C. E. Carlston, "Proverbs, Maxims, and the Historical Jesus," *Journal of Biblical Literature* 99 (1980): 96-97.

to participate in his ministry, Jesus imparted to women a new dignity and role. In so doing, he set a pattern for all his followers.

In what may be the earliest extant ecclesiastical statement of the Christian Church—the confession incorporated by Paul in 1 Corinthians 15:3b-5, with its fourfold declaration concerning our Lord's death, burial, resurrection and appearances—there is no mention of women as witnesses, despite the fact that Mark's Gospel would later highlight their presence at the crucifixion and entombment (15:40-41, 47) and their witness to the resurrection (16:1-8). The testimony of women carried little weight in Judaism,[8] and probably for that reason they are not included in this early Christian confession. But such an attitude did not become entrenched among the early Christians, and soon they expressed a new attitude toward women—one that sprang, I believe, from Jesus and the principles of the gospel.

The letters of Paul speak directly to situations involving the relation of the sexes in the family and the status of women in the church. In 1 Corinthians 11:2-16 Paul deals with a practical problem regarding the decorum of women in worship.

Apparently some women in the Corinthian church, in expressing their rightful Christian freedom, were flouting certain cultural conventions and in the process causing the Christian gospel to be confused with paganism. Perhaps their enthusiastic praying and prophesying with hair hanging loose was reminiscent of pagan prophetesses giving voice to their oracles in disheveled frenzy. Or perhaps their appearance in the congregation with hair cut short and heads uncovered suggested the styles of the city's prostitutes. Commentators vary widely in their understanding of the background of the problem. But the decorum of women in worship was obviously a real problem among Christians at Corinth, for they sought Paul's advice about it. The problem, however, arose precisely because women were taking a responsible part in the public worship of Christians at Corinth—evidently with Paul's blessing. So it was not a question of women praying or prophesying in the congregation, but rather the manner in which they did so.

Paul answers the question with four arguments. He appeals to the

---

[8]See Josephus *Antiquities* IV.219 (IV.8.15): "From women let no evidence be accepted, because of the levity and temerity of their sex."

order established within the Godhead and within creation: "The head of every man is Christ, and the head of the woman is man, and the head of Christ is God" (1 Cor 11:3, with evident reference to Gen 2:21-25). On the basis of such hierarchy within the Godhead and creation—and moving back and forth in his exposition between a metaphorical and a literal meaning for the word "head" *(kephalē)*—he argues that a woman's decorum in Christain worship should be honoring to both God and her husband (vv. 4-9), and that "the woman ought to have a sign of authority on her head" (v. 10b). Yet while he argues for order and decorum in the congregation on the basis of hierarchical orders within the Godhead and creation, Paul also insists, on the basis of eschatological redemption, that "in the Lord, however, woman is not independent of man, nor is man independent of woman,"[9] and that both together find their source in God (vv. 11-12). Paul appears to be saying that though he has argued on the basis of creation for the subordination of women in worship, on the basis of redemption he must also assert their equality.

Hierarchical distinctions because of creation did not mean, for Paul, differing value judgments of a personal (i.e., ontic, "as to being") nature regarding men and women. Nor were even functional distinctions in a hierarchical understanding always held to by Paul. For example, in the doxology of 2 Corinthians 13:14, "the grace of the Lord Jesus Christ" appears before "the love of God," thereby tempering the seemingly rigid order of the Godhead set out in 1 Corinthians 11:3 ("the head of Christ is God") with the redemptive order of 2 Corinthians 13:14 ("the grace of the Lord Jesus Christ, and the love of God, and the fellowship of the Holy Spirit").[10]

In the midst of his first argument from hierarchical order in 1 Corinthians 11, Paul inserts "because of the angels" (v. 10a). What he meant has been hotly debated. Presumably, he was asking that things be done

---

[9]The redemptive context of Paul's thought here is signaled by the expression "in the Lord" (ἐν κυρίῳ), so the statement "woman is not independent of man, nor is man independent of woman" must be seen as going beyond the created partnership of Gen 1:26-27.

[10]Some who want to hold to fixed orders in the Godhead or construct their theology primarily in terms of orders of creation have difficulty with the redemptive order of this doxology. I have known ministers who constantly rephrase it to make it more "theological." But Paul attempted in his thinking and preaching to bring both orders together—although always, I would insist, with an emphasis on the redemptive. So "the Grace" has become the distinctive doxology of the Christian church.

decently and in order because of the presence of angels in the meetings of the Corinthian Christians, much as at Qumran everything was to be done properly in preparation for the eschatological battle and no defiled person was to be allowed to join their ranks "because holy angels march with their hosts" (1QM 7.6). Then Paul argues, much like the Stoics, from "the very nature of things" (vv. 13-15). Finally, he argues from the custom of the churches in general (v. 16), probably having in mind not only the churches of the Gentile mission but also the church at Jerusalem.

Commentators have written much explicating the nuances of these arguments. But all of them as used by Paul in 1 Corinthians 11 essentially *ad hominem* arguments—that is, are meant to appeal to his converts' interests and emotions in terms that they would understand. More important, it needs to be noted that these arguments build up to and conclude with statements about a woman's covering for her head (specifically vv. 10b, 13-15) and that Paul regards such a covering as the woman's "authority" to pray and prophesy in the public meetings of Christians. Whatever may be said about the kind of covering for the woman's head, Paul assumes that she has the right to pray and prophesy in the Corinthian congregation when she has this "sign of authority on her head" (v. 10). Whereas Jewish women were screened off from worship and allowed little or no part in the services, Christian women were free to take a responsible part in the services of the church—a part that was, as F. F. Bruce rightly says, "a substantial step forward in the practical outworking of the principle that in Christ there is neither male nor female."[11]

Because of space limitations, I cannot review all that states or implies in the New Testament regarding the status of women. To some extent that is what I have done in *New Testament Social Ethics for Today*.[12] Suffice it to say that equality and mutuality are also to be found in the phrase "neither . . . male nor female" of Galatians 3:28, in Paul's treatment of marriage in 1 Corinthians 7, in his references to female fellow workers in Romans 16:1-3, 6, 12 and Philippians 4:2-3, and in the

---

[11]F. F. Bruce, " 'All Things to All Men': Diversity and Unity and Other Pauline Tensions," in *Unity and Diversity in New Testament Theology,* ed. R. A. Guelich (Grand Rapids, Mich.: Eerdmans, 1978), p. 95.

[12]R. N. Longenecker, *New Testament Social Ethics for Today* (Grand Rapids, Mich.: Eerdmans, 1984), esp. pp. 74-89.

"house rules" of Colossians 3:18—4:1 and Ephesians 5:21—6:9.

On the other hand, subordination and submission of women to men is prominent in 1 Corinthians 14:34-35 ("Women should remain silent in the churches"), Colossians 3:18 and Ephesians 5:22-24 ("Wives, submit to your husbands"), 1 Timothy 2:11-12 ("A woman should learn in quietness and full submission. I do not permit a woman to teach or to have authority over a man; she must be silent"), Titus 2:5 ("subject to their husbands, so that no one will malign the word of God"), and 1 Peter 3:1-6 ("submissive to your husbands, . . . like Sarah, who obeyed Abraham and called him her master"). To justify such subordination and submission, not only is the created hierarchical order of Genesis 2 cited, as in 1 Corinthians 11:3 ("the head of the woman is man") and 1 Timothy 2:13 ("for Adam was formed first, then Eve"), but also once in 1 Timothy 2:14, Eve's association with the curse and blame for the Fall is appealed to: "Adam was not the one deceived; it was the woman who was deceived and became a sinner."

The data pertaining to the status of women in the Old Testament and Judaism seem easier to understand and control than the data in the New Testament. Yet Christians are chiefly concerned with the New Testament, seeking to understand it on its own terms and in relation to the Old Testament.

III. Some Main Approaches in Explaining the Data
Approaches to the biblical data on the status of women have been many and varied, with no end in sight. In the final section of this paper, in fact, I would like to propose what I believe to be a better understanding than has been given to date.

One popular way of dealing with the data is to understand them in terms of the two creation accounts of Genesis 1 and 2: because they are created in the image of God, women are personally and spiritually equal with men; because of their derivative creation, they are societally subordinate to men. Moshe Meiselman, for example, insists that the Jewish understanding of women is based on the story of creation: "In Jewish thought, the story of creation is not merely of historical interest. Its prime significance is that it puts into perspective certain essential aspects of the human personality. Therefore, an analysis of the creation of woman becomes important for any study of the position of woman in Jewish thought."[13] In the creation narrative Meiselman finds features having to do with equality and mutuality, which he assigns to the private spheres of life, and features having to do with subordination and submission, which he assigns to the public spheres.

Likewise, George W. Knight III sees all the equality emphases of the New Testament in line with Genesis 1:26-27 and all the subordination-istic statements in line with Genesis 2. Knight states, "He [Paul] who can reflect Gen. 1:27 in terms of spiritual equality in Gal. 3:28 (and Col. 3:10, 11) can also reflect Gen. 2:18-25 in speaking of wives being in subjection to their own husbands as the head of the wife (Eph. 5:22-33, see especially verses 22, 23 and 31). Both facets of creation come to their rightful expression."[14] On a woman's role in the church he writes, "1 Timothy 2:11-15 most clearly gives the apostle Paul's verdict and provides his reasons. 1 Corinthians 11:1-16 has explained the significance of one of those reasons. 1 Corinthians 14:33b (or 34)-38 presents the apostle's command and reasons in more general terms."[15]

This has been the traditional approach of almost all Jews and Christians down through the centuries. At times, the woman's greater culpability for the Fall and women as temptresses to sin have been brought into the argument.[16] But the position that advocates women's spiritual equality but societal subordination—venerable though it may be—leaves unresolved the question of how one can speak of a *necessary* subordination of status without also implying a *necessary* inferiority of person.[17]

---

[13]Meiselman, p. xi.

[14]G. W. Knight III, "The New Testament Teaching on the Role Relationship of Male and Female with Special Reference to the Teaching/Ruling Functions in the Church," *Journal of the Evangelical Theological Society* 18 (1975): 83-84. See also his *The New Testament Teaching on the Role Relationship of Men and Women* (Grand Rapids, Mich.: Baker, 1977).

[15]Knight, *The New Testament Teaching*, p. 84.

[16]Neither of these, however, is common today. Knight, for example, on the woman's culpability in 1 Tim 2:14, comments, "Paul does not expand and develop this argument and we must be content with the brevity of his statement"; ibid., p. 85. Strangely, Knight then goes on in the following sentence to speculate on its significance: "One may only conjecture that the apostle is citing this foundational incident as indicating that when the roles established by God in his creative activity and order were reversed by Eve, it manifestly had a disastrous effect."

[17]The emphasis here is on "necessary." Certainly society requires order, with some people functioning as overseers and others as subordinates. But that one gender necessarily must have the one place and the other gender the other place is another matter.

A common way of treating the seeming contradiction between 1 Corinthians 11:5 (when a woman prays or prophesies) and 1 Corinthians 14:34-35 (women are to be silent) has been to posit a difference in the ecclesiastical settings of chapters 11 and 14, with the first referring to more casual and spontaneous gatherings of Christians and the second to the congregation meeting officially as a church.[18] Thus some hold that Paul allowed women to pray or prophesy in the more informal gatherings of believers but prohibited their speaking in the "official" sessions of the church.

Letha Scanzoni and Nancy Hardesty, however, propose a diametrically different conclusion. They argue that the two chapters of 1 Corinthians reflect two parts of the early Christian worship service: the first part, open to all, is reflected in 1 Corinthians 14 (esp. vv. 16, 23-24); the second part, which was only for the baptized and included the observance of the Lord's Supper (cf. the conjunction of 11:17-34 with 11:2-16) is reflected in 1 Corinthians 11.[19] They see Paul as offering strategic advice on the preferred silence of women in the first part of the worship service—when unbelievers, who may have been repelled by questions from women, would have been present—but recognizing the full right of Christian women to pray and prophesy in the congregation when believers met alone. On this view, Paul's statements about the silence of women in the churches in 1 Corinthians 14:34-35 are not absolute commands but rather strategic advice to be considered in the context of the church order of the day.

There is, however, no evidence that the first-century church had such a split service. While circumstantial cases can be built for differing church settings in these two chapters, I believe there are better ways of treating the data.

Others deal with Paul's statements on the equality and subordination of women by understanding the latter as culturally conditioned—due either to external circumstances that were pressing on Christians of that day or to special problems in a particular church, or some combination of both. Peter Richardson views Paul in 1 Corinthians as being of two

---

[18]See, e.g., F. W. Grosheide, *Commentary on the First Epistle to the Corinthians* (Grand Rapids, Mich.: Eerdmans, 1953), pp. 341-42.

[19]L. Scanzoni and N. Hardesty, *All We're Meant to Be* (Waco, Tex.: Word, 1974), pp. 68-69.

minds: desiring to uphold the Christian teaching on freedom and equality yet also wanting not to offend needlessly Jewish scruples or confuse Christianity with paganism.[20] Richardson says:

> In order not to sever all relationships with the Jewish community, Paul advises some concessions, mostly at the level of practices inherited from the oral tradition of Judaism. He wishes to keep himself and the Corinthians sufficiently within Jewish norms to maintain a distinction from the prevailing Greco-Roman behavior. Confusion with Hellenism might occur if women no longer respected the primacy of their husbands. It would not do for a Christian woman to be mistaken for a heathen woman, nor to assert such a degree of freedom that she would be confused with the prostitutes, whether cultic or commercial, who were rather common in Corinth. Too much sexual freedom would create problems for the church's mission to Jews and associate it with the Hellenistic mystery religions.[21]

Likewise, Klyne Snodgrass writes with respect to 1 Corinthians 14:34–35 and 1 Timothy 2:8–15:

> There seem to be special problems in both situations. The problem in 1 Timothy is not as easily identifiable as that in 1 Corinthians 14, but it does seem clear that Christian women were in danger of bringing reproach on themselves, and this situation may have resulted from the newly found status of women in Christianity. These statements should also be seen against the background of the usually negative view of women in the first century and in light of the fact that most women were uneducated. . . . In view of the cultural differences, biblical statements such as Galatians 3:28 and 1 Corinthians 11:15 and the biblical evidence showing women involved in the work of the Gospel, one limits the activity of women in ministry only with great difficulty. . . . The statements in 1 Corinthians 14:34, 35 and 1 Timothy 2:8–12 were necessary for decorum to avoid confusion, arguments, and the violation of the sensitivities of others.[22]

Yet as much as this approach may have in its favor, it is not the whole story. Few, if any, of its advocates have believed that it was, though they may have emphasized it.

---

[20]P. Richardson, *Paul's Ethic of Freedom* (Philadelphia: Westminster, 1979), pp. 63–70.

[21]Ibid., p. 68.

[22]K. R. Snodgrass, "Paul and Women," *Covenant Quarterly* (1976), p. 12.

One further significant and somewhat controversial approach needs to be identified. In 1975, Paul Jewett published *Man as Male and Female*, a re-evaluation of the Genesis creation accounts in the light of the New Testament revelation—particularly in the light of Jesus' attitude toward women and the confessions of the early church.[23] Jewett brings into his argument several vitally important points, such as (1) the clear redemptive note that is sounded throughout the New Testament; (2) the need to take into consideration cultures and circumstances when attempting to understand specific statements within the New Testament; and (3) the need to focus on the principles of the gospel, not just certain of early Christianity's described practices, in seeking to achieve the New Testament ideal of a redeemed humanity in Christ. But these are not his main arguments. The thrust of Jewett's argument is in terms of a better understanding of the creation categories of Genesis 1 and 2 as seen from the perspective of God's later revelation in the New Testament:

> In framing a theology of the man/woman relationship, the basic issue that has to be faced is this: Is the woman, according to the ordinance of creation, subordinate to the man? While the first creation narrative, which includes the fundamental affirmation that Man in the divine image is male and female (Gen. 1:27), contains no hint of such a hierarchical view, the second narrative (Gen. 2:18–23), which we have treated as supplementing the first, allows, if it does not actually imply, that the woman is subordinate to the man. Here we are told that the woman was created *from* and *for* the man. What is the theological significance of this? Does the fact that the man was created first imply the headship of the male? The major theologians of the church have thought so and have reinforced their understanding of this narrative by appealing to the account of the fall as found in Genesis 3.[24]

After a wide-ranging discussion of the biblical texts, most of the associated issues and some historical approaches, Jewett concludes:

> Since the Creator has given us our humanity as a fellowship of male and female, it is only as we achieve the ideal of partnership that we achieve the ideal of humanity. And this partnership is not simply an abstract "ideal," but a concrete reality, since God in Christ has actu-

---

[23]P. K. Jewett, *Man as Male and Female: A Study in Sexual Relationships from a Theological Point of View* (Grand Rapids, Mich.: Eerdmans, 1975).
[24]Ibid., p. 50.

ally begun the creation of a new humanity in which there is no male and female. The historic rivalry between the sexes which has characterized fallen human history, a rivalry in which the man has subjugated the woman, treating her as an inferior, and in which the woman has taken her subtle revenge, is done away in Christ. Admittedly, in a sinful world this new humanity remains a future hope as well as a present reality; yet it is a hope which the church should strive to realize ever more perfectly here and now.[25]

Jewett thus in effect roots the discussion of male–female relationships principally in the creation accounts of Genesis 1 and 2, as have the great majority of interpreters before him. He differs from most who have preceded him, however, in that he overtly attempts to interpret these accounts from a New Testament perspective. Rather than accept a duality of spiritual equality but societal subordination in the two accounts—or, worse yet, that the equality emphasis of Genesis 1:26-27 has been tempered by the subordinationistic thrust of Genesis 2—Jewett views Genesis 1:26-27 as providing the basic datum for a biblical understanding of male-female relationships and insists that whatever thoughts may arise from woman's derivative creation (per Gen 2) or her part in the Fall (per Gen 3) must be in line with this basic understanding of partnership. While I find much in Jewett's argument compelling and attractive, I suggest that there is a better way to look at the biblical data, one that accepts more explicitly a developmental hermeneutic and seeks to work out a thesis more consistently from that approach.

IV. A Developmental Approach

Much of the discussion among evangelicals regarding the status of women has been based on proof texting that assumes a uniformity of teaching and practice throughout the Bible. Scholars have tried to bring the Genesis creation accounts and Paul's statements into harmony—with some analysis of Jesus' attitude toward women often brought in for good measure. The questions become the following: Do Genesis 1 and 2 teach a personal and spiritual equality between the sexes, but also a necessary societal subordination of women to men? Should the subordination features of Genesis 2 be considered normative, with Genesis 1:26-27

---

[25]Ibid., p. 171.

only supplementary; or is Genesis 1:26–27 basic, with all else to be seen in line with its emphases on equality and partnership? Is Paul's teaching and practice best represented in passages such as Galatians 3:28 and 1 Corinthians 7, where equality and mutuality are stressed, or in passages such as 1 Corinthians 14:34–35 and 1 Timothy 2:11–12, where the subordination and submission of women to men are dominant? And what about the attitude of Jesus as portrayed in the Gospels?

A fundamental axiom of Christianity is the integral relation of Old and New Testaments. But while holding to unity, we must also recognize diversity; and while insisting on continuity, we must also affirm development. Elsewhere I have argued that a developmental hermeneutic is important for an understanding of both Christian theology and Christian ethics.[26] Here I would identify four implications of such a hermeneutic for questions having to do with authority, hierarchy and leadership in the Bible, believing that such an approach makes the best sense of the data and guides how we as Christians should think, speak and act on matters pertaining to the relation of the sexes.

Such a developmental approach clarifies the fullness of the redemptive note sounded in the New Testament. Redemptive categories of thought are crucial to a Christian understanding of the status of women. Everything in the Bible has to do with either creation or redemption or both. Creation and redemption categories of thought are inseparable in the Scriptures. Yet without minimizing what God has done by way of creation, the New Testament emphasizes what God has done redemptively in Christ Jesus. A development of revelation in history that has been encapsulated in the Bible may be roughly characterized as follows: in the Old Testament, God the Creator is also God the Redeemer; in the New Testament, God the Redeemer is also God the Creator—and the Re-Creator. This development of revelation within the Scriptures must be constantly borne in mind when treating questions concerning the status of women.

Early Christians generally, and Paul in particular, seemed to work from two categories of thought when facing questions related to the

---

[26]See my *New Testament Social Ethics for Today,* esp. chap. 2, pp. 16–28; see also my "On the Concept of Development in Pauline Thought," in *Perspectives on Evangelical Theology,* ed. K. S. Kantzer and S. N. Gundry (Grand Rapids, Mich.: Baker, 1979), pp. 195–207.

roles of the sexes: (1) that which emphasizes what God has done by creation, wherein hierarchical order, subordination and submission are generally stressed, and (2) that which emphasizes what God has done redemptively, wherein freedom, mutuality and equality take prominence. But holding firm to what God has done by creation, they gave priority to what God has done redemptively in Christ Jesus. In 1 Corinthians 11:3 Paul speaks of a hierarchical order in creation and within the Godhead ("the head of the woman is man, and the head of Christ is God"), but in 1 Corinthians 11:11 he tempers the subordination features of his creation category by a mutuality emphasis that springs from his redemptive category ("in the Lord, however, woman is not independent of man, nor is man independent of woman"). In the doxology of 2 Corinthians 13:14—which, it should be noted, highlights the redemptive notes of "grace," "love" and "fellowship"—he even adjusts the hierarchical order in the Godhead to read "the grace of the Lord Jesus Christ, and the love of God, and the fellowship of the Holy Spirit." Therefore, we may take it that hierarchical order is built into creation by God and must be respected, but a hierarchical ordering of life is not always necessary and status in a functional hierarchy is not necessarily fixed, particularly when redemptive concerns overshadow what is true because of creation. In the Christian life, both creation categories and redemption categories must be taken into account, though with priority given to the latter.

A second implication of a developmental hermeneutic involves where one begins and from what vantage point one views the data. Some begin every topic by investigating Old Testament materials and then find their conclusions confirmed in the New. Others tend to isolate the New Testament from the Old and so determine theological and ethical matters without reference to the Old. A proper Christian approach, I believe, is to begin the study of any issue at that point where progressive revelation has reached its zenith, that is, in the ministry of Jesus as portrayed in the Gospels and the apostolic interpretation of that ministry in the writings of the New Testament. From there we can trace out lines of continuity and development both back into the Old Testament and forward into the patristic period and beyond.

On the question of the status of women, therefore, we must begin as Christians with Jesus' attitude toward women and with the principles of the gospel as proclaimed in the apostolic writings. That is why Galatians

3:28 is so important for our discussions, for there the gospel is clearly stated as having revolutionary significance for the cultural, social and sexual areas of life.[27]

Third, a developmental hermeneutic calls us to distinguish between (1) what the New Testament proclaims about new life in Christ and (2) its description of how that proclamation was practiced in the first century—realizing that the implementation of that proclamation is portrayed in the New Testament as having been only begun and is described as being then worked out in progressive fashion. Thus we must focus our attention on the principles of the gospel message, not just on its first-century implementation. The gospel and the ethical principles that derive from it are presented in the New Testament as normative for every Christian. The way or ways in which the gospel was practiced in the first century, however, should be understood as signposts at the beginning of a journey—signposts that point out the path to be followed if we are to reapply that same gospel in our day.

In regard to the relation of principles and practice in Paul's letters, F. F. Bruce comments on Galatians 3:28: "Paul states the basic principle here; if restrictions on it are found elsewhere in the Pauline corpus, as in 1 Cor. 14:34f. . . . or 1 Tim. 2:11f., they are to be understood in relation to Gal. 3:28, and not vice versa."[28] Likewise Paul Jewett suggests that Christians would do well habitually "to distinguish between what the New Testament *says* about the new life in Christ and the actual *degree of implementation* of this vision in the first-century church." He then applies this hermeneutical rule:

> So far as woman's role in the partnership of life is concerned, it can hardly be the degree of implementation in the New Testament church to which we should look for authoritative guidance in our present moment in history. In its implementation, the New Testament church reflects, to a considerable extent, the prevailing attitudes and practices of the times. Because of this, we should look to the passages which point beyond these first-century attitudes toward women to the ideal of the new humanity in Christ. Only thus can we harness

---

[27]Though many attempt to explain Gal 3:28 in strictly "spiritual" terms, "neither Jew nor Greek, slave nor free" certainly have societal implications—and so, in conjunction with these first two members of the triad, must "male nor female."

[28]F. F. Bruce, *Commentary on Galatians* (Grand Rapids, Mich.: Eerdmans, 1982), p. 190.

the power of the gospel to make all history, not just first-century history, salvation history.[29]

A fourth factor in a developmental hermeneutic involves the effect of circumstances on Christians of the first century as they sought to put into practice the Christian gospel. The New Testament indicates that all of their preaching, teaching and living was expressed in the context of the circumstances they inherited and faced. It was largely because of such circumstances that the Christian gospel, though declared eloquently, was implemented only progressively and often slowly. We may not always be able to spell out precisely the circumstances involved in each case simply because the texts themselves do not tell us and our knowledge of the times is incomplete. But we need to allow for such factors before concluding that contradictions exist or trying to explain every difference on a theological basis.

Admittedly these four hermeneutical rubrics have often been cited separately by others in dealing with the New Testament generally and with various ethical issues in particular. To my knowledge, however, they have never been explicitly associated with a developmental hermeneutic, nor have they been applied in such a united fashion to the question of the status of women.

My claim, of course, is that approaching the biblical data via such a developmental hermeneutic compels us as Christians to stress the redemptive notes of freedom, equality and mutuality that are sounded in the New Testament. Understanding the status of women in this way takes us beyond the public-private dichotomy of the Old Testament and Judaism, but it is in line with the partnership ideal of Genesis 1:26-27. More important, it is based on the recorded attitudes of Jesus toward women and the principles of the gospel.

Much of current secular feminism has its roots in the Enlightenment (humanism), Greek mythology (androgyny), the Baal cult (fertility goddesses) or a bastardized form of Epicureanism (hedonism). Sadly, some of this has spilled over into religious discussions on the status of women. Yet Christians cannot allow such alien counterfeits to divert them from following the example of Jesus and putting into practice as best we can the principles of the gospel. As Christians, we are to express in our lives,

---

[29]Jewett, *Man as Male and Female,* pp. 147-48.

in our churches and in society the fullness of God's revelation as expressed in Christ Jesus and not just to revert to Old Testament patterns or first-century practices. That includes a fuller and more significant application of the gospel principles to the question of the status of women.

Richard N. Longenecker is Ramsay Armitage Professor of New Testament, Wycliffe College, University of Toronto.

RESPONSE

Willard M. Swartley

Richard Longenecker's paper is helpful. I will respond in two parts: first on individual points in his sections I-III and, second, more substantially to section IV.

Evaluative Comments on Sections I-III

1. Longenecker begins with a "duality interpretation" of Genesis 1—2; he says that "ideas of subordination and submission" are implied in the Genesis 2 creation account. Longenecker, however, gives no hard exegetical documentation for this statement. Phyllis Trible's exegetical work on this passage argues for mutuality and leaves no exegetical foundation for subordination, explicit or implicit. Furthermore, at this point Longenecker fails to relate Genesis 2 to Genesis 3. Does not the "fall of humanity" have something to do with the hierarchical order between men and women à la later biblical description?

2. Longenecker's description of the general tendency for women to play strong roles in "private life, but not in public life" should be analyzed in the context of ancient Near Eastern culture generally. Might it not be said that in this pattern Israel is one with its environment but that the exceptions bear witness to something new and revelationally significant in their midst? This question has implications for hermeneutical method.

3. More work needs to be done to assess the influences that led

fourth- and third-century B.C. writers to think of women as morally more responsible for the sinful human condition. These sources introduce into Judaism a disparagement of women that the New Testament usually fights against, but occasionally also reflects.

4. I certainly agree with Longenecker's analysis of Jesus' relationship to women. This indeed represents a revelational breakthrough. I also agree that some statements and actions in the New Testament "appear to promote equality, [unity] and mutuality between sexes; others speak of subordination and submission of women to men."

5. Longenecker identifies the major components of the argument in 1 Corinthians 11 as traditionally read and understood. I am of the opinion, however, that a new reading of that passage, building on Katherine Bushnell's work in 1923, should be considered and tested.[30] The "yes, but" of verse 11 must be heard for its full significance. The final word is not some hierarchical creation order but the new creation reality.

6. In section III, Longenecker has helpfully outlined the various explanations of the data. I would call, however, for further historical work to be done in relation to his statement that "almost all Jews and Christians through the centuries" have supported the subordinationist/hierarchical view. I expect that we have not combed the sources of church history broadly enough. Where do we draw our lines of orthodoxy? The role of women reflected in the Acts of Paul (second-century Asia Minor) would serve an exception to Longenecker's statement; perhaps also the Montanist movement in the second and third centuries. What role did women play in the left wing of the Reformation and in the later Quaker movement headed by George Fox? Also, what role have women played in the pentecostal movement of recent origin? And in smaller groups, such as the Pillar of Fire?

7. I concur with Longenecker in his skepticism about the relatively easy solutions to 1 Corinthians 14:34-35. While the view of "culturally conditioned" is attractive, we must remember that all revelation is embodied within history and culture. Hence, we should not "discount" these texts but rather learn from that particular interaction between gospel

---

[30]Katherine Bushnell, *God's Word to Women* (Oakland, Calif.: K. C. Bushnell, 1923), reprinted by Ray B. Munson, Box 52, North Collins, NY 14111, sections 216-49. See also my summary in *Slavery, Sabbath, War and Women: Case Issues in Biblical Interpretation* (Scottdale, Pa.: Herald Press, 1983), pp. 320-21.

and culture in that specific contextual setting to inform our experiences today. I agree with Longenecker in his appraisal of Jewett's work, but we must remember that Paul did not interpret the Genesis narratives in the same way that Jewett says they should be interpreted. Thus the hermeneutical problem, or challenge, remains.

Longenecker's Proposal for a Developmental Hermeneutic

In this creative and provocative section of his paper, Longenecker tackles the hermeneutical issue that is occasioned by the variety of testimony within the canonical witness. While holding that Jewett's approach is "compelling and attractive," Longenecker proposes "a better way to look at the biblical data," namely, via a "developmental hermeneutic . . . [that] seeks to work out a thesis more consistently." Longenecker then calls the reader's attention to his argument elsewhere[31] for a developmental hermeneutic and then identifies four implications of such a hermeneutic for this issue. By this method, Longenecker intends to present a logical program or philosophical explanation that gives underlying coherence to the diversity of the canonical witness.

My evaluative response to Longenecker's proposal is both positive and critical. On the positive side:

1. The four "implications" or hermeneutical principles are valid in my judgment. They make a convincing case that we should acknowledge the cause of the Bible to be for mutuality and partnership between male and female roles. Statements about male headship and female subordination must be understood as subservient to this central gospel manifesto.

2. Longenecker's first point, that redemptive categories and emphases take priority over creation categories and emphases in our ethical formulations today, correlates well with the concept of a developmental hermeneutic.[32] Longenecker speaks of "progressive revelation" with its apogee in the Incarnation, God's self-disclosure in Jesus Christ. This widely accepted theological tenet provides a revelational basis that enables us to give priority to those biblical teachings that *are said by Scripture* to be the fruit of Christ's redemptive work (e.g., Gal 3:28).

---

[31]Richard N. Longenecker, *New Testament Social Ethics for Today* (Grand Rapids, Mich.: Eerdmans, 1984), pp. 16-28.
[32]Ibid.

At this point I shift to critical response, and these comments cluster around the concept of a "developmental hermeneutic."

3. The term "developmental hermeneutic" needs more careful definition. The word *hermeneutic* denotes human understanding. The assumed relationship between "progressive revelation" and "progressive understanding" needs careful analysis. If the former is itself the basis of the latter, the latter cannot develop essentially beyond the zenith point in divine revelation. If the argument stops here, our theological and ethical insight never surpasses Jesus, a second implication in Longenecker's paper.

In his book, Longenecker speaks of "progressive illumination throughout the past nineteen centuries of the meaning and significance of God's definitive activity in Jesus Christ." After describing three models for understanding "developmental," Longenecker argues for the model of "organic growth." As foundation for this notion he cites Jesus' teaching on the old and new,[33] Jesus' promise that the Spirit will give fuller understanding, the breakthrough in the disciples' understanding after the resurrection and the way in which Gospel writers used the Jesus tradition to address new agendas and challenges.

While this is significant, the individual points do not help us grasp what a "developmental hermeneutic" really is, mostly for the following reasons: (a) The discussion does not deal with the distinction between canonical testimony and postcanonical insight. The biblical citations could be understood as fulfilled in the canonical witness, in both the Epistles and the Gospels. Moreover, the notion of "progressive illumination throughout the past nineteen centuries" is highly questionable. (b) Longenecker never proposes criteria by which to measure progressive development other than the revelational apogee in Jesus Christ. Until this is done—for both revelation and illumination—the notion of a "developmental hermeneutic" lacks accountability.

4. To say that we always begin with the vantage point of Jesus Christ (with which I agree) is the opposite of a developmental hermeneutic.

---

[33]I do not agree with his exegesis of Mt 13:52 (Longenecker, *New Testament Social Ethics*, p. 78). While the Schweizer/Beare suggestion that the old/new polarity is between Jesus and Matthew (which I cannot imagine Matthew thinking!), Longenecker's statement that here *Jesus* speaks of the biblical revelation including his own teaching as the *old* and teachers today applying this to current issues as the *new* simply cannot stand.

5. I agree with Longenecker's excellent third point, that "a developmental hermeneutic calls us to distinguish between what the New Testament proclaims about new life in Christ and its description of how that proclamation was practiced." But I question its coherence with the underlying assumption of progress behind a "developmental hermeneutic." Multiple descriptions of how one central proclamation was fleshed out in varied historical sociocultural contexts do not add up to progressive development, as the divergent applications on this issue within the New Testament testify. If this point truly evidenced a progressive hermeneutic, the later applications, those of the pastoral epistles, would be most definitive for us.

If Longenecker's point is unhooked from the notion that the basic principles were "being then worked out in progressive fashion," his emphasis that these canonical applications "should be understood as signposts at the beginning of a journey" that "point out the path to be followed" is significantly helpful. This means that we should look at biblical diversity as an enriching resource for us, not data that must be harmonized.

Perhaps the questions we bring to this hermeneutical dilemma are the wrong ones. What we regard as a problem needing a solution can function, if we allow it to do so, as signposts for fuller faithfulness. If we really believe in incarnation—that divine revelation came into human history and culture—we can expect and celebrate the diversity of its expressions, all of which stand under the light of God's clearest revelation in Jesus Christ.

On this matter, I cite two paragraphs from my book:

What does Scripture teach us through Paul's use of the rabbinic interpretation of Genesis 2 to speak to the Corinthian situation? In this question the human, cultural dimension is not denied but viewed positively. When one looks at the larger literary context in the epistle (I Corinthians 11—14), it becomes clear that the Scripture as revelation is teaching that cultural patterns are to be respected and utilized, not for reifying them as ends in themselves, but for promoting the larger goals of the gospel: the orderly conduct of worship, the edification of the whole body, and the primacy of love in human relationships. However, in view of other scriptural testimonies which give women prominent roles in early church leadership (thanks to the diversity of the canon), the I Corinthians 11 teaching on male headship should not be translated into a church policy that prohibits women from functioning in church leadership roles.

Using then the missionary factor for hermeneutics—the diversity of expression as faithfulness to the gospel—we must ask: what uses and criticisms of culture in our time and place enable us best to achieve goals central to the gospel, whether these be the goals of I Corinthians 11—14 or those articulated elsewhere in Scripture, including the unity of male and female in Christ (Galatians 3:28)? The divine-human nature of Scripture can then, like its unity in diversity, become an enriching resource for believers who live by its light.[34]

6. Longenecker's fourth principle, which I also espouse, is as much *against* as it is *for* a developmental hermeneutic. The varied circumstances help us understand the specific actualizations of the gospel, but these do not necessarily testify to progressive illumination or an ever more faithful community.

7. The real point of my criticism of a "developmental hermeneutic" is that the modern notion of progress is highly suspect. It may have merit, but its context of significance is nature, not grace. When its use for culture and ethics is examined carefully, both empirically and cross-culturally, it is likely to appear as a Western presumption, for the proposed criteria of measurement are neither self-evident truths nor consensually agreed-upon values. Even the notion of equality, which regularly intrudes into our exegesis of biblical texts on this topic, needs careful scrutiny, both for its empirical meaningfulness and its subtle hijacking of the biblical agenda. The biblical accent, I propose, is regularly *unity* in Christ of hitherto warring or competing sociocultural identities.

Longenecker's four implications are helpful, well-described hermeneutical contributions. Let them stand together and be joined also to others;[35] let us not make them subservient to some optimistic notion of progressive development. In Greek vocabulary, let us flee *chronos* on this matter and cling to *kairos* or *kairoi*,[36] Moses and Jesus Christ, the

---

[34]Swartley, pp. 190–91.

[35]As, for example, those proposed in other papers of this seminar; in my book I draw together twenty-two hermeneutical learnings from the study (pp. 229–34).

[36]Even for "illumination," I propose a breakthrough model that accents moments/experiences of grace and Spirit in achieving clearer understandings of Scripture.

two-language Rosetta stone to which all derived ethical norms are to be held accountable. On this matter, I believe Longenecker and I are essentially agreed.

Willard M. Swartley is professor of New Testament, Associated Mennonite Biblical Seminaries, Elkhart, Indiana.

RESPONSE
Marianne Meye Thompson

Because my field of study is New Testament, I will limit myself chiefly to comments on the data of the New Testament.

First, I affirm what Longenecker acknowledges implicitly, that the key issue in the present discussion is the hermeneutical one. Hermeneutics is basic, not because we need to come up with a theory that will justify our desired conclusions, but because any time we turn to Scripture and ask what it says to the church today, we put our hermeneutical theory into practice, consciously or unconsciously. Nevertheless, hermeneutics is not done in a vacuum, apart from exegesis, and I will raise a few points where I take a different view of the New Testament data or think that further exegetical work can be of service.

The Meaning of Head
A first instance is 1 Corinthians 11:2-16. The meaning of "head" *(kephalē)* is crucial for this passage. Longenecker assumes that *headship* implies hierarchy, an assumption that seems to rest on a translation of *head* as something like "chief." But numerous commentators, including C. K. Barrett, Hans Conzelmann, and J. Murphy-O'Connor, believe that *kephalē* means something more like "source" as in "headwaters." Paul appeals to the creation story of Genesis 2, where woman is taken out of man, and so is her "source," as a basis for his instructions about worship. I grant that the passage assigns to males some sort of "priority," but that is not necessarily "superiority." In contrast to "chain of command" theories, Paul himself did not develop the image of man as

head—no matter how we interpret it—as a basis for urging husbands
to function as decision makers, or for giving them permission to rule
over their wives.

Such is also the case in Ephesians 5:22-24 ("Wives, submit to your
husbands"), which Longenecker points to as an example of woman's
"subordination and submission" alongside the more egalitarian verse,
"Submit yourselves to one another out of reverence for Christ" (5:21).
But there is a very close connection between verse 22, in which there
is no verb, and verse 21 with its exhortation to *mutual* submission,
which serves as the guiding theme. Moreover, the example held up to
husbands is Christ's sacrificial death for the church and the intimate
union that results. The image here is not that of Christ as "Lord" or
hierarch of the church (cf. Col 1:18). Whatever nuance should be assigned to the word *head* and whatever kind of hierarchy one thinks Paul
envisions, it is not one of ruler and subject or of master and servant, and
its application should be in keeping with the thrust of the passage. Thus
the justification for "chains of command" that one often hears, namely,
that "when there is an impasse, someone must make the final decision"
certainly cannot find support in Paul, nor in the relationship of God in
Christ that is Paul's ultimate court of appeal. Such logic is supported
neither by Paul's use of *kephalē* nor by his view of marriage, and it is
dealt a serious blow by the acknowledgment that God distributes the
power of the Christian life, the Holy Spirit, to all.

Authority and Power in the Christian Community

As my second main point, I would like to comment on Longenecker's
observation that it is difficult to control the New Testament data on the
position and status of women. It is helpful to turn to those texts in the
New Testament that address the issues of authority, hierarchy and leadership but that do not *directly* have in view the roles of women in the
home, society and the church. Specifically, I raise the question of authority or power in the community of Christ: what is power and how is
it to be shared and exercised in the Christian community, whether that
community be the church or a marriage?

Following Longenecker's principle that we approach the study of any
issue from the heart of Christian revelation, namely, from the ministry
of Jesus, we note Jesus' own emphasis that relationships between his

disciples were to be characterized not by the exercise of authority but by mutual service. "You know that those who are supposed to rule over the Gentiles lord it over them, and their great men exercise authority over them. But it shall not be so among you; but whoever would be great among you must be your servant, and whoever would be first among you must be slave of all. For the Son of man also came not to be served, but to serve, and to give his life as a ransom for many" (Mk 10:42-45), and the parallel text in Luke 22:27, "I am among you as one who serves." Certainly the power structures in the time of Jesus were male oriented, with power concentrated at the top. Whereas such structures were the norm among the Gentiles, they were not to be the norm among Christ's followers.

The apostle Paul develops at length the character of ministry as self-giving service, summed up when he characterizes his apostolic ministry as literally expendable: "We have this treasure in earthen vessels, to show that the transcendent power belongs to God and not to us" (2 Cor 4:7). The emphasis is not on the one who ministers but on the one who stands behind that minister. Where our power comes from is an extremely important consideration: it is not our own; it does not inhere in us.

Obviously these passages tell us something about ministry but not *who* is to exercise it or *what shape* the expression of that ministry is to take—whether it is to be an "official" church ministry or a ministry common to all as members of the body. Yet the one criterion for exercising any function in the church is that one be given the gift to do it: "Having gifts that differ according to the grace given to us, let us use them" (Rom 12:6). Nowhere does the New Testament say that God gives gifts on the basis of gender.

In *The Ordination of Women,* Paul Jewett states that there are typically three arguments raised against the ordination of women: (1) something in the nature of women forbids it; (2) something in the nature of the priesthood forbids it; (3) something in the nature of God forbids it.[37] Every time I suggest this, someone responds that *none* of these is the problem; the problem is that "*Scripture* forbids it." But if I press them

---

[37]P. K. Jewett, *Man as Male and Female: A Study in Sexual Relationships from a Theological Point of View* (Grand Rapids, Mich.: Eerdmans, 1975).

as to *why* Scripture forbids it, they invariably come back to one of these three points or a combination of the three. Both those who favor women in ministry and those who oppose women in ministry can find suitable proof texts and suitable rationalizations to explain those texts. But if our discussion is ever to move beyond proof texting, we must integrate these texts into a theology of ministry. I suggest that the starting point for such a theology of ministry lies in the God who gives gifts for ministry and in the God who is no respecter of persons.

Creation, Fall, Redemption

Finally, I will comment on the apparent contrast between creation and redemption that Longenecker sets up in his paper. Generally, the essay posits two multifaceted categories and an evolution of emphasis from one to the other. The first, chiefly found in the Old Testament, is rooted in creation and is characterized by the hierarchy of the sexes. The second category finds its chief expression in the New Testament, in redemption and in mutuality of the sexes. Longenecker seems to argue that if we recognize the priority of the New Testament over the Old Testament in the areas of soteriology and ethics—and we surely do recognize this—the recognition of this priority ought to be extended; it ought naturally to suggest a corresponding shift in emphasis in our hermeneutics and practices: A hermeneutic with its center in the New Testament ought to weight redemption more than creation, mutuality more than hierarchy.

Although I like the logic of Longenecker's argument and the consistency it brings to hermeneutics and to the relationship between the testaments, I take issue with the statement that implied in woman's derived creation "are ideas of subordination and submission, even though equality and mutuality are also maintained because of being created in the image of God." Certainly not all commentators read the material this way. Martin Luther asserts that a woman's subordinate role is due *not* to her secondary creation but to the results of sin: "If Eve had persisted in the truth, she would not only not have been subjected to the rule of her husband, but she herself would also have been a partner in the rule which is now entirely the concern of males." "The wife was made subject to the man by the Law which was given after sin." "Eve has been placed under the power of her husband, she who previously was very free and, as the sharer of all the gifts of God, was in no respect inferior to her husband. This punishment, too, springs from original sin." "The female sex has been greatly humbled and afflicted, and it bears a far severer and harsher punishment than the men."[38]

For Luther, man and woman are equal in all ways at creation; the subordination of the woman is due not to creation but to the Fall. In contrast, John Calvin holds that hierarchy is indeed implied in woman's derived creation and says that woman *is* created in the image of God, but only in a secondary sense: "It cannot be denied, that the woman also, though in the second degree, was created in the image of God. . . . We may therefore conclude that the order of nature implies that the woman should be the helper of the man." "Women, being instructed in their duty of helping their husbands, should study to keep this divinely appointed order. . . . For the woman was ordained to be the man's helper, even although he had stood in his integrity." Then, commenting on Genesis 3:15, Calvin writes, "The second punishment which [God] exacts is subjection. She had, indeed, previously been subject to her husband, but that was a liberal and gentle subjection; now, however, she is cast into servitude."[39]

Here are two ways of viewing the Genesis data. On the one hand, Calvin's view is that woman's subjection is part of God's ordering of creation, a corollary of her derived creation and, at least for Calvin, tied to the fact that she is created in God's image only in a "second degree." On the other hand, there is Luther's interpretation that woman's subjection is the result of sin, not properly part of the order of creation. Before the Fall, she is man's full, free and equal partner; only afterward is she subject to him.

Which of these two sixteenth-century contemporaries is the better exegete? I would contend that in this instance Luther has the upper hand and that the derived creation of woman recounted in Genesis 2 does not imply subordination. What is her derived creation intended to imply? First, it shows that she alone of all God's created subjects is a fit companion for man; thus it comes after God has brought all the

---

[38]Martin Luther, *Lectures on Genesis: Chapters 1—5* (St. Louis: Concordia Publishing House, 1958), pp. 203, 138, 202, 200.

[39]John Calvin, *Commentaries on the First Book of Moses Called Genesis*, vol. 1 (Grand Rapids, Mich.: Baker, 1979), pp. 129, 130, 172.

animals to Adam, and none is "fit" or "appropriate" for him. Second, woman's derived creation explains the bonds of marriage: woman was created from man; from one come two. In marriage, they are united once more into one flesh: two become one. Finally, the terminology *(ezer kenegdo),* which the KJV renders as "a help meet for him," we hear as a "helpmeet" or "servant," suggesting a secondary role. But the term *ezer* can also be used in the Old Testament of God himself, who is a help in time of need (Ps 146:5). Woman is thus, for the man, "a helper *of his like."* The primary implication of the formation of the woman out of the man is their unity, their likeness; her being is not alien to his, for she is "bone of his bone and flesh of his flesh." She is a being in which, as soon as he sees her, the man recognizes himself.

It is Genesis 3 that gives the first explicit statement of woman's subjection. Man's "rule" over woman is the woman's punishment. According to the writer of Genesis, this is not the ideal relation of the sexes, just as thorns and thistles in the ground, enmity between human beings and the animal world, and woman's pain in bearing children are not God's created ideal. Although the phrase "to rule over" need not connote "tyranny of power," it does reflect the position of the woman in the ancient world as wholly subject to the man.

Let me return to the development that Longenecker traces from the Old Testament to the New Testament and particularly to the development he describes from a dominance of the categories of creation to a dominance of the categories of redemption. It makes more sense to me exegetically and theologically to see the movement not as bipolar, from creation to redemption, but as tripolar, from creation to the Fall and from the Fall to redemption. It is not the creation of woman but rather human sinfulness that led to woman's subject status. If Christ has truly come to redeem us from sin *and its results,* the hope of redemption must also extend to our fallen human relationships in general and to the relationship between man and woman. In the words of Isaac Watts, "He comes to make his blessings flow/Far as the curse is found."

Marianne Meye Thompson is assistant professor of New Testament, Fuller Theological Seminary, Pasadena, California.

6

WHAT DOES *KEPHALĒ* MEAN IN THE NEW TESTAMENT?

Berkeley & Alvera Mickelsen

THE BELIEF OF some Christians that the Bible teaches a hierarchy, with men in a role of authority over women (basically over all women and very specifically over their wives) is based largely on two references by Paul to males (or husbands) as the "head" of women (or wives), 1 Corinthians 11:3 and Ephesians 5:23.

In 1 Corinthians 11:3, Paul writes, "the head of every man is Christ, and the head of the woman is man, and the head of Christ is God" (NIV). Ephesians 5:23 says, "For the husband is the head of the wife as Christ is the head of the church, his body, of which he is the Savior" (NIV).

The American Heritage Dictionary gives as one meaning of *head,* "one who occupies the foremost position; leader, chief, or director."[1] We use *head* frequently this way in our everyday speech: "He is the head of his company," or "He is the department head." To understand what the apostle Paul really meant when he wrote about man or husband being the head of the woman or the wife in 1 Corinthians and Ephesians 5, we must carefully examine the meaning of the word *kephalē* ("head") in the Greek of Paul's day.

The Challenges of Translation
The most complete Greek–English lexicon (covering Homeric, classical and *koinē* Greek) in current existence is a two-volume work of more

---

[1] William Morris, *The American Heritage Dictionary of the English Language* (Boston: Houghton Mifflin Co., 1980).

than 2,000 pages compiled by Liddell, Scott, Jones and McKenzie, published first in 1843.[2] It is based on examination of thousands of Greek writings from the period of Homer (about 1000 B.C.) to about A.D. 600—a period of nearly 1,600 years, including the Septuagint and New Testament times. This lexicon lists, with examples, the common meanings of *kephalē.* The list includes more than 25 possible figurative meanings in addition to the literal meaning of physical head of man or beast. The list does *not* include "authority," "superior rank," "leader," "director," or anything similar as a meaning. There is an older Greek–Latin thesaurus published in 1851 but written primarily in the sixteenth century.[3] It also gives no meanings such as "authority over" or "supreme over." Apparently, ordinary readers of Greek literature during New Testament times would not think of "final authority," "superior rank" or "director" as common meanings for the word translated "head."

The entry looks somewhat like this in the 1940 edition of the Liddell, Scott, Jones and McKenzie lexicon:

I. 1. Physical *head* of man or beast. Frequently used with preposition such as "down over the head," or "above the head" or "from head to foot" or "head foremost" or "thrust headlong." [In our day we would say "head first."]
   2. As the *noblest* part, periphrasis for the whole person.
   3. *Life,* as in "staking their heads on . . ."
   4. In imprecation, as in "on my head be it!" [or Paul's response in Acts 18:6 to the Jews who opposed him in Macedonia, "Your blood be upon your heads!"]
II. Of things, extremity.
   a. In botany, *head* of garlic, tubers.
   b. In anatomy, *base* of heart, but also *apex;* of muscles, *origin.*
   c. Generally, *top, brim* of vessel; *coping* of a wall; *capital* of a column.
   d. In plural, *source, origin* of a river, but singular, *mouth;* generally, *source, origin, starting point.*
   e. *extremity* of a plot of land.

---

[2]Henry George Liddell and Robert Scott, *A Greek-English Lexicon,* revised by Henry Stuart Jones, with the assistance of Roderick McKenzie (Oxford: Clarendon Press, 1940), 1:944-45.
[3]Henrico Stephano, *Thesaurus Graece Linguae,* ed. Carolus Hase, Guilielmus Dindorfius and Ludovicus Dindorfius (Paris: Excuderbot Ambrosius Firmin Didot, 1851), pp. 1495-99.

III. a *bust* of Homer.

IV. wig, head-dress.

V. Metaphorical

    a. pièce de résistance [i.e., main dish of a meal]

    b. crown, completion, consummation.

    c. sum, total

    d. band of men; right hand half of phalanx

    e. Astronomy, Aries [as the gable of the world]

The lexicon gives references to Greek literature for each of these meanings. The lexicographers (with various editions spanning more than 100 years—from 1836 to 1940) apparently found no examples in their study of Greek literature where *kephalē* could have only the meaning "one having authority," "supreme over" or anything similar. (Where other recognized meanings are possible, one cannot assume that the word *kephalē* means chief, authority or superior rank.) These scholars living in the 1800s and early 1900s surely could not be accused of being blinded by the "feminist movement" and thus ignoring references in Greek that supported *kephalē* as meaning authority.

The most common lexicon used by pastors and teachers of the Bible in our day is the *koinē* Greek lexicon by Arndt and Gingrich, commonly known as Bauer's.[4] This lexicon is less than half the size of Liddell, Scott, Jones and McKenzie. The following is a basic condensation of the entry for *kephalē* in Bauer:

> [*kephalē*, *ēs*, *hē*,] (Homer, + inscriptions, papyri, Septuagint, Enoch, Epistle of Aristotle, Philo, Josephus) 1. lit.—a. actually of the *head* of man or beast [followed by thirty-six lines of entry giving examples of this obvious meaning, ranging from the New Testament to Aesop's fables].
>
>   b. metaph. . . . Christ the [*kephalē*] of the [church] thought of as a [*sōma* ("body")] Col 1:18; cf. Col 2:19.
>
>   2. fig.—a. In the case of living beings, to denote superior rank. (cf. Artem. 4:24. p. 218 where [*kephalē*] is the symbol of the father; Judg 11:11; 2 [Sam] 22:44) *head* (Zosimus of Ashkelon [500 A.D.]

---

[4]Walter Bauer, *A Greek-English Lexicon of the New Testament and Other Early Christian Literature,* trans. and adapted by William F. Arndt and F. Wilbur Gingrich, 2nd ed., revised and augmented by F. Wilbur Gingrich and Frederick W. Danker (Chicago: University of Chicago Press, 1979), p. 430.

hails Demosth. as his master: ["O divine head"] [Biogr. p. 297]; of the husband in relation to his wife 1 Cor 11:3b; Eph 5:23a. Of Christ in relation to the church Eph 4:15; 5:23b. But Christ is the head not only of the church but of the universe as a whole, *["head over all things"]* Eph 1:22, and of every cosmic power . . . *the head of all might and power* [or all rule & authority]. Col 2:10. The divine influence on the world results in the series (for the growing distance from God with corresponding results); . . . God the *[kephalē]* of Christ, Christ the *[kephalē]* of the man, the man the *[kephalē]* of the woman, 1 Cor 11:3c, a, b.

b. of things *the uppermost part, extremity, end, point . . .[kephalē gōnias]* the *cornerstone* (forming the farthest extension . . . of the corner, though Joachim Jeremias . . . thinks of it as the *keystone* or *capstone* above the door; . . . Mt 21:42; Mk 12:10; Lk 20:17, . . . Ac 4:11; 1 Pt 2:7; B[arnabas] 6:4 (all [quoting] Psalm 118:22 [LXX Ps 117:22]).

Under section two, where Bauer gives "superior rank" as a meaning for *kephalē,* he cites only two references from secular Greek. One comes from Zosimus and is dated A.D. 500—at least 400 years *after* the New Testament was written. (Our question is *not* what *kephalē* meant in A.D. 500 but rather what Paul meant when he used *kephalē* when writing his letters to the churches in the first century.) Bauer's only other reference to secular Greek to support the meaning of "superior rank" is to Artemidorus in the second century, where *kephalē* is used as a symbol of the father. What Artemidorus said (Lib K, Capt 2, Para 6,) was "He [the father] was the cause *(aitos)* of the life and of the light for the dreamer [the son] just as the head *(kephalē)* is the cause of the life and the light of all the body." He also said: "the head is to be likened to parents because the head is the cause [source] of life." Bauer's reference may be an example of a lexicographer reading his own cultural understanding (i.e., fathers have "superior rank") into the text.

Under definition "2. fig.," Bauer also gives two references to the Septuagint—the Greek translation of the Hebrew Old Testament that was completed between 250 and 150 B.C. He points to Judges 11:11 as an example of *kephalē* meaning superior rank: "the people made him [Jephthah] head and leader over them." Here the Septuagint translators used *kephalē* to translate the Hebrew word *ro'sh* ("head"). The Hebrew text follows *ro'sh* with another word, *qatzyn,* meaning chief or ruler. For *qatzyn,* the Septuagint uses *hēgeomai* ("be a leader") in Manuscript A and *archēgos* ("captain, leader, chief prince") in Manuscript B. These words would clarify for Greek readers the meaning of *kephalē* in this case. The Greek concept of *kephalē* as top or crown (from the basic concept of extremity) would also make the meaning clear.

Bauer also points to the Septuagint translation of 2 Samuel 22:44 to defend "superior rank" as a meaning for *kephalē:* "Thou didst keep me as the head of the nations; people whom I had not known served me." Again, the meaning of "top or crown" for *kephalē* would make good sense. The passage thus speaks of Judah as the top or crown of the pagan countries that surrounded it.

To support the meaning of "superior rank" for *kephalē,* Bauer lists five passages from Paul's letters in the New Testament where Bauer personally thinks *kephalē* means this. The two passages that speak of the man (or husband, for the same Greek word is used for both) as the "head" of the wife (or woman—same Greek word for both) are among the five passages listed by Bauer. Is Bauer justified in claiming that in these five passages, the apostle Paul used *kephalē* with the meaning of "superior rank" or "authority over," although that was not an ordinary meaning of the word?

Those who, like Bauer, insist that *kephalē* means "superior rank" say that since *kephalē* is used with that meaning in the Greek translation of the Old Testament, that meaning must have been familiar to Greek-speaking people in New Testament times. The facts do not support this assumption.

The Septuagint was prepared by a large group of Hebrew-Greek scholars for the thousands of Jewish people who lived outside of Palestine. For these Jews, Greek was their first and sometimes only language, and they could not have read a Hebrew Old Testament even if one had been available. They used the Septuagint in their synagogues. For all the early churches outside Palestine, the Septuagint translation *was* the Old Testament, for it was written in the only language they knew.

We studied all the instances in which the Hebrew word *ro'sh* (meaning "head") appears in the Old Testament and how it was translated in the Septuagint. *Ro'sh* occurs approximately 600 times and the Aramaic word *re'sh* occurs 14 times. Usually *ro'sh* or *re'sh* simply means the physical head of a person or animal, the same meaning that the Greek word *kephalē* usually has in the New Testament. In the 239 instances when *ro'sh* refers to a physical head, the Septuagint translators nearly always translated it with *kephalē*. But like our English word *head*, *ro'sh* sometimes had metaphorical or figurative meanings, including leader or someone in authority, or beginning, as in *ro'sh hashshanah* (Ezek 40:1, "at the beginning of the year").

About 180 times, the Hebrew word *ro'sh,* meaning "head," clearly refers to a "chief something"—a chief man, chief city, chief nation, chief priest, that is, the leader or authority figure in a group. Apparently, this meaning for *ro'sh* was as common in ancient Hebrew as it is in English today. But, as we have seen from the Liddell, Scott, Jones and McKenzie lexicon, that was not a common meaning in the Greek language of New Testament times. The findings of these lexicographers are confirmed when we examine the Greek words that the translators of the Septuagint used when the Hebrew word *ro'sh* means leader or chief. In the 180 instances when *ro'sh* means leader or chief, the Septuagint translators rarely used *kephalē*. *Archōn,* meaning ruler, commander or leader, was used 109 times (about 60 per cent). Apparently the translators believed that *archōn* rather than *kephalē* more accurately conveyed the meaning of the Hebrew *ro'sh* when it meant ruler or leader.

Translators today face similar problems. If an English writer says, "he was hotheaded," translators to another language probably could not use the literal words for *hot* and *head* and still convey the author's meaning of "violent temper." In the same way, Septuagint translators of *ro'sh* knew that the literal *kephalē* (head) might not give the correct idea because *kephalē* did not mean "leader" or "authority" to ordinary Greek readers. For example, Joshua 23:2 reads, "Joshua summoned all Israel, their elders and heads *[ro'sh]* their judges and officers. . . ." But the Septuagint translators did not use *kephalē* for "heads" in this passage. They used a form of *archōn,* "their elders and *leaders* (or rulers)." The word *ro'sh* also appears in 1 Chronicles 8:10, 13 and 28 in the phrase "heads of fathers' houses." In each instance, the Septuagint translators used a form of *archōn* rather than *kephalē*.

Although *archōn* was the most common word used for *ro'sh* when it meant chief or authority, it was not the only one. The translators occasionally used thirteen other words. Some appear in Deuteronomy

1:13-15, where *heads* appears three times: "Choose wise, understanding and experienced men, according to your tribes, and I will appoint them as your heads. And you answered me, 'The thing that you have spoken is good for us to do,' So I took the heads of your tribes, wise and experienced men, and set them as heads over you. . . ."

Obviously *heads* in this passage meant superior rank or authority. But the Septuagint translators did not use *kephalē* in any of the three places. Instead, they used the Greek words *hēgoumenous, hēgeisthai* and *chiliarchos*. The verb *hēgeomai* means to rule or have dominion. The noun *chiliarchos* means to be a leader, a commander of a thousand soldiers. Among the fourteen words used to translate *ro'sh, kephalē* does appear eighteen times. But these incude six passages that have variant readings. Four others involve a head-tail metaphor that would not make sense without the use of head in contrast to tail. For example, Deuteronomy 28:44 says, "He shall be the head and thou shalt be the tail."

That leaves only eight instances (out of 180) where the Septuagint translators clearly chose to use *kephalē* as a translation for *ro'sh,* when *ro'sh* meant chief or leader. They include the two quoted by Bauer (Judg 11:11; 2 Sam 22:44—2 Kings 22:44 LXX); plus Psalm 18:43 (LXX 17:44); Isaiah 7:8-9 (three times); Jeremiah 31:1 (LXX 38:7); Lamentations 1:4 (LXX 1:5). Why did those eight remain? We don't know. Perhaps not all the translators were equally skilled or conscientious in struggling for different Greek words that would accurately carry the meaning of leadership or authority, and they chose the easier way of putting down the literal transference of *ro'sh* to *kephalē.* Translation is hard work. Or perhaps they assumed that the Greek metaphorical meaning of top or crown would accurately carry the meaning of leader or chief, one prominent, one looked up to.

Septuagint translators used fourteen different Greek words to translate *ro'sh:*

1. *archōn* (meaning ruler, commander, leader) _____ 109 times
2. *archēgos* (captain, leader, chief, prince) _____ 10 times
3. *archē* (authority, magistrate, officer) _____ 9 times
4. *hēgeomai* (to be a leader, to rule, have dominion) _____ 9 times
5. *prōtos* (first, foremost) _____ 6 times
6. *patriarchēs* (father or chief of a race, patriarch) _____ 3 times
7. *chiliarchēs* (commander) _____ 3 times

8. *archiphulēs* (chief of a tribe) _____ 2 times
9. *archipatriotēs* (head of a family) _____ 1 time
10. *archō* (verb; ruler, be ruler of) _____ 1 time
11. *megas, megalē, mega* (great, mighty, important) _____ 1 time
12. *proēgeomai* (take the lead, go first, lead the way) _____ 1 time
13. *prōtotokos* (firstborn or first in rank) _____ 1 time
14. *kephalē* (where *head* can mean top or crown) _____ 8 times
 kephalē (in head-tail metaphor) _____ 4 times
 kephalē (where manuscripts have variant readings) ____ 6 times
 ro'sh (not translated) _____ 6 times

Eliminating the head-tail metaphors (where nothing but *kephalē*, the Greek word for "head," would make sense) and the instances where manuscripts have variant readings, we are left with the eight instances (less than 4 per cent) in which *kephalē* translates *ro'sh* where the metaphorical meaning implies "leader or chief." In these instances, the context permitted the Greek meaning of "top or crown" (extremity) to convey the leader idea. Most of these eight passages are in relatively obscure places in the Old Testament. Early Christians could have gone to church for years without ever hearing these passages where *kephalē* meant something different from the usual Greek meanings.

Kephalē would have been the natural word to use in all 180 instances if the word had been commonly understood to mean "leader or chief." Its rare usage indicates that translators knew that *kephalē* did not commonly carry this meaning. They also recognized that translation demands exact equivalents whenever possible rather than inexact approximations. Since the Septuagint translators recognized that *kephalē* did not carry the Hebrew meaning of leader, authority or superior rank, we must be sure that *we* do not read our similar English meaning of head into the Greek word.

The apostle Paul was a Greek-speaking Jew (he grew up in the Greek-speaking city of Tarsus); indeed, Greek was his native language. He knew both Hebrew and Greek, but he wrote his epistles to Greek-speaking churches in areas where most of the converts (including Jews of the dispersion) knew only Greek. A man of his superb intellectual ability and intense passion to spread the gospel would likely use Greek words with Greek meanings that his readers clearly understood.

Examination of the seven passages where Paul used *kephalē* in reference to Christ indicates that, when they are read with common Greek meanings of *kephalē,* we see a more exalted Christ than when we read "head" primarily with the meaning of "authority over." When Christ is spoken of as the head of the church, it may refer to him as the church's source of life, as its top or crown, as its exalted originator and completer. These rich meanings are lost when "authority" or "superior rank" is considered the only meaning for head.

Christ unquestionably *does* have authority over the church and over all the world, but that authority is established in *other* passages of Scripture, such as Matthew 28:18, "And Jesus came and said to them, 'All authority *[exousia]* in heaven and on earth has been given to me' "; Matthew 9:6, "The Son of man has authority *[exousia]* on earth to forgive sins"; and John 5:26–27 "The father . . . has given him authority *[exousia]* to execute judgment, because he is the Son of man."

In two of the seven passages, Paul used *kephalē* in reference to Christ as the head of the church and man (or husband) as head of the woman (or wife). The church has traditionally read all these passages with the English meaning of head or authority rather than with the Greek meanings of head. This misreading of the Greek word has been used to teach that male dominance over women was ordained by God, when Paul may have been saying something quite different.

In the remainder of this paper we will examine each of the seven passages where Paul speaks of Christ as the head of the church (the body). Does the context in each case support one of the ordinary Greek meanings of *kephalē* rather than the "superior rank" meaning associated with the English word *head* and the Hebrew *ro'sh*?

Head = Source of Life

1. *Colossians 2:19 (context 2:16–19).* Christians are told to hold fast "to the Head, *from whom* the whole body, nourished and knit together through its joints and ligaments, grows with a growth that is from God" (emphasis added). This passage points to Christ as the source of life. Similarly Greeks spoke of Zeus as source *(kephalē)* and beginning *(archē):* "From whom [Zeus] all things have been made" (Orphic fragments).

2. *Ephesians 4:15 (context 4:11–16)* is very similar to Colossians 2:19 (above), with the same Greek meaning of "source of life." It reads, "We

are to grow up in every way into him who is the head, into Christ, *from whom* the whole body, joined and knit together by every joint with which it is supplied, when each part is working properly, makes bodily growth and upbuilds itself in love" (emphasis added). This passage stresses the unity of head and body, and it presents Christ as the nourisher and source of growth.

Strangely, Bauer classifies this passage as meaning "superior rank," although he does not so classify the very similar Colossians 2:19.

Head = Top or Crown (Extremity)

3. *Colossians 2:10 (context 2:6-15).* "For in him the whole fulness of deity dwells bodily, and you have come to fulness of life in him, who is the head of all rule and authority." Paul uses two Greek metaphors here—the head-body metaphor, with the church coming to "fulness of life" in Christ (the nourisher, enabler), and the metaphor of top or crown (Christ the head of all rule and authority). *Head,* meaning "top or crown," emphasizes Christ's position by virtue of the cross and resurrection. He is victor, crowned with glory and honor (Heb 2:9; Ps 8:5). Only Jesus, the God-man, can have such a position because of his unique work.

4. *Ephesians 1:20-23.* This passage presents an exalted picture of Christ and his authority over everything in creation, "when he raised him from the dead and made him sit at his right hand in the heavenly places, far above all rule and authority and power and dominion, and above every name that is named, not only in this age, but also in that which is to come, and he has put all things under his feet and has made him the head over all things for the church, which is his body, the fulness of him who fills all in all."

Verses 20 and 21 clearly establish the absolute authority of Christ over everything. Paul then returns to his favorite head-body metaphor, this time adding "feet" to the picture. The authority of Christ, established in verses 20 and 21, is extended to every extremity from crown (head) to feet—including the church, which is his body. This church, his body, is described as "the fulness of him who fills all in all." The church is a part of this glorious, exalted Christ.

Head = Source, Base, Derivation

5. *1 Corinthians 11:3 (context 11:2-16).* Here *head* seems to carry the

Greek concept of source, base or derivation. "Now I want you to know that the head of every man is Christ, and the man is head of woman, and God is head of Christ." (For some unknown reason, the RSV reads "the head of a *woman* is her *husband.*" Since the same Greek word is used for *woman* and *wife,* and for *man* and *husband,* there is no excuse for this inconsistency. Either it should read "the head of a *wife* is her husband" or "the head of the woman is man." For reasons of context, we agree with the NIV and KJV readings, "the head of the woman is man.")

In this chapter, Paul discusses how men and women should pray and prophesy in public church gatherings. Paul is not discussing marriage— he did that in 1 Corinthians 7. The instructions here apparently involve customs, dress and hair style in Corinth and the tendency of the Corinthian church to be disorderly. The discussion centers on women's and men's head coverings or hair styles (veils are not mentioned in the Greek text). Paul says in verse 8 that "man was not made *from* woman, but woman *from* man." In verse 12 he also says that "woman was made *from* man" (emphasis added). This strongly suggests that Paul was using "head" in verse 3 with the Greek meaning of "source, origin, base, or derivation." Man was the "source or beginning" of woman in the sense that woman was made from the side of Adam. Christ was the one through whom all creation came, as Paul states in 1 Corinthians 8:6b, "Jesus Christ, through whom are all things and through whom we exist." God is the source of Christ, as taught in John 8:42, "I proceeded and came forth from God."

When we recognize the Greek metaphorical meaning of source or origin in the word *kephalē* as Paul explains it in verses 8 and 12, 1 Corinthians 11:3 does not teach a chain of command. Paul's word order also shows he was not thinking of a chain of command: Christ, head of man; man, head of woman; God, head of Christ. Those who make it a chain of command must rearrange Paul's words. In fact, Paul seems to go out of his way to show that he was not inputing authority to males when he says in verse 12, "For as woman was made from man, so now man is born of woman. And all things are from God."

Careful examination of Bauer's entry on 1 Corinthians 11:3 (which he uses as an illustration of *kephalē* meaning "superior rank") indicates the result (or perhaps the cause) for his believing that "superior rank" is a

meaning of *kephalē*. Bauer says that the series here indicates "the growing distance from God with corresponding results." On Bauer's view,
men are automatically closer to God than women are by virtue of their
being male.

Head = Exalted Originator and Completer

6. *Colossians 1:18 (context 1:14-20)*. Who is the Christ in whom we
have redemption? He is the "head" (originator and completer) of the
body, the church. "He [Christ] is the head of the body, the church; he is
the beginning, the first-born from the dead, that in everything he might
be pre-eminent." In this passage, Paul practically defines his Greek
meaning for *head,* "the beginning, the first-born from the dead." Christ
is the beginning or first cause and through him God reconciles all things
to himself (v. 20).

Here *kephalē* fits clearly the Greek meaning of source or beginning.
Bauer does not list this passage among those meaning "superior rank."

Head = One Who Brings to Completion

7. *Ephesians 5:23 (context 5:18-23)*. In this passage, "head" in a
head-body metaphor shows the unity of husband and wife and of Christ
and the church. "For the husband is head of the wife as Christ is head
of the church, his body." Paul often uses the head-body metaphor to
stress the unity of Christ and the church. In fact, this unity is the prevailing theme of the letter to the Ephesians and forms the context for
this passage. The head and body by nature are dependent on each other.

The oft-quoted verse 23 ("The husband is the head of the wife as
Christ is head of the church, his body") follows a section in which Paul
explains what it means to be filled with the Spirit. The last evidence of
being Spirit-filled is "submitting yourselves to one another out of reverence for Christ." This is addressed to *all* Christians and obviously
includes husbands and wives. As part of this mutual submission of all
Christians to each other, wives are to submit to their husbands as to the
Lord. The word for "submit" does not appear in verse 22 in the better
Greek manuscripts. The text says only "wives to your husbands." The
meaning is brought down from verse 21 and therefore must refer to the
same kind of submission demanded of all Christians in "submit yourselves to one another out of reverence for Christ."

To stress the oneness of husband and wife, Paul then returns to his favorite head–body metaphor: "For the husband is head *[kephalē]* of his wife as Christ is head *[kephalē]* of the church, his body."

Paul emphasizes this unity of husband and wife and of Christ and the church by quoting Genesis 2:24: "For this reason, a man shall leave his father and mother and be joined to his wife and the two shall be one flesh. This is a great mystery, but I am speaking about Christ and the church" (Eph 5:31–32). There surely is no hierarchy in Genesis 2:24. If Paul were teaching headship as authority or hierarchy, he probably would have quoted Genesis 3:16: "Your desire shall be for your husband, and he shall rule over you."

Paul develops his head–body metaphor of interdependence at length in 1 Corinthians 12:22–27. If he thought of "head" as the part of the body that had control or authority over the rest of the body, would it not appear in this long passage? We know that the brain largely directs the body. But Paul did not use that concept in his metaphor. He refers to various parts of the head: ears (12:16), eyes (12:16), nose (12:17). The head as a whole is mentioned only in verse 21: "The eye cannot say to the hand, 'I have no need of you,' nor again the head to the feet, 'I have no need of you.'" (Head and feet represent the extremities.) Paul ends his discussion with his basic teaching of the unity and mutual dependence of all parts on each other: "If one member suffers, all suffer together; if one member is honored, all rejoice together." He never suggests that "head" has authority over other parts of the body.

Of course, Christ *does* have authority over the church. But most of the passages that present Christ as head of the church do not emphasize the authority of Christ over the church but rather the oneness of Christ and the church. In Ephesians 5:18–33, this oneness is applied to husband and wife.

If we are to see a meaning in *head* in Ephesians 5:23 beyond the head–body metaphor of mutual dependence and unity, we must do so on the basis of the immediate context. Christ's headship of the church is illustrated thus: "Christ loved the church and gave himself up for her . . . that he might present the church to himself in splendor . . . holy and without blemish." Christ gave himself up to enable believers (the church) to become all that we are meant to be. As Christ gave himself up by death for the church, to enable the church to become what it was meant to be, so the husband is to give himself up to enable (bring to completion) all that his wife is meant to be.

The husband is to *nourish* and *cherish* his wife (v. 29) as he does his own body, even as Christ nourishes and cherishes the church. This concept of sacrificial self-giving so that a spouse can achieve full potential has been expected of the wife in our society. Here Paul gives that responsibility to the husband! Of course, "giving oneself sacrificially for the other" is a model example of the submission that wives and husbands are to have toward each other, as Paul taught in Ephesians 5:21.

These are the only passages in the New Testament where *kephalē* is used metaphorically. They include the five given by Bauer as examples of *kephalē* meaning "superior rank," although such a meaning does not appear in secular Greek of New Testament times. If Paul had been thinking about an authority or leader, there were easily understood Greek words that he could have used and that he did use in other places. He used *exousia* ("authority") in Romans 13:1-2 and *archōn* in Romans 13:3.

In these seven passages where Paul used *kephalē* metaphorically, we see a more exalted, complete Christ when *kephalē* is read with Greek meanings that would have been familiar to the first readers.

We cannot legitimately read an English or Hebrew meaning into the word *head* in the New Testament when both context and secular Greek literature of New Testament times indicate that meanings such as "superior rank" or "authority over" were not what Greeks usually associated with the word and probably were not what the apostle Paul had in mind. Our misunderstanding of these passages (especially 1 Cor 11:3 and Eph 5:23) has been used to support the concept of male dominance that has ruled most pagan and secular societies since the beginning of recorded history.

Even more important, this misunderstanding has robbed us of the richer, more exalted picture of Christ that Paul was trying to convey to us. This exalted Christ who is top or crown of all creation is the one who brings his church to completion and enables the church to follow his example of servant leadership.

Berkeley Mickelsen is professor of New Testament, Bethel Theological Seminary, St. Paul, Minnesota. Alvera Mickelsen is assistant professor of journalism, Bethel College, St. Paul, Minnesota.

RESPONSE
Ruth A. Tucker

The Mickelsens do a commendable job in searching out the meanings of the word *kephalē*. Their research, like that of some other recent scholars, counters the notion that *kephalē*, when used for male-female relationships, should be translated "superior rank"—a rendering that has been used to limit the role of women in both marriage and ministry. I was disappointed, however, not to find a concise summation of their conclusions as to how the concept of headship relates to male-female distinctions and to the role of women in marriage and ministry. Throughout church history, these very issues related to the application of the concept of headship have been most significant. Whether a woman could remarry after divorce, whether she could perform the sacrament of baptism and whether she could teach in the church were all argued on the basis of headship. The questions relating to headship are as important today as they have been at any time in church history: What distinctions between the sexes does headship imply? What practical applications can we derive from these distinctions?

Throughout church history, the practical applications of the concept of headship have at times been crucial. No doubt the most far-reaching application of headship is found in Mormon polygamy. The Mormons' defense of this practice was based on the biblical concept of headship. A pamphlet entitled "The Peace Maker, or the Doctrines of the Millennium," printed by the Mormon Press in 1842, argues that polygamy is the only way to re-establish the true church on earth. In this true church, the husband was to be the head of the wife, even as Christ was head of the church, and the truest picture of that relationship was polygamy. According to the argument, "woman's unnatural usurpation of power in the family has led to ungoverned and ungovernable children, and male desertion of their families." The remedy was simple. "Polygamy would allow men to reassert their proper authority and leadership. It would free them from the unnatural sexual influence women held over men in a monogamous system."[5] Interestingly, the Mormons were not the only religious group to associate polygamy with male authority and headship. Certain of the Anabaptists similarly argued for polygamy, as did some early Lutherans and Puritans.

The vagueness of the biblical meaning of headship and thus the lack of understanding of that concept have opened the door to some unusual and unwarranted interpretations and applications over the course of Christian history. It would be difficult, therefore, to exaggerate the importance of this study. Indeed, it is essential that all available evidence be brought to bear on our conclusions. The Mickelsens have added much to our understanding, but there are significant areas that need to be investigated further.

As a historian, I feel that the area I am most qualified to discuss in relationship to the word *kephalē* and the concept of headship pertains to the historical implications that are woven throughout the Mickelsen's paper. Although they do not give us any specifics as to how the word *kephalē* or the concept of headship has been interpreted in church tradition, they do say, in reference to Ephesians 5 and 1 Corinthians 11, "The church has traditionally read all these passages with the English meaning of head or authority rather than with the Greek meanings of head." If by use of the word *traditionally* they mean the whole of church history, it would seem that they are suggesting that the church from the beginning has held an untenable position. Are they suggesting that we ignore the views held by the fathers—those closest in time to the Scriptures themselves? If, on the other hand, by using the word *traditionally* the Mickelsens mean only recent tradition that has been directly affected by the "English meaning," I submit that it is essential that we find out what the earlier tradition has to offer, giving particular attention to the fathers. In fact, I believe that historical theology in general should be more closely integrated with hermeneutics.

Clement, Tertullian and Cyprian

In my research in the patristic writings, I found no discussion of the word *kephalē*, but there were a number of references to headship. I looked

---

[5]Lawrence Foster, *Religion and Sexuality: The Shakers, the Mormons, and the Oneida Community* (Urbana: University of Illinois Press, 1984), p. 176.

particularly at the passages that referred to 1 Corinthians 11 or Ephesians 5. In many, the understood meaning of headship must be inferred from the way that the concept was applied. Clement of Alexandria (ca. 155–220) conceded that there was a spiritual equality of man and woman, but he went on to say that "she is destined for child-bearing and housekeeping. 'For I would have you know,' says the apostle, 'that the head of every man is Christ; and the head of the woman is the man.' "6 Why a woman would be destined for childbearing and housekeeping because her head is man is not explained. Could it be that such activities (by their very nature private and perhaps viewed as dishonorable) were appropriate only for a woman, since she did not have the pre-eminence in the marriage relationship?

Tertullian (ca. 169–215), more than other ante-Nicene fathers, associates the term *head* with the meaning "source" or "author." He arrives at the meaning by a two-step process. He implies that since (1) the primary meaning of *head* is "authority" and (2) the idea of authorship can be derived from "authority," *head* means "author." This somewhat confusing discussion of the term *head* occurs in his argument against Marcion's dualism, where Tertullian insists that the creator God of the Old Testament is the same as the Christ of the New Testament. In doing so he states: " 'The head of every man is Christ.' What Christ, if He is not the author of man? The *head* he has here put for *authority;* now 'authority' will accrue to none else than the 'author.' Of what man indeed is He the head? Surely of him concerning whom he adds soon afterwards: 'The man ought not to cover his head, forasmuch as he is the image of God.' Since then he is the image of the Creator . . . how can I possibly have another head but Him whose image I am? For if I am the image of the Creator, there is no room in me for another head."7

This quote, perhaps more than any other, sheds light on the interpretation of *kephalē* in 1 Corinthians 11 only a little more than a century after it was written. It would have been logical for Tertullian to simply say that the "head" (Christ) is the same as the "author" (source, originator or creator), but instead he argues the point indirectly by saying that the "head" (Christ) is the "authority." From there he goes on to

---

6 *The Stromata, or Miscellanies* 4.8 [in *The Ante-Nicene Fathers,* ed. Alexander Roberts and James Donaldson (Grand Rapids, Mich.: Eerdmans, 1951), 2:420].
7 *Against Marcion* 5.8 [*Ante-Nicene Fathers* 3:445].

argue that "authority will accrue to none else than the author." The correctness of his logic here is not the issue. What is significant is the fact that Tertullian arrives at the meaning of *head* as "author" only by building on what he perceives to be the primary meaning, "authority."

Bishop Cyprian of Carthage (ca. 200–258), in commenting on Ephesians 5, makes a close parallel between the physical head and the concept of headship and emphasizes the unity and oneness of the husband-wife relationship. "The apostle declares that the man is the head of the woman, that he might commend chastity in the conjunction of the two. For as the head cannot be suited to the limbs of another, so also one's limbs cannot be suited to the head of another: for one's head matches one's limbs, and one's limbs one's head; and both of them are associated by a natural link in mutual concord, lest, by any discord arising from the separation of the members, the compact of divine covenant should be broken."[8] This statement stands out as one of the few references in the early church to headship where the implied meaning of "superior rank" or "authority" is entirely absent.

Apostolic Constitutions

The *Constitutions of the Holy Apostles,* or simply the *Apostolic Constitutions*—a fourth-century, eight-volume work that deals primarily with the church worship and ministry of the times—offers further insight on the meaning of *head.* Here "superior rank" could be inferred from the application given. "Let the wife be obedient to her own proper husband, because 'the husband is the head of the wife.' But Christ is the head of that husband who walks in the way of righteousness; and 'the head of Christ is God,' even His Father. Therefore, O wife, next after the Almighty, our God and Father . . . and His beloved Son . . . fear thy husband, and reverence him, pleasing him alone. . . ."[9] Here, because of the principle of headship, the wife is enjoined to obey, fear and reverence her husband.

Another reference to headship in the *Apostolic Constitutions* sees even more clearly to carry the idea of authority: "We do not permit our women to teach in the Church,' but only to pray and hear those that

[8] *Of the Discipline and Advantage of Chastity* 5 [*Ante-Nicene Fathers* 5:589].
[9] *Constitutions of the Holy Apostles* 1.3.8 [*Ante-Nicene Fathers* 7:394].

teach. . . . For 'if the head of the wife be the man,' it is not reasonable that the rest of the body should govern the head."[10]

Another reference to headship in the *Apostolic Constitutions* relates to administering baptism. Again, the meaning of authority is assumed.

Now, as to women's baptizing, we let you know that there is no small peril to those that undertake it. Therefore we do not advise you to it; for it is dangerous, or rather wicked and impious. For if the "man be the head of the woman," and he be originally ordained for the priesthood, it is not just to abrogate the order of the creation, and leave the principal to come to the extreme part of the body. For the woman is the body of the man, taken from his side, and subject to him, from whom she was separated for the procreation of children. For says He, "He shall rule over thee." For the principal part of the woman is the man, as being her head. But if in the foregoing constitutions we have not permitted them to teach, how will any one allow them, contrary to nature, to perform the office of a priest? For this is one of the ignorant practices of the Gentile atheism, to ordain women priests to the female deities, not one of the constitutions of Christ."[11]

Ambrose and Augustine

In the late fourth century, Ambrose, the great bishop of Milan, associated the concept of headship with apparent physical (and perhaps emotional) strength. "She who was created to be a helper to man requires male protection! 'The head of woman is man.' (I Cor. 11:3)."[12]

The Ambrosiaster, a fourth-century commentary on the Pauline Epistles incorrectly believed to have been written by Ambrose, refers to headship in order to argue that men are not under the law, at least in regard to divorce and remarriage, as women are. After categorically forbidding a woman under any circumstance to remarry following a divorce, the commentary addresses the same issue with respect to men: "for it is permissible for a man to marry a wife, if he has divorced a sinful wife, because a man is not bound by the law as a woman is; for a man

---

[10]Ibid., 3.1.6 [*Ante-Nicene Fathers* 7:427-28].

[11]Ibid., 3.1.9 [*Ante-Nicene Fathers* 7:429].

[12]*On Paradise,* Corpus Scriptorum Ecclesiasticorum Latinorum 32.1.280, cited in Elizabeth A. Clark, *Women in the Early Church* (Wilmington, Del.: Michael Glazier, 1983), p. 30.

is head over woman."[13]

Augustine understood the concept of headship in terms of the pre-eminence of the husband and the subjection of the wife. In his essay *On Continence*, he argues against the dualism—the "utter madness"—of the Manicheans and others who viewed the flesh, and thus the marriage relationship, as wholly evil. In response, he wrote that "all the things are good, when" they "observe the beauty of order." What is this order? According to Augustine, it is an order of "certain [things] set over [other things] by way of pre-eminence," and "certain [things] made subject [to other things] in a becoming manner." How does he illustrate this? "Let wives be subject unto their own husbands . . . because the husband is the head of the wife."[14] So it would seem that Augustine understood headship in terms of pre-eminence or authority.

Calvin

Although the patristic writings have the greatest bearing on this discussion, I believe that it is also important to look at the writings of Calvin—the most eminent theologian between Augustine and modern times, whose writing bears directly on this subject. Calvin surprisingly appears to have a very flexible outlook, particularly in his commentary on 1 Corinthians. In reference to headship in 11:3, he asserts that "Christ is the head of the man and of the woman without any distinction, because as to that, there is no regard paid to male or female; but as regards external arrangement and political decorum, the man follows Christ and the woman the man." So "this inequality exists," according to Calvin, because Paul "does not disturb civil order or honorary distinctions, which cannot be dispensed with in ordinary life."[15]

How did Calvin himself apply the passage? Did he disturb civil order? Certainly not. In fact, his application of the concept of headship in the church was as narrow as any of the so-called traditionalists. In discussing 1 Corinthians 14:34, he brings up the subject of teaching and states:

[13]*The Ambrosiaster* 1341a, in *The Faith of the Fathers*, trans. W. A. Jurgens (Collegeville, Minn.: Liturgical Press, 1979), 2:178.
[14]*On Continence* 23, in *A Select Library of the Nicene and Post-Nicene Fathers of the Christian Church*, ed. Philip Schaff (Buffalo: Christian Literature Co., 1887), 3:388.
[15]John Calvin, *Commentary on the Epistles of Paul the Apostle to the Corinthians*, trans. John Pringle (Grand Rapids, Mich.: Eerdmans, 1948), pp. 353-54.

"For how unseemly a thing it were, that one who is under subjection to one of the members, should preside over the entire body! It is therefore an argument from things inconsistent—If the woman is under subjection, she is, consequently, prohibited from authority to teach in public. And unquestionably, whatever even natural propriety has been maintained, women have in all ages been excluded from the public management of affairs. It is the dictate of common sense, that female government is improper and unseemly."[16]

Calvin's understanding of the term *head* in Ephesians 2:22 is relevant to the issue. Speaking of Christ, Paul states, "And gave him to be the head." Calvin interprets *head* to mean authority: "He was made the head of the Church, on the condition that he should have the administration of all things. The apostle shows that it was not a mere honorary title, but was accompanied by the entire command and government of the universe. The metaphor of a head denotes the highest authority."[17]

In conclusion, it is my impression that whatever the word *kephalē* meant to the apostle Paul as he wrote 1 Corinthians 11 and Ephesians 5, it was generally interpreted by the church fathers and by Calvin to mean authority, superior rank or pre-eminence. These findings bring into question some of the Mickelsens' assumptions—particularly that the "superior rank" meaning of *kephalē* is not "one of the ordinary Greek meanings" but rather a "meaning associated with the English word *head.*" More research needs to be done in this area, but it seems clear that the fathers used this so-called English meaning long before they could have in any way been influenced by the English language.

Ruth A. Tucker is visiting professor, Trinity Evangelical Divinity School, Deerfield, Illinois.

---

[16]Ibid., p. 468.
[17]John Calvin, *Commentaries on the Epistles of Paul to the Galatians and Ephesians,* trans. William Pringle (Grand Rapids, Mich.: Eerdmans, 1948), p. 217.

RESPONSE

Philip Barton Payne

Nowhere do the practical consequences of the Bible's teaching about women come closer to home than in the phrase "the husband is the head of the wife" (Eph 5:23). With so much at stake, the Mickelsens are to be commended for examining the meaning of the word *kephalē* ("head") in the Greek of Paul's day. The lexicon of Liddell and Scott is the right place to start. The Mickelsens' investigation of the Septuagint demonstrates that its translators were on the whole quite aware that *kephalē* was *not* an appropriate word to choose to translate "head" when the Hebrew word *ro'sh* ("head") implied a position of authority. Finally, they give attention to the context of each Pauline passage where *kephalē* occurs, providing a reasonable interpretation of each of them in harmony with the range of meaning of *kephalē* recognized in the Greek of Paul's day.

An Understated Case

The Mickelsens actually understate their case from Greek usage. Including its 1968 supplement, the Liddell and Scott lexicon lists forty-eight separate English equivalents of figurative meanings of *kephalē*. None of them implies leader, authority, first or supreme. To confirm that "authority" was not in the usual connotative range of *kephalē*, I consulted three prominent specialists in ancient Greek literature.[18] They all agreed that the idea of "authority" was not a recognized meaning of *kephalē* in Greek.

An examination of other Greek lexicons further supports the Mickel-

---

[18]David Armstrong of the University of Texas at Austin and Michael Wigodsky and Mark Edwards of Stanford University.

sens' thesis. None of the following lexicons lists any examples related to "leader" or "authority": Moulton and Milligan, Friedrich Preisigke, Pierre Chantraine.[19] and E. A. Sophocles gives only one such example from A.D. 952.[20] S. C. Woodhouse lists twenty Greek equivalents for "chief" (p. 129) and twenty-six Greek equivalents for "authority" (p. 54), but *kephalē* is not listed as an equivalent for either of these or for "leader."[21]

Heinrich Schlier, describing *kephalē* in the *TDNT,* lists twenty-seven possible English translations of metaphorical meanings of *kephalē* outside the New Testament, none of which conveys the idea of "authority."[22] He concludes "that in secular usage *kephalē* is not employed for the head of a society. This is first found in the sphere of the Gk. OT. . . . [And the idea of obeying the head] does not go beyond the LXX view. This is true only of much later and relatively infrequent combinations like 'head of the priesthood.' "[23] Stephen Bedale states, "In normal Greek usage, classical or contemporary, *kephalē* does not signify 'head' in the sense of ruler, or chieftain, of a community."[24] C. K. Barrett asserts that the meaning "ruler . . . was not a native meaning of the Greek word."[25]

The ancient Greek world through the time of Paul commonly believed that the heart, not the head, was the center of emotions and spirit, the

---

[19]James Hope Moulton and George Milligan, *The Vocabulary of the Greek Testament Illustrated from the Papyri and Other Non-literary Sources* (London: Hodder & Stoughton, 1930), p. 342; Friedrich Preisigke, *Worterbuch der griechischen Papyrusurkunden mit Einschluss der griechischen Inscriften Ausschriften Ostraka Mumienschilder usw. aus Ägypten,* 4 vols. (Berlin: Selbstverlag der Erden, 1935), 1:790–91 (under *kephalē* the meaning *Oberhaupt* ["chief"] is listed, but no examples are given, the only meaning in this entry that does not quote at least one example); Pierre Chantrain, *Dictionaire étymologique de la langue Grecque: Histoire des mots,* 5 vols. (Paris: Éditions Klincksieck, 1968-80), 2:522.

[20] E. A. Sophocles, *Greek Lexicon of the Roman and Byzantine Periods (from B.C. 146 to A.D. 1100)* (New York: Frederick Ungar, 1887), p. 662.

[21]S. C. Woodhouse, *English–Greek Dictionary—a Vocabulary of the Attic Language* (London: Routledge & Kegan Paul, 1982).

[22]Heinrich Schlier, κεφαλή, *Theological Dictionary of the New Testament,* 10 vols, ed. Gerhard Kittel and Gerhard Friedrich, trans. Geoffrey Bromiley (Grand Rapids, Mich.: Eerdmans, 1964–76), 3:673-81.

[23] *TDNT* 3:674, 676.

[24]Stephen Bedale, "The Meaning of κεφαλή in the Pauline Epistles," *Journal of Theological Studies* 5 (1954): 211.

[25]C. K. Barrett, *The First Epistle to the Corinthians* (New York, Harper & Row, 1968), p. 248.

"central governing place of the body."[26] Aristotle held that the heart was not only the seat of control but also the seat of intelligence. Classicist Michael Wigodsky of Stanford is probably correct that many, even the doctors with the most advanced anatomical understanding of the brain, did not really believe that the brain exerted more control over the body than the heart.[27] Such a notion seemed to contradict the nearly universal belief that, since the life is in the blood, the heart must be the center of life. Thus, it is hardly surprising that the idea of authority was not normally associated with the word for "head" in Greek thought.

The Mickelsens' criticism of Bauer's treatment of *kephalē* is well founded. The inappropriateness of citing the Zosimus statement as an example of *kephalē* denoting "superior rank" is not due only to its late date. It is virtually certain that this passage does not imply a position of authority over anyone. Stanford classicist Mark Edwards stated that *hō theia kephalē* in the Zosimus document is a salutation implying dignity, not authority.[28] Presumably the Demosthenes referred to is the great Athenian orator (384–22 B.C.), who could not have had a position of authority over Zosimus since Demosthenes had died over 800 years earlier.[29]

Bauer's most important reference, Ps.-Aristotle, *De Mundo* 6.4, does not even contain the word *kephalē*! Yet the idea of ruler or chief being conveyed in Greek so exactly fits our idea of "head of a household" that the Oxford series translator felt it best to insert the word *head*.[30] This passage clearly shows, however, that the ideas of "source," "nourisher"

---

[26]Aristotle *De Motu Animalium* 2.703a.35, translation from *The Works of Aristotle*, ed. J. A. Smith and W. D. Russ (Oxford: Clarendon, 1908–52). Typically, Aristotle wrote of the heart as the "primary or dominating part . . . the centre wherein abides the sensory soul." *De Partibus Animalium* 3.4.665b, 3.10.672b.17. Apparently, "having found the brain to be devoid of sensation, he concluded that it could not be associated with it. The function of the brain was to keep the heart from overheating the blood"; Charles Joseph Singer and Abraham Wassestein, "Anatomy and Physiology," in *The Oxford Classical Dictionary*, ed. N. G. L. Hammond and H. H. Scullard, 2nd ed. (Oxford: Clarendon, 1970), p. 59.

[27]Conversations with the author at Stanford University, September 27 and October 4, 1984.

[28]LSJ gives eight examples of *kephalē* used as a salutation in which *kephalē* is periphrastic for the whole person, including a virtually identical prose example from the fourth century A.D. *Orationes* 7.212a of Julianus Imperator: *tēs theias kephalēs*.

[29]Conversation with the author at Stanford University, September 28, 1984.

[30]E. S. Forster, *Aristotle (Ps.) De Mundo* (Oxford: Clarendon, 1914), p. 398a, 8.

and "having the highest place" were very important to the Greek mind and were prominent in their most exalted descriptions of God.

Several factors indicate that Paul probably did not consider the brain the control center of the body and that medical evidence was not the source of his use of the head-body metaphor. He does not use words for "brain" or "nerves" or offer any evidence that he differentiated sensory and motor functions. Furthermore, "no parallels have as yet been traced in the books of the scientists to his statements (Eph 5:23, 29; 4:15-16; Col 2:19) about the capability of the 'head' to 'save,' 'provide for,' 'care for' or 'sustain' the body . . . [or to] the idea of 'growth *from* the head' [or to the head as the source] of life."[31]

Rather, Paul seems to associate intelligence and control of the body with the heart in such expressions as "their foolish heart was darkened" (Rom 1:21), "the law written in their hearts" (Rom 2:15), "it is with your heart that you believe" (Rom 10:9-10), "no heart has conceived God's plans" (1 Cor 2:9), "he who has decided in his own heart" (1 Cor 7:37) and "may the eyes of your heart be enlightened to know" (Eph 1:18).[32] Nowhere does he associate the mind with the head.

The Mickelsens are to be commended for drawing attention to the significant fact that in the overwhelming majority of instances where the Hebrew Old Testament referred to a physical head it is translated *kephalē* in the Septuagint. Septuagint translators chose *kephalē* to render *ro'sh* when it refers to a physical head in 226 of its 239 occurrences.[33] In sharp contrast, Septuagint translators chose *kephalē* to render *ro'sh*

---

[31]Markus Barth, *Ephesians 1—3* (Garden City, N.Y.: Doubleday, 1974), p. 191.

[32]See also "stubborn and unrepentant heart" (Rom 2:5); "do not say in your heart" (Rom 10:6-8); "by smooth talk and flattery they deceive the hearts" (Rom 16:18); "the motives of the hearts" (1 Cor 4:5); "the secrets of his heart will be disclosed" (1 Cor 14:25); "make music in your heart" (Eph 5:19); "call on the Lord out of a pure heart" (2 Tim 2:22).

[33]Hatch and Redpath list only 292 instances of *kephalē* translating *ro'sh* and ten instances translating the Aramaic *re'sh* (six more are in variants of the same verses already cited). Of these, 226 are instances of *kephalē* translating *ro'sh* or its Aramaic equivalent when they refer to a physical head, some of which imply a figurative meaning as well. Although it is a very small minority and does not affect the Mickelsens' overall thesis, there are thirteen instances where *ro'sh* refers to a physical head but is not translated *kephalē* in the LXX. In two of these it is translated by another Greek word for "head," *koryphē,* which denotes the "top of the head" or "crown" (LSJ 983): Prov 1:9 and Ezek 8:3. Once it is translated "neck," *trachēlos,* changing "bow the head" to "bow the neck," Is 58:5. Twice it is omitted as understood: "crown her [head]" in Esther 2:17 and "cover their heads,"

when it refers to a leader in only about a dozen of its 180 occurrences. My independent analysis of all these occurrences of *ro'sh* agrees exactly with the Mickelsens' total of 180. Half of these are found only in a single variant manuscript or were required to preserve a "head–tail" contrast.

The Mickelsens have stated their case conservatively. Only two of the occurrences of *kephalē* in Isaiah 7:8–9 refer to leaders; the other two, to capital cities. The reference to Israel as "head among the nations" in Jeremiah 31:7 probably refers to her exalted position in God's sight, for she did not have leadership or rule over the nations.[34]

In each of its four occurrences, the meaning of "head and tail" is explained in the immediate context. The Hebrew explanation in Isaiah 9:15, "palm branch and reed," reinforces the same message conveyed by "head and tail." In the Septuagint, "palm branch and reed" is replaced by "beginning and end." In so doing, the translator transformed the meaning of this verse from the Hebrew sense of "leader and subordinant" to the Greek sense of "beginning and end."

The Mickelsens correctly note five occurrences of *kephalē* as a variant reading where *ro'sh* meant "leader." In three of these instances *kephalē*

omitted from Jer 14:3 since it would be redundant with the identical expression in 14:4. In two instances the translator apparently thought "head" referred to the person as a whole (Job 10:15; Lam 2:10b). Six times *ro'sh* was translated with words conceptually unrelated to "head." Three times it is translated *archē*, Gen 40:13, 20, 20, here meaning "office," losing the nuance of the Hebrew idiom "to lift up the head." Once it is translated "wings" (Ezek 1:22b, perhaps to avoid redundancy with "head" in 1:22a), once "sacrifice" (Job 20:6), and once "cut off his head" is euphemistically translated "turned him" (1 Sam 31:9 = 1 Kings 31:9 LXX).

34"Head in Jer 31:7 is singular in both Greek *[kephalēn ethnōn]* and Hebrew *[ro'sh]*, not plural as in the NASB "the chiefs of the nations." C. F. Keil observes that "the head of the nations" signifies "the first of the nations . . . , i.e., the most exalted among the nations. Such is the designation given to Israel, because God has chosen them before all the nations of the earth to be His peculiar people . . . , made them the highest over (. . . Deut xxvi:19) all nations" (C. F. Keil and F. Delitzsch, *Commentary on the Old Testament in Ten Volumes*, vol. 8 *Jeremiah, Lamentations* [Grand Rapids, Mich.: Eerdmans, n.d.], p. 20). Similarly, John Bright writes, "*the first of the nations.* Apparently a popular, and prideful, term for Israel" (*The Anchor Bible: Jeremiah* [Garden City, N.Y.: Doubleday, 1965], p. 281). F. Cawley and A. R. Millard write, "*Chief,* i.e. in the Lord's estimation" ("Jeremiah," in *The New Bible Commentary: Revised*, ed. D. Guthrie et al. [Grand Rapids, Mich.: Eerdmans, 1970], p. 645). R. K. Harrison also writes, "Israel has pride of place among her neighbours" (*Jeremiah and Lamentations: An Introduction and Commentary* [London: Inter-Varsity, 1973], p. 136).

clearly means "leader" (Judg 10:18; 11:8; 11:9). All of them are in a single section shorter than a chapter, and all occur only in one manuscript (A). Thus they can reasonably be attributed to a single scribe unaware that this idiom was foreign to Greek. The only other similar case is in the same manuscript where *kephalē* as a variant reading refers to a "chief place" (1 Kings 20:12 = 3 Kings 20:12 LXX).

In the fifth such occurrence, 1 Kings 8:1, the two manuscripts that did include *kephalē* in the translation completely avoided the idea of "leader." Thus, "head of the tribes" is replaced with "heads [meaning tops] of the staffs" they carried. When the Old Testament meaning of *ro'sh* was "leader," the Septuagint translators realized quite clearly that this would not be conveyed by *kephalē,* so they resorted to some other translation in 171 cases out of 180.[35] This occurred in spite of the strong tendency in the Septuagint for "Greek words to extend their range of meaning in an un-Greek way after the Hebrew word which they render."[36] Thus we have strong evidence of the high degree to which "head" meaning "leader" was recognized by these translators to be foreign to Greek.

Just because the Old Testament was the Bible for the early church does not mean that the primarily Greek congregations to which Paul wrote were familiar with the Hebrew connotation of head as "leader." The Old Testament they had was the Septuagint, and as we have seen, its translators very rarely used the Greek word for *head* in contexts where it meant "leader." The Mickelsens are correct that none of them are well-known passages. The most common error in interpreting "head" in the Pauline passages is to read back into them the meaning "leader." The Mickelsens follow proper procedure in looking for Paul's meaning in the commonly recognized pool of connotations that *kephalē* carried then. If Paul does use *kephalē* with the meaning "leader," he is the only New Testament writer to do so, even though most of the New Testament writers use more Hebraic Greek than he does. For example, "head of the house" is a very

---

[35]The nine exceptions are Judg 11:11; 2 Sam 22:44; Ps 18:43; Is 7:8, 9; Lam 1:5 and three of the head-tail metaphors: Deut 28:13, 44; Is 9:14. The variant text instances are not included since the majority of the manuscripts do not use *kephalē* in these verses. There are only three other passages where *kephalē* might be construed to refer to the idea of leader (Deut 32:42; 1 Chron 12:19; Ps 140:10), but in each instance an examination of the context and parallels makes it virtually certain that *kephalē* refers to the physical head.

[36]Peter Walters, *The Text of the Septuagint: Its Corruptions and Their Emendations,* ed. D. W. Gooding (Cambridge: At the University Press, 1973), p. 143.

common expression throughout the Gospels, but *kephalē* is never used to convey this meaning.[37]

A Point of Departure

Essentially, I agree with the Mickelsens' underlying treatment of the Pauline "head" passages. But their separation of Paul's meanings into six categories is unnecessarily confusing. At several points, it reads into the image more than the context seems to indicate. Nor is it obvious that such elaborate meanings fit easily into the major Greek connotations given by *kephalē*. Their first two categories, "source of life" and "top or crown," are adequate to cover all ten of the occurrences in question. In eight of them, the basic connotation of *kephalē* for Paul seems to be "source," and since the relationships in view are personal, it is the source of life that is primarily in view. The remaining two are the parallel passages, Colossians 2:10 and Ephesians 1:22, where *top* or *crown* fits the context.

Examples of *kephalē* meaning "source of life" include Philo (first century A.D.), *The Preliminary Studies* 61 ("And of all the members of the clan here described Esau is the progenitor *[genarchēs]*, the head *[kephalē]* of the whole creature") and *On Rewards and Punishments* 125 ("the virtuous one, whether single man or people, will be the head *[kephalē]* of the human race and all the others like the limbs of a body which draw their life from the forces in the head *[kephalē]* and at the top"). F. H. Colson notes, "The allegorical meaning seems to be that . . . the *[spoudaios,* "the virtuous one"] is the source of spiritual life to all who . . . are true members of the body." Philo stated that this section (XX) is not about external blessing, victories over enemies, honors or offices, but rather about personal matters (118) and virtue for service to others (119). Thus, for him to say that "this virtuous one, whether single man or people, will be the head of the human race," refers (as in 123) not to political authority but to being the source from which they "draw their life."

Other examples occur in Artemidorus Daldiani (second century A.D.), *Oneirocritica* 1.2 ("Another man dreamt that he was beheaded. In real life, the father of this man, too, died; for as the head *[kephalē]* is the

---

[37]See, e.g., NASB's translation of Mt 10:25; 13:52; 24:43; Lk 12:39; 13:25; 14:21.

source of life and light for the whole body, he was responsible for the dreamer's life and light. . . . The head *[kephalē]* indicates one's father"), 1.35 ("the head *[kephalē]* resembles parents in that it is the cause *[aitia]* of one's living") and 3.66 ("The head *[kephalē]* signifies the father of the dreamer. . . . Whenever, then a poor man who has a rich father dreams that his own head has been removed by a lion and that he dies as a result, it is probable that his father will die. . . . For the head *[kephalē]* represents the father; the removal of the head *[kephalē]*, the death of the father").

A further example of *kephalē* used to mean "source of life" occurs in *Orphic Fragments* 21a ("Zeus is the head, Zeus the middle, and from Zeus all things are completed"). "Zeus is the head" poetically balances and sets the stage for "from Zeus all things are completed." The sequence is both temporally and logically balanced. Zeus as the fountain-head or source actively brought all things into being in the past, and he will actively bring all things to completion in the future. Thus, unless *[kephalē]* means "source" this poetic balance is lost. Significantly, another word for "source," *archē*, replaces *[kephalē]* in some manuscripts. *On the World*, a treatise attributed to Aristotle and probably written in the first century A.D., cites this saying to prove that Zeus is the source of all things: "Zeus himself is the source of all. Therefore it is properly said by the Orphics . . . Zeus is head, Zeus the center, from Zeus comes all that is." Similarly, Eusebius in *Preparation for the Gospel* 3.9, written early in the fourth century A.D., cites this famous saying to show that Zeus was believed to be the creator, "The authors of the Orphic hymns supposed Zeus to be the mind of the world, and that he created all things therein, containing the world in himself. Therefore in their theological systems they have handed down their opinions concerning him thus:

Zeus was the first, Zeus last, the lightning's lord,
Zeus head, Zeus centre, all things are from Zeus . . .
Zeus alone first cause of all."[38]

---

[38]The sources of the above translations are, in the order cited: *Philo with an English Translation by F. H. Colson*, Loeb (Cambridge, Mass.: Harvard University, 1939), vol. 4, p. 489 and vol. 8, p. 389. Artemidorus Daldianus, *The Interpretation of Dreams = Oneiro-critica*, trans. Robert J. While (Park Ridge, N.J.: Noyes, 1975), pp. 16–17, 34, 175–76; cf. *Artemidori Daldiani Onirocriticon Libri V*, ed. Roger A. Pack (Leipzig: Teubner, 1963), pp. 7, 9, 43, 234. Otto Kern, *Orphicorum Fragmenta* (Berlin: Weidmannsche Verlagsbuch-

In 1 Corinthians 11:3, Paul affirmed that Christ is the "head," the source of life, of every man. As the Creator, Christ gave life to Adam and so to every man. Thus Paul refers to the creation in verse 9 and verse 12.[39] Developing his thought in the temporal sequence in which these events occurred, Paul then affirms that the man is the "head," the source of life, of woman. The article before man may suggest the first man, Adam, from whom woman came. Accordingly, Paul affirms in verses 8–9 that woman was created from man and in verse 12 that "woman came from man."

Third, in this temporal sequence, Paul refers to the Incarnation, "God is the head of Christ." The eternal second person of the Trinity came forth from the Godhead in the Incarnation (Jn 1:14; 8:42). Thus it is proper to speak of his source as God.[41] In the Incarnation Christ was given human life by God for the purpose of saving his people (Mt 1:21–23; Lk 1:54–55; 2:30–32; 3:6).[42] Note that Paul did not specify that the *Father* is the head of Christ but simply says that "God" is the head of Christ.[43] This fits perfectly with "head" in the sense of source since Christ came forth from the Godhead. Under the interpretation that "head" means "authority," the present tense of *estin* requires that Christ now in the present time after his resurrection and ascension is under the

---

handlung, 1922), p. 91, cited in C. K. Barrett, *1 Corinthians*, 248; cf. *TDNT* 3:676. "On the World" is cited by M. L. West, *The Orphic Poems* (Oxford: Clarendon, 1983), p. 89. Eusebius, *Preparation for the Gospel,* trans. Edwin Hamilton Gifford, 2 vols. (Grand Rapids, Mich.: Baker, 1981): 1:109; cf. Larry Alderink, *Creation and Salvation in Ancient Orphism* (Missoula, Montana: Scholars Press, 1981), pp. 28–31. Catherine Kroeger drew my attention to Artemidorus *Onirocriticon* 1.2 & 35 and the quotations in "on the World" and in Eusebius. Adelaide Pearson showed me the Philo passages.

[39]"Everything is from God" (1 Cor 11:12) makes it clear that God is also the source of every woman.

[40]God did not give Adam authority over woman in the creation accounts of Genesis, nor is Adam given authority over women today. These problems with the "authority" interpretation are not avoided by taking "the man" as generic for all men. The Bible never states that all women are to be under the authority of all men or should submit to all men. The story of Ananias and Sapphira in Acts 5 shows that a wife should not even submit to her own husband in every situation.

[41]1 Cor 8:6 states, "all things came from God" and 11:12 of this very passage says, "all this comes from God."

[42]Possibly implied in the definite article with Christ.

[43]In contrast to 1 Cor 15:24. Yet it seems invariably to be interpreted as specifying God the Father by those who say that "head" means authority.

authority of God.[44] Such a view has been condemned throughout most of church history as subordinationist Christology. The Arians used this "head as authority" interpretation as a favorite proof that Christ is inferior to the Father.[45]

Understood as referring to "source of life," the threefold head relationships make an appropriate theological introduction to this whole passage. It is Christ's coming forth from the Godhead to do his saving work that has given us direct access to God. This introduces Paul's insistence that a head covering, which symbolizes a denial of the direct access to God that Christ has provided (see 2 Cor 3:12-18), is a dishonor to the man's head.[46] Again, man's source in God's special creative act provides the theological foundation for Paul's comment (in v. 7) that man is the image and glory of God. Similarly, the idea that woman was formed out of man provides the framework from which Paul states that the woman is the glory of man. If Paul's introduction in verse 3 were a statement of authority relations, it would not provide as appropriate a background for theological development of this nature. The rest of the passage dis-

---

[44]Archibald Robertson and Alfred Plummer, *The First Epistle of St. Paul to the Corinthians*, ICC, 2nd ed. (Edinburgh: T. & T. Clark, 1914), p. 229, insist that this interpretation "implies more than the inferiority of Christ's human nature." Those who advocate the meaning "authority" usually point to Jesus' voluntary submission to the Father in his incarnate life in the past (e.g., Richard C. Lenski, *The Interpretation of First and Second Corinthians* (Minneapolis: Augsburg, 1934), pp. 439-40; Charles Hodge, *An Exposition of the First Epistle to the Corinthians* (1864, reprint ed., Grand Rapids, Mich.: Eerdmans, 1969), p. 207, and/or in the future (e.g., James Hurley, *Man and Woman in Biblical Perspective* [Grand Rapids, Mich.: Zondervan, 1981], p. 164). Note Hurley's omission from his quote from Bedale, pp. 214-15, of "this principle of subordination . . . *includes sonship of the Christ himself* . . . in the order of being." But the verse refers to the present, and now Christ is "over every power and authority" (e.g., Col 2:10; Eph 1:21-22; Mt 28:18) and will not turn all authority over to God the Father until the future consummation according to 1 Cor 15:24-28.

[45]Robertson and Plummer, *First Corinthians*, p. 229. The theological dangers of the view that "head" means authority are examined in detail by C. H. Sherlock, "On God and Gender," *Interchange* 22 (1977): 93-104, who cites on p. 96 George W. Knight III's affirmation of the "ontological relationship of pre-incarnate and submissive Sonship," as "most certainly" entailing that Christ is inferior to God.

[46]"Head" here can be understood physically, or as a symbol of the person, or it can appropriately imply the dishonor such a covering implies to God (just called man's head in v. 3) or possibly to Christ (though this Letter precedes the other passages where Paul states that Christ is the head of the body). A multiple sense may have been intended by Paul.

cusses head coverings. He argues as follows: since man is the source from which woman came, she should show him appropriate respect. Paul argues similarly in 1 Timothy 2:12 on the basis of woman's being formed from man that it is improper for women to teach men in a domineering autonomous manner.[47]

It is largely because the meaning of "authority" has been read into *head* in verse 3 instead of "source of life" that the affirmation of the woman's authority in verse 10 has been regarded as so abrupt (or even interpreted as the man's authority) and why verses 11-12 are seen as a retreat from what Paul had just said. Note that verse 11 reads, "However, *woman* is not independent of man," and only after stating this adds, "nor is man independent of woman." This order is significant since if verse 10 were affirming man's authority (as some translations imply by adding to the Greek "*a sign of* authority"), verse 11 should have said, "However, *man* is not independent . . ." Instead, as one would expect after a bold affirmation of woman's authority, Paul immediately cautions *women* lest they draw improper conclusions from their authority to cover their heads as they see fit. Mistranslation of verse 10 has contributed to two further mistranslations of Paul's conclusion. Verse 15 should read that the woman has been given long hair *instead of (anti)* a prayer shawl, and verse 16 that the churches have *no such (toiautēn) custom* as requiring a prayer shawl (*peribolaion,* named only in v. 15). James Hurley has argued convincingly that these are the correct translations and that the head covering Paul recommended for women was not a veil but hair modestly done up over the head.[48]

The interpretation of *head* in this passage as a chain of command or hierarchy demands rearrangement of the sequence that Paul gives. The context does not develop the idea of authority except to affirm the authority of the woman over her own head in verse 10. These factors and the statements of the interdependence of man and woman in verses 11-12 tell strongly against the "authority" interpretation. It is hardly surprising that many scholars have concluded that *head* in verse 3 means "source," including many who believe on other grounds that Paul

---

[47]Or possibly "seductive" manner; see Catherine C. Kroeger, "Ancient Heresies and a Strange Greek Verb," *The Reformed Journal* (March 1979), pp. 12-15.
[48]James Hurley, "Man and Woman in 1 Corinthians" (Ph.D. diss., Cambridge University, 1973), pp. 43-71; *Man and Woman in Biblical Perspective,* pp. 168-71, 254-71.

taught that men should have authority over women in social relationships.[49]

In Colossians 1:18, Paul seems to have defined "head" for us: "[Christ] is the head of the body, the church, who is the beginning, the first-born from the dead, so that in everything he might have first place." The word here for "beginning," ἀρχή, commonly refers to originating power, source or origin, and this sense fits the context perfectly. Christ is the source of the church, the one who gave it life and sustains its life. The idea of Christ as the source is repeatedly emphasized in Colossians 1:15-20: "by him all things were created . . . all things were created by him . . . in him all things hold together. And he is the head of the body . . . who is the beginning."[50] The Mickelsens have already shown why Colossians 2:19 and Ephesians 4:15 are widely regarded as meaning that Christ as "head" of the body is its "source of life."[51] Paul again explains his use of *head* in Ephesians 5:23, here through apposition.[52]1 Immediately following "Christ the head of the church" is a phrase with the identical grammatical construction, "he the savior of the body":

---

[49]See, e.g., Herman Ridderbos, *Paul: An Outline of His Theology,* trans. John Richard de Witt (Grand Rapids, Mich.: Eerdmans, 1975), pp. 379-82; Barrett, 1 Corinthians, p. 249; Bedale, "The Meaning of *kephalē,*" pp. 214-15.

[50]This passage is surrounded with statements about Christ's work that gave life to the church: "redemption, the forgiveness of sins" (v. 13), "reconciliation . . . making peace through his blood shed on the cross" (v. 20).

[51]See, e.g., J. B. Lightfoot, *Saint Paul's Epistles to the Colossians and to Philemon* (London: Macmillan, 1882), p. 200: "The *source* of all (ἐξ οὖ) is Christ Himself the Head. . . . In the Colossian letter the vital connexion with the Head is the main theme. . . . the discoveries of modern physiology have invested the Apostle's language with far greater distinctness and force than it can have worn to his own contemporaries." M. Carson, *The Epistles of Paul to the Colossians and Philemon* (Grand Rapids, Mich.: Eerdmans, 1960), p. 76: "certain main ideas are apparent. These are —the source of the life of the body, the growth of the body, and its unity. The source of the life of the body is Christ." Ralph P. Martin, *Colossians and Philemon* (Grand Rapids, Mich.: Eerdmans, 1973), pp. 92-93: "vital contact with the source of life and nourishment . . . living union." Note also that in Col 2:19 the idea of losing connection with one's source fits the context perfectly. Similarly, in Eph 4:15-16, which is all part of one sentence in Greek, it fits that believers are to "grow up into him who is the head." The context of neither verse develops the idea of Christ's lordship.

[52]"The placing of a word or expression beside another so that the second explains and has the same grammatical construction as the first." David B. Guralnik, ed., *Webster's New World Dictionary of the American Language,* 2nd ed. (New York: Collins/World, 1974), p. 67.

Christos kephalē tēs ekklēsias
autos sōtēr tou sōmatos.

Christ the Savior is the life giver, the source of life for his body. The whole passage develops this thought. Verse 25 states that Christ "gave himself up for her." Christ the Savior is the continual source of life for the church.[53] This meaning, "source of life," is in harmony with the meaning of *head* that Paul used in 4:15. Christ is depicted as the continuing source of life and growth of the church.[54] "Source of life" is the aspect of the analogy between Christ and the believing husband that Paul develops in this passage: "Husbands, love your wives, just as Christ loved the church and gave himself up for her" (v. 25). Husbands are to be a source of life for their wives even if it means giving up their own lives for them. Just as Christ sustains the life of the church through his love—feeding and caring for her—so the husband is to love his wife (vv. 25, 28-29).

In verses 28-32, Paul further develops the head-body metaphor by highlighting the unity of head and body.[55] As Christ and the church are one body, so husband and wife are one flesh. Paul calls wives to submit to their husbands because "the husband is head of the wife as Christ is the head of the church, the Savior of the body."[56] She is to submit to him because he is a source of life for her and because she is one flesh with him.[57] Paul bases his appeal for submission on the loving nature of the head-body relationship in which the head is a source of life.

---

[53]See "to us who are *being* saved" (1 Cor 1:18; 2 Cor 2:15). Such a usage is proper to the meaning of the term σωτήρ. It is translated "preserver" in the similar passage in Aristotle *De Mundo* 6.4.397b. 20-21, "for God is in very truth the preserver (σωτήρ) and creator (γενέτωρ = "giving birth") of all. . . ."

[54]Nicander Epicus *Alexipharmaca* 215: "the head sustains/holds together (συνέκει) the whole body."

[55]This passage is an original inspiration. Nowhere does the Old Testament speak of Israel as "members of God's body." Thus it cannot be properly argued that "head" here is an allusion to an Old Testament image and so incorporates the Hebrew connotation of "leader"; cf. Barth, *Ephesians 1—3*, p. 184.

[56]This submission is one example of the mutual submission required throughout the entire body as the grammar of Eph 5:18-23 requires. Husbands as well as wives are called to "submit to one another." See the defense of this by Barth, *Ephesians 4—6*, pp. 607-11.

[57]Paul develops this meaning of "head" in the passage both in relation to Christ and to the husband. The reference to head and body in v. 23 is not an isolated one. This whole

The Mickelsens' analysis that Colossians 2:10 and Ephesians 1:22 should be understood as referring to Christ as "crown" or "top" makes good sense. It is also true, however, that the very nature of the things over which Christ is top ("all rule and authority") made it sufficiently clear to his Greek audience that Christ's being top entails his having authority. It is rather like our English expressions "she is the head (or top) of her class" or "that shot-putter is at the top of his field." Do we conclude that one of the meanings of *head* is "highest grade point average"? Should "best shot-putter" be added to the dictionary meanings of *top?* Of course not! In each case the nature of the grouping over which someone is head or top determines what is involved in being top. Paul's Greek audience would not have recognized the idea of authority if the context had not specified the group over which Christ is top includes all rule and authority. The context as a whole entails the natural implication that Jesus is in the top position of authority.[58] The context of Ephesians 1:22 emphasizes Christ's top position in such expressions as "God raised him . . . seated him at his right hand in the heavenly realms" (v. 20), "far above all authority . . ." (v. 21),[59] "God placed all things under his feet," and he is "head over all things to the church" (v. 22).[60]

I conclude that *head* throughout the Pauline Epistles carries the nor-

---

passage develops it as Paul's repeated references to the body in vv. 28, 29, 30 show. The reference to Christ and his body in v. 30 continues the picture of Christ as the source of life. Eph 5 does not develop the idea of Christ or the husband having authority. It does not say that we are to submit to Christ because he has authority over us or that wives are to submit to their husbands because they have authority over them. As J. Armitage Robinson says, "Not headship here, but identity, is the relation in view" (*St Paul's Epistle to the Ephesians* [London: James Clarke, n.d.]), p. 124.

[58]This distinction is rather like Bedale's classification of the meaning of *head* in 1 Cor 11:3 as "source," yet also affirming on p. 215 that it "carries with it the idea of 'authority.' " Exegetically and theologically I disagree with Bedale's opinion of what *head* as "source" "carries with it" in 1 Cor 11:3. In Col 2:10 and Eph 1:22, however, the context does show that *head* as "top" or "crown" does carry with it the idea of authority.

[59]ὑπεράνω, cf. Artemidorus Daldianus 2.9: "the head *rises above (ὑπερέχει)* the whole body."

[60]ὑπέρ, its only occurrence with *head* in the Pauline Epistles. The idea of a gift to the church seems to be primary; see Barth, *Ephesians 1—3*, p. 158; George Howard, "The Head/Body Metaphors of Ephesians," *NTS* 20 (1974): 353. Similarly, in Col 2:13-15, Paul directly associates Christ's victory over the powers through the cross with his function of giving life to the church. These should not be thought of as separate accomplishments.

mal Greek connotations of "source" and "top." Paul's primary and original contribution to the use of *head* was in creating the dynamic metaphor of Christ, the head of the church, which is his body. There are variations on the nuances of this metaphor, that Paul develops in different passages, but the central meaning is constant. For Paul, Christ as the "head" of the body is its "source of life." As the continual source of life and upbuilding of the church, Christ models how a husband should relate to his wife.

Philip Barton Payne is visiting professor of New Testament, Gordon-Conwell Theological Seminary, South Hamilton, Massachusetts.

DIFFICULT PASSAGES IV

7

WOMEN, SUBMISSION AND MINISTRY IN 1 CORINTHIANS

Walter L. Liefeld

1 CORINTHIANS 11:2-6 and 14:33b-40 are important and complex passages.[1] It is especially important when interpreting the sections on women to guard against letting our own horizon and ideas about women skew our interpretation.[2]

The approaches to the New Testament passages on women range from the traditionalist retention of the commands in their precise form (with perhaps some leniency with regard to veils) to the idea that Paul is reverting to his upbringing, arguing on Jewish grounds,[3] and thus we are not bound to follow his ideas. In between are proposals that Paul is writing under divine inspiration but providing correctives in transitory situations. These correctives provide a model for churches of all ages

---

[1] For inclusion in this volume, this paper has been considerably abridged and simplified.

[2] It is obvious in reading Linda Merchante's survey of commentaries on 1 Corinthians 11:2-16 that the passage is something of a touchstone in evaluating the attitude of commentators to women (*From Hierarchy to Equality, A Comparison of Past and Present Interpretations of 1 Cor 11:2-16 in Relation to the Changing Status of Women in Society* [Vancouver: G-M-H Books, Regent College, 1978]).

[3] Paul King Jewett, *Man as Male and Female* (Grand Rapids, Mich.: Eerdmans, 1975); Virginia Ramey Mollenkott, *Women, Men and the Bible* (Nashville: Abingdon, 1977). Cf. Pagels: "His response, apparently, is to revert abruptly to Jewish conventional wisdom, appealing to authority and to 'nature,' to warn that women's activity must be kept within the confines of the natural and social order, custom, and convention" (Elaine H. Pagels, "Paul and Women: A Response to Recent Discussion," *American Academy of Religion Journal* 42 (1974): 543-44.

to follow, but the specifics may be pertinent only to the circumstances in the churches of Paul's day.

Even this median approach is followed in different ways. Some see Paul applying God's Word to a *cultural situation;* others see him addressing an internal *church circumstance* discernible in the text itself. Richard and Catherine Kroeger, for example, emphasize cultural life at Corinth, with all its immorality and boisterous religious practices. In contrast, Mary Evans explores a situation behind chapter 11 that is suggested by the Corinthians passage itself. She proposes that women either (1) were "flouting convention and possibly Paul's direct instructions in order to claim an equality that was not rightly theirs," or (2) "were worried that by following convention women were denying the equality of status with men that was now theirs in Christ."[4]

The difference between what is *cultural* and what is *circumstantial* is often overlooked. Some scholars find it difficult to accept the idea that any biblical instruction is culturally conditioned, while many others think it is possible to separate the abiding principle from the cultural background. Between these positions is the acknowledgment that some biblical instructions apply to specific circumstances that may or may not relate to a cultural situation. Wherever those circumstances exist, even in different cultures, the instructions apply. Where the circumstances vary, the application will vary. In neither case is Scripture tied to culture. However, the effort to explain the text in terms of culture need not involve a wrong hermeneutic. The Word of God is not detached from the world to which it came. It is able to *speak to* real life situations without its doctrines being *influenced by* the culture it addresses. Some scholars have difficulty here.[5]

We have noted thus far three positions: (1) The instructions about women are to be followed in the same form in which they appear in the New Testament, (2) These instructions are to be followed in principle,

---

[4]The Kroegers' contributions will be cited later. Mary J. Evans's work is *Women in the Bible* (Downers Grove, Ill.: InterVarsity, 1984), p. 92.

[5]Susan Foh, for example, fails to take into account that there is a difference between purely doctrinal topics, such as justification, and those that have a sociocultural aspect, such as the role of women: "If Paul's teaching about women in the church is cultural, maybe his teaching on justification or his faith in God is too" (*Women and the Word of God: A Response to Biblical Feminism* [Grand Rapids, Mich.: Baker, 1980], p. 46).

with the specifics depending on how close the contemporary situation is to the ancient one. (3) The instructions about women reveal Paul's pre-Christian ideas and are not to be followed at all. This disagreement among scholars indicates the need of a continuing study of the text itself, to which we now turn.

1 Corinthians 11:2-16

The point of entrance to the immediate passage is verse 2, but we must approach that entrance along the walkway of 10:23—11:1. Paul has just urged limitation of one's freedom in order not to hinder others from accepting the gospel (chapters 8-10). He is apparently modifying the principle of liberty in Galatians in certain respects: (1) In Galatians he affirmed freedom regarding table fellowship, but in 1 Corinthians he restricts certain associations and foods. Even what is "permissible" may not be "beneficial" (10:23-30). (2) Although in Galatians he insisted on his status as an apostle and on his freedom from the law, in 1 Corinthians he is willing to "become as a Jew" and as "under the law" to "win some" (9:22). (3) He taught in Galatians that there is "neither male nor female," but in 1 Corinthians he introduces certain limitations on women. We may reasonably ask whether this last modification also involves avoiding something that might obstruct the gospel. There are two reasons to suppose this. (1) Immediately before the passage under consideration Paul reaffirms that what he does is for the glory of God and for the good of others (10:31—11:1). (2) 11:2-16 is connected with the preceding discussion and theme by the Greek conjunction *de,* which is seldom used to introduce a totally new topic.

Paul's introductory words, "I praise you," in verse 2 show unmistakably that in spite of the need of correction the Corinthians were doing something right. This becomes even more clear when we note that in contrast verse 17 has, "I do not praise you." Even though they were observing the Lord's Supper, their behavior was so wrongly motivated that Paul could not praise them. We may assume, therefore, that in verses 2-16 they *were* carrying on Paul's teachings (literally, "traditions").[6] The only "tradition" discernible in this section is men and women exercising their

---

[6]Elisabeth Schüssler Fiorenza thinks this "emphasizes that Paul is not referring here to any particular abuse but is introducing regulations and customs which were observed in other Christian communities" (*In Memory of Her* [New York: Crossroad, 1983], p. 226).

spiritual gift in prophesying. This stands in parallel with the tradition (v. 23) of the Lord's Supper in the next section. We can therefore assume (in contrast to some interpretations) that they were right in allowing women to prophesy. There can be little doubt that this was a church meeting, since Paul has already spoken of the Lord's Table in chapter 10. Also he connects this section with the following one on the Lord's Supper by means of the "praise/praise not" structure, and he mentions angels, who were thought, by some Jews at least, to be present when God's people gathered for worship. Therefore attempts to explain away the public prophetic ministry of women in church are unconvincing.

Because Paul's reference to headship in verse 3 introduces his argument, it is important that we do not, through dogmatic assumptions, jump to conclusions as to the meaning of that concept. The most common understanding of it today is probably still the traditional one, that it teaches a divine order of authority or, as it has been called by some, a "chain of command." There are three reasons to reject that supposition.

1. The links in the "chain" would be out of sequence. Paul does not proceed from the Father to Christ to man to woman, but rather goes from Christ to woman to man to God.

2. The argument that follows is not based on the idea of a command structure. The order one finds in this passage has to do first with the interrelationships between pairs (Christ/man, etc.), and second with arrangement and decorum (cf. 14:33, 40), but not with some military-like structure.

3. We must not prejudge the Greek word *kephalē* and assume that it has to mean "ruler." Its meaning must have been understood by both writer and reader. Paul's affirmation in verse 3 is in accord with his general desire to discuss matters on the basis of common knowledge and understanding.[7] It is possible that several levels of meaning then develop as the argument proceeds. We need to avoid two errors. One is the semantic fallacy of importing the *total* range of meanings of a given term into the context at hand.[8] The other is assuming at the outset

---

[7] Cf. "We know . . ." in 8:1, 4. This is a concession to those who boasted in knowledge, but it is supplemented by, "But not everyone knows this . . ." in verse 7; also "I do not want you to be ignorant" in 10:1.

[8] James Barr, *Semantics of Biblical Language* (London: Oxford University Press, 1961), pp. 218–22. Cf. Anthony Thiselton's comments on this in *New Testament Interpretation*, ed. I. Howard Marshall (Grand Rapids, Mich.: Eerdmans, 1977), p. 84.

some single *narrow* meaning that fits our concept, irrespective of whether or not it is well attested in literature contemporary with the New Testament. We need to ask (1) What meaning(s) would both sender and recipient most likely have in mind, given the subject matter of the passage? (2) What meaning(s) best fit the context?

There are a number of studies on *kephalē*. The most thorough study I know of that deals with biblical theology was completed in 1966, *The [KEPHALĒ] Concept in the Pauline Tradition with Special Emphasis on Colossians,* by R. Weldon Crabb.[9] My own research has been aided by the independent studies of three students, mainly on the Septuagintal evidence.[10] The most recent contribution is an exhaustive survey of computer-generated lists, summarized by Wayne Grudem.[11] But the study that has had the most effect in recent years is the 1954 article by Bedale, who proposed the meaning "source."[12]

Although Crabb does not think *kephalē* was used prior to our period to denote "the head or chief of persons,"[13] he holds that the idea of "first," "foremost," and even "determiner" is present. He notes that when the Septuagint translated the Hebrew *ro'sh,* "head," it usually used the Greek word *archē* ("beginning," "rule," "authority") rather than *kephalē* if the meaning was "beginning of" or "first."[14] Worthy of more attention than Crabb gives it is that when *ro'sh* meant "ruler," it was likely to be translated by *archōn,* a common word for ruler, not *kephalē*. On the basis of such information, one could conclude that unless Paul was thinking in the Hebrew, not the Greek, idiom, it is unlikely that he used *kephalē* in the sense of "ruler." Crabb suggests that in 1 Corinthians, Paul has authority in mind because he is opposing the authority of Christ against that of Paul's opponents.[15]

---

[9]R. Weldon Crabb, "The ΚΕΦΑΛΗ Concept in the Pauline Tradition with Special Emphasis on Colossians" (Ph.D. diss., San Francisco Theological Seminary, 1968).

[10]Unpublished papers by Jack Hoyt, James Ramsak and David Banks, written with special reference to the Septuagintal evidence.

[11]Wayne Grudem, "Does κεφαλή Mean 'Source' or 'Authority Over' in Greek Literature? A Survey of 2,336 Examples," *Trinity Journal* New Series 6 (Spring 1985): 38–59.

[12]S. Bedale, "The Meaning of κεφαλή in the Pauline Epistles," *JTS* New Series 5 (1954): 211–15; compare the modification of this in Berkeley and Alvera Mickelsen, "The 'Head' of the Epistles," *Christianity Today,* 1981, pp. 264–67.

[13]Crabb, *ΚΕΦΑΛΗ,* p. 7.

[14]Ibid., p. 21.

[15]Ibid., p. 83.

The meaning "source," adduced by Bedale as a clue to some of Paul's passages, lacks clear evidence. Grudem disputes even the couple of instances usually cited, and his research of over 2,000 occurrences of *kephalē* has failed to turn up any other examples of the meaning "source."[16] If Grudem's research is as sound as it seems, those who would claim such a meaning in the New Testament have to rely only on the context, not on any external evidence prior to the first century. In opposition to that theory, Grudem provides a number of instances, including some from the first century, of *kephalē* being used in the sense of rulership or authority. But one later piece of evidence concerning the idea of source is virtually overlooked in the discussions: Tertullian's explanation (late second century) of a head having "authority" in the sense of being an "author." Man is the "author" of woman in that she was "taken out of man."[17]

There is not much evidence for *any* single metaphorical use of *kephalē* above the others. Perhaps Paul begins 1 Corinthians 11 by using *kephalē* in a less technical sense than either authority or source, introducing those overtones only later as he writes about woman's authority in verse 10 and about woman coming from man and vice versa in verses 11–12. In my judgment, it is not only methodologically correct but also proves exegetically fruitful to keep to the mainstream of Greek and Septuagintal thought and see *kephalē* as that part of the body that was (1) *prominent,* because, given the ancient mode of dressing from neck to foot, most easily observed, (2) *representative* of the whole body and, less frequently, (3) the *eminent* or most honored part of the body. In the very next chapter Paul says that "the head cannot say to the feet, 'I don't need you,' " and goes on to imply that the feet are less honorable than the head (1 Cor 12:21–24). This reinforces the fact that Paul has in mind the common perceptions of honor and dishonor with respect to the head. In my judgment, however, it is no longer possible, given Grudem's research, to dismiss the idea of "rulership" from the discussion.

Essential to the flow of thought in this section is a prominent vocabulary of glory/honor and shame/disgrace. In this context it makes more sense to understand *kephalē* as meaning the "prominent," or "hon-

[16]Grudem, "Does κεφαλή mean 'Source'?" pp. 38–46.
[17]Tertullian *Against Marcion* 5.8.

ored" member than as "source" or "ruler." But even if fault can be found with such terminology, clearly Christ receives glory or shame from man, man receives glory or shame from woman, and God receives (only) glory from Christ (v. 3). Seen this way, the order of the clauses in 11:3 makes sense, with the climax coming, not with the lowest element in some "chain of command" (which, on that theory, would have been "and man is the head of woman" but with the highest element in a succession of "honored members" ("and the head of Christ is God").

In this connection, the omission of a reference in verse 7 to woman as the image of God is due probably to Paul's desire to emphasize the idea of woman as the glory of man, rather than to any negation of the statement in Genesis 1:27 that man and woman were made in the image of God. Also the use of *anēr* ("male") here in 1 Corinthians, rather than *anthrōpos,* as in Genesis 1:27, is due to the parallel structure with *gynē,* woman. The idea in both Genesis and in the New Testament is not inferiority but complementarity.[18]

Space does not allow a list of the Greek terms, but a careful survey of this passage even in English will reveal the significant repetition of words such as *glory* and *disgrace.* The terms reveal Paul's underlying concern that Christians maintain an orderly worship that brings glory to God, and not incur disgrace through practices or appearances that were considered shameful. The idea also occurs in chapter 14 about women's silence: "If they want to inquire about something, they should ask their own husbands at home; for it is disgraceful for a woman to speak in the church" (14:35).[19]

Another word group related to this is one having to do with "propriety, decorum, presentability."[20] It also occurs in 1 Corinthians 12:23. Note

---

[18]The term *complementarity* could perhaps take its place along with, or in place of, Mercadante's term *friendship* (*From Hierarchy to Equality,* pp. 166–69).

[19]The theme of shame is a significant one in Scripture. Cf. H. C. Kee, in *On Language and Culture,* ed. M. Black and W. A. Smalley (The Hague: Mouton, 1974), pp. 133–47. One of the four categories Kee finds in the New Testament is "shameful behavior," for which he lists 1 Corinthians 11:4 and 14:35. I see these, however, as part of the larger group of terms pertaining to honor and shame, which form a pattern essential to the understanding of this entire section of 1 Corinthians.

[20]Walter Bauer, William F. Arndt and F. Wilbur Gingrich, *A Greek-English Lexicon of the New Testament,* rev. by F. Wilbur Gingrich and F. W. Danker (Chicago: University of Chicago Press, 1979), s.v. "εὐσχημοσύνη"; cf. s.v. εὐσχημόνως and εὐσχήμων.

that for our study the adverbial form occurs in 14:40, which concludes the discussion of order in the church. The word *order* also appears in that verse. With this we must connect the use of the verb, "to set in order," in 11:34, which concludes the section on the Lord's Supper ("And when I come I will give further directions"). The Greek compounds that Paul has chosen to use show that the order expressed is that of structure rather than of commanding. When all this is taken together with the previous words about glory, honor, shame and dishonor, a clear picture emerges. Paul is urging a sensitivity to contemporary moral conventions, which were commonly expressed in the very words Paul uses.

This picture develops even further when we read the following quotations, which illustrate two secular viewpoints about women in public. Although they are separated by two centuries, both of them reveal ancient attitudes about women's public behavior that cannot be ignored in this study. Plutarch (A.D. 46–120) wrote:

> Theano [the wife of Pythagoras], in putting her cloak about her exposed her arm. Somebody exclaimed, "A lovely arm." "But not for the public," said she. Not only the arm of the virtuous woman, but her speech as well, ought to be not for the public, and she ought to be modest and guarded about saying anything in the hearing of outsiders, since it is an exposure of herself; for in her talk can be seen her feelings, character, and disposition.[21]

The idea of exposure of a woman's inner person underlies the restriction of public speech as well as the physical covering. What makes this passage so significant for us is that it links together the two elements of our 1 Corinthians 11 passage, women's public *appearance* and women's public *speech*.

The second quotation is by the historian Livy from a speech by the elder Cato shortly before 200 B.C. The occasion was the discussion of a law (the "Oppian Law") that severely limited women's public appearance and activities. The Roman matrons were demonstrating against this and "could not be kept at home by advice or modesty or their husbands orders." They "dared even to approach and appeal to the consuls." Their actions were considered "shameful." They should not have been "running out into the streets and blocking the roads and

---

[21]Plutarch *Moralia* ["Conjugal Precepts," also known as "Advice to Bride and Groom"] 31.

speaking to other women's husbands." Cato says he should have said to them, "Could you not have made the same requests, each of your own husband, at home?" The speech continues to oppose women's public appearance and speaking, accusing them of seeking not only liberty but license.[22]

Although the status of women was changing in the Roman Empire during the first century, the attitudes expressed in Cato's speech undoubtedly persisted among many, with Plutarch in the first century bearing witness to this.

We thus see two overlapping background patterns: (1) a moralistic view that women should not express themselves visually or vocally in public because that would be a disgrace and (2) a hostile view of women who might lose control of their emotions and should be kept "in their place." Paul was certainly aware of both of these patterns. Given his concern to avoid anything that might appear disgraceful and thus hinder the gospel, we may be reasonably sure that he had both in mind when writing the Corinthians.

When we further link this with Paul's principles in Titus 2, we see a wider pattern. Women should "be subject to their husbands, so that no one will malign the word of God" (Tit 2:5). Titus was also to instruct the young men to be self-controlled "so that those who oppose you may be ashamed because they have nothing bad to say about us" (vv. 6-8). Finally, slaves were to be "subject to their masters in everything . . . so that in every way they will make the teaching about God our Savior attractive" (vv. 9-10). Clearly Paul puts the subjection of women and that of slaves in the same category in that passage. The reason for that subjection was to *avoid social criticism* that might hinder the gospel. Those interpreters who say that culture has nothing to do with such instructions have missed the thrust of these verses. They would certainly not say Paul was teaching that slaves should, as a universal and permanent theological principle, live in subjection. The subjection of slaves—and of women—was to communicate the value of the gospel to their society. This is also made explicit in 1 Peter 3:1-2 (see all 2:13-20). If this impinged on the equality taught in Galatians, it was for the cause of the gospel. A Christian woman must not bring shame on her

---

[22]Livy 34.2.1-14.

husband, either by inappropriate dress (1 Cor 11) or inappropriate speech (1 Cor 14).

The above considerations of headship and avoidance of shame may now be brought together with the idea of glory in verse 7. While one may think of the term *glory of* in either of two ways, receiving glory from another or giving glory to another, the idea here seems to be the latter (see 1 Thess 2:20; 2 Cor 8:23).[23] Thus, for Christ to be the glory of God means that he gave glory to God (see Jn 17:4). In 1 Corinthians 11:15 woman does have glory herself, exhibited in her long hair, but in verse 7 she brings glory to man. She can bring glory or shame to her own head, or to her husband as head, just as he can bring glory or (if he covers his head) shame to his head, Christ. It is not a matter of mere "reflection" of glory, as though woman does not reflect the glory of God as well as man does.

The following quotation from a treatise written in the second or third century B.C. illumines Paul's concern that the woman honor her husband: "In general a woman must be good and orderly [cf. 1 Corinthians 14:34, 40]. . . . A woman's greatest virtue is chastity. Because of this quality she is able to *honour* and to cherish *her own particular husband*" (italics mine).[24] Jaubert has pointed to the Septuagint translation of Proverbs 11:16 as a fine biblical example of a woman bringing glory *(doxa)* to her husband.[25] An English translation would be, "A thankful woman brings (lit., "raises") glory to a husband." The Septuagint adds: "A woman who hates justice is a throne of dishonor."

Women were undoubtedly praying and prophesying at Corinth. As to the nature of prophecy in the New Testament church, we have some guidance from 14:3, 5, 12, 26, 31. It is that which strengthens, encourages, comforts, edifies and instructs. There is no mention here of prophecy in the sense of biblical revelation (like the "writing prophets" of the Old Testament) or of prediction (like that of Agabus, Acts 11:27-28; 21:10-11). Nor do these prophets seem to be different from the other gifted people (in contrast to the prophets mentioned in Ephesians 2:20

---

[23]Cf. Morna D. Hooker, "Authority on Her Head: An Examination of 1 Cor 11:10," *New Testament Studies* 10 (1963-64): 410-41.

[24]Quoted in Mary R. Lefkowitcz and Maureen B. Fant, *Women's Life in Greece and Rome* (Baltimore: Johns Hopkins University Press, 1982), p. 104, par. 107.

[25]Annie Jaubert, "Le voile des femmes," *New Testament Studies* 18 (1972): 419.

who were the "foundation" of the church). To interpret 1 Corinthians 13:8-13 as implying that all prophecy has ended with the completion of the New Testament canon misses the eschatalogical thrust of verse 12 (seeing "face to face" and knowing "fully"). To be sure, prophecy in the sense of biblical revelation has ended. But the kind of prophecy mentioned in 1 Corinthians 11 and 14 is not an infallible biblical revelation but a message from God that needed to be evaluated (14:29). The higher one values that kind of prophecy, the higher one must evaluate the ministry of the women who prophesied. And the higher one values their ministry then, the higher should be their privilege of ministry today, even if the precise form is no longer thought to be valid.[26]

There is neither space nor need to discuss here the issue of veil versus hair style. But lest there be any question that a woman's appearance, including hair style and the use of jewelry, is closely connected with her morals in the ancient world, we may cite the article, "Women's Adornment," by David Scholer.[27] He provides numerous quotations that show beyond doubt how significant the connection was. Richard and Catherine Kroeger, James Hurley and others have provided useful compendia of ancient source material on hair styles and coverings.[28] Jaubert also

---

[26]See especially David Hill, *New Testament Prophecy* (Atlanta: John Knox, 1979); Wayne A. Grudem, *The Gift of Prophecy in 1 Corinthians* (Washington: University Press of America, 1982); David E. Aune, *Prophecy in Early Christianity* (Grand Rapids, Mich.: Eerdmans, 1983).

[27]David Scholer, "Women's Adornment," *Daughters of Sarah* 6 (1980): 3-6.

[28]Some see Paul as advocating wearing a veil, as Jewish women did; others see him as advocating the wearing of the hair bound up in a modest manner (without jewels, 1 Timothy 2:9, which incidentally would not have been seen anyway if the hair were covered). Among the many discussions of the issue, we may cite James B. Hurley, who takes the second position, "Did Paul Require Veils or the Silence of Women? A Consideration of I Cor 11:2-16 and I Cor 14:33b-36," *Westminster Theological Journal* 35 (1973): 190-220. He claims that hair style had significance in ancient times in a way that coverings did not. Cf. Joseph A. Fitzmyer, "A Feature of Qumran Angelology and the Angels of 1 Cor 11:10," *Essays on the Semitic Background of the New Testament* (Missoula, Mont.: Scholars Press: 1974, [reprint of his article in *New Testament Studies* 4 (1957-58): 45-58, with additions]), pp. 193-94. This is a concise statement supporting the meaning "veil." Robin Scroggs provides two instances of altered hair style in relevant literature. In *Joseph and Aseneth*, the Egyptian woman, now a Jewish convert, covers her head. The archangel Michael, who had appeared to her with instructions to put on clothes of joy rather than mourning, comes again, with the word that she should remove the covering, since she is a holy virgin and her head "is as that of a young man." In the other instance, the *Acts of Paul and Thecla*, Thecla offers to cut her hair short and follow Paul. He refuses, because

provides some targumic evidence regarding the significance of an uncovered head.[29]

Since the publication of an article by Morna Hooker twenty years ago, reinforced by the more recent contribution by Jaubert, 1 Corinthians 11:10 has commonly been understood to mean that the woman *possesses* authority.[30] Earlier it was thought that the meaning was to have a *symbol* of the *husband's* authority on her head. In 1907 W. M. Ramsay called this passive sense "a preposterous idea which a Greek scholar would laugh at anywhere except in the New Testament, where (as they seem to think) Greek words may mean anything that commentators choose."[31] His opinion is finally being given recognition.[32]

The most straightforward meaning of the expression taken alone would probably be that the woman ought to have authority over her own head, that is, authority to make decisions about her head (in this context most likely on the subject of veiling). It would be difficult, however, to conclude that all of Paul's theology in this passage and his arguments about glory, shame and the importance of showing honor to one's husband lead simply to a statement that a woman can do as she pleases in this respect. There is also the possibility that "head" could refer back to a woman's husband, who was just declared to be her "head," but the idea of a woman having authority over her husband is foreign to the context. Therefore, it is more in accord with the context

---

the time is not yet right, but later, after she is baptized, she puts on a man's garment and goes looking for Paul. He tells her to become a teacher in the church (Robin Scroggs, "Paul and the Eschatological Woman: Revisited," *American Academy of Religion Journal* 42 [1974]: 537–38). Clearly the idea of role exchange is linked with hair style and with conversion. This fortifies the idea, also found in Richard and Catherine Kroeger's work, "Sexual Identity in Corinth," *Reformed Journal* 28 (December 1978): 11–15, of a sex role exchange against which Paul is working. See also W. J. Martin, "I Corinthians 11:2–16: An Interpretation," in *Apostolic History and the Gospel,* ed. W. W. Gasque and R. P. Martin (Grand Rapids, Mich.: Eerdmans, 1970), pp. 231–41; James Hurley, "Did Paul Require Veils?"

[29]Annie Jaubert, "Le voile des femmes," p. 421.

[30]Morna D. Hooker, "Authority on Her Head: An Examination of I Cor 11:10," *New Testament Studies* 10 (1963/64): 410–16.

[31]W. R. Ramsay, *The Cities of St. Paul* (New York: Hodder and Stoughton, 1907), p. 203.

[32]Stephen B. Clark thinks the word can be assigned the meaning Ramsay gave it without losing the idea that it is the husband's authority (*Man and Woman in Christ* [Ann Arbor, Mich.: Servant, 1980], p. 171). But it is the phrase *echein exousian,* "to *have* authority," that signifies the active meaning, not just the word itself.

to propose that the authority possessed by the woman is the right to pray publicly.

Conceivably there is a double meaning here. Why does Paul say "authority over her *head*? Is it that he is affirming both that she *has* authority to speak and that she ought to have a symbol that would *give* her that right? This would be a modest hair style or covering that would deflect accusations of shameful behavior in public. In the larger context of this passage, we find *exousia* used five times in 9:1-12 in the sense of "right." Chapters 8-14 pertain in part to the limiting of rights and freedom that the believer possesses for the sake of winning others to the gospel and not stumbling the "weak." Paul thus is affirming that women do have a God-given right to pray and prophesy (cf. Acts 2:17f.), but that they can exercise that right only if they do so without causing social offense by bringing shame to their husbands through uncovered heads.

Richard and Catherine Kroeger's proposal that Paul is writing over against the pagan Corinthian practice of a ritual sex change also has value and is not incompatible with what I have argued here.[33] Likewise the idea that Paul is guarding against anything that blurs the distinction between male and female, in view of the homosexuality that was rampant, claims serious consideration.[34]

Passing by the issue of the angels, we come to a crucial point in the passage in 11:11. The introductory word, "nevertheless" *(plēn)*, is a strong adversative. It can also have the sense of "only," "but," "however." In our text, it appears without any accompanying word of further modification, which makes it stronger than a mere limitation or exception. It could range from a complete reversal of the previous argument to simply indicating that the freedom of the woman expressed in verse 10 does not mean complete independence from her husband.

In my understanding, Paul has argued up to now for an accommodation to Jewish and also decent pagan standards of female decorum. He has based this on the principle of headship, which justifies such an accommodation in order to avoid disgrace. There is nothing to fault in Paul's theology in verses 1-10. He maintains the biblical distinction of

---

[33]Richard and Catherine Kroeger, "Sexual Identity in Corinth."
[34]This would be in accordance with his views in Romans 1:26-27.

the sexes. He opposes homosexuality and all excesses, whether of pagan worship or transgression of basic morals. But the argument has led, not to some permanent law, but to a social accommodation. In verses 11–12 Paul moves, as it were, from Judaism to Christianity, from the Old Testament to the New.

Paul's argument in verses 11–16 runs, as I understand it, somewhat as follows in paraphrase:

Although I have argued strongly up to this point for accommodation, willing to be under the law to win some for the Lord, *nevertheless* we need to affirm the truth as it is in Christ. Spiritually there is no distinction, no priority. So my instructions about hairstyle are *not* an inviolable rule; you must judge this matter for yourselves. Let's restate the matter in *reverse* fashion, looking at the custom of women leaving their hair down and uncovered from *their* point of view, not their husband's. What is proper? What is disgraceful? Consider the nature of things and you will understand. Also the long hair a woman has makes an extra covering unnecessary; in itself it is a covering, modestly bound up, of course. And looking at it from the woman's point of view, it not only is a matter of honoring her husband, but of her own glory. But if someone wants to be contentious about all this, remember that while this is a matter of custom, not law, none of our churches has any such custom of leaving the head uncovered.

The foregoing paraphrase can serve as my interpretation of the text. Two points may be further explained. The word *nature* as used here does not mean "custom," as some think, although there is a relationship in ancient thought between nature, law and custom. In Paul's thought here the law of nature combines with both the law of God and the informal laws of custom as indicating proper hair attire. Koester has shown that the word for "nature," *physis,* was used in Stoic literature to describe hair and beard style as being appropriate to one's sex, though noting that Paul's use of *physis* in his argument is "a typical one in popular philosophy and is not specifically Stoic."[35] Paul's use of *physis* should not, however, be taken to mean that the way one wears or covers one's hair is so tied to nature that it can never change. Leviticus 19:27 commands "Do not cut the hair at the sides of your head or clip off the

---

[35]Helmut Koester, in G. Kittel and G. Friedrich, *TDNT* 9:273, cf. 263.

edges of your beard" as one of a series of injunctions based on the
holiness of God. Yet obviously sideburns and beards carried a significance in that society that they do not today. In the same way, what was
according to "nature" for Stoics and others in Paul's day is not necessarily so today, even though the basic fact remains that a woman's hair
tends to grow longer than a man's.

The second point has to do with the word *synētheia* in verse 16.
Unlike *physis* this word does have the common sense of "custom." It is
translated "practice" in NIV and can also mean "habit." The very use of
this word throws emphasis on the principles behind the headcovering
rather than on the headcovering itself. Perhaps it is wrong to think of
Paul's closing argument here as weak, as some have, but the fact remains that Paul does not come down as heavily as he would have were
it a crucial doctrinal issue. The Corinthians are to weigh matters and,
on balance, accept the custom.

1 Corinthians 14:33b-40

Not only does the injunction for women to be silent in 1 Corinthians
14:33-34 seem to contradict the idea in chapter 11 that women were
prophesying, but it also seems to run counter to other New Testament
accounts of women prophesying (among other ministries) as a mark of
the new age (Acts 2:17-18). The most common approach, of course, has
been to affirm women's essential equality while holding to a functional
subordination.[36]

The argument that it is just as appropriate to take the silence of
women as normative and their prophetic activity in chapter 11 as ab-
errant ignores the weight of the evidence. Also the argument that we
do not have any direct statement that women spoke *in church* is weak
since Acts does not provide enough samples of church meetings to form
a basis for judgment.[37] There is no reason to assume that the "sons and
daughters" who prophesied did so only apart from the church. Therefore, while we should approach 1 Corinthians 14 on its own terms, we

---

[36]Linda Mercadante has noted this in her survey of commentaries on 1 Corinthians 11:2-
16 *(From Hierarchy to Equality).*
[37]It could be understood that Agabus prophesied in a church meeting in Acts 20:7-12,
since he was "standing up" (more unusual inside) and since his prophecy was followed
by a church decision.

should honestly recognize that only it and 1 Timothy 2:8–15 in all of the New Testament specifically restrict the ministry of women.

Some scholars have argued, because of the displacement of the passage to a later point in some early texts, that 1 Corinthians 14:34–35 was not originally in Paul's writings.[38] Others have argued that the teaching is not Paul's own, but an opinion he wishes to refute.[39] I find inadequate support for either of these alternatives. What Paul negates by his use of the adversative Greek particle ē is *not* the *command* in verses 34–35 but the assumed *disobedience* of it, just as in the structurally similar passage 6:18–19.[40]

But what *law* is Paul referring to when he says "as the law says?" No single Old Testament text stands clearly behind this prohibition, though Genesis 1 and 2 as well as 3:16 have been suggested as possibilities. I find two other alternatives more likely.

1. Paul may be referring in general to Jewish and Gentile laws that restricted the public participation of women. Seen this way, Paul is not exalting rabbinic tradition as an ultimate authority but using law generally as representative of general restrictions on women in first-century society.[41]

2. Paul may instead be referring to a general understanding in Old Testament times that women should not usurp male authority. The problem with this suggestion is the implication that Paul was teaching a patriarchal perspective. But the citation of a particular instance may clarify the scene. In Numbers 12:1–15 Miriam and Aaron complained against Moses, and Miriam (but not Aaron) became a leper. Miriam was

---

[38]See the Nestle-Aland textual apparatus for the relevant data. William O. Walker, Jr., "The 'Theology of Women's Place' and the 'Paulinist' Tradition," in *Semeia* 28 (1983): 101–12, presents reasons for this reconstruction of sources.

[39]A recent proponent of this view, which goes back at least to Kathryn Bushnell, is David W. Odell-Scott, "Let the Women Speak in Church: An Egalitarian Interpretation of 1 Cor 14:33b–36, *Biblical Theology Bulletin* 13 (1983): 90–93; Cf. Neal M. Flanagan and Edwina Hunter Snyder, "Did Paul Put Down Women in 1 Cor 14:34–36?" *Biblical Theology Bulletin* 11 (1981): 10–12.

[40]Odell-Scott does not discuss the use of the Greek particle in question in 1:13; 6:2, 9, 16, 19; 9:6, 8, 10; 10:22; 14:36. I question his interpretation of the passage he does discuss.

[41]The rabbinic restrictions are well known; pagan examples of such limitations were given above. Note especially the 3rd to 2nd century B.C. Treatise attributed to the Pythagoreans: "For public law prevents women from participating in these [Cybeline] rites." Of course, such laws were changing, but Paul might have been generalizing as to public opinion.

a prophetess (like Deborah, Judges 4:4, and Huldah, 2 Kings 22:14; 2 Chronicles 34:22), but when she countered the authority of Moses, she transgressed. She was a leader (Mic 6:4) but should not have "judged" the prophet Moses (Deut 18:15).[42] So, Paul's argument might run, women in the church can prophesy but should not judge the words of others. They should be "in submission" just as Miriam should have been to the leadership of Moses. This fits in well but does not require that the limitation placed on women in chapter 14 was with regard to the "judging" of the prophets.

A few further exegetical observations are in order. In view of its overall New Testament usage, it seems unwise to see the verb *laleō* ("speak") as carrying any special meaning here, such as "chatter." Similarly, though *sigaō* refers to absolute silence, its use in verses 28 and 30 with regard to prophets and tongues-speakers suggests that the silence imposed on women in verse 34 is not a universal silence but one dictated by circumstances, in this case the time for judging the prophecies.[43] Women were thus free to prophesy, but, according to this interpretation, were not free to judge the words of the prophets.

This accords best, in my judgment, with the prohibition against asking questions. In the ancient world, questions were a means of teaching. They were also a means of challenging. The similarity of verse 35 to the quotation from Cato given above is striking: "Could you not have made the same requests, each of your own husband, at home?" It is difficult to know, however, if Paul would have had this in mind.

Paul's reason is that women should be in submission. Although in virtually every other use of the verb *submit* in the New Testament there is mention of to whom one should submit, there is none here. It is quite possible that we have an absolute use of the term in the middle voice with the meaning "be submissive in attitude." This could be a carry-over from the idea of a wife being in submission to her husband. In that case the question of single women arises. It is possible that Paul wanted all women to be in a submissive attitude, so that married women would not be in the position of opposing their husbands' prophetic words.[44]

---

[42]I am indebted to David Banks for his presentation of this idea in an unpublished paper on women in 1 Corinthians.

[43]Wayne Grudem, *The Gift of Prophecy,* pp. 245-55.

[44]See E. Earle Ellis, "The Silenced Wives of Corinth," in *New Testament Textual Criticism,* ed. E. J. Epp and G. D. Fee (New York & Oxford: Clarendon Press, 1981), pp. 213-20.

It is equally possible that Paul had general submission to the orderly principles of Christian ministry in mind. The word *hypotassō* ("submit, be subject") occurs earlier in the passage: "The spirits of the prophets are subject to the control of the prophets. For God is not a God of disorder but of peace." So verse 34 might mean that women, like the prophets, should be submissive for the sake of order.

A final exegetical observation centers on verses 39-40. Clearly verse 39 is a summary of our present chapter 14, but only two topics receive mention: prophesying and tongues. There is no mention of the silence of women. We may infer from this that the topic is not major in Paul's thinking. He concludes with the statement that everything should be done "in a fitting and orderly way," an expression that we noted earlier has more social than doctrinal overtones.

As we seek to explore the implications of this passage for today, there are three facets of *social background* we ought to keep in mind:

1. As pagan converts to Christianity, many Corinthians would have had a vivid memory of the orgiastic madness of much of their previous worship. This has been presented vividly in the works of Richard and Catherine Kroeger.[45] It is almost inconceivable that the cultic frenzy, exchange of sex roles, including hair style, change of clothing, and authoritarian attitudes on the part of women would not have had some effect on the Corinthian church. With Paul's convictions regarding homosexuality, he must have viewed the exchange of sexual roles with horror. Whether he viewed the blurring of sexual distinctions as such in the same way is questionable.[46]

2. Coexistent with this sordid background of pagan excesses was a sense of decorum and propriety. This is seen in certain other pagan rites, such as those of Isis, but also in a more rigid form in the writings of the moralists, in both Latin and Greek. Paul's concerns about honor and shame, propriety and order certainly recall this background. We saw this

---

[45]Richard and Catherine Kroeger, "Pandemonium and Silence at Corinth," *Reformed Journal* 28 (June 1978): 11-15; "Sexual Identity in Corinth," *Reformed Journal* 28 (December 1978): 11-15.

[46]Elisabeth Schüssler Fiorenza, *In Memory of Her* (New York: Crossroad, 1983), pp. 229-30, based on the research of Josef Kuerzinger into the meaning of *choris* in v. 11, "Frau und Mann nach 1 Kor 11.11f.," *Biblische Zeitschrift* 22 (1978): 270-75. She notes that Jerome Murphy-O'Connor accepts Kuerzinger's idea that the word means basically "different from" rather than "without," but she does not think this obliterates all distinctives.

also in the quotations above from Plutarch and from Cato.

3. The ancient Greeks, as Sigountos and Shank have shown, accepted women *prophets* but not women *teachers*.[47] I hold that social perception is a key element in Paul's teachings. Considering the elevated status of teachers within Judaism, we can easily see why, even though women were accepted by the church, their public function might have been limited.

Regarding the particular *circumstances* that existed within the Corinthian church, several theories attempt to account for the theological problems and the opponents that Paul faced. The gnostic question is not as relevant to our section as it is to other parts of the correspondence. The presence of "enthusiasts" in the congregation is more so. The Corinthians were "carnal" in that they were immature and quick to take sides against each other.[48] According to chapter 11 they were also carnal in their disorderliness at the Lord's Table, both with respect to their insistence on "having their say" and with regard to their attitudes at the love feast. Some interpreters reason that women's participation in prophesying was itself part of the general carnal disorder in the Corinthian church and therefore by no means an example for us. Over against this, however, in addition to Paul's "I praise you" in verse 2, is the improbability that Paul would have wasted so much time and space on regulating that practice, only to condemn it three chapters later.

Another issue regarding circumstances, mentioned earlier, concerns the possibility that chapters 11 and 14 deal with two different meetings of the church. Could women speak at one meeting but not the other? Previous attempts to show the existence of such a pattern of meetings have not been successful, but a work by G. Almlie ought to be consulted.[49] Of course, even if there were two different meetings, the

---

[47]James G. Sigountos and Myron Shank, "Public Roles for Women in the Pauline Church: A Reappraisal of the Evidence," *Journal of the Evangelical Theological Society* 26 (1983): 283-95.

[48]1 Corinthians 1:11-12; 3:1-4. For a major study of the sociological background of the troublesome divisions in the Corinthian church see Gerd Theissen, *The Social Setting of Pauline Christianity* (Philadelphia: Fortress Press, 1982).

[49]One attempt to resolve the apparent contradictions between chapter 11 and chapter 14 is that of Gerald L. Almlie, "Women's Church and Communion Participation: Apostolic Practice or Innovative Twist?" *Christian Brethren Review* 33 (1982): 41-55. Through the generally accepted practice of assuming a change of topic and perhaps a correction

silence of women at one of them still needs to be explained. It is possible that Paul did not want women to speak when the public were present, as is the case in chapter 14 (see v. 23), for reasons we have suggested above.

Regarding the *theological background,* it is sometimes wrongly assumed that to appeal to the social background automatically involves dismissing Paul's theological assumptions and argument. Bertil Gärtner argues that if the teaching in 1 Corinthians 14:34 and 1 Timothy 2:12 "is only a casual directive intended to correct some irregularities then current in the external order, then the New Testament does not present any teaching concerning the office of men and women."[50] But in fact, he says, it is a "normative teaching." He is correct in his statement but incorrect in his comprehension. Paul *is* giving normative teaching. But the normative teaching is not women's silence, it is how God's people are to behave in the world of the first-century church and therefore in any other similar circumstance. The normative teaching is how to apply the various principles of God's Word, in this case, the headship of man (properly understood), the avoidance of shame, and the avoidance of anything that would hinder the acceptance of the gospel. Further, Paul is dealing with a problem far deeper than the participation of women. Elisabeth Schüssler Fiorenza's statement is worth pondering: "Paul's major concern . . . is not the behavior of women but the protection of the Christian community. He wanted to protect the Christian community from being mistaken for one of the orgiastic, secret, oriental cults that undermined public order and decency."[51]

In conclusion, Paul is not writing to impose an arbitrary permanent restriction of women's ministry. Just as he counseled submission on the

---

through the use of *peri de,* and by outlining a chiastic structure in chapter 11, he moves toward the conclusion that two different meetings are in view in the two chapters. He supports this by appealing to the fact that the Jerusalem Christians worshiped at the temple as well as in homes, and by hypothesizing that at Troas Paul preached in the *circumstances* of their gathering for the Lord's Supper, but not at the time *when* they observed the Lord's Supper. He does this by taking the participial construction, "coming together" (to break bread), as circumstantial, not temporal. The New Testament evidence is slender, as is the historical evidence, for two separate meetings. His argument that there is a difference between priesthood and ministry carries more weight.

[50]Bertil Gärtner, "Didaskalos: The Office, Man and Woman in the New Testament," *Concordia Journal* 8 (1982): 52-60.

[51]E. Schüssler Fiorenza, *In Memory of Her,* p. 232.

part of slaves in order to make the gospel attractive, so, in order to avoid maligning that gospel through appearing to dishonor their husbands, he counsels women to accommodate to contemporary standards of decency. Feverish pagan practices must be avoided, along with anything that suggests homosexuality. In spite of true spiritual equality (Gal 3:28), restrictive measures are advisable to avoid violating the principle of headship. Such a violation would occur if women brought shame on their husbands. Therefore, just as Paul became as under the law to win those who actually were under that law, he counsels an accommodation, a reversion to Jewish (and some pagan) customs of decency. Paul is not teaching us that women are inferior, nor that they do not have freedom to pray and prophesy publicly, nor that they must wear a first-century coiffure or veil. Rather he is teaching us how to apply biblical principles to social perceptions and social relationships. He is also teaching that women indeed do have "authority," the right to pray and prophesy in the assembly of God's people, even in a society where these practices were controversial. These teachings should encourage the church both to guard the right of women to prophesy in the Lord's name and to preserve the honor of that name as we declare to contemporary society the Christian dignity of women.

Walter L. Liefeld is professor of New Testament, Trinity Evangelical Divinity School, Deerfield, Illinois.

RESPONSE
Alan F. Johnson

Walter Liefeld is to be commended for his competent, fresh, balanced, exegetical treatment of 1 Corinthians 11 and 14. His work advances our understanding of these passages and should set the standard for future exegetical research, especially in chapter 11.

I understand Liefeld's thesis for chapter 11 to be this: Paul in this chapter is not teaching that the man or husband has authority over the woman in some hierarchical chain of command. Rather he is correcting an abuse in the manner in which men and women were participating in public worship in the church. Sensing from a social standpoint that covered men or uncovered women bring dishonor or shame to their heads when they pray or prophesy publicly, the apostle instructs the Corinthians not to follow a practice that will cause the gospel to be maligned or jeopardized. Paul argues on strictly Jewish grounds for the headcovering restriction on women as they minister publicly (vv. 3–10), but then concedes that in Christ there is no difference or priority spiritually between men and women and that the woman has a natural covering provided by God in her long hair. Nevertheless, the Corinthians are to accept the custom of women being covered. This thesis, it seems to me, is essentially the point of view argued by Balch *(Let Wives Be Submissive . . .)* in his study of 1 Peter.[52]

With the broad outlines of Liefeld's thesis I am in substantial agreement. I will comment briefly on details of the case, pointing out minor differences or raising a question or two.

The Exegesis of 1 Corinthians 11

Locating chapter 11 in the larger context of 8–10, Liefeld has shown us that the same concerns of the apostle carry over into this section. Paul has argued in the previous chapters for a limitation of Christian liberty so that other believers are not offended and nonbelievers are not hindered from accepting the gospel ("all things to all people that by all means I may win some"—9:22). Paul also wants to do all things for the "glory of God" (10:31—11:1). Proper decorum in public worship (11:2-16) relates to these same themes of accommodation of liberty in order not to cause offense and to do what brings glory to God. This context sheds light on the intent and character of Paul's corrective teaching in this section.

With the study and conclusions on *kephalē* I agree. I am now convinced that *kephalē* does not mean "ruler" or "leader." The text is not describing a hierarchical chain of command from God to Christ to husbands to wives. The chain is out of sequence; the corresponding parallel sets of terms—"man is the glory of God," "woman is the glory of the

---

[52]David Lee Balch, *Let Wives Be Submissive, The Domestic Code in 1 Peter* (Chico, Calif.: Scholars Press, 1981).

man"—emphasize more the idea of honor or representative relationship than authority over, and the word *kephalē* in the LXX is seldom a translation of *ro'sh* where *ro'sh* clearly means "ruler" or "authority over someone" (*archōn* is usually the translation).

Furthermore, the paper is certainly correct to raise some questions about understanding *kephalē* as "source" or "origin." Despite the attempts of Scroggs and Bartchy to argue this sense of the word, the linguistic evidence is too meager and the view presents problems theologically as Liefeld has noted.[53] In addition to the problem of God being the "source of" Christ, which the essay notes, I would also see a problem with Christ as the "source of" every man (even every Christian man). Only in some remote sense as Christ the creator of men or Christ the source of men's divine life could we understand Paul's reference.[54] While some support for this idea is to be found in verses 8 and 12 in Paul's statements that the woman is derived from the man in creation, it is by no means clear that *kephalē* should therefore be understood simply as source. It is at best a secondary sense given a new meaning in verses 11–12.

Liefeld concludes that *kephalē* means "eminent" or "prominent" or "honored" member in relationship to the other. This explanation commends itself as superior to the idea either of authority or source. The head receives glory or honor from that member to whom it stands in this special relationship. In public ministry and worship neither the man nor the woman is to violate the standards of the expected social decorum and bring shame on that member who stands as the honored or eminent partner. All of this sounds strange to our ears in the twentieth-century Western world. Perhaps we have in *kephalē* the modern equivalent of "pride and joy" in someone. God is the "pride and joy" of Christ; Christ is the "pride and joy" of every Christian husband because Christ is the perfect model of the husband's relationship to his wife in self-sacrificing love and service (Eph 5:25); and the husband is the "pride and joy" of his wife in that though she is equal and complementary to him,

[53]Scott Bartchy, "Power, Submission and Sexual Identity among the Early Christians," *Essays on New Testament Christianity*, ed. C. Robert Wetzel (Cincinnati, Ohio: Standard, 1978); Robin Scroggs, "Paul and Eschatological Woman," *JAAR* 40 (1972): 283–303.
[54]Bartchy, "Power, Submission," p. 79.

she honors him as the exemplar from which she was created (Gen 2).[55] But I am bothered by the lack of any direct source for Paul's *kephalē* imagery. Where does he find this connection between *kephalē* and male eminence?

Liefeld's description of the Greco-Roman cultural situation pertaining to women's conduct in public vis-a-vis their husbands' honor or shame is quite germane. Titus 2:5 provides a parallel situation where Paul more explicitly says that women are to submit to their husbands because otherwise the word of God would be maligned due to the social standards of propriety of that day. This argument sounds very much like that which Balch has argued for in 1 Peter *(Let Wives Be Submissive . . .)*. Balch argues that just as lack of submissiveness of wives to their husbands (expressed by proper social decorum in the first century) would cause offense to the gospel, so the opposite would occur today if an outsider came into one of the traditionally male-dominated services where women never speak or minister. It would surely be interpreted as demeaning to women and cause hindrance to the gospel.[56]

I wish Liefeld had shed more light on the Jewish customs with reference to females in public and in worship. His emphasis on the Greco-Roman texts was excellent, but is nothing known about Jewish decorum standards?

To determine whether Paul has some veil or headcovering in view or merely hair style, it might be worth noting that Derrett denies that shaving a woman's head (vv. 5-6) signified a punishment for social misbehavior as it does in the Western idea. In Derrett's view, the reason women should be covered is not primarily to show respect, but because long tresses were a sign of sexual attractiveness. If the woman untied her hair and uncovered it in public, her husband suffered and was put to shame. He had a right to expect that her hair would be covered in public. On the other hand, the woman's long hair was a sign of her sexuality and when she wanted to make a special vow, she sacrificed her long hair by shaving it or cropping it close. "A woman (perhaps a widow) who had her head shaven or shorn *could* appear with her head

---

[55]This idea was sparked by Derrett's observation that "glory of" someone means "pride of" someone (J. Duncan Derrett, "Religious Hair," *Studies in the New Testament*, I (Leiden: Brill, 1977), p. 172.

[56]Balch, *Let Wives*, pp. 120-21.

uncovered in public, and no doubt often did so with pride."[57] This point needs to be explored further.

What about Liefeld's handling of the difficult section in verses 11-16? He argues that until verse 11 Paul has been arguing for accommodation in the church to Jewish and pagan standards of social decorum. Paul's accommodation was based on Jewish grounds which included the principle of the husband's headship. Now with the strong adversative *plēn* in verse 11, Paul wants to move beyond Judaism to the Christian response. What he has said in verses 2-10 can be justified, but he now wants his readers to understand that "in Christ" there is no distinction between man and woman; there is no priority of one over the other. His haircovering advice, Paul affirms, is not a theological matter; the Corinthians must judge for themselves. From the woman's perspective, her long hair is given to her by God as a covering so that no further covering is necessary (providing the hair is bound up). From her point of view, the long hair should create no shame for her husband and at the same time her long hair brings honor to herself. Paul then concludes by mildly suggesting that the Corinthians should consider the practice of the other churches which have no custom of women praying and preaching with improperly covered heads.

This interpretation of Liefeld has much to commend it. It takes seriously the adversative particle *plēn* which begins the section. According to Bauer-Arndt-Gingrich, among other usages the particle may signal either breaking off the subject to emphasize what is really important (see Eph 5:33) or breaking off the subject to pass to a new subject (see Luke 22:21). Since the matter of coverings is again mentioned by Paul in verse 13 it would seem that here Paul is breaking off the subject to emphasize what is really important.

The expression "in the Lord" (v. 11) in Paul often means "from the Christian perspective" (see Col 3:20). This indicates some advance in the argument while not denying the validity of what Paul already argued. Admittedly this is a difficult section to harmonize with the former verses.

I find this ingenious reconstruction quite attractive. That a change of some sort is signaled by the *plēn* (v. 11) is clear. But does this change

---

[57]Derrett, "Religious Hair," p. 172.

mean that Paul is now adopting the Christian woman's point of view? Liefeld's approach explains some of the changes of viewpoint in this section compared with Paul's previous statements, and I cannot offer any substantial argument against it. Further discussion will help us to see if this view can stand and be more widely adopted.

The Exegesis of 1 Corinthians 14

We turn now to the thornier problem of chapter 14:33b-34. Paul seems, on first reading, to deny absolutely the right of wives to speak publicly in the church—something he has apparently stated they have the right to do (if properly covered) in chapter 11. The resolution of this apparent absurdity has taken a number of forms as Liefeld cites. Some argue that women are equal to men but functionally subordinate; others that silence is normative for women and their prophetic speaking in chapter 11 is to be seen as abnormal or that there is no evidence that women ever spoke in church. Others suggest displacement and hostile source theories. To these could be added Earle Ellis's marginal gloss view.[58] Liefeld rejects all of these. He then evaluates the theory of Odell-Scott and others that Paul here introduced a Jewish point of view with which Paul disagrees. I believe Liefeld's case against this view is right and that we should not accept it as Paul's intent.

Liefled then offers his own view of the "law" in verse 34b as the laws of both Jews and Gentiles that restricted the public participation of women, or more likely the general understanding in Old Testament times that viewed male authority as determining the limits of participation of women. However, to my knowledge we have no other New Testament usage of *nomos* that would fit this suggestion.

Liefeld shows that the "speaking" was of a particular kind, that is, that which involved critically evaluating the prophets' words. The silence was not absolute, therefore, and allowed women to pray and prophesy in their turn just as the men did. Why then the restriction? Hurley, following the same view up to this point, says it is because this practice is inconsistent with male authority and female subordination in the church. Liefeld answers that the instruction of Paul is due to his accom-

---

[58]Earle E. Ellis, "The Silenced Wives of Corinth" in *New Testament Textual Criticism*, E. J. Epp and G. D. Fee, eds. (Oxford: Clarendon, 1981), pp. 213-20.

modation to Jewish and pagan social norms of decorum that frowned on women teaching in public. In light of this social phenomena, as well as the Corinthian church's problem of enthusiasm, Liefeld feels we must separate Paul's overarching theological principles that everything should be done to avoid shame and discredit to the gospel from the specific cultural forms of decorum relevant to the first century, including what was honorable or shameful for women to do. With this I am in complete agreement. However, I am not sure what Liefeld believes about the submission of wives to husbands. Was this a binding theological principle like the headship of the husband or a temporary accommodation to the social norms of the day? Or does Christianity modify the headship–submission principle but still leave it as normative? I'm not sure what Liefeld's answer would be.

Let me close with two final comments. First, whether we agree with Liefeld's analysis or not, he is not arguing for the relativity of Paul's teaching. He holds to the total truthfulness of all scriptural teaching. The theological teaching is normative for all ages and just as binding on the church today as it was in Paul's day. But theological principles were embodied in certain cultural specifics of Paul's day, such as the wearing of coiffures and the silence of women in teaching roles to avoid social impropriety. When we see these improprieties as different in different times and places, thus requiring a change in these cultural specifics, we do not breed relativism but rather honor the Word of God as capable of addressing every age and society. To wed the Word of God to its cultural specifics is to imprison the Word in the biblical world.

It is my opinion, in the light of Leifeld's exegesis, with which I substantially agree, that we cannot, on the basis of passages in 1 Corinthians, deny women full participation in any form of ministry that does not create a demonstrable social offense to their husbands or an impediment to the societies' acceptance of the Christian gospel.

Alan F. Johnson is professor of New Testament and theological ethics at Wheaton College, Wheaton, Illinois.

8

GALATIANS 3:28: CONUNDRUM OR SOLUTION?

Klyne R. Snodgrass

THE STUDY OF Galatians 3:28 is both exciting and frustrating. On the one hand, the verse is the most socially explosive statement in the New Testament. On the other hand, the context gives little help in interpreting these words, and a bewildering array of possibilities for interpretation appear both in technical and in nontechnical studies.

The problems are caused by two main facts. First, the words about slave and free and about male and female appear abruptly and without apparent relation to the situation in the Galatian church. Second, some of Paul's other statements—such as 1 Corinthians 11:2-16; 14:33-36; Ephesians 5:22-33; and 1 Timothy 2:8-15—seem to contradict Galatians 3:28. What is the relation between this passage and the other texts? Is Galatians 3:28 more important than the others, or has its significance been overestimated? The attempts to explain the setting and the role of Galatians 3:28 have left a trail that is not particularly flattering to biblical and theological studies. Any attempt at biblical studies involves some reading between the lines, but too often our studies have focused more attention on the material between the lines than on the lines themselves. This text, like some others, has become a hermeneutical skeleton key by which we may go through any door we choose. More often than not, Galatians 3:28 has become a piece of plastic that people have molded to their preconceived ideas.

We are made painfully aware of this when we examine the treatment of our text in the arguments for slavery in nineteenth-century America.

Galatians 3:28 was used to prove that the distinctions that slavery creates are insignificant and that the same doctrine should hold for both slaves and masters.[1] The parallel words in Colossians 3:11 were used to show that the presence and favor of God are not limited to "any outward condition," and therefore slaves should be content with their position.[2] The argument for slavery was bolstered by the parallel and "obvious" necessity to subjugate women. Without qualms the argument was given by, of all people, Charles Hodge: "In this country we believe that the general good requires us to deprive the whole female sex of the right of self-government. They have no voice in the formation of the laws which dispose of their persons and property. When married, we despoil them almost entirely of a legal existence, and deny them some of the most essential rights of property."[3] I do not mean to belittle people of another era, but it is both humbling and frightening to see what has been done in the name of good exegesis.

Options for Interpretation
Before analyzing the text, an overview of approaches will be helpful. Because of the seeming contradiction with what Paul writes elsewhere, the underlying question determining every interpretation is "How seriously did Paul believe what he wrote in Galatians 3:28?" Could Paul have really meant it when he wrote, "There is neither Jew nor Greek, there is neither slave nor free, there is not male and female"? In interpreting 3:28, the approaches group themselves into rather limited options. One may say: (1) Paul did not really mean these words, (2) he meant them only partially, (3) his theology developed in one direction or the other or (4) he meant exactly what he said. Most interpreters choose either the second or the fourth option.

Those who believe that Paul did not really mean these words usually argue that 3:28 is a pre-Pauline formula that Paul has inserted at this

---

[1]George D. Armstrong, *The Christian Doctrine of Slavery* (New York: Negro Universities Press, 1969), pp. 65, 123. (Originally published in 1857 by Charles Scribner.)

[2]John Henry Hopkins, *A Scriptural, Ecclesiastical, and Historical View of Slavery* (New York: Negro Universities Press, 1969), pp. 139-40. (Originally published in 1864 by W. S. Pooley & Co.)

[3]Charles Hodge, "The Bible Argument on Slavery," *Cotton Is King, and Pro-Slavery Arguments*, ed. E. N. Elliott (Augusta: Pritchard, Abbott & Loomis, 1860; reprinted 1968), p. 863. See also p. 379.

point in his letter and that Paul quoted the words without intending them to be taken at face value for the community. Marie de Merode believes that 3:28 is more liberal than Paul would like and reflects a theology of women in the primitive community *before* Paul.[4] J. C. O'Neill omitted this verse from his discussion of Galatians because he felt that it expressed the view of the post-Pauline church.[5] Others see 3:28 as a cry of the enthusiasts[6] or of the Gnostics,[7] which Paul either has to adapt or refute. One might compare this with the argument of Brinsmead, even though he maintains that Paul believes that these words have social consequences. Brinsmead says that 3:28 is used polemically by Paul and that he has taken the language from his opponents. A "unification" saying associated with Matthew 22:30 and parallel passages suggests that in Galatia (as in Corinth) there was concern for the attainment of the future angelic state. Paul used these words to show that the attainment of this androgynous state was through baptism.[8]

The second option, that Paul meant these words only in part, may fairly be called the traditional position. On this approach the claim is

---

[4]Marie de Merode, "Une théologie primitive de la femme?" *Revue théologique de Louvain* 9 (1978): 180–81.

[5]J. C. O'Neill, *The Recovery of Paul's Letter to the Galatians* (London: SPCK, 1972), p. 55.

[6]Siegfried Schulz, "Evangelium und Welt: Hauptprobleme einer Ethik des Neuen Testaments," *Neues Testament und christliche Existenz,* ed. Hans Dieter Betz und Luise Schottroff (Tübingen: J. C. B. Mohr, Paul Siebeck, 1973), pp. 491–94; cf. Ernst Käsemann, *Jesus Means Freedom* (Philadelphia: Fortress Press, 1970), pp. 64–65.

[7]Walter Schmithals, *Gnosticism in Corinth,* trans. John E. Steely (Nashville: Abingdon Press, 1971), p. 239. See also Dennis Ronald McDonald, *There Is No Male and Female: Galatians 3:26–28 and Gnostic Baptismal Tradition* (Ph.D. diss., Harvard University, 1978). McDonald argues that 3:28 points beyond Paul's own prevailing view. For him, the words in 3:26–28 derive from a baptismal "garment/two-are-one tradition" that is reflected in Gnosticism, especially the Gospel of the Egyptians (see n. 42 below). Paul then is viewed as opposing the theology and anthropology of that tradition in 1 Corinthians. The glaring weakness of McDonald's approach is his assumption that the Gnostic version found in the Gospel of the Egyptians is earlier than and independent from Gal 3:28. If Gal 3:28 is the source of the various "gnostic" statements—as seems likely—then the whole theory is unnecessary.

[8]Bernard Hungerford Brinsmead, *Galatians—Dialogical Response to Opponents* (Chico, Calif.: Scholars Press, 1982), pp. 154–61. Wayne A. Meeks ("The Image of the Androgyne: Some Uses of a Symbol in Earliest Christianity," *History of Religions* 13 [1973–74]: 203, n. 153) seems to suggest also that he does not believe Paul meant these words: "It also appears therefore if we are to take [1 Cor] 11:7 at face value, that Paul himself did not—or did not always—accept the androgynous interpretation of Genesis 1:27 which, we have concluded, lay behind the baptismal language of Galatians 3:28."

usually made that 3:28 is a soteriological statement and has nothing to do with social issues: the text speaks *coram Deo* ("before God"), but it has nothing to do with nations or slavery[9] or with positions assigned in creation.[10] Therefore, this "purely religious" text has no direct consequences for the arrangement of church offices or political society.[11] At times the language is shocking. Lenski writes, "The gospel changes nothing in the domain of this world and this natural life," then seemingly catches himself and adds, "In a way the gospel effects changes also in this domain. It has driven out slavery and has elevated the status of woman."[12]

This approach often takes a rather ironhanded view that Scripture cannot contradict Scripture and quickly excludes any option that would allow even a surface contradiction with other texts.[13] James Hurley went so far as to say that 3:28 deals with the question "Who may become a son of God, and on what basis?" and does not deal with relations within the body of Christ.[14] Not all those taking this approach would say that 3:28 is without social implications, but they still would not see it as affirming any kind of social equality for male and female.[15] Obviously those who take this approach de-emphasize the importance of the verse for understanding male and female relations in this age. For them

---

[9]Ernest de Witt Burton, *A Critical and Exegetical Commentary on the Epistle to the Galatians* (Edinburgh: T. & T. Clark, 1921), pp. 206-7; cf. Madeleine Boucher, "Some Unexplored Parallels to I Corinthians 11:11-12 and Galatians 3:28: The New Testament on the Role of Women," *CBQ* 31 (1969): 57-58; and Averil Cameron, "Neither Male nor Female," *Greece and Rome*, 2nd series, 27 (1980): 64-65. Cameron even said that it is a false assumption to think that Christianity offered something special for the underdog.

[10]Fritz Zerbst, *The Office of Woman in the Church*, trans. Albert G. Merkens (St. Louis: Concordia, 1955), p. 35.

[11]Albrecht Oepke, *Der Brief des Paulus an die Galater*, 2nd ed. (Berlin: Evangelische Verlagsanstalt, 1960), p. 61; Heinrich Schlier, *Der Brief an die Galater* (Göttingen: Vandenhoeck & Ruprecht, 1962), p. 175, n. 4.

[12]R. C. H. Lenski, *The Interpretation of St. Paul's Epistles to the Galatians, to the Ephesians, to the Philippians* (Minneapolis: Augsburg, 1937), p. 189.

[13]Susan Foh, *Women and the Word of God* (Phillipsburg, N.J.: Presbyterian and Reformed, 1979), pp. 27, 140-41. See also James B. Hurley, *Man and Woman in Biblical Perspective* (Grand Rapids, Mich.: Zondervan, 1981), pp. 127-28.

[14]Hurley, *Man and Woman*, pp. 126-27.

[15]See Stephen B. Clark, *Man and Woman in Christ* (Ann Arbor, Mich.: Servant Books, 1980), pp. 151-52; or John Jefferson Davis, "Some Reflections on Galatians 3:28, Sexual Roles, and Biblical Hermeneutics," *JETS* 19 (1976); 202-3.

it is not the primary passage for discussing the relation of male and female. In fact, it is not even a key text.[16] Focus is usually placed instead on 1 Corinthians 11 and 14 and 1 Timothy 2.[17]

The third option, that there was development in Paul's thought in one direction or the other, possibly should not be singled out since many interpretations in option four also include the idea of development. However, some interpretations focus so explicitly on development that they deserve attention as a separate category. Robert Jewett views Paul as starting out in his earliest letters (the Thessalonian correspondence) with patriarchal ideas, then moving to a position of "equality in principle with residual patriarchy," (Galatians, Philippians and some of the Corinthian correspondence)[18] and finally moving to a position of consistent equality (in Philemon, Romans and the remaining Corinthian correspondence).[19] He, like others, understands 3:28 to refer to androgyny.[20] However, some other scholars see the development moving in the opposite direction. The emergence of the house codes and the strictures placed on women in 1 Corinthians are viewed as corrections necessitated by problems that were caused by 3:28.[21] Hans Dieter Betz says that Paul's treatment of women in 1 Corinthians may imply that he has retracted his position in Galatians.[22]

The fourth option, that Paul meant what he said in 3:28, is held by a variety of scholars, who have differing views as to the relation between 3:28 and what Paul says elsewhere. Those who have difficulty dealing with tension in a writer's thought tend to assign contradictory state-

---

[16]Clark, *Man and Woman in Christ,* p. 138.

[17]Charles Caldwell Ryrie, *The Place of Women in the Church* (New York: Macmillan, 1958), p. 76, who does not emphasize 1 Cor 11; George W. Knight III, "The New Testament Teaching on the Role Relationship of Male and Female with Special Reference to the Teaching/Ruling Functions in the Church," *JETS* 18 (1975): 1, 4–11. Note the attention given to 1 Tim 2 by Hurley.

[18]Jewett identifies seven different letters in 1 and 2 Corinthians.

[19]Robert Jewett, "The Sexual Liberation of the Apostle Paul," *JAAR* 47 (supp.) (1979): 55–87.

[20]Ibid., pp. 64–69.

[21]James E. Crouch, *The Origin and Intention of the Colossian Haustafel* (Göttingen: Vandenhoeck & Ruprecht, 1972), pp. 27, 141–45; cf. Peter Richardson, *Paul's Ethic of Freedom* (Philadelphia: Westminster, 1979), pp. 70–72. (Almost the first half of Richardson's book is focused on Gal 3:28.)

[22]Hans Dieter Betz, *Galatians* (Philadelphia: Fortress, 1979), p. 200.

ments to redactors or later authors. Typically, 1 Corinthians 14:33-36 and possibly 11:2-16 are viewed as interpolations, while Ephesians, Colossians and the Pastorals are considered to be the work of Pauline disciples. In this way, Paul's thought can be relieved of any difficulty.[23] Some argue that Paul saw the implications of his statement for Jews and Gentiles but did not see the implications so clearly for slaves and even less so for women.[24] Paul Jewett, among others, argues that Paul is merely inconsistent. Galatians 3:28 is his best Christian thinking and is in accord with the first creation narrative and the teaching of Jesus, but his other statements are holdovers from his rabbinic training and the second creation narrative.[25] Scholars such as Richard Longenecker and Scott Bartchy view Galatians 3:28 as a normative text while texts such as 1 Corinthians 14 and 1 Timothy 2 are descriptive or deal with problems in the early church.[26] Only slightly different is the language that sees 3:28 as a statement of what ought to be, while other texts deal with the reality of life as Paul knew it,[27] or the argument that 3:28 is the primary passage for dealing with male and female in the church and that all other texts must be seen as descriptions or applications of it.[28]

---

[23]See, for example, Robin Scroggs, "Paul and the Eschatological Woman," *JAAR* 40 (1972): 283-303; Gerhard Dautzenberg, "Da ist nicht männlich und weiblich," *Kairos* N.F., 24 (1982): 199; L. Legrand, "There Is Neither Slave nor Free, Neither Male nor Female: St. Paul and Social Emancipation," *Indian Theological Studies* 17 (1981): 156; Elisabeth Schüssler Fiorenza, *In Memory of Her* (New York: Crossroad, 1983), pp. 245-46. (She does retain 1 Cor 14:33-36 as part of Paul's letter; see p. 230.)

[24]W. M. Ramsay, *A Historical Commentary on St. Paul's Epistle to the Galatians* (London: Hodder & Stoughton, 1899), pp. 386-87; Evelyn and Frank Stagg, *Woman in the World of Jesus* (Philadelphia: Westminster, 1978), p. 165; cf. Richardson, *Paul's Ethic*, pp. 60, 75-78; and Paul K. Jewett, *Man As Male and Female* (Grand Rapids, Mich.: Eerdmans, 1975), p. 142.

[25]P. Jewett, *Man As Male and Female*, p. 112; cf. R. Scroggs, "Woman in the N.T.," *IDB Supplementary Volume* (Nashville: Abingdon, 1976), p. 967.

[26]Richard N. Longenecker, *New Testament Social Ethics for Today* (Grand Rapids, Mich.: Eerdmans, 1984), pp. 84-86 (over half of Longenecker's book is devoted to Gal 3:28); Scott Bartchy, "Power, Submission, and Sexual Identity among the Early Christians," *Essays on New Testament Christianity*, ed. C. Robert Wetzel (Cincinnati: Standard Publishing, 1978), pp. 58-59.

[27]Thomas R. W. Longstaff, "The Ordination of Women: A Biblical Perspective," *ATR* 57 (1975): 322-27; cf. J. Louis Martyn, "Galatians 3:28, Faculty Appointments and the Overcoming of Christological Amnesia," *Katallagete* 8 (1982): 41-44.

[28]William Houghton Leslie, *The Concept of Woman in the Pauline Corpus in Light of the Social and Religious Environment of the First Century* (Ph.D. diss., Northwestern University,

Cautions and Procedural Suggestions

We all have our canon within the canon, which is just another way of saying that we are attracted to those verses in Scripture that express what we already believe—even if we do not put our beliefs into practice. Even where we decide that a text is normative and that other texts are descriptive—which we certainly must—we cannot ignore the descriptive texts. We must try to explain what those descriptive texts are attempting to accomplish in their context. We must also determine what truth from those texts is still pertinent in our own time in similar contexts. Nothing may be labeled "cultural" and forgotten. All the Bible is culturally conditioned; that is, it arises from within a culture and is addressed to a culture. Still, *all* the Bible is instructive for us.

In this connection, we must allow Paul to be Paul. He was not addressing our situation or our set of questions. We only distort his thinking when we transfer it directly to our time. Would Paul be able to deal easily with our concept of ordination? He might well need time to get accustomed to the idea. We may legitimately ask *why* Paul was not dealing with our concerns, but to attempt to make him a twentieth-century Christian is as erroneous as trying to make ourselves into first-century ones.[29]

As we approach Galatians 3:28, we must not attempt to answer all questions about male and female relations from this one text. Is it really fair to say that nothing more is to be said after Galatians 3:28?[30] This verse by itself cannot answer all our questions with satisfaction for all persons concerned. Other pertinent texts must be placed alongside Galatians 3:28 in a reasonable biblical theology of women.

On the other hand, there are writers who seem highly defensive in discussing 3:28, as if its words could not reasonably be given serious attention without damaging the scheme of things. Such defensiveness only shows how concerned we are to preserve our order—this world's order. Galatians 3:28 *is* the most socially explosive text in the New Testament, and if given its due, it will confront and change our lives and

---

1976), pp. 27-29; cf. Krister Stendahl, *The Bible and the Role of Women* (Philadelphia: Fortress, 1966), pp. 32-37; and F. F. Bruce, *The Epistle to the Galatians* (Grand Rapids, Mich.: Eerdmans, 1982), p. 190.

[29]See Stendahl, *The Bible and the Role of Women*, p. 17.

[30]P. Jewett, *Man As Male and Female*, p. 142.

communities. The only question is *how* socially explosive it is. If this text directs us away from the divisions of society, how far down the road in the other direction does it take us? Some Christians—those in Corinth and some Gnostics—apparently took its teaching too far, and we have much too much evidence of those who did not take it far enough.

We will have to exercise care in determining the relation of Galatians 3:28 to other literature. Parallels within the New Testament, Judaism and Hellenism can easily be used as the key to interpret Galatians. The danger is in reading between the lines rather than reading the lines themselves.

Finally, as concerned as we are about such issues as women in ministry, we need to remind ourselves that the right of women to minister is not the gospel. The *kerygma* must always center on the death and resurrection of Jesus Christ and the freedom found in Christ. I am convinced that if that message is given its proper focus it will lead to the ministry of women as it did in the New Testament, but we cannot afford to substitute our issues for the saving gospel of Jesus Christ.

Background and Parallels to Galatians 3:28

One intriguing aspect of Galatians 3:28 is the number of texts in the ancient world that use similar wording. Many people have assumed that Paul's statement was consciously framed to negate or reflect the concerns of the other sayings.[31] The most pertinent of the parallels is a male thanksgiving that is known both in the Hellenistic and Jewish worlds. The Hellenistic versions are attributed variously to Socrates, Plato and Thales, and in them the speaker gives thanks "that I was born a human being and not an animal, that I was born a man and not a woman, and that I was born a Greek and not a barbarian."[32]

The Jewish version of this thanksgiving, which may well be modeled on the Hellenistic,[33] states: "R. Judah used to say, A man is bound to say

---

[31]Raphael Loewe, *The Position of Women in Judaism* (London: SPCK, 1966), p. 43; Oepke, *Der Brief an die Galater,* p. 90; Bruce, *Epistle to the Galatians,* p. 187.

[32]Diogenes Laertius 1.33; also in Lactantius *The Divine Institutes* 3.19 with an additional thanksgiving for being born an Athenian and in the time of Socrates; and in Plutarch *Lives, Caius Marius* 46.1, but without the thanksgiving that he was born a man and not a woman. Instead, the third thanksgiving is that "his birth had fallen in the times of Socrates."

[33]Bruce, *Epistle to the Galatians,* p. 187; and Meeks, *Image of the Androgyne,* pp. 167-68. But see David Kaufmann, "Das Alter der drei Benedictionen von Israel, vom Freien und

the following three blessings daily: [Blessed art thou . . .] who hast not made me a heathen, who hast not made me a woman, and who hast not made me a brutish man."[34] The same prayer is still in use in Jewish liturgies today.[35] The prayer does not appear to have been intentionally misogynist,[36] for it attempts to thank God for the privilege of learning and keeping the law. The three contrasted groups either did not have that privilege or were excused from the observance of certain requirements.[37]

Whether Galatians 3:28 was written consciously to negate this prayer is difficult to determine. Several commentators reject the suggestion, particularly because the Jewish blessing uses the usual Hebrew word for woman *(ishah)* while the equivalent to the word used by Paul would be *neqebah.*[38] I do not consider this to be conclusive and think that we must allow the possibility that the thanksgiving in either its Hellenistic or Jewish form may have been known and intentionally negated by the

---

vom Mann," *Monatsschrift für Geschichte und Wissenschaft des Judentum* N.F. 1 (1893): 14-18. There is also evidence of a Persian version of the thanksgiving. See Theodor Zahn, *Der Brief des Paulus* (Leipzig: A. Deichert'sche Verlagsbuchhandlung, 1907), p. 187; and James Darmesteter, *Une prière Judéo-Persane* (Paris: Librairie Léopold Cerf, 1891), p. 9, no. 10.

[34]bMenaḥoth 43b, a fourth element is attributed to R. Aḥa b. Jacob, that God has not made him a slave. On being asked if that is not the same as a woman, he replied that a slave is more contemptible. The thanksgiving appears as well in Tosephta Berakoth 7.18 and in pBerakoth 9.1.

[35]See S. Singer, *The Standard Prayer Book* (New York: Bloch, 1943), p. 6. Instead of the line "who hast not made me a woman," the women are to say "who hast made me according to thy will."

[36]Bruce, *Epistle to the Galatians,* p. 187; Leslie, *Concept of Woman,* p. 32; Clark, *Man and Woman in Christ,* pp. 147-49.

[37]One has only to be reminded of the Court of Women in the Temple. See also Sotah 3.4, "If any man gives his daughter a knowledge of the Law it is as though he taught her lasciviousness"; Berakoth 3.3, "Women and slaves and minors are exempt from reciting the *Shema'* and from wearing phylacteries . . . "; Berakoth 7.2, "Women or slaves or minors may not be included [to make up the number needed] for the Common Grace"; Sukkah 2.8, "Women, slaves, and minors are exempt from [the law of] the *Sukkah*"; Aboth 3.6, "If ten men sit together and occupy themselves in the law, the Divine Presence rests among them"; and Kiddushin 1.7, which states that positive ordinances that depend on the time of year for observance are not required of women. Positive ordinances not depending on the time of year and the negative ordinances are to be observed by women.

[38]Scroggs, "Paul and the Eschatological Woman," p. 292, n. 29; and Leslie, *Concept of Woman,* p. 32; cf. Betz, *Galatians,* p. 185, n. 26; and Henning Paulsen, "Einheit und Freiheit der Söhne Gottes—Gal 3:26-29," *ZNW* 71 (1980): 85.

Christian saying. At least these thanksgivings indicate the kinds of attitudes and divisions that the early church rejected.

A number of other parallels from the Hellenistic and Jewish worlds focus on the equality of male and female or other contrasted pairs, but I do not see them as having direct relevance for the analysis of Galatians 3:28.[39] Although the Hellenistic parallels are early enough, the Jewish ones appear to be quite late. These documents underscore the longing in the ancient world—at least in some quarters—for the divisions in humanity to be healed so that a more sane society could emerge.[40] Some of the parallels that are religiously oriented focus only on the attitude of God, but Paul treats the new position of those baptized into Christ.[41] Galatians 3:28 says a lot more than "God is no respecter of persons." The concern in Galatians is for the new status and oneness that exist in Christ.

A number of interesting parallels that appear in the postapostolic period deserve attention, but I do not believe that these parallels give us direction about Paul's intention with the Galatians. Some speak of the cessation of divisions, including the division of humanity into two sexes. The Gospel of Thomas, logion 22, is typical: "They said to Him: Shall we then, being children, enter the Kingdom? Jesus said to them: When you make the two one, and when you make the inner as the outer and the outer as the inner and the above as the below, and when you make the male and the female into a single one, so that the male will not be male and the female (not) be female, when you make eyes in the place of an eye, . . . then shall you enter [the kingdom]." This concern for the reuni-

---

[39]See Wilhelm Dittenberger, *Sylloge Inscriptionum Graecarum* (Hildesheim: George Olms Verlagsbuchhandlung, 1960), no. 985; English trans. in *Hellenistic Religions,* ed. Frederick C. Grant (New York: Liberal Arts Press, 1953), pp. 28–30: "granting access. . . both to free men and women, and to household slaves." The mention of women, however, seems to have been restored to the text. See also Plato *Laws* 7.804D–805D; *The Republic* 5.451D–452A; Plutarch *Moralia* 329A-D. Among the Jewish sources see GenR 8.9; 22.2; and *Seder Eliahu* 7, 10, and 14 (see S-B, III, 563). *Seder Eliahu* 7, e.g., reads: "I call heaven and earth to witness that whether Gentile or Israelite, man or woman, slave or handmaid reads this verse, *northward before the Lord,* the Holy One, blessed be he, remembers the binding of Isaac the son of Abraham *northward before the Lord.*"

[40]See Betz, *Galatians,* pp. 191–92; and H. C. Baldry, *The Unity of Mankind in Greek Thought* (Cambridge: At the University Press, 1965).

[41]Ben Witherington III, "Rite and Rights for Women—Galatians 3:28," *NTS* 27 (1981): 593.

fication of the sexes into an androgynous being is found frequently in "gnostic" texts.[42]

The focus of these texts on androgyny and the Jewish speculation on Adam's being an originally androgynous creation have led some people to conclude that the tradition recorded in Galatians 3:28 was originally intended in an androgynous fashion.[43] Support is often found for this view in the confusion of sexual roles dealt with in 1 Corinthians, but the problem in 1 Corinthians does not seem to have been androgyny. If it were, would not Paul have addressed it more directly and would he not have said as much to the men as to the women? The problem in Corinth seems rather to have been an attempt on the part of women to obliterate the distinctions between the sexes, not to unite them into one. Also, the wording in 3:28 is not like the later texts that read "neither male nor female." Although nearly all the major translations (KJV, ASV, NEB, NIV, RSV) render Galatians 3:28 this way, Paul wrote "There is not male *and* female" (ouk eni arsen kai thēly), marking out this third pair as different from the other two and making an allusion to the words of Genesis 1:27. I see little reason to interpret 3:28 with any androgynous overtones.[44] As Robin Scroggs points out, the Gnostics wanted to obliterate the distinctions between the sexes, but Paul was passionate in maintaining the distinctions while rejecting any value judgment based on them.[45]

One other set of parallels is of major significance for our study—the parallels within the Pauline corpus. Several other texts repeat the con-

---

[42]See *The Tripartite Tractate* 1.5 (NHL, p. 95), "For when we confessed the kingdom which is in Christ, we escaped from the whole multiplicity of forms and from inequality and change. For the end will receive a unitary existence just as the beginning, where there is no male nor female, nor slave and free, nor circumcision and uncircumcision, neither angel nor man, but Christ is all in all"; see also the Gospel of Thomas 114; the Gospel of Philip, 118, 78-79; the Gospel of the Egyptians as cited in Clement of Alexandria *Strom* 3.92 (see Hennecke, NTA, I, 168); *Prot.* 112.3; Hippolytus *The Refutation of All Heresies* 5.2; Acts of Thomas 129. A similar saying appears in 2 Clement 12.2.

[43]Brinsmead, *Galatians*, pp. 150-51; Betz, *Galatians*, pp. 195-200; R. Jewett, "Sexual Liberation," pp. 65-69; and Meeks, "Image of the Androgyne," passim, esp. pp. 185-86.

[44]See also Bruce, *Epistle to the Galatians*, p. 189; P. Jewett, *Man As Male and Female*, pp. 24-28, 142; and Fiorenza, *In Memory of Her*, pp. 211-12. Fiorenza points out that the allusion to Gen 1:27 in Mk 10:6 and parallels is understood of the first couple (Adam and Eve) and not of an androgynous being. The allusion in Rom 1:27 would point in the same direction.

[45]Scroggs, "Paul and the Eschatological Woman," p. 283, n. 1.

Galatians 3:26-28
26For you are all children of God through faith in Christ Jesus, 27for you who were baptized into Christ have put on Christ. 28There is neither Jew nor Greek; there is neither slave nor free; there is not male and female, for you are all one in Christ Jesus.

1 Corinthians 12:13
13For also in one Spirit we were all baptized into one body—whether Jews or Greeks, whether slaves or free people, and we all drank one Spirit.

Colossians 3:9-11
9Do not lie to each other since you have stripped off the old being with its deeds and have put on the new which is being renewed into knowledge in accordance with the image of the one who created it, where there is not Greek and Jew, circumcision and uncircumcision, barbarian, Scythian, slave, free, but Christ is all things and in all.

1 Corinthians 7:17-27
17Nevertheless, let each person live as the Lord assigned and as God called. I am giving this direction in all the churches. 18Was a man already circumcised when he was called? He should not become uncircumcised. Was a man uncircumcised when he was called? He should not become circumcised. 19Circumcision is nothing and uncircumcision is nothing, but keeping the commands of God is what counts. 20Each person should remain in the calling in which he was called. 21Were you called as a slave? Don't let it bother you, but if you are able to become free, do so. 22For the one in the Lord who was called as a slave is the Lord's free person. Likewise the one who was free when called is Christ's slave. 23You were bought with a price! Do not become slaves of people. 24Brothers, each person should remain before God in the situation in which he was called. 25Concerning virgins I do not have a command from the Lord, but I give my opinion as one who is faithful because of the mercy of the Lord. 26I think it is good because of the present distress for a man to remain as he is. 27Are you joined to a wife? Do not seek to be free. Are you free from a wife? Do not seek one.

1 Corinthians 11:11-12
11But neither is the woman anything apart from the man nor is the man anything apart from the woman in the Lord. 12For just as the woman came from the man, thus also the man is born through the woman, but all things are from God.

Romans 10:12-13
12For there is no distinction between Jew and Greek, for the same Lord is over all, being rich to all who call upon him, 13for everyone who calls upon the name of the Lord will be saved.

Table 1. Parallel Passages on Women from Paul's Letters

cerns that are found in Galatians 3:28 and deserve our full attention (see table 1).[46]

None of the other passages is identical to Galatians 3:28, but the repetition of themes and expressions provides much information for understanding Paul. The texts in 1 Corinthians 12:13 and Colossians 3:9–11 are the closest to Galatians 3:28. The Colossians text does not mention baptism explicitly, and the Corinthians text does not mention "putting on," but one can easily understand why many scholars see this as a pre-Pauline baptismal formula.[47] Other scholars think that Paul himself formulated these sayings.[48] Either way, these sayings demonstrate how important in Paul's mind are the words of Galatians 3:28. *Far from being a statement that Paul is uncertain about, it is his basic summary of what it means to be a Christian.* This is verified by the climactic positioning of each of these statements, particularly Galatians 3:28, as the center or climax of the Epistle.[49]

In analyzing the parallel passages, note that the third pair in 3:28 (male and female) is not mentioned in 1 Corinthians 12 or Colossians 3. Of the six sayings in table 1, five mention that the division between Jew and Greek is obliterated in Christ, four mention slave and free, and three mention male and female in some way (but no text repeats explicitly the comment on male and female in 3:28). People frequently suggest that the male/female contrast is not repeated in 1 Corinthians because the problem in Corinth was caused by women over the distinction of the sexes.[50] This seems likely, but 1 Corinthians 7:17–27 seems

---

[46]Fiorenza, *In Memory of Her*, p. 267, would also see Eph 2:11-22 as referring to Gal 3:28.

[47]Michel Bouttier, "Complexio Oppositorum: Sur les formules de I Cor. XII.13; Gal. III.26-8; Col. III.10,11," *NTS* 23 (1976): 3-5; Betz, *Galatians*, p. 184; Scroggs, "Paul and the Eschatological Woman," p. 291; and Fiorenza, *In Memory of Her*, p. 208. Note the switch to the second person plural, the mention of baptism, and that slave/free and male/female do not relate to the context. Longenecker, *New Testament Social Ethics*, p. 31, suggests that the baptismal formula is contained in vv. 27-28.

[48]Bruce, *Epistle to the Galatians*, p. 187; cf. Meeks, "Image of the Androgyne," pp. 181-82; Legrand, "There Is Neither Slave nor Free," p. 138; Dautzenberg, "Da ist nicht männlich und weiblich," p. 201.

[49]Charles B. Cousar, *Galatians* (Atlanta: John Knox Press, 1982), p. 83; Betz, *Galatians*, p. 181, describes these verses as the center of the *probatio* section of Galatians.

[50]Scott Bartchy, *ΜΑΛΛΟΝ ΧΡΗΣΑΙ: First Century Slavery and I Corinthians 7:21* (Missoula, Mont.: Society of Biblical Literature, 1973), p. 130; Stendahl, *The Bible and the Role of Women*, p. 35; Longenecker, *New Testament Social Ethics*, p. 75; and Peter Stuhl-

to be an explanation based on Galatians 3:28. This will be significant for interpretation.

Meaning and Significance

Galatians 3:26-29 functions as the climax of the epistle, a hinge between 3:7-25 and 4:1-7, since both sections focus on the change that has taken place with the coming of faith (3:21-25; 4:1-7).[52] Paul's point is that faith in Christ has brought a new status (children of God) and a new existence (incorporation into Christ). The text implies that Christians are the body of Christ and stresses the unity achieved in this new existence.[53] This section identifies what it means to be in Christ.[54] Each of the three pairs in 3:28—Jew and Gentile, slave and free, male and female—encompasses all humanity.[55] The parallel structure found in 3:26 and 3:28b emphasizes that all have the same status as children of God and that all enjoy the unity that is in Christ.

Bonnard's summary catches the intention of the text well. The Galatians suffered from an inferiority complex and sought in the law a way to make their divine sonship more impressive. But baptism is the end of such religious and social supports. In baptism, each person is stripped of any dignity due him or her and reclothed with the sole dignity of Christ.[56]

The text expresses the unity and equality that all persons experience in Christ. No one is better for being circumcised or Jewish, nor are such persons set apart in some way from others in Christ. This is Paul's real concern, but he includes the two other categories, slave/free and male/

---

macher, *Der Brief an Philemon,* 2nd ed. (Benziger Verlag, 1981), p. 47. The omission from Colossians is not because of the House Codes, for the slave/free pair is included and yet slaves are addressed in the House Codes.

[51]Richardson, *Paul's Ethic,* p. 53; Bartchy, *MAΛΛON XPHΣAI* pp. 129-30, 162-65; and Fiorenza, *In Memory of Her,* pp. 218-19; Dieter Lührmann, "Wo man nicht Sklave oder Freier ist," *Wort und Dienst* 13 (1975): 61; and Hartwig Thyen, ". . . nicht mehr männlich und weiblich . . . : eine Studie zu Galater 3, 28," *Als Mann und Frau geschaffen,* ed. Frank Crüsemann and Hartwig Thyen (Gelnhausen: Burckhardthaus-Verlag, 1978), pp. 157, 174.

[52]Paulsen, "Einheit und Freiheit," p. 75.

[53]I would suggest that *Christou* in v. 29 should be understood as a partitive genitive.

[54]Dautzenberg, "Da ist nicht männlich und weiblich," p. 183; Bouttier, "Complexio Oppositorum," p. 6. Betz, *Galatians,* pp. 182-85, seems to have gone too far in referring to this section as a "macarism."

[55]Dautzenberg, "Da ist nicht männlich und weiblich," p. 183.

[56]Pierre Bonnard, *L'épitre de Saint Paul aux Galates* (Neuchatel: Delachaux & Niestlé, 1953), pp. 77-79.

female, to emphasize the point. Being baptized into Christ institutes a new value system in which religious, social and sexual differences do not play a part. The issue is not merely that all are accepted by God on the same terms. The point that the text makes is that something new has come into being in Christ. The new creation has its foundation in the oneness of God (3:20) and in the death and resurrection of Christ.[57] James Hurley is wrong when he says that Paul is not reflecting on relations within the body of Christ.[58] If the concern is unity, that is precisely what Paul is reflecting on.

Dautzenberg correctly suggests Joel 2:28-32 as the background for Galatians 3:28 (see Acts 2:17-21 and Rom 10:12-13).[59] In Joel 3:1-5, women and slaves are included as equal recipients of the Spirit's eschatological activity. Galatians 3:28 and Acts 2 both point to the same event, the new age breaking into the old. Traditionalists are often concerned about creation and doing justice to an order set up by the Genesis narratives. The idea of hierarchy does not emerge from Genesis 1 or 2, however, but from Genesis 3 and from various New Testament texts. Paul obviously did not give up on the idea of hierarchy, and I would argue that equality and hierarchy are not necessarily antithetical ideas. Nevertheless, what did change for Paul and must change for every Christian is the understanding of hierarchy. Christianity redefines hierarchy in terms of love, servanthood and mutual submission. If the new age has broken in, we cannot allow ourselves to continue to be determined by the old. Only Christ can legitimately determine our existence and our relationships.

Still, some people point out that the three categories are not alike.[60] One is religious, one is social and one is sexual. Often, but not necessarily, this observation is linked to an attempt to maintain a hierarchical relation of the sexes. Similarly, people correctly underscore that Paul's words do not remove the distinctions between the categories.[61] Paul took pride in being Jewish and consistently addressed Jews as Jews and Gentiles as Gentiles. He would not say, "There is no advantage in being

---

[57]See Volker Stolle, "Die Eins in Gal 3, 15-29," *Festgabe für Karl Heinrich Rengstorf zum 70,* ed. W. Dietrich and H. Schreckenberg (Leiden: E. J. Brill, 1973), pp. 204-13.

[58]Hurley, *Man and Woman,* p. 127.

[59]Dautzenberg, "Da ist nicht männlich und weiblich," p. 197.

[60]Davis, "Some Reflections on Galatians 3:28," p. 203; Foh, *Women and the Word,* pp. 141-42.

[61]Cousar, *Galatians,* pp. 85-86; Witherington, "Rite and Rights," p. 598.

a Jew," just when it seemed that he would. On the other hand, he would not grant that Jews excel or have some special standing (see Rom 2:25—3:9). Being Jewish has some advantage, but it does not count for anything in Christ (Phil 3:4-11). The way that Jews and Gentiles relate to each other in Christ has nothing to do with their religious past. Paul's confrontation with Peter over eating with Gentiles (Gal 2:11-14) underscores how far-reaching are the *social implications* of his religious statement. Being in Christ did not change a Jew into a Gentile; rather, it changed the way that Jews and Gentiles relate to each other. The only thing that counts is faith working through love, a new creation, or having put on Christ—all ways of saying the same thing (see Gal 5:6; 6:15; 3:27, respectively). The Jew/Gentile issue is *the* issue that dominated Paul's concerns throughout much of his ministry. For him, to act as if one's religious past or national heritage made some difference was to deny the gospel. On this issue, Paul was an agitator to make sure that the gospel was not sacrificed.[62]

The issue is much the same with slavery, even though it receives much less attention from Paul. The distinctions between slave and master still remained at that time, but the value placed on the distinction was ignored by Paul. The only thing determinative for life is Christ. Why Paul did not campaign against slavery and the abuse of women more directly will be considered later; however, Paul's thought with regard to slavery is much more revolutionary than is usually acknowledged, even with the house codes attempting to redefine what it meant to be a slave. That Paul could ask Philemon to receive Onesimus back as a brother *both in the flesh and in the Lord* (v. 16) shows how seriously the words of Galatians 3:28 should be taken. How sad that it took centuries for his thought to run its full course![63]

With regard to male/female relationships, the situation is different because it deals with the obvious physical distinction of sexuality. The allusion to Genesis 1:27 and the change of the wording to kai ("and") are important for interpretation.[64] The change shows that Paul was aware

---

[62]Legrand, "There Is Neither Slave nor Free," p. 155.

[63]On the issue of slavery, see Bartchy, *ΜΑΛΛΟΝ ΧΡΗΣΑΙ*; Richardson, *Paul's Ethic*, pp. 40-56; and Longenecker, *New Testament Social Ethics*, pp. 48-69.

[64]*Contra* Longenecker, *New Testament Social Ethics*, p. 75 n. 6, who does not see the change as having any effect on the meaning.

that this category is different. I do not see an intended contrast between the order of creation and the order of redemption.[65] Paul does not set the one against the other anywhere else; rather, redemption includes creation within its scope.[66] Paul's point is not that gender distinctions are obliterated. Elsewhere he argues strenuously for maintaining a distinction between the sexes (see 1 Cor 11:2-16). If we are correct to see 1 Corinthians 7:17-27 as a parallel, "there is not male and female" says that being in Christ and relationships in Christ are not based on the marriage relationship and kinship ties.[67] Whether a person is married is insignificant. The standing of a woman in the Christian community is not linked to a man; she, like every man, has her standing only because of Christ and, like every man, she as an individual partakes of the new unity in Christ. Being in Christ does not change a woman into a man any more than it changes Gentiles into Jews, but it changes the way that men and women relate to each other just as it changed the way that Jews and Gentiles relate. The differences are not denied, but valuation or status based on the difference is rejected. Social implications are necessarily involved.

The context of Galatians must be remembered when we consider the significance of the statement about male and female.[68] Paul's opponents argued that Gentiles should be circumcised and keep the law. Circumcision dominates the whole discussion as a supposed entrance requirement or a mark of higher position (2:3, 7-9; 5:2-3, 6, 11-12; 6:12-13, 15). Paul's opponents ignore the place of women entirely. In their eyes women did not exist as individuals in their own right.

The discussion of the position of women in Judaism is somewhat disconcerting at this point, for little information is given on how women had a standing within the community relative to circumcision. If circumcision is a mark of the covenant, how were women included? The documents tell us very little, but then they were written from the stand-

---

[65]*Contra* Stendahl, *The Bible and the Role of Women,* p. 32; and Thyen, ". . . nicht mehr männlich und weiblich," pp. 109-11.

[66]Witherington, "Rite and Rights," p. 598.

[67]See Bartchy, *MAΛΛON XPHΣAI,* pp. 129-32, 162-65. Bartchy's application of the A-B-A pattern to 1 Cor 7 is helpful, and Gal 3:26-29 seems to function as the B in a similar pattern in Galatians. On the connection to 1 Cor 7:17-18 and the interpretation of "male and female" with reference to marriage, see Witherington, "Rite and Rights," pp. 599-600, and Fiorenza, *In Memory of Her,* pp. 218-19.

[68]Witherington, "Rite and Rights," pp. 594-95.

point of men.[69] Apparently, a woman had her standing in Judaism only because of her relation to her father or her husband. Clarence Vos argues that the woman was viewed as involved in the circumcision of the male.[70]According to bBerakoth 17a, women gain merit by making their sons go to the synagogue to learn Scripture and their husbands to the Beth Hamidrash to learn Mishnah and waiting for their husbands to return. However, Christianity did not suddenly grant women access to God that they did not have in Judaism. Women belonged to the covenant in Israel, and Dautzenberg is correct to emphasize that neither the Old Testament nor Judaism saw the categories slave/free or male/female as significant for salvation. Women and slaves still belonged to Israel, even if their relation to the law was different from that of free men.[71]

The significance of this for our purposes is that one cannot speak of Galatians 3:28 as if it merely pertains to salvation. The verse points to something new established by Christ for each category, and each statement reacts against the old valuations. Gentiles, slaves and women are granted access and standing in Christ on the same footing and with the same valuation, privileges and responsibilities as Jewish and free men. Whereas circumcision was a mark of separation, baptism expresses the new unity of these persons in Christ.

Whatever else is done with the other texts concerning women,[72] justice must be done to the newness proclaimed in Galatians 3:28. Without attempting to deny the distinctions between the sexes, we err greatly if we do not insist on equal standing for women with men in Christ. To deny the social implications of this text is a ploy that will not work. Nothing about the Christian faith may be labeled "merely *coram Deo*"

---

[69]See Jacob Neusner, *Method and Meaning in Ancient Judaism* (Missoula, Mont.: Scholars Press, 1979), pp. 85, 96, and *A History of the Mishnaic Law of Women*, pt. v (Leiden: E. J. Brill, 1980), pp. 159-60, with regard to the Mishnah. He states that in this context women meant no more than rocks or trees or study of the Torah. Women were "abnormal" and are discussed in the Mishnah only because of their relation to men.

[70]Clarence Vos, *Woman in Old Testament Worship* (Delft: Verenigde Drukkerijen Judels & Brinkman, n.d.), pp. 49-50, 59.

[71]Dautzenberg, "Da ist nicht männlich und weiblich," p. 195.

[72]My views on the other texts are expressed briefly in "Paul and Women," *Covenant Quarterly* 34 (1976): 3-19. Despite the errors of some Christian feminists, I object to the claim of A. Duane Litfin ("Evangelical Feminism: Why Traditionalists Reject It," *BibSac* 136 [1979]: 258-71) that the feminist position results from nonevangelical presuppositions about Scripture.

("in the eyes of God"), and I do not know any other subject on which people argue in this fashion. If one thinks that Paul's statement did not have social implications in his own day, the ministry of women in the early church and 1 Corinthians 7 prove otherwise. In 1 Corinthians 7, Paul carefully balances his statements ten times so that the same thing said of one sex is repeated explicitly of the other. He says that the husband does not have authority over his body but rather his wife does (7:4)—a startling statement, particularly in the context of the ancient world. Here as elsewhere Paul grants equal footing for the woman and denies the prerogatives of the male.

Some traditionalists grant that Galatians 3:28 speaks of newness in the male and female relationships, but they view these words as descriptive of the *eschaton:* this is what life will be like after Christ's return. They say, however, that we still live in the old age, the age of sin, and therefore the words of 3:28 cannot be implemented on a practical level. This will not do: Christians are still residents of the old age, but they are people for whom the new age has already dawned. Our task is to actualize the new age in the midst of the old. We cannot allow ourselves to be ruled by sin and the old age, but only by Christ and the presence of the new age.

That Paul did not spell out the implications for slaves and women more than he did is not too surprising if one allows for his concern for missions. Other factors, no doubt, were the fear of social upheaval and the fear that the Christian movement would be seen as a political force and, as a result, would be stamped out. Possibly the expectation of the *parousia* was a factor too.[73] Another obvious reason why male/female and slave/free issues did not receive the attention that the Jew/Gentile issue did is that there was no one saying "You must be a free person or a male to become a Christian." The gospel was not at stake. The categories of slave/free and male/female were not a threat to the understanding of the gospel, as the Jew/Gentile issue was.

Galatians 3:28 does not spell out what roles and functions will look like where "there is no male and female." Other texts will have to be treated fairly and in keeping with their purposes. Decisions made in the Christian community about roles and functions, however, must do jus-

---

[73]See, e.g., Leslie, *Concept of Woman,* pp. 46–50; Longenecker, *New Testament Social Ethics,* p. 55; Richardson, *Paul's Ethic,* pp. 41–42, 76–78.

tice to the equal standing and value of women in Christ. I view 1 Corinthians 14:33b-36 and 1 Timothy 2:11-15 as statements necessitated
by specific problems in Corinth and Ephesus, respectively, and as
shaped by an ancient culture. These texts do not become less important
than Galatians 3:28, but they are less direct in their application. Although we value certain parts of the Bible more highly than others, we
must not neglect to hear those less attractive texts and understand what
purpose they have in Scripture and for us.

Whatever else is said about these other texts, Galatians 3:28 is no conundrum. The words appear abruptly because Paul intends them to support his position. Even Paul's opponents might have acknowledged the
formula. Paul viewed it as incontestable.[74] Slave/free and male/female
were included to strengthen his argument about Jew and Gentile. In 1
Corinthians 7:17ff., Jew/Gentile and slave/free are used to confirm his
statements about male and female. Galatians 3:28 does function as a
solution for Christians, for it is part of a statement of the gospel promising
new status and new existence. While not answering all our questions
about the roles of women in our society, Galatians 3:28 prohibits the
valuations and divisions of the old order and insists on equal standing and
unity in Christ.

Some want to deny women ecclesiastical equality while granting
them civil and social equality. This will not do. Those who think that they
are upholding tradition by allowing women to prophesy or testify, but
not preach, do not realize how much our churches and society have
changed. This is not the traditional position. Not too long ago the argument was whether women should even speak in mixed public assemblies.[75] The issue is not society, however, but Scripture. I do not

---

[74]Lührmann, "Wo man nicht Sklave," pp. 57, 59, 61.

[75]In 1885, e.g., the eligibility of women delegates to the Southern Baptist Convention was
challenged, and as a result the constitution was changed to read "brethren" instead of
"members." In 1918, the word was changed to "messengers" to open the door to women;
however, also in 1918, a woman made some explanatory comments at the convention,
which caused considerable debate as to whether women should be allowed to speak. (See
Juliette Mather, "Women, Convention Privileges of," *Encyclopedia of Southern Baptists*
Nashville: Broadman Press, 1958], p. 1543.) In 1905 the noted grammarian A. T. Robertson
wrote an introduction to a book opposed to the idea of women preaching, in which he
spoke disparagingly of " 'testifying' and public speaking on the part of women in our
religious meetings." (See William Patrick Harvey, *Shall Women Preach?* [Louisville: Baptist
Book Concern, 1905], p. 2.)

think that there is a legitimate way that one can separate "prophesying" (which women were doing in Corinth; see 1 Cor 11:5) from "authoritative teaching and preaching."[76] If women and men stand on equal footing in Christ, ecclesiastical equality certainly cannot be denied.

In 1853, Luther Lee preached the sermon at the ordination of Antoinette Brown, the first woman fully ordained in a recognized American denomination. His text was Galatians 3:28.[77] If this text represents a salvation-historical turning point,[78] which I think it does, his choice was an appropriate one. If God has poured out his Spirit on both the sons and the daughters (Acts 2:17ff.), it will not do for us to erect a modern-day "court of the women" for our churches. The old distinctions and valuations based on sexuality do not count. There is no male and female anymore, for you all are one in Christ Jesus.

Klyne R. Snodgrass is professor of biblical literature, North Park Theological Seminary, Chicago, Illinois.

RESPONSE
Susie C. Stanley

I agree with Snodgrass that Galatians 3:28 "is the most socially explosive statement in the New Testament." My remarks will focus on the social implications of this verse and affirm that Galatians 3:28 is the solution, not the conundrum; but before doing that, I would like to comment on two points of Snodgrass's presentation.

First, Snodgrass cautions that "the right of women to minister is not the gospel. The *kerygma* must always center on the death and resurrection of Jesus Christ and the freedom found in Christ." Why this caution? True, we must keep first things first. Yet can we separate the good news of the gospel from the fact that the "freedom found in Christ" includes the freedom for all believers, men and women, to share that

---

[76]Against Hurley, *Man and Woman,* pp. 235–53.
[77]Luther Lee, "Woman's Right to Preach the Gospel," *Five Sermons and a Tract by Luther Lee,* ed. Donald W. Dayton (Chicago: Holrad House, 1975), pp. 77–100.
[78]Stuhlmacher, *Philemon,* p. 48.

good news? Snodgrass suggests that if the message of the *kerygma* is "given its proper focus it will lead to the ministry of women as it did in the New Testament." Following his reasoning, then, those groups where women have not been accepted as full-fledged ministers of the gospel are churches that have not given proper focus to the *kerygma*. If we limit the proclamation of the *kerygma*, we are subverting the opportunity to realize the hope of the *kerygma* in Christian fellowship.

Second, I would like to add another voice to the discussion of the background of Galatians 3:28. Dennis MacDonald argues that Galatians 3:28 represents Paul's "radical alterations of a saying found in the Gospel of the Egyptians, 2 Clement, and the Gospel of Thomas."[79] MacDonald refers to this saying as the "garment/two-are-one tradition":

When you tread upon the garment of shame,

and when the two become one.

[and the outside as the inside]

and the male with the female

neither male nor female.[80]

Paul's version of this tradition in Galatians 3:28 counteracts the Gnostics' negative view of the body and also their conception of androgyny. MacDonald concludes, "[Paul] altered the saying so that putting off the garment of shame became putting on Christ, and the two sexes becoming one became all social groups becoming one in Christ. . . . Baptism was the symbol by which the individual expressed membership in a new creation, a unified community."[81]

Contrary to some arguments, we do have evidence that male/female equality was implemented in the New Testament era. Paul affirmed that "in Christ there is no male and female" in concrete ways. He greeted ten women colaborers in Romans 16. Priscilla, Phoebe and Lydia are only a sampling of the litany of women who labored with Paul as protecters, teachers, deacons and apostles. Paul's widespread actions confirmed that he meant what he said in Galatians 3:28. Elisabeth Schüssler Fiorenza contends that "new behavior was engendered by this baptismal

---

[79]Dennis R. MacDonald, "Making the Two One: Androgyny and Social Unification in Paul" (unpublished manuscript, 1984), chap. 1, p. 13. In the revised version of his paper, Snodgrass mentions MacDonald in a footnote.

[80]Ibid., chap. 3, p. 1.

[81]Ibid., chap. 5, p. 2.

declaration [Galatians 3:28], at least with respect to women who exercised leadership roles in the house churches and mission of the early Christian movement."[82]

History of Interpreting Galatians 3:28

Hermeneutics involves looking at what the text meant when originally written, what it has meant in the history of interpretation and what the text means now. I will touch briefly on the history of the interpretation of Galatians 3:28 from the nineteenth century to the present. Those who caught a glimpse of the liberating vision that Galatians 3:28 generates endeavored to implement it in church and in society.

In the nineteenth century, members of the holiness movement were the ones who most often wrested ministry from the male domain and encouraged women to claim all the gifts of the Holy Spirit. Holiness adherent Adam Clarke's commentary on Galatians 3:28 was often quoted: "Under the blessed spirit of Christianity, women have equal *rights,* equal *privileges,* and equal *blessings;* and let me add, they are equally *useful.*"[83]

Snodgrass also referred to Luther Lee's use of Galatians 3:28 at Antoinette Brown's ordination. Lee preached, "In the Church of which Christ is the only head, males and females possess equal rights and privileges. . . . To make any distinction in the church of Jesus Christ, between males and females, purely on the ground of sex is virtually to strike this text from the sacred volume, for it affirms that in Christ there is no difference between males and females, that they are all one in regard to the gospel of the grace of God."[84] Lee's was not a lone voice; others also used Galatians 3:28 to support their arguments favoring women in ministry. Catherine Booth and Phoebe Palmer published writings in 1859. In "Female Ministry," Booth asserted, "If this passage does not teach that in the

---

[82]Elisabeth Schüssler Fiorenza, *In Memory of Her; A Feminist Theological Reconstruction of Christian Origins* (New York: Crossroad, 1983), p. 209.

[83]Adam Clarke, *The New Testament of Our Lord and Savior Jesus Christ, the Text Carefully Printed from the Most Correct Copies of the Present Authorized Translation, including the Marginal Readings and Parallel Texts: With a Commentary and Critical Notes; Designed As a Help to a Better Understanding of the Sacred Writings,* vol. 2, *Romans to the Revelations* (New York: Abingdon, n.d.), p. 402.

[84]Luther Lee, "Woman's Right to Preach the Gospel," *Five Sermons and a Tract by Luther Lee,* ed. Donald W. Dayton (Chicago: Holrad House, 1975), pp. 80-81.

privileges, duties, and responsibilities of Christ's Kingdom, all differences of nation, caste, and sex are abolished, we should like to know what it does teach."[85] Palmer quoted Galatians 3:28 several times in *The Promise of the Father*.[86] For Palmer, the promise of the Father that both sons and daughters would prophesy when God's spirit was poured out (Joel 2:28–29) was fulfilled at Pentecost.

Two Free Methodist pastors used Galatians 3:28 urging their denomination to ordain women. The Reverend W. A. Sellew's pamphlet was entitled "Why Not? A Plea for the Ordination of Those Women Whom God Has Called to Preach the Gospel."[87] The Reverend B. T. Roberts, in *Ordaining Women*, devoted a chapter to the verse stressing its importance, "Make this the KEY TEXT upon this subject, and give to other passages such a construction as will make them agree with it, and all is harmony."[88] Roberts further argued, "So we must give this verse its full, natural, comprehensive, broad meaning. We must understand it to teach, as it actually does, the perfect equality of all, under the Gospel, in *rights, privileges,* without respect to nationality, or condition, or sex."[89]

The Reverend W. B. Godbey, a Methodist evangelist, wrote the following on Galatians 3:28, "This brief and terse statement of the Holy Ghost forever sweeps from the field all the world-wide controversy relative to woman's gospel rights."[90] Alma White, converted under Godbey's preaching, was inspired by a Black pastor who walked by her house one day and quoted Galatians 3:28. She reminisces in her autobiography, "A breeze from the ocean of God's love wafted his message to my soul,

---

[85]Catherine Booth, "Female Ministry: Woman's Right to Preach the Gospel" (London, 1859; reprint, New York: Salvation Army, 1975), p. 17.

[86]Phoebe Palmer, *The Promise of the Father: A Neglected Specialty of the Last Days* (Boston: Henry V. Degen, 1859; reprint, Salem, Ohio: Schmul Publishers, n.d.), pp. 10, 59, 161, 166–67, 364.

[87]W. A. Sellew, "Why Not? A Plea for the Ordination of Those Women Whom God Has Called to Preach the Gospel" (North Chile, N.Y.: Earnest Christian Publishing House, 1894).

[88]B. T. Roberts, *Ordaining Women* (Rochester, N.Y.: Earnest Christian Publishing House, 1891), p. 55. F. F. Bruce agrees, "Paul states the basic principle here; if restrictions on it are found elsewhere in the Pauline corpus, as in I Cor. 14:34f. . . . or I Tim. 2:11f., they are to be understood in relation to Gal. 3:28, and not vice versa." *The Epistle to the Galatians* (Grand Rapids, Mich.: Eerdmans, 1982), p. 190.

[89]Roberts, *Ordaining Women,* p. 58.

[90]W. B. Godbey, *Commentary on the New Testament,* vol. 4, *Corinthians-Galatians Paul, the Champion Theologian* (Cincinnati: M. W. Knapp, 1898), p. 499.

bringing encouragement and cheer. I felt that God makes no distinction between the sexes, whatever the verdict of man may be."[91] White became an evangelist and founded the Pillar of Fire Church. In her tract "Woman's Ministry," she wrote, "Paul says that in Christ there is neither male or female, showing that in the gospel dispensation both men and women have the privilege of expounding the Word of God and of teaching it to others."[92] White also addressed the broader ramifications of Galatians 3:28 in *Woman's Chains,* a magazine she published which favored women's rights in church and state and included support of the Equal Rights Amendment.

Thus many persons used Galatians 3:28 to legitimate the equality of women in the church, and some applied the vision of Galatians 3:28 beyond the walls of the church.[93] I focus now on those who used this verse to argue for the equality of women in the state, primarily in the struggle for suffrage. Caught up in the millennialist spirit of the times, the suffragists were motivated to usher in the biblical vision of equality.

Struggle for Suffrage

Elizabeth Wilson wrote *A Scriptural View of Woman's Rights and Duties* in 1849, one year after the first women's rights convention. Commenting on Galatians 3:28, she wrote, "There are no exclusively privileged classes among Christ's disciples—no monopolists—not only is there no distinction of eternal salvation between male and female, for that was preached in the garden of Eden. Not only have women the same right to the saving ordinances of the gospel as men, but they have the same rights and privileges."[94] At the third national women's rights convention, held in Syracuse, New York, in 1852, the record tells of two participants who referred to Galatians 3:28. Abby Price spoke of it and Genesis 1:27-28 as "explicit declarations of equality."[95] Antoinette Brown, less than

[91] Alma White, *The Story of My Life and Pillar of Fire,* 5 vols. (Zarephath, N.J.: Pillar of Fire, 1935-43), 1:311.

[92] Alma White, "Woman's Ministry" (London: Pillar of Fire, n.d.), p. 7.

[93] B. T. Roberts also expanded the argument to include women's rights in the political arena.

[94] Elizabeth Wilson, *A Scriptural View of Woman's Rights and Duties* (Philadelphia: Wm. S. Young, 1849), pp. 172-73.

[95] *History of Woman Suffrage,* vol. 1-3, ed. Elizabeth Cady Stanton, Susan B. Anthony, Matilda Joslyn Gage, 1881-86; vol. 4, ed. Susan B. Anthony and Ida Husted Harper, 1902; vols. 5-6, ed. Ida Husted Harper, 1922; 1:532.

one year before her ordination, offered the following resolution at that convention, "Resolved, That the Bible recognizes the rights, duties and privileges of woman as a public teacher, as every way equal with those of man; that it enjoins upon her no subjection that is not enjoined upon him, and that it truly and practically recognizes neither male nor female in Christ Jesus."[96] Lucy Stone responded to an antisuffragist at a later convention, "The gentleman says he believes in Paul. So do I. When Paul declares that there is neither Jew nor Greek, neither bond nor free, male or female in Christ, I believe he meant what he said."[97]

In 1866, Mrs. Cutler commented on the development of the implications of Galatians 3:28: "The great Christian doctrine of the equality of all before God, who is declared to be no respecter of persons, is the axe laid at the root of the tree of prejudice, which has for such long ages brought forth injustice and oppression in a multitude of forms. Our good and great men are reading with anointed eyes the declaration, 'There is neither Jew nor Greek, neither bond nor free,' and we may hope they will soon read the final assertion 'Neither male nor female, for ye are all one in Christ Jesus.' "[98] The Reverend Mary Safford shared the same hope when she preached during a convention worship service in 1904.[99]

Male supporters of women's suffrage also quoted Galatians 3:28. In his first speech before a women's rights convention, the Reverend Henry Ward Beecher declared in 1866, "the nation can never become what it should be, until there is no distinction made between the sexes as regards the rights and duties of citizenship—until we come to the 28th verse of the third chapter of Galatians."[100] The Reverend Gilbert Haven, the Methodist bishop who had also been an abolitionist, favored suffrage and called Galatians 3:28 Paul's "greatest doctrine of Woman's Rights."[101]

Julia Ward Howe, author of "The Battle Hymn of the Republic" and a suffragist, was a key speaker at the national suffrage convention in 1906.

---

[96]Ibid., 1:535-36.
[97]Ibid., 1:650. This is the most explicit example of the fourth option for interpreting Galatians 3:28 that Snodgrass described.
[98]Ibid., 2:916.
[99]Ibid., 5:98.
[100]Ibid., 2:161.
[101]Ibid., 2:399.

Her comments included the following: "The weapon of Christian warfare is the ballot, which represents the peaceable assertion of conviction and will. Society everywhere is becoming converted to its use. Adopt it, you women, with clean hands and a pure heart! Verify the best word written by the apostle: 'In Christ Jesus there is neither bond nor free, neither male nor female, but a new creature,' the harbinger of a new creation!"[102] Also at the 1906 convention, a resolution referred to Galatians 3:28 as a point of the suffragists' creed and invited Christian ministers' cooperation. Cooperation was evident. In the same year, Bishop John Bashford authored the leaflet "The Bible for Woman Suffrage."[103]

Use of Galatians 3:28 to support women's rights did not end when women gained the vote in 1920. Senator Kaneaster Hodges of Arkansas, in a U.S. Senate debate in 1978, quoted it in support of the Equal Rights Amendment.[104] At an ERA benefit in Denver several years ago, cards were on a booktable with the ERA printed on one side and Galatians 3:28 on the other, making the connection between the two explicit.

Mary Daly speaks of "would-be pacifiers of women" who quote Galatians 3:28 as an example of those who refuse "to look at concrete oppressive facts."[105] Such a viewpoint corresponds to Snodgrass's second option, in which Galatians 3:28 is understood only in a spiritual sense. Contrary to Daly, I have found this text to be a rallying cry in the movement for women's rights and the recovery of the New Testament practice of women in ministry.

While MacDonald focuses on the original meaning of Galatians 3:28, he realizes "by including sexual equality in the pairs of opposites to be united in Christ, [Paul] has inspired in subsequent Christian tradition innumerable quests for egalitarian communities."[106] The history of the interpretation of Galatians 3:28 involves such quests. The women's

---

[102]Ibid., 5:186–87.

[103]John Bashford, "The Bible for Woman Suffrage" (Warren, Ohio: National American Woman Suffrage Association, 1906). A similar leaflet, probably published by the Woman's Christian Temperance Union, was "The Bible on Women Voting" by Catherine McCulloch (Evanston, Ill., n.d.).

[104]Marvella Bayh and Mary Kotz, *Marvella: A Personal Journey* (New York: Harcourt Brace Jovanovich, 1979), p. 291.

[105]Mary Daly, *Beyond God the Father: Toward a Philosophy of Women's Liberation* (Boston: Beacon, 1973), p. 5.

[106]Dennis R. MacDonald, "Making the Two One," chap. 5, p. 7.

rights movement provides one example of a quest for an egalitarian community on a grand scale. Galatians 3:28 has been a key text in this movement. Likewise, in the church, this text has been a biblical verification of the calling to ministry that women have experienced through the Holy Spirit. We in evangelical churches should affirm the equality in ministry advocated in Galatians 3:28.

Lillie McCutcheon, a prominent Church of God pastor, refers to God as an "Equal Rights Employer." She argues, "Dual standards for male and female are not a part of the gospel. . . . Qualifications for service are synonymous for all. Spiritual gifts are not in two listings designating some for men and the inferior gifts for women. It is written, 'There is neither Jew nor Greek, there is neither bond nor free, there is neither male nor female: for ye are all one in Christ Jesus.' "[107]

I align myself with the tradition. Like the suffragists and others before me, I am continually inspired to implement the vision of Galatians 3:28.

Susie C. Stanley is professor of church history, Western Evangelical Seminary, Portland, Oregon, and an ordained minister in the Church of God (Anderson).

RESPONSE

W. Ward Gasque

It is salutary to find someone who puts things exactly the way you would put them if you had his or her breadth of scholarship and ability of articulation. This is my position as I respond to Klyne Snodgrass. In my opinion, he has said just about all there is to say on the text at hand! In my response, I shall underline several of his points and expand one or two.

Galatians 3:28 As a Starting Point
First, he has demonstrated the impossibility of interpreting Galatians

---

[107]Lillie McCutcheon, "Lady in the Pulpit," *Centering on Ministry* (Winter 1980), p. 5.

3:28 as a soteriological statement unrelated to social issues. Even if Paul could think of individual salvation apart from the social context of the body of Christ (that new humanity that God is bringing into being), the apostle certainly does not think in these terms in Galatians 3. Rather, he is focusing on the new social reality created by our baptism into Christ.

Paul's concern is with the practical implications of this new social reality, a church in which Jews and Gentiles, slaves and free persons, men and women, are here and now fellow members, sharing equal rights and obligations. In the epistle to the Galatians, Paul presses the implications of this for Jewish-Gentile relations—the specific issue facing the Galatian churches—but the radical implications of the other two parallel pairs in Paul's triad are equally clear.

Second, Snodgrass demonstrates that Galatians 3:28 is at the heart of Paul's theological concern and cannot be relegated to the periphery of his thought, any more than it can be limited to "religious" matters. Rather, it represents the climax of Paul's argument in his letter and is a focus of his theologizing throughout his writings. It is hermeneutically illegitimate to set up as theologically normative passages such as 1 Corinthians 14:34-35 and 1 Timothy 2:11-12, where Paul is dealing with concrete local situations. To do so sets aside the thrust of this clear statement of theological principle. Richard Longenecker recognizes this in his exposition of the major contours of Paul's social ethic, and he organizes his material around this very text.[108]

Galatians 3:28 is the necessary theological starting place for any discussion on the role of women in the church. Here is an unequivocal statement of absolute equality in Christ in the church. Paul excludes all discrimination against Gentiles, slaves or women. Whatever distinctions might be made by the Jewish synagogue, by Roman law or by general society outside the church, Paul emphatically asserts that these cease to be relevant in church fellowship. Other texts must not be used to undermine this fundamental theological affirmation. F. F. Bruce points out, "Paul states the basic principle here; if restrictions on it are found elsewhere in the Pauline corpus, as in 1 Cor. 14:34f. . . . or 1 Tim. 2:11f.,

---

[108]Richard N. Longenecker, *New Testament Social Ethics for Today* (Grand Rapids, Mich.: Eerdmans, 1984).

they are to be understood in relation to Gal. 3:28, and not *vice versa*."[109]
By taking Galatians 3:28 as the starting place for Paul's view on women,
it becomes extremely difficult, if not impossible, to come to the traditionalist conclusion.

Third, Snodgrass shows why we must reject the view of Paul Jewett
and others who say that here Paul speaks as a consistent Christian and
elsewhere (e.g., 1 Cor 11; 14; Eph 5; 1 Tim 2) as a Jewish rabbi. Recent
New Testament research clearly shows that Paul never ceased to be a
Jewish rabbi following his conversion to Jesus Christ. He always writes
from this perspective. This is as true of Galatians 3:28 as it is of any other
passage by Paul. In my view, this text cannot be understood apart from
Paul's being brought up to offer the traditional synagogue thanksgiving,
thanking God that he had been born a Jew, rather than a Gentile; a free
man, rather than a slave; and a man, rather than a woman. In Galatians
3:28, Paul takes the traditional triad and turns it on its head, but his
theological exposition only makes sense in terms of his rabbinic heritage. This passage, as much as others used by the traditionalists to
undercut the social implications of this statement by Paul, is culturally
conditioned. As Snodgrass comments, however, "All the Bible is culturally conditioned, but all of it is instructive for us.

Full Equality in the Church

Paul, as Snodgrass notes, fought hard for the rights of Gentiles to full
equality in the church. This is what Galatians is all about. To accept
Gentiles into the church as second-class citizens, or to insist that one
had to become a Jew in order to become an authentic Christian, denied
the heart of the gospel. Paul could not tolerate a compromise on this
issue.

But why did he not fight equally hard for the rights of women and
slaves? The answer is, as Snodgrass observes, there was no movement
in the early church to deny equal status in the church to women (or to
slaves). All the evidence is to the contrary: women were engaged in
significant ministries in the church, even in roles of leadership. Women
shared the common gift of the Holy Spirit, exercised the spiritual gifts

---

[109]Bruce adds, "Attempts to find canon law in Paul, or to base canon law on Paul, should
be forestalled by a consideration of Paul's probable reaction to the very idea of canon law."
F. F. Bruce, *The Epistle to the Galatians* (Grand Rapids, Mich.: Eerdmans, 1982), p. 190.

that they had received for the benefit of the whole church, shared in the diaconate, engaged in pioneer evangelism and teaching, and took full responsibility for their own spiritual development. There is no evidence that anyone during Paul's lifetime sought to deny Christian women their rightful place in the church. Therefore, there was no need for Paul to defend what needed no defense.

But what about the apparent contradiction between the affirmation of women's equality in Galatians 3:28 and the apparent limitation of women's freedom in passages such as 1 Corinthians 11 and 14 and 1 Timothy 2? The answer is rather simple: the danger for the church in Paul's day lay in the exact opposite direction from the church in our day; that is, there was the danger that it might press the principle of Christian freedom too far. Rather than defending the status quo (as is often the case with the church in our day), the first-century church called into question many of the fundamental structures of contemporary society. First-century Christians might—and many did—push their new-found freedom to extremes. Liberty could easily degenerate into license.

We see many examples of this in both the Corinthian and Ephesian churches. Our precious heritage of freedom in Christ, says Paul, should not become a stumbling block in the way of anyone's coming to faith or to Christian maturity. There is a law higher than the law of liberty: it is the law of love. Thus, in 1 Corinthians 11, Paul exhorts the women not to abandon their veils as they lead in prayer and proclaim the word of the Lord in gatherings for worship. In 1 Corinthians 14, Paul is concerned for order in public worship, not with canon law: all things are to be done decently and in order (1 Cor 14:40); a chaotic worship service builds up no one, even if it is motivated by a concern for liberty. In 1 Timothy 2, Paul faces a situation in which liberty has gone awry: some women have begun to use their freedom to teach heresy (and, perhaps, also to live immorally). Now, says Paul, the freedom of women in the Christian community must not be used as a cloak for the undermining of the Christian gospel.

From the vantage point of Galatians 3:28, the texts used to defend the traditionalist point of view are seen to be, in reality, applications of other theological principles—namely, the principle that the law of love takes precedence over the law of liberty, the principle that communal worship should edify the entire body, the principle that the truth of the gospel takes precedence over local customs and practices—rather than contradictions to the affirmation by Paul of the equality of women in the church.

Although Paul may be a far more complex thinker than some of his most devoted disciples would have wished, he did not speak with a forked tongue. The freedom that he gives to women with his right hand he does not take away with his left. In Galatians 3:28, Paul opens wide the door for women, as well as for Gentiles and slaves, to exercise spiritual leadership in the church. It is my conviction that it is a door that no man can shut without severely hurting the church's life and witness in the world.

W. Ward Gasque is vice principal and professor of New Testament, Regent College, Vancouver, British Columbia.

9

1 TIMOTHY 2:9-15 & THE PLACE OF WOMEN IN THE CHURCH'S MINISTRY

David M. Scholer

EVANGELICALS WHO oppose or limit the participation of women in preaching, teaching or exercising authority in the church consider 1 Timothy 2:11-12 the clearest and strongest biblical text in support of their position.[1] Although 1 Corinthians 14:34-35 appears to be absolute on prohibiting women from speaking in the church and cites "the law" as sanction for this view, this text is not cited as frequently and forcefully, probably because it is obvious that 1 Corinthians 11:5, indicating that women do pray and prophesy, in some way qualifies the prohibition of 1 Corinthians 14:34-35.[2] In contrast, 1 Timothy 2:11-12 appears to have no qualification of any kind and a sanction is provided by a clear allusion to Genesis 2—3 (1 Tim 2:13-14). This passage has been addressed in numerous articles stemming from the evangelical communities, both

---

[1]See, e.g., G. W. Knight III, *The New Testament Teaching on the Role Relationship of Men and Women* (Grand Rapids, Mich.: Baker, 1977), p. 29, who lists this text as the one "which most clearly gives both the apostle Paul's verdict and his reason"; and the space given to this passage in J. B. Hurley, *Man and Woman in Biblical Perspective* (Grand Rapids, Mich.: Zondervan, 1981), pp. 195-233.

[2]For further comments on this see D. M. Scholer, "Women in Ministry, Session Six: 1 Corinthians 14:34, 35," *Covenant Companion* 73, no. 2 (February 1984): 13-14.

from those who oppose or limit the participation of women in ministry[3] and from those who support full participation of women in ministry.[4]

This essay provides exegetical and hermeneutical considerations on 1 Timothy 2:9-15 that are crucial to a responsible, contextual interpretation of this Pauline text and to its consistent application to the place of women in the church within the context of faith and commitment to biblical authority.[5]

To carry out this purpose, this essay focuses on (1) the historical

---

[3]Evangelical articles that oppose or limit the participation of women in ministry are: G. L. Archer, "Does 1 Timothy 2:12 Forbid the Ordination of Women?" *Encyclopedia of Bible Difficulties* (Grand Rapids, Mich.: Zondervan, 1982), pp. 411-15; G. W. Knight III, "AYΘEN TEΩ in Reference to Women in 1 Timothy 2.12," *New Testament Studies* 30 (1984): 143-57; D. J. Moo, "1 Timothy 2.11-15: Meaning and Significance," *Trinity Journal* 1 (1980): 62-83; "The Interpretation of 1 Timothy 2.11-15: A Rejoinder," *Trinity Journal* 2 (1981): 198-222; C. D. Osburn, "AYΘENTEΩ (1 Timothy 2:12)," *Restoration Quarterly* 25 (1982): 1-12; A. J. Panning, "AYΘENTEIN—a Word Study," *Wisconsin Lutheran Quarterly* 78 (1981): 185-91; B. W. Powers, "Women in the Church: The Application of 1 Timothy 2:8-15," *Interchange* 17 (1975): 55-59.

[4]Evangelical articles that support full participation of women in ministry are: J. J. Davis, "Ordination of Women Reconsidered: Discussion of 1 Timothy 2:8-15," *Presbyterian Communique* 12, no. 6 (November/December 1979): 1, 8-11, 15 (reprinted in R. Hestenes, ed.) *Women and Men in Ministry* [Pasadena: Fuller Theological Seminary, 1980], pp. 37-40); N. J. Hommes, "Let Women Be Silent in the Church: A Message Concerning the Worship Service and the Decorum to Be Observed by Women," *Calvin Theological Journal* 4 (1969): 5-22; K. W. Hoover, "Creative Tension in 1 Timothy 2:11-15," *Brethren Life and Thought* 22 (1977): 163-66; C. C. Kroeger, "Ancient Heresies and a Strange Greek Verb," *Reformed Journal* 29, no. 3 (March 1979): 12-15 (reprinted in Hestenes, ed., *Women and Men in Ministry*, pp. 60-63); R. and C. C. Kroeger, "May Women Teach? Heresy in the Pastoral Epistles," *Reformed Journal* 30, no. 10 (October 1980): 14-18; V. R. Mollenkott, "Interpreting Difficult Scriptures," *Daughters of Sarah* 5, no. 2 (March/April 1979): 16-17 (reprinted 7, no. 5 [September/October 1981]: 13-16); P. B. Payne, "Libertarian Women in Ephesus: A Response to Douglas J. Moo's Article, '1 Timothy 2:11-15: Meaning and Significance,'" *Trinity Journal* 2 (1981): 169-97; M. D. Roberts, "Woman Shall Be Saved: A Closer Look at 1 Timothy 2:15," *TSF Bulletin* 5, no. 2 (November/December 1981): 4-7; D. M. Scholer, "Exegesis: 1 Timothy 2:8-15," *Daughters of Sarah* 1 (May 1975): 7-8 (reprinted in Hestenes, ed., *Women and Men in Ministry*, p. 74); "Women in Ministry, Session Seven: 1 Timothy 2:8-15," *Covenant Companion* 73, no. 2 (February 1984): 14-15; "Women's Adornment: Some Historical and Hermeneutical Observations on the New Testament Passages," *Daughters of Sarah* 6, no. 1 (January/February 1980): 3-6; A. D. B. Spencer, "Eve at Ephesus (Should Women Be Ordained As Pastors According to the First Letter to Timothy 2:11-15?)" *Journal of the Evangelical Theological Society* 17 (1974): 215-22; "Paul, Our Friend and Champion," *Daughters of Sarah* 2, no. 3 (May 1976): 1-3.

[5]In spite of genuine historical, literary and theological problems, I remain convinced that the Pastoral Epistles (1 and 2 Timothy, Titus) are best accounted for as coming from Paul

context of the passage gained by using the often-neglected 1 Timothy 2:15 as a key to uncovering the social-historical context and (2) the particular arguments of those who see this text as a primary basis for excluding or limiting women in ministry.

The approaches that neglect this text[6] or dismiss it because it does not correspond well with one's "genuine" Pauline "canon within a canon"[7] are rejected here. Such approaches usually see 1 Timothy 2:9-15 as a post-Pauline critique of the "genuine" Paul on women's place in the church. My approach assumes much more complexity both for Paul's thought and for the variety of situations that he addresses.

Exegetical Considerations

1. *1 Timothy 2:15—the Heresy at Ephesus and the Purpose of 1 Timothy*. The discussion of 1 Timothy 2:9-15 and its bearing on the place of women in the church often focuses immediately or only on verses 11-12 (or vv. 11-14) to the exclusion of verses 9-10 and especially of the notoriously difficult verse 15. For example, George W. Knight's book, which considers 1 Timothy 2:11-15 the clearest biblical evidence for his position, never discusses verse 15 per se.[8] Susan Foh ends her discussion of 1 Timothy 2:8-15 by saying: "The last verse (v. 15) in this section is a puzzle and a sort of non sequitur."[9] Such neglect shows an irresponsible and symptomatic neglect of reading texts in their contexts.

---

or from someone under his general supervision. This is not the place to rehearse the arguments. In any event, 1 Tim 2:9-15 is part of the church's New Testament canon and must be dealt with as such; I reject the view (e.g., Powers [see n. 3] and Hommes [see n. 4] that 1 Tim 2:9-15 deals only with the marriage relationship and not the place of women in the church. For me, the specific language and the context make this clear.

[6]E. M. Tetlow, *Women and Ministry in the New Testament* (New York: Paulist, 1980), e.g., does not mention this text at all in her book.

[7]See, e.g., R. Scroggs, "Paul and the Eschatological Woman," *Journal of the American Academy of Religion* 40 (1972): 283-303: "To separate the establishment Paul from the historical Apostle is reasonably simple. . . . The Pastorals are thus immediately discarded and, for our purposes, hopefully forgotten" (p. 284). Scroggs (and others) also reject 1 Cor 14:34-35 as non-Pauline. At least two scholars have argued, further, that it is thus logical to regard 1 Cor 11:3-16 as non-Pauline as well and do so regard it: W. O. Walker, Jr., "1 Corinthians 11:2-16 and Paul's Views Regarding Women," *Journal of Biblical Literature* 94 (1975): 94-110; and G. W. Trompf, "On Attitudes toward Women in Paul and Paulinist Literature: 1 Corinthians 11:3-16 and Its Context," *Catholic Biblical Quarterly* 42 (1980): 196-215.

[8]Knight, *The New Testament Teaching*.

[9]S. T. Foh, *Women and the Word of God: A Response to Biblical Feminism* (Grand Rapids, Mich.: Baker, 1980), p. 128.

Verse 15 is clearly the climactic resolution of the whole unit.[10] The subject introduced in verse 9 is "likewise *women.*" The explicit noun (*woman* or *women*) is repeated in verses 10, 11 and 14 and is implied throughout. The sentence of verse 15 is connected with the preceding by *de* ("yet") and the opening verb depends on the previous sentence for its subject *hē gynē* ("the woman"). One frequently mentioned problem with verse 15 is that the first verb *sōthēsetai* ("will be saved") is singular, whereas the second verb *meinōsin* ("to abide or remain") is plural. This demonstrates the obvious connection between verse 15 and 2:9-14—Eve (v. 13) represents woman (v. 14) /women (vv. 9, 10, 11); thus, the grammatically natural shift in verse 15 from the singular (woman as womankind) to the plural (individual women).

Not only is verse 15 clearly part of the 2:9-15 unit, but it is also its climax. It provides, within the structure of Paul's argument, a positive conclusion to the negative statements in 2:11-14. Therefore, until verse 15 is adequately addressed, there is no legitimate entrée to the rest of the paragraph (2:9-14).

The opening clause, "woman will be saved through childbirth" (v. 15a) often reads with great difficulty for Protestant evangelical interpreters; thus, the New International Version translates it: "But women will be kept safe through childbirth." Of course, *sōzein* ("to save") can have a range of meanings, but in such Pauline contexts the virtually inevitable sense is that of the salvation of God in Christ. This sense of salvation is confirmed by the next clause, "if they continue in faith, love and holiness with propriety" (NIV), which would make little sense otherwise.

One relatively common attempt to resolve the difficulties is to assume that the singular subject of "will be saved" is Eve and the "childbearing" is the birth of the Messiah Jesus, implying that Eve's sin (2:14) is reversed with the coming and work of Christ.[11] Such a view, however, founders on the most likely meaning of *teknogia* ("childbearing and -rearing"; see 1 Tim 5:14) and the inapplicability of this reading of 2:15 with reference to 2:13-14.[12]

---

[10]In spite of the punctuation in N-A[26] and the arguments of some, I reject the view that 1 Tim 3:1a ("This is a faithful saying") is the conclusion of 2:9-15 or any part of it. I understand it to be the introduction to 3:1b.

[11]See, e.g., Spencer, "Eve at Ephesus"; and Roberts, "Woman Shall Be Saved."

[12]For significant lexical data, see C. Spicq, *Les épîtres pastorales*, vol 1 (Études Bibliques; 4th ed.; Paris: Gabalda, 1969), pp. 382-83; see also Moo, "1 Timothy 2:11-15," p. 71.

In view of the vocabulary, structure and contextual location of 2:15, this conclusion to the discussion of the place of women in the church must mean that women find their place among the saved (assuming, of course, their continuation in faith, love and holiness) through the maternal and domestic roles that were clearly understood to constitute propriety *(sōphrosynē)* for women in the Greco-Roman culture of Paul's day.[13]

The concern for propriety in verse 15 appears also in verse 9 at the beginning of this paragraph in connection with women's dress and adornment. This concern in verses 9-10 is another aspect of a woman's domestic role of decency and propriety in Greco-Roman society at that time.

These concerns in 2:9-15 for propriety in women's behavior imply that, in 1 Timothy and, more generally, in the Pastoral Epistles, Paul is addressing a challenge to their behavior . This is confirmed by the context of similar passages. These other texts focus on what is appropriate behavior for women and for domestic life, particularly with reference to the opposition (heresy) that Timothy and Paul faced and in terms of Paul's concern for the church's social reputation within Greco-Roman society.

The emphasis in 2:15 takes on a special focus when it is noted that the opponents, against whom Paul is writing and warning Timothy, forbid marriage (1 Tim 4:3). Thus, it is not surprising that Paul dwells on marriage concerns in his long paragraph on widows in the church (1 Tim 5:3-16). He stresses that widows under sixty years of age should not be put on the roll of widows (5:11) but should marry, have children and manage their homes (5:14). This appeal is explicitly set against an alternative behavior: "They get into the habit of being idle and going about from house to house. And not only do they become idlers, but also gossips and busybodies, saying things they ought not to" (5:13 NIV).[14] Paul finds such behavior so unacceptable that he describes it as following Satan (5:15). The widows sixty years of age and older can be placed on the roll of widows provided that their lives have been marked by good works (5:10), a characteristic explicitly called for in 2:9-10 and implied in 2:15.

This concern is also explicit in Titus 2:3-5. Older women are to be

---

[13]For the cultural context see S. B. Pomeroy, *Goddesses, Whores, Wives and Slaves: Women in Classical Antiquity* (New York: Schocken, 1975); and D. L. Balch, *Let Wives Be Submissive: The Domestic Code in 1 Peter*, Society of Biblical Literature Monograph Series 26 (Chico, Calif.: Scholars, 1981).

[14]See a similar concern in Philo *De specialibus legibus* 3.169-71.

exemplary in behavior and committed to teaching younger women what is good (2:3-4). What the younger women are to be taught corresponds to what is said in 1 Timothy 2:15, 9-10 and 5:9-15: they are to love their husbands and children, be subject to their husbands and be domestic.[15] The concern for propriety is also expressed (2:4-5).

Concern for proper domestic life is also noted in texts directed to male leaders within the church. Bishops (1 Tim 3:4-5), deacons (1 Tim 3:12) and elders (Tit 1:6) must be persons whose home and family life are respectable and in order.

These texts and others express concern for the reputation of the church within the larger Greco-Roman society:[16] "a good reputation with outsiders" (1 Tim 3:7); "to give the enemy no opportunity for slander" (1 Tim 5:14); "so that . . . our teaching may not be slandered" (1 Tim 6:1); "so that no one will malign the word of God" (Tit 2:5); "so that those who oppose you may be ashamed because they have nothing bad to say about us" (Tit 2:8) and "so that in every way they [slaves] will make the teaching about God our Savior attractive" (Tit 2:10). Certainly this concern lies behind Paul's first agenda item in 1 Timothy in which the rationale is "that we may live peaceful and quiet lives in all godliness and holiness. This is good, and pleases God our Savior, who wants all persons to be saved" (2:2-4).

This concern for public reputation, model domestic life, and appropriate decorum and maternal-domestic roles for women clearly implies that the opposition (heresy) that Paul and Timothy faced in Ephesus constituted an assault on marriage and what were considered appropriate models for women in that society. As noted above, the heresy prohibited marriage (1 Tim 4:3). Apparently, the false teachers encouraged women to leave their homes and meet together (see 1 Tim 5:13-15 and the implied converse of Tit 2:4-5). Part of the heresy evidently involved what Paul called "worldly old wives' tales" (*tous bebēlous kai graōdeis mythous*—1 Tim 4:7).[17] This accounts for Paul's emphasis on

---

[15]On the meaning of the term see Bauer⁵-Gingrich-Danker, p. 561; note that this is a Hellenistic term.

[16]Biblical quotations are from the NIV with occasional alterations to make the language inclusive.

[17]The translation is that of Bauer⁵-Gingrich-Danker, p. 138. Note that the term γραώδης (characteristic of old women) is a Hellenistic and Stoic term and is used only here in the New Testament (Bauer⁵-Gingrich-Danker, p. 167).

godly living and right teaching for older women in 1 Timothy 5:9-10 and Titus 2:3-4.

Such inferences are confirmed by the description of the false teachers and their methods in 2 Timothy 3:1-9. They "worm their way into homes and gain control over weak-willed women *gynaikarion*,[18] who are loaded down with sins and are swayed by all kinds of evil desires, always learning but never able to acknowledge the truth" (3:6-7).

1 Timothy 2:15, then, in its immediate and larger context within the Pastoral Epistles, opens the way for understanding the paragraph on the conduct of women in the church in 1 Timothy 2:9-15. It addresses a particular situation of false teaching in Ephesus that assaulted and abused what was considered appropriate and honorable behavior for women.[19]

To see 1 Timothy 2:9-15 as addressing a particular heresy focused on women and women's roles raises the whole issue of the purpose of 1 Timothy (as well as 2 Tim). The purpose of 1 Timothy is to combat the Ephesian heresy that Timothy faced. Paul addresses this heresy immediately after the formal beginning of the letter (1:3-7). Apart from the final "grace be with you" (6:21b), the letter ends with explicit concern about the false teaching (6:20-21). Paul mentions false teachers frequently throughout the letter (1:18-20; 4:1-8; 5:16; 6:3-10; see also 2 Tim 2:16-18; 3:1-9; 4:3-4, 14-15).[20]

It is within this understanding of the purpose of 1 Timothy that 1 Timothy 3:14-15 should be understood: "I am writing you these instruc-

---

[18]See Bauer⁵-Gingrich-Danker, p. 168: this term is a relatively uncommon word found almost entirely within the Hellenistic period.

[19]The heresy is some type of ascetic-gnosticizing movement within the church (1 Tim 1:3-7; 6:20-21) but cannot be more specifically defined. There is no clear or particular evidence that connects this heresy with any pagan worship in Ephesus and its sexual activities and connotations. For background on the Artemis/Diana cult in Ephesus see the references given in Moo, "1 Timothy 2:11-15," p. 81, n. 118. Two especially useful articles bearing on the heresy and women in the Pastoral Epistles are: R. J. Karris, "The Background and Significance of the Polemic of the Pastoral Epistles," *Journal of Biblical Literature* 92 (1973): 549-64; and J. M. Bassler, "The Widows' Tale: A Fresh Look at 1 Timothy 5:3-16," *Journal of Biblical Literature* 103 (1984): 23-41. See also the earlier study of J. M. Ford, "A Note on Proto-Montanism in the Pastoral Epistles," *New Testament Studies* 17 (1970/71): 338-46.

[20]See G. D. Fee, *1 and 2 Timothy, Titus,* Good News Commentary (San Francisco: Harper & Row, 1984) for a presentation of 1 Timothy as an ad hoc letter dealing with a particular problem of heresy.

tions so that . . . you will know how people ought to conduct themselves in God's household. . . ."

Scholars such as George Knight and James Hurley understand 1 Timothy 3:14-15 as *the* purpose of 1 Timothy and infer from it that Paul is giving a suprasituational "church manual." Thus, Hurley begins his chapter on 1 Timothy 2:8-15 with a unit entitled "The Announced Purpose of 1 Timothy" and writes that Paul "considered what he said normative beyond the immediate situation" and "indicates that his instructions should have a general rather than closely limited application."[21] Knight also begins his treatment of 1 Timothy 2:8-15 by noting that 1 Timothy 3:14-15 determines its character.[22]

Yet it is presumptuous to take 1 Timothy 3:14-15 out of the context of the whole letter and make it the proof of a transsituational reading of 1 Timothy. Rather, 3:14-15 should be seen as a summary statement of the specific directions given for meeting a particular problem of heresy that Timothy was facing in Ephesus at that time.[23]

Therefore, 1 Timothy should be understood as an occasional ad hoc letter directed specifically toward enabling Timothy and the church to avoid and combat the false teachers and teaching in Ephesus. This false teaching appealed strongly to women and led them so astray that traditional values of marriage and the home were seriously violated.

2. *1 Timothy 2:9-10.* The paragraph on the place of women in the church begins with 1 Timothy 2:9. The opening clause is somewhat unclear, although it is related to 2:8 by *hōsautōs* ("likewise"). In 2:8 Paul instructs men on the proper posture and attitude for prayer. This relates

[21]The unit is in Hurley, *Man and Woman,* pp. 195-97; the quotations are from p. 196.

[22]Knight, *The New Testament Teaching,* pp. 29-30.

[23]The understanding of the purpose of the Pastorals and the heresy faced by them is different from the situation proposed in the intriguing book by D. R. MacDonald, *The Legend and the Apostle: The Battle for Paul in Story and Canon* (Philadelphia: Westminister, 1983). In brief, MacDonald argues that the complexity of Paul led in two post-Pauline directions on women in the church. The Pastorals represent the domestication of the gospel; the Acts of Paul represent the "socially radical" Paul on women. In fact, MacDonald argues that the Pastorals are directed against the traditions that ultimately surface in the Acts of Paul and that, therefore, what is "heresy" from the Pastorals' perspective is what is the "positive" view of women in the Acts of Paul. In spite of the difference between MacDonald's and my assessment of the opponents of 1 Timothy and the Pastorals, his book is useful in getting at the particular social-historical context of the Pastorals.

to the theme of prayer introduced in the previous paragraph (2:1–7). Whether verse 9 should be understood specifically as an instruction to women at prayer or as a general instruction on women's adornment and dress cannot be resolved, although the latter may be slightly more likely.[24] In any event, the context is the church.

With the perspective of 1 Timothy 2:15 and the purpose of the entire epistle seen as combating false teaching, 2:9–10 is clearly as serious a set of injunctions in the context as 2:11–12.[25] The instructions regarding women's dress and adornment are given without qualification. Most important, 2:9–10 is similar to 2:15 in affirming high standards of cultural decency so that the church will be above reproach. These standards contrast the values encouraged by the opposing heretical teachings.

This assumption is confirmed when the injunctions regarding women's adornment and dress are seen within the larger societal contexts of the church, in terms of both Jewish and Greco-Roman cultures.[26] The extrabiblical literature from these cultural contexts also favors modesty and rejects expensive clothing, hair styling, gold jewelry and pearls. These Jewish and pagan passages regularly condemn such external adornment and argue that a woman's inner beauty and chastity should be her real adornment.

More important, in virtually all the Jewish and pagan texts, the rejection of external adornment was part of a woman's submission to her husband and a recognition of her place among men in general. Using external adornments such as pearls, gold jewelry, hair styling and ex-

---

[24]See Moo, "1 Timothy 2:11–15," p. 63.

[25]Contrast this with S. B. Clark, *Man and Woman in Christ: An Examination of the Roles of Men and Women in Light of Scripture and the Social Sciences* (Ann Arbor: Servant Books, 1980), p. 194: "We should not place too much emphasis on the exhortation to women to adorn themselves modestly and sensibly. This exhortation is not the heart of the passage." This certainly begs the issues at hand and decides on grounds totally apart from the text or 1 Timothy that the "heart" of the passage is elsewhere (i.e., 2:11–12).

[26]For a more extensive treatment of this point with the citation of numerous primary texts see Scholer, "Women's Adornment." This article provides the detailed evidence for this section on 1 Tim 2:9–10 in this essay. The texts include 1 Enoch 8:1–2; Testament of Reuben 5:1–5; Pseudo-Phintys and Pseudo-Perictione (Neo-Pythagorean texts from about the second century B.C.); Seneca, *To Helvia on Consolation* 16.3–4; Musonius Rufus 3.17–20; Juvenal 6.457–59, 501–3, 508–9; Plutarch, *Advice to Bride and Groom* 26; 30–32; and *Sentences of Sextus* 235; 513.

pensive, provocative clothing indicated two undesirable characteristics—material extravagance and sexual infidelity.

Thus, the progression of thought in 1 Timothy 2:9-15 moves from concern for women's adornment (vv. 9-10) to concern for women's submission and silence in public worship (vv. 11-12). These are two sides of the same coin in the cultural settings of the first century A.D., which assumed male dominance and a belief in women's subordination and inferiority.

In view of this unity of 2:9-12 and the conclusion in 2:15, there is no exegetical, historical or hermeneutical basis to regard 2:9-10 as normatively different from 2:11-12. Nevertheless, most evangelicals, including those who see 2:11-12 as warrant for limiting women in ministry, take the injunctions against women's adornment in 2:9-10 to be culturally relative and do not seek to apply them in the unqualified terms in which they are stated. Furthermore, many who discuss 2:11-12 as warrant for limiting women in ministry do not even consider 2:9-10 in their discussion, or they treat it rather briefly.[27]

The point is that 2:9-10 is intended to protect women from the enticements of the false teachers (see esp. 1 Tim 4:1-3; 6:3-10) and the temptations of sexual infidelity within Greco-Roman culture to which the false teaching could lead. Thus, 2:9-10 is part of Paul's specific response to the false teaching in Ephesus that had been directed especially at women who had been made vulnerable by their treatment as inferior or marginal in their society. Paul encourages dress and adornment for women that corresponds to the "high moral standards" of Jewish and pagan society and, therefore, presents the church as of good reputation and without offense.

3. *1 Timothy 2:11-12 and the Pauline Context of Women's Participation in the Church's Ministry.* To the degree that 2:15 and 2:9-10 are limited to the threat and presence of the false teachers in Ephesus and are set within particular cultural values, so also are the injunctions to

---

[27]Note that Moo, "1 Timothy 2:11-15," and Knight, *The New Testament Teaching,* include only 2:11-15 in their discussions. Foh's section entitled "1 Timothy 2:8-15" (pp. 122-28) does not, in fact, treat 2:9-10. Hurley's chapter on 1 Tim 2:8-15 (pp. 195-233) includes only a page and a half on 2:9-10 (pp. 198-99). In my judgment, Hurley understands to some degree the "culturally conditioned" character of 2:9-10, but he is not consistent in understanding the whole of 2:9-15 on the same model.

silence and submission in 2:11-12.[28] All are part of the same paragraph.

The injunctions of 2:11-12 correspond with the generally accepted norms of behavior and expectations for women in both Jewish and Greco-Roman cultures.[29] Thus, the statements of 2:11-12 reinforce honorable patterns of behavior in response to the false teaching and its abusive use of women. The statements of 2:9-10 and 2:15 do the same.

The statements of 2:11-12 are thus ad hoc instructions intended for a particular situation in Ephesus of false teaching focused on women. These statements are not to be understood as universal principles encoded in a suprasituational "church order manual" that limit women in ministry in all times and places. Rather, the instructions of 2:11-12 are directed against women who, having been touched or captivated by false teachings, are abusing the normal opportunities women had within the church to teach and exercise authority.

This interpretation is grounded in three basic perspectives. First, the immediate context (2:9-15) and the larger context of 1 and 2 Timothy show that the fundamental issue being addressed throughout 1 Timothy is the false teaching plaguing the church in Ephesus. This false teaching and its teachers had women as a particular focus and encouraged them to radically violate appropriate and honorable behavior patterns for women. Thus, it is reasonable to assume that this situation occasioned the specific remarks of 2:11-12.

Those who see 2:11-12 as excluding or limiting women in ministry usually object to such a historical reconstruction. They argue that if Paul had intended 2:11-12 to mean that women who were involved in the false teachings should be prohibited from teaching or exercising authority in the church, he could easily have said so at this very point. More-

---

[28] I reject the suggestion that Paul's "I do not permit" (οὐκ ἐπιτρέπω 2:12) is a basis for limiting 2:11-12 because it is only opinion. Paul often expresses his apostolic authority in personal terms (e.g., 1 Cor 7:40; 7:12). See the "debate" over ἐπιτρέπω in Payne, pp. 170-73, and Moo, "interpretation," pp. 199-200. I side with Moo and do not rest my case for a limited application of 2:11-12 on Payne's observations on this point.

[29] For the cultural context of the customary prohibition on women's public speaking, see the citations in nn. 13, 14, 19 and 26. The contention of Moo, "1 Timothy 2:11-15," p. 81, that due to trends in the Hellenistic period and especially the presence of the cult of Artemis/Diana in Ephesus, women engaging in public teaching would not be offensive is too simplistic and too narrow a view of all the evidence regarding the place of women in Greco-Roman culture.

over, Paul could have mentioned cultural values of importance to the church.[30]

Such an objection does not take seriously the character of 1 Timothy as an occasional letter or the full context of 1 and 2 Timothy. Such an objection assumes that 2:11-12 is one unit in a series of timeless, universal principles set within a document on church order. The commands of 2:11-12, however, occur within a specific paragraph, the climax of which (2:15) already indicates a specific situation. The larger context of 1 and 2 Timothy confirms this. Thus, 2:11-12 must always be understood within these contexts, as well as the larger Pauline context. To assert that Paul did or could have easily written for the sake of twentieth-century interpreters begs the whole question of the contextual and historical situation addressed in 1 Timothy. Paul is not obligated to give a full account of the whole social context shared by him and his original readers. Paul did not do that in his complex discussion of eating meat offered to idols and of abuses in church worship directed to Corinth (1 Cor 8—10; 12—14). Those texts also have interpretive ambiguities that must be resolved by social-historical reconstruction. The complete literary context and the shared experience and knowledge of author and first readers made such discussion unnecessary.

Another objection is that if Paul's purpose was to stop heretical teaching within the church's worship, then the male false teachers should have been included within the injunctions of 2:11-12.[31] This assumes that the male false teachers participated in the church's regular worship at the same level as the women who were touched by the false teachings. Nevertheless, the context of 1 and 2 Timothy suggests that the women involved were special targets of the male false teachers and were probably used by them as a means of infiltration. Certainly Paul does not condone or ignore false teachers simply because they are men; the rest of 1 and 2 Timothy makes that clear. Furthermore, this objection does not recognize that 2:11-12 is part of a paragraph (2:9-15) that is devoted exclusively to the issue of women in the Ephesian church. The abuses of men are handled elsewhere in the letter.

Another factor basic to the interpretation of 2:11-12 concerns Paul's

---

[30]See, e.g., Moo, "Interpretation," p. 203; Knight, *The New Testament Teaching*, pp. 31-32; Hurley, p. 203.
[31]See, e.g., Moo, "Interpretation," p. 203.

use of the unusual word *authentein* (translated "to have authority over" RSV) in the second injunction (2:12). This is the only occurrence of this word in Paul's writings and, indeed, in the entire New Testament. The word is not frequently used in ancient Greek literature. The precise meaning of *authentein* and its use in 2:12 cannot be completely resolved at this time; scholars are currently in an extended debate on the issue.[32]

Traditionally, *authentein* has been understood to connote a sense of "to domineer" or "to usurp authority" and the term is even associated with murder.[33] Although not all of the evidence and arguments have been fully assessed, two points seem relatively certain. First, the term is unusual. If Paul were referring to the normal exercise of authority, his otherwise constant *exousia/exousiazō* ("authority/to exercise authority") vocabulary would most likely have been used. The choice of such an unusual term itself indicates that Paul intended a different nuance or meaning. Second, in spite of Knight's efforts to the contrary, many uses of the term seem rather clearly to carry the negative sense of "domineer" or "usurp authority."[34] Thus I see the injunctions of 2:11-12 as directed against women involved in false teaching who have abused proper exercise of authority in the church (not denied by Paul elsewhere to women) by usurpation and domination of the male leaders and teachers in the church at Ephesus.[35]

The most crucial factor in understanding 2:11-15 is the matter of Paul's practice with regard to women's ministry in the church. Careful analysis of Acts and Paul's letters demonstrates that women engaged in the gospel ministry in Paul's churches just as men did.[36] Scholars such

---

[32]See the articles devoted to this term listed in nn. 3 and 4 by Knight, "ΑΥΘΕΝΤΕΩ"; Panning; Osburn; and Kroeger, "Ancient"; see also the essay by Kroeger on this term included in this book.

[33]See Osburn, "ΑΥΘΕΝΤΕΩ," pp. 2-8, for a brief summary of the evidence with primary text reference.

[34]See Osburn, "ΑΥΘΕΝΤΕΩ"; Kroeger, "Ancient"; and Kroeger's essay in this book.

[35]If it were ever established that the term means only neutral or positive authority, the interpretation of 2:11-12 argued here would not be lost; the first and third perspectives would still establish the case.

[36]For detail on all these texts, see D. M. Scholer, "Paul's Women Co-Workers in the Ministry of the Church," *Daughters of Sarah* 6, no. 4 (July/August 1980): 3-6; "Women in Ministry, Session Three: Its Basis in the Early Church," "Session Four: Its Basis in Paul (Part One)," *Covenant Companion* 73, no. 1 (January 1984): 12-13; and "Women in Ministry, Session Five: Its Basis in Paul (Part Two)," *Covenant Companion* 73, no. 2 (February 1984): 12-13. See also the other essays in this book that deal with the Pauline texts in question.

as Moo and Hurley argue that since none of the Pauline texts explicitly state that women "taught" or "exercised authority," the case for women in ministry at this level has not been established and the supposed evidence is irrelevant. This approach does not take seriously the depth of evidence available.[37] For example, even though Philippians 4:2-3 does not say that Euodia and Syntyche "taught," Paul's description of their ministry implies that they taught and did so with authority.

Moo, Hurley and others also discount the evidence on women in the ministry in Paul's churches on another ground. Their approach posits two levels of authority. They insist that the women noted in Romans 16:1-16 and Philippians 4:2-3 and the activity indicated in 1 Corinthians 11:5 show that women participated in the ministry of the church, but not at the level of authority prohibited by 1 Timothy 2:11-12. Such an approach imposes on the New Testament a concept of two levels of authority that is never indicated in the Pauline texts. Furthermore, this approach assumes that the structures reflected in 1 and 2 Timothy were normative in all Paul's churches. This assumption is rendered virtually untenable by 1 Corinthians alone, not to mention other letters of Paul.[38] For example, Hurley and Moo allow that even if Junia (Rom 16:7) were a woman designated as an apostle, she would not be an example of a woman having authority (in the sense of 1 Tim 2:12) in the church because it would be clear that the use of the term *apostle* here would have a very general, nonauthoritative sense![39]

Other unwarranted means have been used to maintain 1 Timothy 2:11-12 as a "timeless absolute" prohibiting or limiting women with regard to teaching and exercising authority. One argument, noted first by Origen in his commentary on 1 Corinthians, says that 1 Timothy 2:12 does not exclude *private* instruction women give to men, with Priscilla's teaching of Apollos in Acts 18:26 as the example.[40] Such an argument

[37]For one example, cf. Scholer (articles cited in n. 36) on Junia as apostle in Romans 16:7 with Hurley, pp. 121-22; and Moo, "1 Timothy 2:11-15," p. 76, "Interpretation," pp. 207-8. This would apply to all the women noted in Rom 16:1-16 and Phil 4:2-3.
[38]For an extended critique of these two arguments against the significance of the Pauline data on women in ministry, see D. M. Scholer, "Hermeneutical Gerrymandering: Hurley on Women and Authority, *TSF Bulletin* 6, no. 5 (May/June 1983): 11-13.
[39]Hurley, *Man and Woman,* p. 122; Moo, "Interpretation," p. 208.
[40]Origen *Commentary on 1 Corinthians* 74 (the text of this fragment is in C. Jenkins, "Origen on I Corinthians," *Journal of Theological Studies* 10 [1908/09]: 41-42).

does not address the fact that even such private teaching was certainly authoritative.

A final matter concerns the debate over whether women's engaging in prophecy (1 Cor 11:5, 14; Acts 2; 21:8-9) indicates that women taught with authority in the church. Hurley and Moo, for example, sharply distinguish between prophecy and teaching, claiming that prophecy does not constitute the authoritative teaching ruled out by 1 Timothy 2:11-12.[41] Defining *prophecy* is difficult, but recent major studies of prophecy in the early church, such as those by D. Hill and D. Aune, clearly indicate that prophetic utterances and prophecy did function as authoritative teaching within Paul's churches.[42] This is certainly how prophecy should be regarded in 1 Corinthians 11–14, where Paul extols prophecy as the most desirable gift and activity for the edification of the church. Paul's definition of prophecy in 1 Corinthians 14:3 makes it, along with the whole argument of 1 Corinthians 14:1-25, a functional equivalent of authoritative teaching.[43]

A recent study by James Sigountos and Myron Shank adds a new argument to the relationship between prophecy and teaching. These scholars argue that Paul could allow women to prophesy and to pray and yet forbid them to teach because such a distinction was common in Greco-Roman society.[44] Although there has not yet been time to evaluate carefully the evidence they cite, it is dubious that they have made their case with respect to the Pauline literature. In some of the Greco-Roman texts they cite, prophecy is distinct from teaching be-

---

[41]Hurley, *Man and Woman*, pp. 120-21, 188-94; Moo, "1 Timothy 2:11-15," pp. 73-75, "Interpretation," pp. 206-7.

[42]D. Hill, *New Testament Prophecy*, New Foundations Theological Library (Atlanta: John Knox, 1981); D. Aune, *Prophecy in Early Christianity and the Ancient Mediterranean World* (Grand Rapids, Mich.: Eerdmans, 1983); see also T. W. Gillespie, "Prophecy and Tongues: The Concept of Christian Prophecy in Pauline Theology" (Ph.D. diss., Claremont Graduate School, 1971).

[43]I find it telling that Hurley does not cite 1 Cor 14:3 or deal with Paul's positive emphasis on prophecy for edification in his book; see again Scholer, "Hermeneutical," and the excellent critique of Moo in J. G. Sigountos and M. Shank, "Public Roles for Women in the Pauline Church: A Reappraisal of the Evidence," *Journal of the Evangelical Theological Society* 26 (1983): 283-95 (the critique is found on pp. 285-86). These authors conclude that prophecy was at least as authoritative in Paul as was teaching.

[44]Sigountos and Shank, "Public Roles," pp. 283-95. For the record, Sigountos and Shank, p. 294, do not see 1 Tim 2:11-12 as prohibiting or limiting women in ministry today.

cause prophecy is mindless or beyond rational control. This analysis, however, does not fit Paul, since the apostle argues vigorously (1 Cor 14) that prophecy *was* edifying speech that appealed to the rational thought of both speakers and hearers.

4. *1 Timothy 2:13-14.* The rationale for the injunctions stated in 2:11-12 is given in 2:13-14 in two parts: (1) Adam was created prior to Eve and (2) it was Eve, not Adam, who was deceived and who transgressed. Those who believe that the statements in 2:11-12 are general and universal and that they limit women in ministry usually place great stress on the allusions to Genesis 2—3 found in 2:13-14.[45] Several issues arise in assessing the meaning and significance of Paul's use of Genesis 2—3 at this point.

The discussion is introduced with *gar* ("for"). It is unclear whether the term here is meant to be causal (the position favored by Moo and others) or explanatory (the position that I favor). One's reading of the flow of the entire paragraph is the ultimate factor in deciding the meaning.

Those who find the allusion to Genesis 2—3 a reason for giving 1 Timothy 2:11-12 timeless validity assume that any injunction followed by a scriptural allusion is absolute. There is, however, no internal Pauline evidence that a Genesis allusion for the injunctions of 2:11-12 gives them greater universal significance than, for example, injunctions about widows in 1 Timothy 5:3-16, which do not include a Genesis allusion.

Furthermore, the Genesis allusion in 2:13-14 is often considered to be an especially authoritative sanction because it derives from so-called creation ordinances. Of course, this applies only to the first sanction (2:13); the second sanction (2:14) is drawn from the account of the sin that violated the original situation. An argument drawn from the Genesis 3 account of sin does not necessarily give a Pauline injunction universal validity. After all, Paul's allusion to Genesis 1 in Galatians 3:28 must mean that, among those in Christ, the original mutuality and equality and the shared authority established in creation (Gen 1:26-28) is restored.

---

[45]See, e.g., Knight, *The New Testament Teaching,* p. 32 ("No more basic and binding reason could be cited"); Moo, "1 Timothy 2:11-15," pp. 68-71; and Hurley, who has "an excursus on Genesis 1—3 and Paul's use of it" in the midst of his chapter on 1 Tim 2:8-15 (*Man and Woman,* pp. 204-21).

The allusion in 1 Corinthians 11:7-9 to Genesis 2 (which is before sin enters) indicates that arguments from the so-called creation ordinances can be used by Paul to support an injunction with clear historical-cultural limitations. The purpose of 1 Corinthians 11:3-16 (seen esp. in vv. 4-5, 6, 7, 10, 13 and in the climax in 16) is to argue that women ought to have their heads covered in worship whenever they engage in prayer or prophecy. The purpose of this passage is not a presentation of male headship;[46] rather, that point is one of the several arguments used (along with nature, church practice, Genesis and Christ's subordination to God) for the point that women should have covered heads in worship. The majority of evangelicals subscribing to biblical authority (including those who find in 1 Tim 2:9-15 a basis for excluding or limiting women in ministry) understand the specific point of 1 Corinthians 11:3-16 to be no longer directly applicable in our culture, at least in practice if not also in formal interpretation.[47] Such recognition indicates that Genesis 2 can be used by Paul to argue for a command that is historically and culturally limited.

It is important, however, in understanding 1 Timothy 2:13-14 to examine the specific data that Paul uses from Genesis. What seems overwhelmingly clear is that Paul is *selective* in his use of Genesis material.

That Adam was created prior to Eve (2:13) is drawn from Genesis 2; the creation account in Genesis 1 does not set priorities in the creation of the two sexes.[48] Galatians 3:28 establishes that Paul knew the language of Genesis 1:27. Paul also selected Genesis 2 rather than Genesis 1 in his discussion in 1 Corinthians 11:7-9. There, too, Paul asserts that Adam was created before Eve. In the 1 Corinthians text, Paul is even more selective in asserting that the man "is the image and glory of God; but the woman is the glory of man" (11:7). Although Paul does not deny that woman also was created in the image of God (Gen 1:26-27; 5:1-2),

---

[46]See, e.g., Knight, *The New Testament Teaching,* pp. 32-34; Hurley, *Man and Woman,* p. 182 ("The basic command . . . at issue is the appointive headship of men"), p. 184.

[47]As implied in this paragraph, some persons who concede this limitation for 1 Cor 11:3-16 have then attempted to argue that the headcovering for women was never the main point of the passage anyway.

[48]On the interpretation of Gen 1—3 itself, see D. M. Scholer, "Women in Ministry, Session One: Its Basis in Creation," *Covenant Companion* 72, no. 22 (December 15, 1983): 14; and P. Trible, *God and the Rhetoric of Sexuality,* Overtures to Biblical Theology (Philadelphia: Fortress, 1978).

he deliberately chooses to mention only that the man is in God's image in order to more clearly buttress his argument for head coverings for women. Paul, however, does qualify his Genesis argument in 1 Corinthians 11:7-9 by his parenthetical, strong counterassertion in 11:11-12 of the mutual interdependence of man and woman in the Lord, a text parallel to Galatians 3:28.

In 1 Timothy 2:13, Paul selects data from Genesis 2 to state that man was created before woman. In contrast to 1 Corinthians 11:3-16, 1 Timothy 2:9-15 has no qualifying assertion. Nevertheless, Paul clearly selected his Genesis material to explain 2:11-12.

More complex is Paul's selectivity with regard to Eve's deception and sin (2:14) drawn from traditional Jewish interpretation of Genesis 3. The account in Genesis 3 allows for different emphases. Genesis 3:1-7 makes it clear that woman and man sin together: the serpent addresses the woman with the plural "you," and Genesis 3:6 states that the man was with the woman in the event.[49] On the other hand, Genesis 3 has the woman eat the fruit first and she alone acknowledges deception (v. 13).[50]

In the Jewish tradition, Genesis 3 was usually understood to emphasize Eve's culpability for sin and death. One of the better-known texts, Sirach 25:24, asserts: "From a woman sin had its beginning, and because of her we all die" (RSV). Philo says that the serpent speaks to the woman because she "is more accustomed to be deceived than man. . . . She easily gives way and is taken in by plausible falsehoods which resemble the truth."[51] Various other Jewish texts make similar statements about Eve.[52]

That Paul is selective in his use of Eve in 1 Timothy 2:14 seems clear from at least three other Pauline texts. In 2 Corinthians 11:3, Eve's deception is a negative model, warning all Corinthian believers—men and women—against false teaching. This shows that Paul did not limit Eve's deceivability to women. In both Romans 5:12-14 and 1 Corinthians 15:21-22, the apostle attributes sin and death to Adam, not Eve.

---

[49]The phrase about the man's presence with the woman has been omitted, without warrant, in some Bible translations.

[50]Philo, *Allegory on the Law* 3.61, made this observation.

[51]Philo *Questions on Genesis* 33 *(LCL)*.

[52]See, e.g., Philo *On Creation* 156, 165; 4 Maccabees 18:6-8; *The Life of Adam and Eve*.

This emphasis is also known, although to a lesser extent, in Judaism.[53] Clearly, the contextual needs of the argument determine what part of the Genesis narrative Paul uses and emphasizes.

Paul's selective and wide range of arguments is well known. He even uses some that may have reflected beliefs and practices he did not approve. In 1 Corinthians 11:3-16, Paul uses at least five arguments to buttress his point. In 1 Corinthians 15:12-57, Paul employs several arguments for the future bodily resurrection, including one based on a practice and belief in baptism for the dead (v. 29), with which he could have hardly agreed. In 2 Corinthians 11—12, he rhetorically uses an argument against his opponents of personal boasting in spite of his own objections to doing it. Paul consciously gathered and used arguments that suited the point he wished to make.

Thus, 1 Timothy 2:13-14 should be understood as an explanatory rationale for verses 11-12 that uses data from Genesis 2—3 selectively to suit the needs of the argument at hand.[54] The women who were falling prey to the false teachers in Ephesus were being deceived and were transgressing as Eve did.[55] The rationale using Eve's deception in verse 14 is, therefore, ad hoc and occasional and is no more a "timeless" comment about women than the use of the same point in 2 Corinthians 11:3. In both cases, Paul was warning against false teachers and false teaching.[56]

If one assumes that 1 Timothy 2:11-12 is a "universal, timeless absolute" and that 2:13-14 as a scriptural allusion is an "absolute" authority, one faces the uneasy possibility that 2:14 implies that women are by nature deceivable in a way that men are not.

The ancient Jewish traditions current in Paul's time did hold that

---

[53] 2 Baruch 23.4.
[54] I would paraphrase the beginning of 1 Tim 2:13-14 as follows: "For the Scripture provides a way of supporting these injunctions [2:11-12] in that Adam. . . ."
[55] There is not sufficient evidence, in my judgment, to identify the false teaching in Ephesus as Gnosticism in a complete enough sense to hold that, as in some forms of developed Gnosticism, Eve was a "hero" of the false teachers and thus account for Paul's statements about Eve here.
[56] Moo, "1 Timothy 2:11-15," p. 70, e.g., gives indirect consent to the selective nature of 2:13-14 by commenting that "in attributing blame to woman here, Paul in no way seeks to exonerate man . . . : he concentrates upon the woman because it is her role which is being discussed."

women were inherently more deceivable. From this came numerous consequences about the inferiority and subordination of women.[57] Both Moo and Hurley struggle with this. In his first article on 1 Timothy 2, Moo had written that "it is difficult to avoid the conclusion that Paul cites Eve's failure as exemplary and perhaps causative of the nature of women in general and that this susceptibility to deception bars them from engaging in public teaching."[58] After being criticized for this remark, Moo claims misrepresentation but admits that "the difficulties with viewing v. 14 as a statement about the nature of women are real."[59] Moo then endorses Hurley's resolution, that it is "very unlikely that Paul meant to say . . . that all women are too gullible to teach."[60] Rather, Hurley argues that Paul's point is that Adam sinned deliberately, thus demonstrating that God had given to him (thus to men) the capacity to be a religious leader. Actually, this appears simply to be another way to say that, conversely, women do not have this capacity and are thus more deceivable than men. The implications are disturbing and contradict the reality of the whole of biblical teaching, church history and human experience.[61]

Hermeneutical Considerations

I will briefly identify five specific hermeneutical considerations that are crucial to the interpretation and application of 1 Timothy 2:9-15, especially within the evangelical traditions.

1. *Starting Points and Balance of Texts.*[62] Two hermeneutical axioms have wide, general acceptance: (1) clearer texts should interpret less clear or ambiguous texts and (2) any viewpoint that is claimed to be "biblical" should be inclusive of all the texts that speak to that particular

---

[57]Here see esp. L. Swidler, *Women in Judaism: The Status of Women in Formative Judaism* (Metuchen, N.J.: Scarecrow, 1976).

[58]Moo, "1 Timothy 2:11-15," p. 70.

[59]Moo, "Interpretation," p. 204; cf. Payne, "Libertarian Women," pp. 175-76.

[60]Hurley, pp. 214-16, esp. p. 215.

[61]Clark, *Man and Woman,* pp. 201-5, is an example of another attempt to cope with Eve's deception in 2:14 as a rationale for 2:11-12. He argues for a typological interpretation that, he claims, does not hold that women are necessarily deceivable but posits that Eve as a type who was deceived has set the scriptural pattern for the subordinate, nonteaching place of women. The explanation seems strained and also has disturbing implications.

[62]See D. M. Scholer, "Women in Ministry, Session Eight: Summary—Consistency and Balance," *Covenant Companion* 73, no. 2 (February 1984): 15.

issue. We need to recognize, however, that these axioms are often used with assumptions that are not explicit.

One such assumption that underlies most uses of 1 Timothy 2:11-12 to exclude or limit women in ministry is that this is *the* clear text through which all other New Testament texts on women in the church must be read. If 1 Timothy 2:11-12 is the starting point, the conclusion is inevitable. But the New Testament does not specify particular starting points for many issues. For example, on the matter of the so-called eternal security of believers, does one read Hebrews 6:4-6 "through" Romans 8:28-39, or should the Romans text be read "through" the one from Hebrews?

Why should we assume that 1 Timothy 2:11-12 is the controlling text through which other texts on women must be read? That passage cannot be divorced from its immediate paragraph of verses 9-15. If one reads the whole paragraph, the "simple clarity" of 1 Timothy 2:11-12 is called into question. F. F. Bruce writes on Galatians 3:28: "Paul states the basic principle here: if restrictions on it are found elsewhere in the Pauline corpus [e.g., 1 Tim 2:11-12] . . . they are to be understood in relation to Gal. 3:28, and not *vice versa.*"[63]

The balancing of texts is especially crucial for interpreting 1 Timothy 2:9-15 because the larger Pauline context and practice with regard to women in the ministry of the church confirms the understanding that the 1 Timothy text is limited to a problematic situation and is not a denial of Pauline practice.

2. *The Danger of Equivocation.* Anyone who argues for the "timeless," absolute character of any scriptural injunction should be prepared to take such a text without qualification or equivocation. For those who use 1 Timothy 2:11-12 to exclude or limit women in ministry, the passage often seems to "prove too much." Those who claim its absoluteness began to equivocate as early as Origen and John Chrysostom.[64]

Hurley, for example, argues that 1 Timothy 2:11-12 clearly prohibits

---

[63]F. F. Bruce, *The Epistle to the Galatians: A Commentary on the Greek Text,* The New International Greek Testament Commentary (Grand Rapids, Mich.: Eerdmans, 1982), p. 190.

[64]For Origen, see no. 40; John Chrysostom *Homily* 3.1 (on Rom 16.6); see J. LaPorte, *The Role of Women in Early Christianity,* Studies in Women and Religion, no. 7 (New York and Toronto: Edwin Mellen, 1982), pp. 122-23.

women from authoritatively teaching men. Yet he would allow women to teach on the mission field, in regular worship if under the authority of an elder, and in Bible study groups and the like.[65] He assumes that the only teaching of men prohibited to women in verses 11-12 is that committed to the office of elder. Others who see the passage as prohibiting women from teaching men often see no problem in women writing theological books or teaching in theological seminaries.[66]

Yet 1 Timothy 2:11-12 is not directed at only a certain level of persons (ordained elders rather than missionaries, a distinction that would be very difficult to maintain within Paul's churches) or at only one form of teaching (such as preaching in distinction from writing). It is rather an unqualified prohibition, the limits of which are found only in its specific sociohistorical purpose.

3. *Consistency.* Forced consistency is not a desirable hermeneutical axiom. Instead, one must achieve interpretive consistency through giving each text its integrity. Such consistency demands that 1 Timothy 2:9-10 and 15, for example, be taken with the same seriousness and be interpreted with the same procedures as 2:11-12.

The issue of consistent interpretation throughout 1 Timothy needs to be addressed. Foh's *Women and the Word of God,* for example, has a chapter entitled "What the New Testament Says about Women," which discusses 1 Timothy 2:8-15 but never touches 1 Timothy 5:3-16, a passage nearly twice as long, which is devoted exclusively to the place of women in the church. Similarly, Hurley's *Man and Woman in Biblical Perspective* devotes thirty-nine pages to 1 Timothy 2:8-15 but only twenty-nine lines on three scattered pages to 1 Timothy 5:3-16. Certainly, those who see the purpose of 1 Timothy as a "timeless" church manual should hold that 1 Timothy 5:3-16 be applied as literally and absolutely as 2:11-12. Such inconsistency suggests that their agenda is much more than a concern for biblical authority and for accurate biblical teaching.

4. *The Cultural Conditioning of the Text and the Interpreter.*[67] The

---

[65]Hurley, *Man and Woman,* pp. 242-52.

[66]See Payne, "Libertarian Women," pp. 174-75, for comments on this.

[67]My concerns here are developed much more fully in D. M. Scholer, "Unseasonable Thoughts on the State of Biblical Hermeneutics: Reflections of a New Testament Exegete," *American Baptist Quarterly* 2 (1983): 134-41. Some of the language in this section is taken verbatim from this article.

concept of genuinely objective biblical interpretation is a myth. All interpretation is socially located, individually skewed, and ecclesiastically and theologically conditioned. Nowhere is all of this more clear than on the issue of understanding biblical teaching on the place of women in the church's ministry. Generally, persons raised within holiness, pentecostal and certain Baptist traditions experienced women teaching authoritatively in the church long before they were equipped to interpret 1 Timothy 2:11-12 and never found that passage a problem. Conversely, persons raised in many Reformed traditions knew long before they were equipped to interpret 1 Timothy 2:11-12 that women were to be excluded from authoritative teaching in the church. They grew up finding the verses clear support for what they believed.

All biblical interpreters, regardless of where they now stand on the issue of women in ministry, have been deeply influenced by both the sexism and misogyny of our culture and also the currents of nineteenth-century women's rights and twentieth-century feminist movements.[68]

One should not despair over the reality of the cultural conditioning of interpreters. Rather, all interpreters should openly recognize this and proceed with caution, humility and a commitment to as high a level as possible of interpretive integrity and consistency as well as sensitivity to the historical settings of the biblical texts.

Not only are interpreters conditioned. The authors of biblical texts also lived and thought within particular historical-social settings. The biblical texts themselves are addressed to various historical settings for many different purposes. Thus, the Bible as God's Word is God's communication *in* history, not above it or apart from it. In this sense, the entire Bible consists of historically conditioned (i.e., culturally conditioned) texts.

Such an understanding of the Bible does not deny that many biblical texts are statements or contain principles of a directly transcendent or universal character, even if they have a particular setting in history and culture that *can* be explored and explained.

It is not easy to determine which biblical texts are so relative to their own cultural settings or are so limited to their own historical circum-

---

[68]One certainly ought to read the searching critique of androcentric biblical interpretation found in the first section of E. S. Fiorenza, *In Memory of Her: A Feminist Theological Reconstruction of Christian Origins* (New York: Crossroad, 1983), pp. 1-95.

stances that they do not have or cannot have transcultural claims as normative texts. The task is complex, but unless we struggle to develop consistent principles for making such determinations, our inherited traditions, theological presuppositions or personal prejudices will dictate what is and what is not culturally relative.[69]

5. *History of Interpretation.* Those who interpret 1 Timothy 2:9-15 as a historically limited, ad hoc text and who support full participation of women in every aspect of ministry are often charged with theological flaws or deviations. First, they are accused of capitulating to the influence of secular feminism. Second, they are accused of denying or weakening biblical authority.

A few vignettes and a quick look at the history of the interpretation of 1 Timothy 2:9-15 show the inappropriateness of such charges. Such an approach to 1 Timothy 2:9-15 is hardly novel. The first book published in English defending full and equal participation of women in ministry was written by a Quaker, Margaret Fell, in 1666.[70] Fell argued that 1 Timothy 2:11-12 was directed only against the deviating women described in 1 Timothy 5:11-15.

In the nineteenth century, at least thirty-six defenses of women in ministry were published in English.[71] Probably the most significant of these for 1 Timothy 2:9-15 are those of Antoinette L. Brown, Luther Lee, Phoebe Palmer, Catherine Booth and A. J. Gordon.[72] They all argued,

---

[69]Elsewhere (Scholer, "Unseasonable," pp. 139-40), I have developed eight guidelines for attempting to distinguish between what is culturally relative and what is transculturally normative in Scripture texts.

[70]M. Fell, *Women's Speaking Justified, Proved and Allowed of by the Scriptures* . . . (London, 1666; reprinted Amherst: Mosher Book & Tract Committee, New England Yearly Meeting of Friends, 1980).

[71]N. A. Hardesty, *Women Called to Witness: Evangelical Feminism in the 19th Century* (Nashville: Abingdon, 1984), pp. 162-64.

[72]A. L. Brown, "Exegesis of 1 Corinthians xiv, 34, 35; and 1 Timothy ii, 11, 12," *Oberlin Quarterly Review* 3 (1849): 358-73. Brown wrote this as a paper at Oberlin, where she was the first woman to complete the theological course there (in 1850), although the school would not grant her the degree. L. Lee, *Woman's Right to Preach the Gospel* (Syracuse, N.Y.: Author, 1853). This was the sermon preached at A. L. Brown's ordination on September 15, 1853, at South Butler, New York. Brown was the first woman ordained by a standard church body in the United States. This sermon has been reprinted in D. Dayton, *Luther Lee: Five Sermons and a Tract* (Chicago: Holrad House, 1975). P. Palmer, *Promise of the Father; or, A Neglected Specialty of the Last Days* (Boston: Henry V. Degen,

within a context of commitment to biblical authority, that 1 Timothy 2:9-15 was limited to a particular situation. They all noted the significance of the verb *authentein* in 1 Timothy 2:12 and the importance of other Pauline data that showed women as participants in ministry. Although none developed these observations on 1 Timothy 2:9-15 fully, they noted these points within the context of biblical exegesis that sought to be faithful to biblical theology and authority.

Early in the twentieth century, two books by women had considerable influence on the issues of women in ministry. Katherine Bushnell published a series of 100 Bible studies in book form, which was, to a large extent, summarized and popularized by Jessie Penn-Lewis.[73] Both stressed that, because of the evidence that women did engage in ministry in Pauline churches, 1 Timothy 2:11-12 was a temporary prohibition due to the perilous situation for women in society at that time and place.

In our own time, a staggering number of evangelical scholars and writers—many of whom are especially known for their defense and support of biblical authority—have understood 1 Timothy 2:9-15 as a limited text. The following representative list includes men and women in scholarly and popular works with a wide range of publishers, denominations and theological traditions: Paul K. Jewett, Leon Morris, Robert K. Johnston, John J. Davis, Donald G. Bloesch, F. F. Bruce, Dorothy Pape, Patricia Gundry, Dennis Kuhns, Don Williams, Shirley Stephens, Margaret Howe, Myrtle Langley, Mary J. Evans, Ward Gasque, Klyne Snod-

---

1859; reprinted Salem, Ohio: Schmul, 1981), pp. 24-25, 48-50. Palmer was a prominent Methodist evangelist. C. Booth, *Female Ministry; or, Woman's Right to Preach the Gospel* (London, 1859; reprinted [partially] New York: Salvation Army Supplies Printing and Publishing Department, 1975). Booth and her husband founded the Salvation Army. A. J. Gordon, "The Ministry of Woman," *Missionary Review of the World* 7 (1894): 910-21; reprinted in [Fuller] *Theology, News and Notes* 21, no. 2 (June 1975): 5-9; *Gordon College Alumnus* 8, no. 1 (1978): 3-4, 8-9; *Equity* 1, no. 1 (July/August 1980): 26-31; and as Gordon-Conwell Theological Seminary Monograph no. 61 (1974). Gordon was a Baptist pastor in Boston, who founded what became Gordon College and Gordon Divinity School (later Gordon-Conwell Theological Seminary).

[73]K. C. Bushnell, *God's Word to Women: One Hundred Bible Studies on Woman's Place in the Divine Economy* (place and date uncertain; reprinted North Collins, N.Y.: Ray B. Munson, ca. 1975); J. Penn-Lewis, *The "Magna Charta of Woman" according to the Scriptures* (Bournemouth: Overcomer Book Room, 1919; reprinted Minneapolis: Bethany Fellowship, 1975).

grass, Alvera and Berkeley Mickelsen, Philip Siddons and Aida Spencer.[74]

This demonstrates that the approach advocated in this essay and by many other persons grows out of deep respect and concern for sound biblical exegesis and a vital commitment to biblical authority for the church. Only the ill-informed could suggest that such exegesis depends on or even takes its initiative from secular feminism or that this "cloud of witnesses" are "soft" on biblical authority.

Conclusion

Through the exegetical and hermeneutical considerations offered here, four basic conclusions have emerged.

1. *1 Timothy 2:9-15 should be understood as a unifed paragraph on the place of women in the church in Ephesus.* It provided instructions for and was limited to a particular situation of false teaching.

2. *1 Timothy 2:11-12 cannot legitimately be divorced from its immediate context of 1 Timothy 2:9-15 or its larger literary context of 1 and 2 Timothy, including significant texts such as 1 Timothy 5:11-15 and 2*

---

[74]Paul K. Jewett, *Man As Male and Female: A Study in Sexual Relationships from a Theological Point of View* (Grand Rapids, Mich.: Eerdmans, 1975); Leon Morris, "The Ministry of Women," *Women and the Ministries of the Church,* ed R. Hestenes and L. Curley (Pasadena: Fuller Theological Seminary, 1979), pp. 14–25; Robert K. Johnston, "The Role of Women in the Church and Family: The Issues of Biblical Hermeneutics," in *Evangelicals at an Impasse: Biblical Authority in Practice* (Atlanta: John Knox, 1979), chap. 3, 48–76; Davis, "Ordination of Women Reconsidered"; D. G. Bloesch, *Is the Bible Sexist? Beyond Feminism and Patriarchalism* (Westchester: Crossway, 1982) (Bloesch does see 1 Tim 2:9–15 as a limited text, but for other reasons he qualifies the degrees to which women should participate in ministry); Bruce, *Galatians,* p. 190; "Women in the Church: A Biblical Survey," *Christian Brethren Review* 33 (1982): 7–14; D. R. Pape, *In Search of God's Ideal Woman: A Personal Examination of the New Testament* (Downers Grove, Ill.: InterVarsity, 1976), pp. 149–208; P. Gundry, *Woman Be Free!* (Grand Rapids, Mich.: Zondervan, 1977), pp. 74–77; D. R. Kuhns, *Women in the Church,* Focal Pamphlets no. 28 (Scottdale/Kitchener: Herald, 1978), pp. 48–52; D. Williams, *The Apostle Paul and Women in the Church* (Van Nuys: BIM, 1977), pp. 109–14; S. Stephens, *A New Testament View of Women* (Nashville: Broadman, 1980), pp. 145–47; E. M. Howe, *Women and Church Leadership* (Grand Rapids, Mich.: Zondervan, 1982), pp. 45–53; M. Langley, *Equal Woman: A Christian Feminist Perspective* (Basingstoke: Marshall Morgan & Scott, 1983), pp. 55–56; M. J. Evans, *Woman in the Bible* (Downers Grove, Ill.: InterVarsity, 1984), pp. 98–105; W. W. Gasque, "The Role of Women in the Church, in Society, and in the Home," *Crux* 19, no. 3 (1983): 3–9; K. Snodgrass, "Paul and Women," *Covenant Quarterly* 34, no. 4 (November 1976): 3–19; A. and B. Mickelsen, "May Women Teach Men?" *Standard* 74, no. 4 (April 1984): 34, 36–37; P. Siddons, *Speaking Out for Women—A Biblical View* (Valley Forge, Penn.: Judson, 1980), pp. 82–85; Spencer, "Eve at Ephesus."

Timothy 3:6-7. Paul's words in 1 Timothy 2:9-15 must also be placed in the context of all other Pauline data on the participation of women in ministry.

3. *It should be acknowledged within the evangelical communities that the type of interpretation of 1 Timothy 2:9-15 offered here and by many others is a completely acceptable and legitimate option within the framework of evangelical theological and ecclesiastical traditions and institutions.* Those who see in 1 Timothy 2:11-12 an exclusion or limitation of women in ministry cannot with integrity say or imply that those who understand 1 Timothy 2:9-15 as a historically conditioned and limited text have thereby denied or weakened a strong commitment to biblical authority or to responsible biblical interpretation.

4. *All persons concerned with biblical interpretation must admit the reality of agenda other than simply a commitment to biblical authority and biblical teaching.* Faithfulness to Scripture and desire to interpret accurately what the Bible teaches are genuine. Nevertheless, commitment to biblical authority and the sheer existence of particular texts, such as 1 Timothy 2:11-12, do not account for all that is happening within the evangelical discussion. The virtual neglect of 1 Timothy 5:3-16, equivocations in the application of 1 Timothy 2:11-12 and the very nature of the controversies over women in ministry within the evangelical communities demonstrate that there are many motivations and interests that deeply touch our interpretations of Scripture.

David M. Scholer is Dean of the Seminary and Julius R. Mantey Professor of New Testament at Northern Baptist Theological Seminary, Lombard, Illinois.

RESPONSE

Walter L. Liefeld

Scholer's essay is the finest treatment from this viewpoint of the passage in question that I have seen. He faces the hard issues and gives attention to the entire context of 1 Timothy. He clearly states his case and his methodology. He contributes much to the historical background, specifically, the problem of false teaching in the church at Ephesus. I make my comments with full appreciation of Scholer's contribution.

Scholer's major concern is that the passage be studied in its full context. Strangely, he says that "the paragraph on the place of women in the church begins with 1 Timothy 2:9." But in the Greek syntax, verse 9 is a dependent clause, subordinate to verse 8. In addition, the word *hōsautōs* ("likewise") provides an immediate clue that the teaching of verse 9 is parallel to that in verse 8. Instructions are to both men and women, showing appropriate behavior of each. Therefore, even though the topic of women begins with verse 9, the *paragraph* does not. This is not a minor matter, for to handle the text with integrity we must see the whole picture of the relationships between men and women. Scholer correctly stresses the importance of verse 15. He points out the importance of the last word, *sōphrosynē* ("propriety"). He does not, however, exegete the verse as a whole. Also the meaning of women being "saved" is significant. As for the interpretation of "childbirth," Scholer mentions only two interpretations, rejects one, chooses the other and omits any discussion of these or other alternatives.

Scholer counters the premise that the main purpose of this epistle is expressed in the middle of the book (3:14ff.) and affirms, as I do, that the main purpose is to oppose heresy. However, in the only passage in the Pastoral Epistles that combines a clear reference both to heretical teachings and to women, women are not the promulgators but the *victims* of false teaching (2 Tim 3:6-7). The question still remains, therefore, why Paul does not leave matters with the general prohibition against false teaching in 1 Timothy 1:3-4, but adds a paragraph directed specifically against women teachers. He thus restricts the recipients, rather than the originators, of the false doctrine. Of course, since the women—whether because of poor education, pagan influence or whatever—were being easily deceived in that culture, that fact connects with the reference in 2:14 to the deceiving of Eve. But that relates to the problem of women being deceived rather than to the problem of heresy itself.

Scholer correctly points out that the paper by Sigountos and Shank claims too much. But it is true that there is a difference between teaching and prophesying, both in the ancient secular world and in Christianity. We cannot proceed as though prophecy were, even in its instructional aspect, the same as the ministry of teaching or were equally authoritative. That would be incorrect for the following reasons: (1) Paul frequently differentiates between prophecy and teaching. (2) Edification is indeed mentioned as one of the *effects* of prophecy (1 Cor 14:4, 14) but not as its main purpose or function. (3) Prophecy uttered in the Corinthian church could be judged by the others; this would not have been so had it been authoritative teaching. (4) Paul felt at liberty not to allow the prophecy of Agabus to affect his decision. (5) Important as prophets became in the early church, certainly in the Didache, it was the teachers who transmitted the doctrinal traditions in the New Testament period.

All this is to suggest that any study of the passage at hand should seriously evaluate the contention of some that Paul allowed women to prophesy but not to teach. Scholer rejects this possibility and dismisses Moo and Hurley without discussing their arguments. He cites two "major" works in his favor—unfortunately, without providing their supporting arguments or page references to their discussions. One of these is David Aune's massive work. Aune says that "teaching was a function exercised by apostles and prophets as well as 'teachers' " (p. 217). This is in the context of a discussion of *itinerant* prophets. In support of the authority of prophets, Aune states that although 1 Thessalonians 5:20 enjoins Christians not to look down on prophesying (which suggests that its authority was not universally assumed), and although the prophets had to undergo testing, such uncertainty occurs only in cases of conflict between the prophets and other leaders. Wayne Grudem (to cite an opposite opinion) states that the testing referred to in 1 Corinthians is of the prophecies, not of the prophets themselves, who were fully accepted in the community (*The Gift of Prophecy in 1 Corinthians* [Washington, D.C.: University Press of America, 1982], pp. 62–67). Grudem also claims that it is the presence of an *apokalypsis* ("revelation") that distinguished prophecy from teaching. This, however, would neither render the ministry "mindless," like some ancient prophecies, nor deny its edificatory value, but it would indicate an identifiable difference between prophecy and teaching. We cannot assume that women were teaching authoritatively in the early church simply on the ground that teaching was included in prophesying. Nor can we therefore assume a text that seems to forbid them from teaching could not possibly mean that. This is not to reject Scholer's argument as a whole, but just to evaluate one element in it.

Scholer devotes many pages to the careful discussion of issues, to background, to hermeneutical considerations (including the history of interpretation) and to various elements of verses 9-15, but relatively few to verses 11-12, the crux of the passage. He sets the problematic verses in their proper context and background. Space limitations required that this goal be gained at some sacrifice of adequate exegetical attention to the verse itself. The crucial word *authentein* is treated in only a brief section, with detailed study left to Kroeger. Scholer does point out that if Paul had wanted simply to speak of the ordinary exercise of authority, there were other, less ambiguous ways of doing it. The word *hēsychia* ("quietness" or "silence") receives only a few lines. Although this might seem necessary so that he could deal more adequately with the text as a whole, the significance of *hēsychia* lies not only in how the word itself is translated, but in how it is used in the total structure. Note the repetition of the word and the way it brackets the sentence:

a woman / *in quietness* / let her learn / in all submission,

to teach / to a woman / I do not permit,

nor to *authentein* a man / but to be *in quietness*

Scholer does not discuss the word *didaskein* ("teach"). But it deserves more attention than it usually receives in proportion to *authentein*. His attention to the historical background could have been strengthened by added information on the status of the teacher. We know that teachers were accorded great honor in Judaism, in the greater Greco-Roman world and in the early church. Furthermore, Christian teachers were involved in a most significant and sensitive task, that of transmitting the traditions of Jesus and of the early apostles. Given the widespread feeling against women teachers in the ancient world, documented by Sigountos and Shank as mentioned before, it would not be surprising if the Christian church were hesitant to have their sacred traditions publicly conveyed by women. There is new evidence that some women were given titles of honor in Judaism. There is, however, enough evidence that women were considered unfit even to be taught the Torah to suggest that the Christians would have thought it wise for men to convey the teachings of Christ. Also, the perception of the transmitter of the tradition as a witness to that tradition may have made the ministry of women in that role a liability in a world that would not accept the testimony of women. This may explain why Paul did not mention that women were the first at the tomb when he cited witnesses in 1 Corinthians 15.

In the early church, the *didasko* ("to teach") word group gave way to the *katecheo* ("to orally instruct") word group. This change may have been related to the increase in the availability of the Scriptures. Some functions of the teacher in the New Testament period seem to have been taken over by the catechist, who repeated the doctrines that were by now well defined and accepted. Scholars should research whether teaching in the New Testament period had a dimension of authority that it no longer has, now that the Scriptures are so widely available and the doctrines of the church established. Was the prohibition against women teaching indeed limited to a historical situation, as Scholer suggests, although perhaps not to the specific instance he (or Kroeger) would propose? Was the prohibition against a kind of teaching that no longer exists except in frontier situations?

Scholer has cited Douglas Moo at various points, often favorably, but he does not interact with Moo's significant articles on this passage. In my judgment, Scholer is weak in his attempt to deal with the basing of Paul's instruction regarding women teaching on the biblical reference to the deceiving of Eve. He says *gar* ("for") can be causal or explanatory. This is a crucial issue, but Scholer merely cites scholars on both sides without indicating their reasons. He asserts that "the ultimate factor" in the decision is "one's reading of the flow of the entire paragraph." But surely the accumulated knowledge of the use of *gar* in Greek literature has something to do with its use in any given passage. Moo offers evidence that the explanatory use is rare. He also mentions that in the Pastoral Epistles alone *gar* follows an imperative idea twenty-one times and apparently has a causal sense. It is important to know whether Paul is quoting the Eve passage as a foundation, in a causal sense for his command, or whether it is merely explanatory or illustrative. If it is causal here, it seriously affects Scholer's argument.

Scholer rightly argues, and at length, that Paul's use of the Eve passage is selective. He shows that Paul can apply a biblical quotation or allusion to a practice that is not intended to be universal. Yet Scripture sometimes marshals theological truths and biblical allusions or quotations to give instruction not simply on how to handle a particular situation, but on how to handle similar situations as long as this civilization endures. Yet in some cases (perhaps this one), if we take a command in the explicit form in which it was given, we may, in a different culture or circumstance, distort the principle that underlies the command. This is not the same as situational ethics, and it does not mean painting Scripture with the whitewash of culture. It does mean that by sound exegesis and the illumination of the Spirit we should be able to find and apply biblical principles in an appropriate way. But what is needed is evidence from within Scripture itself that the command is given for a specific historical circumstance and for a specific reason. Without controls, of course, this procedure can be wrongly used to do away with commands that are intended to be universal and permanent.

Walter L. Liefeld is professor of New Testament, Trinity Evangelical Divinity School, Deerfield, Illinois.

10

1 TIMOTHY 2:12— A CLASSICIST'S VIEW

Catherine Clark Kroeger

NO PASSAGE HAS been used more consistently than 1 Timothy 2:12 to prohibit the leadership of women in the church. Two activities were denied the women of Ephesus by the verse: *didaskein oude authentein,* traditionally translated "to teach" and "to exercise authority." *Didaskō* ("to teach") is used of various types of instruction; but in the Pastoral Epistles, both *didaskō* and *didaskalos* ("teacher",) generally refer to the content of the message whether orthodox or heterodox.[1] Possibly the prohibition applies more to the message than to the act of teaching itself. *Authenteō* has a significant range of meanings: (a) to begin something, to be primarily responsible for a condition or action (especially murder); (b) to rule, to dominate; (c) to usurp power or rights from another; (d) to claim ownership, sovereignty or authorship.[2]

I propose that 1 Timothy 2:12 forbids false teaching by Paul's oppo-

---

[1]Karl H. Rengstorf, "διδάσκω, διδάσκαλος," *TDNT* 2:135, 147, 158.
[2]The major discussions through approximately A.D. 1400 may be found in Phrynichus (ed. G. Rutherford), nr. 96, p. 201; scholion on Thucydides 3.58.5; scholion on Euripides' *Andromache* 172; scholion on Aeschylus' *Eumenides* 42; Harpocration (ed. Bekker) 1.15.9; Alexander Rhetor (ed. Spengel), p. 2· Hesychius; Moeris; Thomas Magister (see also "Despoteia"); *Etymologicum Magnum;* Śuidas.

nents, just as do 1 Timothy 1:3-4 and Titus 1:10-14. My thesis is that
the first verb *didaskō* prohibits the erroneous teaching, whereas the
second verb *authenteō* represents either a ritual act or a doctrinal tenet
propounded by the heretical teachers who constitute a very great problem for the writer of the Pastorals. The verse may have been directed
against the promulgation of a proto-Gnostic type of cosmology.

The Religious Environs of Ephesus

Both Timothy and Titus were told to stop the false teachers, but in 1
Timothy 2:12, Paul himself prohibits the teaching by women. This interdiction occurs in a passage filled with directives in the first person
(1:12-18, 20; 2:1, 8) and may indicate that these problems and the need
for their resolution were especially acute. Gordon Fee has recently demonstrated that the Pastorals were written in large part to deal with those
who radically rejected orthodox doctrine.[3] The opponents were part of
the Christian community; otherwise, they could not have been expected
to heed the directives of Timothy and Titus. They had a Jewish background, albeit a deviant one (1 Tim 1:7; Tit 1:10, 14), but there must also
have been one or more distinctly non-Judaeo-Christian strands in the
eclectic movement that so exercised the apostle and troubled the
church at Ephesus.

The religious elements that existed in Ephesus and its environs may
have played a part in the heresy attacked in the Pastorals and specifically in the prohibition against women teaching. The history of Anatolia
(Asia Minor) and of Ephesus, including its religion, has excited little
interest in the English-speaking world. With the exception of a fine
numismatic monograph in 1945, 1908 saw the last publication of a
scholarly book in English dealing with the major local deity, Artemis of
Ephesus, and her great temple.[4]

---

[3]Gordon D. Fee, *1 and 2 Timothy, Titus: A Good News Commentary* (San Francisco: Harper
& Row, 1984), "Introduction," pp. xx-xxiii and throughout. See also Acts 20:17-31, esp.
29-30; 1 Cor 16:8-9; Eph 4:14; 5:6-12; Rev 2:6.
[4]Bluma Trell, *The Temple of Artemis at Ephesus: Numismatic Notes and Monographs*
(New York: The American Numismatic Society, 1945). D. C. Hogarth, *The Archaic Arte-
misia: Excavations at Ephesus* (London: British Museum, 1908) deals almost exclusively
with archaeology and art objects including treasure hordes. See too the forthcoming
volume edited by Martin Price, *The Archaic Temple of Artemis at Ephesus* (papers delivered at a colloquium held at the British Museum, March 1984) to be published by the

Before the advent of the Greeks to Ephesus about 1000 B.C., the site already had a well-established shrine to a mother-goddess and a sacred village built around it in typically Anatolian fashion.[5] Tradition held that the site had been dedicated to Artemis by the Amazons, those legendary female warriors who may have been a reality in one of the great migrations of grasslands peoples that swept the eastern Mediterranean world.[6] These Amazons were said to have dwelt at Ephesus along with Lydians, Carians and Lelegians.[7] From the beginning, women—especially those of nearby Lydia—were attached as priestesses to the Ephesian cult.[8] Strabo reported that virgins were compelled to minister along with the priests,[9] perhaps in the same manner as women were required to give themselves to ritual prostitution in other temples throughout Asia.[10]

The neighboring peoples, the Lycians, Carians and Phrygians were likewise prominent in the cult of the Ephesian Artemis. The ancient historian Herodotus believed that both the Lelegian Carians and the Lycians derived from Cretan stock, an observation borne out by linguistic similarities.[11] Like the Cretans, these peoples also venerated a pow-

---

British Museum. C. Picard, *Ephese et Claros, recherches sur les sanctuaires et les cultes de l'Ionie du Nord* (Paris: Thorin et Fontemoing, 1922) is still held to be the most complete discussion of the cult. An extremely helpful modern article is that of Richard Oster, "The Ephesian Artemis as an Opponent of Early Christianity," *Jahrbuch für Antike und Christentum,* Jahrgang 19 (1976): 24–44. Anton Bammer, *Das Heiligtum der Artemis von Ephesus* (Graz, Austria: Akademische Druck-u. Verlagsanstalt, 1984). Robert Fleischer, *Artemis von Ephesos und verwandte Kultstatuen aus Anatolien und Syrien,* Etudes Preliminaires aux religions orientales dans l'empire romain 35 (Leiden: Brill, 1973) provides extensive numismatic, archaeological and art historical evidence.

[5] W. M. Ramsay, *Cities and Bishoprics of Phrygia* (Oxford: Clarendon Press, 1895), p. 134; *Historical Geography of Asia Minor* (London: John Murray, 1890), p. 7.

[6] Callimachus *Hymn to Diana* 237.

[7] Pausanias 7.2.4.

[8] Aristophanes *Clouds* 599–600, *Lysistrata* 1310 ff.; Athenaeus 14.635–36.

[9] Strabo *Geography* 14.1.23. The term *virgin* appears to imply the absence of bonds to a husband rather than lack of sexual activity (W. K. C. Guthrie, *The Greeks and Their Gods* [Boston: Beacon Press, 1955], p. 102). While women were bound by obligations to a husband, they were forbidden entry to the Artemisium, the great temple of Artemis of Ephesus (Artemidorus of Ephesus *Oneirocr.*4.4). For a married woman who was considered a virgin during a period of cult prostitution, see Ramsay, *Cities,* 1:94 ff., 115.

[10] Herodotus 1.93.199; Athenaeus 12.11.a–b; Strabo *Geography* 11.14.16.

[11] Herodotus 1.171–73; Martin P. Nilsson, *A History of Greek Religion,* tr. F. J. Fielden, 2nd ed. (reprint, New York: W. W. Norton, 1964), p. 11.

erful female deity who elevated the status of women.[12] Artemis herself
was known as the "Cretan Lady of Ephesus,"[13] and was worshiped with
the same rites in Crete as in Ephesus.[14] This is significant for the Pastorals since the letters deal with similar religious problems in both Ephesus and Crete.

Before the Christian era, Cretans and Ephesians alike gave to Artemis
the Asian title Oupis, while the Lydians of Sardis invoked her as Artimuk
Ibsimsis (i.e., Ephesus) to guard their dead.[15] W. K. C. Guthrie viewed the
Ephesian Artemis as perpetuating the non-Greek character of the female
deity whose realm had included Greece, Crete and western Asia Minor
before the coming of the Indo-Europeans.[16] On the mainland of Greece,
the patriarchal religion of the invaders triumphed over the older matriarchal one; and Artemis, along with other mother-goddesses, fell to a position secondary to the Greek male gods. At Ephesus, however, she re-
tained her original nature as mother of all living things, closely associated
with the other great mother-goddesses of Anatolia. Her devotees believed
that from her all life began and to her all returned. Tombs were cut in the
shape of the womb and filled with images of the goddess.[17]

The Ephesian Artemis represents the most powerful expression of the
Great Mother, who took no second place to a male god. In the second
century A.D., Pausanias reported that there was a shrine to Artemis Ephe-
sia in every Greek city throughout the Mediterranean region and that in
private devotion she was the most worshiped of the gods.[18] Yet she never

[12]Plato *Protag.* 342E. See Mary May Downing, "Prehistoric Goddesses: The Cretan Challenge," *Journal of Feminist Studies in Religion* 1 (1985): 7-22.

[13]A. Boeckh, *Corpus Inscriptionùm Graecarum* (Berlin, 1828-1877), no. 6797.

[14]Diodorus of Sicily 5.77.3-8.

[15]Alexandros Aitolos (ed. Powell) *fragment* 4, 5; Callimachus *Hymn* 3.204; Macrobius *Saturnal.* 5.22.4-6; Picard, *Ephese et Claros,* pp. xvi-xvii, 364, 468-74; George Hanfmann, *Sardis from Prehistoric to Roman Times* (Cambridge: Harvard Univ. Press, 1983), pp. 51, 64-65; A. B. Cook, *Zeus: A Study in Ancient Religion* (reprint ed., New York: Biblio and Tannen, 1964), 2:1228.

[16]Guthrie, *The Greeks and Their Gods,* pp. 99-106. For the conflict of matriarchal and patriarchal religion, see Jane Ellen Harrison, *Themis: A Study of the Social Origins of Greek Religion,* 2nd ed. (reprint, Hyde Park, N.Y.: University Books, 1966), pp. 498-506. See also Pausanias 4.32.6.

[17]Maarten J. Vermaseren, *Attis and Cybele,* tr. M. H. Lemmers (London: Thames and Hudson, 1977), pp. 15-16; James Mellaart, *Catal Huyuk, A Neolithic Town in Anatolia* (New York: McGraw-Hill, 1967).

[18]Pausanias 4.31.8.

surrendered her Asian character to that of her Greek manifestation as virgin huntress.[19] The Ephesian goddess was at home not on Mount Olympus among the Greek gods, but on the mountains of Asia Minor.

The Meaning of Authenteō

If the religious environment surrounding 1 Timothy 2 is important, so is the language. Authenteō, translated "to usurp authority" in the King James Version, is a Greek verb so rare that it appears nowhere else in the entire New Testament. The concept of ruling or exercising authority over another occurs frequently in the New Testament, but always with other words. The French etymologist Pierre Chantraine suggested that authentēs, the noun from which the verb authenteō is derived, had essentially the significance of the person beginning or being responsible (aitios) for an action, situation or state. From this stemmed two other basic meanings, namely, to be in charge or rule over something and to be ultimately responsible for a terrible crime, usually murder.[20] In this way, Chantraine resolved an etymological problem that had perplexed scholars since late antiquity. How could the same word denote both murderer and ruler? In the earliest usages, the concept of murder was almost always involved. The concept of ruling came later. For the verb

---

[19]For ancient commentaries on the dichotomy, see Minucius Felix Octavius 21.225 [Ante-Nicene Fathers, p. 185]; St. Jerome Commentary on St. Paul's Epistle to the Ephesians 26.441.

[20]"Nous admettons donc: . . . que le sens originel est 'celui qui accomplit un acte, qui en est l'auteur, que est responsable,' d'ou l'emploi pour designer un chef; que le sens de 'meurtrier' est issu du premier. . . . Le seul moyen de couvrir, comme il est necessaire, les emplois franchement differents de authentes est de marquer que ce terme exprime la responsabilité du sujet dans l'accomplissement d'un acte ou d'une fonction" (Pierre Chantraine, "Encore Authentes," Aphieroma ste mneme tou M. Triantaphyllidis [Salonica, 1960], pp. 89, 93. George W. Knight III ("Authenteō in Reference to Women in 1 Timothy 2.12," New Testament Studies 30 [January 1984]: 143–57) does not appear to be familiar with this article but relies heavily on Paul Kretschmer, "Authentes," Glotta 3 (1912) 289–93. For other discussions in this century, see Louis Gernet, "Authentes," Revue des Etudes Grecques 22 (1909): 13–32; M. Psichari, "Efendi," in Melanges de philologie et de linguistique offerts a M. L-Havet (Paris: Hachette, 1908); A Dihle, "Authentes," Glotta 39 (1960): 77–83; A. J. Festugiere, La Revelation d'Hermes Trisgimeste, 4 vols. (Paris: Lecoffre, 1953), 3:1677 n. 4; Bentley Layton, "The Hypostasis of the Archons," Harvard Theological Review 69 (1976): 71 n. 158; Walter Scott, Hermetica (Oxford, 1925) 2:17–18, 68 n. 30; A. D. Nock, Corpus Hermeticum 1.2, 13.15 note; Fredrich Zucker, "Authentes und Ableitungen," Sitzungsberichte der Sachsischen Akademie der Wissenschaften zu Leipzig, Philologisch-historische Klasse, Band 107, Heft 4 (1962): 3–26.

authenteō, there is only one attested use in the sense of "to murder."

Let us turn to the value that Chantraine held to be most basic, that of originating something or being responsible for it. By the New Testament era, *authentēs* was already being used to denote an originator or instigator.[21] The related adjective, *authentikos,* like the English "authentic," implies something original or genuine. In the sense "to begin something, to take the initiative, or to be primarily responsible for it," the verb *authenteō* is even used by the early church fathers for the creative activities of God.[22] John Chrysostom (late fourth century) discusses the replacement of Judas in the book of Acts and writes, *"Protos tou pragmatos authentei"* ("He was primarily responsible for the matter").[23] In a discussion of lapsed brethren, Athanasius (mid-fourth century) suggests leniency for those who defected under compulsion but had not themselves instigated *(authenteō)* the problem: *"Tois de mē authentousi mēn tēs asebeias parasyreisi de di'ananken kai bian."*[24]

Authenteō, as well as the related *authentizō,* could also mean "to take a matter or inheritance into one's own hands."[25] It was equated with *autodikein* ("to have one's own law courts or to take the law into one's own hands").[26] For example, a bishop was asked to take a difficult marital situation in hand, and the pope to take a matter under his jurisdiction.[27] In the sixth century, Lydus used the verb in the sense of taking the initiative, in a manner that combined the concepts both of starting something and of having the authority to do so.[28]

In the late Renaissance, an era when scholars studied classical texts more thoroughly than is customary today and had materials to which we no longer have access, another definition was cited by lexicog-

---

[21]Josephus *Wars* 1.582; Polybius 12.14.3; 22.14.2; Diodorus of Sicily 16.61. "*Authentes* implique ici une nuance de pure responsabilite, d'auteur responsable" (Psichari, "Efendi," p. 426).

[22]Eusebius *de ecclesiastica theologia* 3.5; J. P. Migne, *Patrologia Graeca* (Paris, 1857–66), 24:1013A; Dihle, "Authentes," pp. 82 n. 2, 83 n. 1.

[23]John Chrysostom *Homily* 3.3 on Acts (ed. Montfaucon 9.26D).

[24]Athanasius *Epistle to Rufinus* (ed. Migne 26.1180C).

[25]*Berliner griechische Urkunden (Aegyptische Urkunden aus den königlichen Museen zu Berlin),* vol. 1 (1895), no. 103.3, 8 (p. 122).

[26]Thomas Magister (ed. Ritschl) 18.8; Moeris (ed. Piers), p. 58.

[27]*Berliner griechische Urkunden* 103; Basil *Epistle* 69.4.389A.

[28]Johannes Laurentius Lydus, *de Magistratibus populi Romani,* ed. R. Wuensch (Leipzig: Teubner, 1903), 3:131.

raphers: *praebeo me auctorem* ("to declare oneself the author or source of anything"). *Authenteō*, when used with the genitive, as it is in 1 Timothy 2:12, could imply not only to claim sovereignty but also to claim authorship. "To represent oneself as the author, originator, or source of something" was given in various older dictionaries that I have been able to consult, such as the widely used work of Cornelis Schrevel and the still-fundamental *Thesaurus Linguae Graecae* by Stephanus.[29] The earliest of these entries date back to the Renaissance, the latest to the last century. This value disappeared from classical dictionaries about the time when the translation of 1 Timothy 2:12 was being challenged by feminists.[30]

The differentiation between being an originator and professing to be one is a valid point. In several texts, the meaning is strengthened by the sense of asserting oneself to be the author or source of something. For instance, Saint Basil was in anguish because the rumor had gone out that he had anathematized his old friend Dianius. Where was he supposed to have proclaimed the anathema? he asked. In whose presence? Was he merely following someone else's lead, or did he himself instigate the outrage or even profess himself *(authentōn)* to be its author *(katar-*

---

[29]George Dunbar, *A Greek-English Lexicon,* 3rd ed. (Edinburgh: MacLachian and Stewart, 1850); Benjamin Hederich, *Graecum Lexicon Manuale* (London: Wilks and Taylor, 1803); T. Morrell, *Lexicon Graeco-Prosodiacum* (Cambridge: J. Smith, 1815); John Pickering, *Greek Lexicon* (Boston: Wilkins, Carter and Co., 1847); Johann Scapula (fl. 1580), *Lexicon Graeco-Latinum* (Oxford: Clarendon Press, 1653); Cornelis Schrevel, *Lexicon Manuale Graeco-Latinum et Latino-Graecum* (Edinburgh: Bell and Bradfute, 1823); *The Greek Lexicon of Schrevelius Translated into English with Many Additions* (Boston: Cummings, Hilliard and Co., 1826); Stephanus, *Thesaurus Graecae Linguae,* ed. Dindorf (Paris: Didot, 1831-65).

[30]By the midnineteenth century, feminists were raising questions as to the meanings of certain words in the text of 1 Tim 2:12 and as to other possible interpretations. In 1849 Charlotte Brontë had one of her heroines discuss the words of Saint Paul in this passage: "I account for them in this way: he wrote that chapter for a particular congregation of Christians, under peculiar circumstances; and besides, I dare say, if I could read the original Greek, I should find that many of the words have been wrongly translated, perhaps misapprehended altogether. It would be possible, I doubt not, with a little ingenuity, to give the passage quite a contrary turn: to make it say, 'Let the woman speak out whenever she sees fit to make an objection;'—'it is permitted to a woman to teach and to exercise authority as much as may be. Man, meantime, cannot do better than hold his peace,' and so on" (Charlotte Brontë, *Shirley* (1849, reprint ed., London: Thornton, 1899), 2:17. It is after the appearance of well-articulated arguments such as this that the definition disappears from standard lexical works. I am indebted to Joyce Penniston for calling this work of Brontë to my attention.

chōn kai authentōn tou tolmētos)?[31] *Authentōn* is the climax of this carefully constructed progression. It moves from a passive role to an active one and then to claiming responsibility for that role of instigator. Constantine's Edict speaks of God who proclaims himself to be the author of judgment *(tēs de kriseos authentei ho hypsistos theos).*[32] Leo wrote to Pulcheria of Eutychus, the self-avowed author *(authentountos)* of the dissension in the church at Constantinople.[33]

Thus there is support for *authenteō* as meaning "to proclaim oneself the author or originator of something." If we apply this meaning of *authenteō* to 1 Timothy 2:12, we would have "I do not allow a woman to teach nor to represent herself as the originator or source of man." This then might be a prohibition against a woman teaching a mythology similar to that of the Gnostics in which Eve predated Adam and was his creator. Certain Gnostic myths also included the notion that Adam, who had been deluded, was liberated by the Gnosis of his more enlightened spouse.

Eve and Questions of Origin

The question of origins and first causes was a lively one throughout the ancient world, and the false teachers of the Pastorals were deeply involved in a divisive controversy over genealogies (Tit 3:9).

Who we were and whence we came. . . .

Where we have been cast. . . .

What is generation and what regeneration . . .[34]

were concerns not only of the Gnostic but of other philosophic systems as well. Prominent in such thinking was the "feminine spiritual principle," as Plato called it.[35] The goddess Isis was represented as proclaiming herself "the one who was in the beginning, the one who first came into existence on earth." "I am all that has been and is and will be, and my robe no mortal has yet uncovered."[36] She was said to have generated a

---

[31]Basil *Epistle* 51.1.

[32]Eusebius *Vita Constantini* 2.48.

[33]Leo the Great *Epistle* 30.1.

[34]Clement of Alexandria *Excerpta ex Theodoto* 78.2. These excerpts are identified as being from the Anatolian branch of Valentinianism.

[35]Plato *Timaeus* 49A, 51A; Plutarch *Moralia* 372B, 1014D, 1015D, 1023A. See J. Gwyn Griffiths, *Plutarch's de Iside et Osiride: Introduction, Translation and Commentary* (Cardiff: University of Wales Press, 1970), pp. 58, 502ff.

[36]Plutarch's *Moralia* 354C, 376B; see also Proclus, *In Platonis Timaeum Comentarii*, ed. Diehl (Leipzig: Teubner, 1903) 1:98, and Griffiths, *Plutarch's de Iside*, pp. 283ff., 521ff.

son without male assistance and declared, "I have played the part of a man though I am a woman."[37] Plutarch, who began his writing career about A.D. 55, was deeply devoted to Isis. Yet he repudiated the belief held by others that the seed of woman was "power and primal cause."[38]

The concept of woman and her seed as first cause was in harmony with the religious views of Asia Minor and especially of Ephesus, where the maternal principle reigned supreme. W. M. Ramsay maintained that it was not by accident that the Virgin Mary was declared *Theotokos* ("bearer of God") at Ephesus, where Artemis had herself borne the same title.[39] Other Anatolian mother-goddesses had no husbands but did possess weak, young and rather effeminate consorts, often sons whom they themselves generated without the assistance of male procreational activity.[40] Artemis, the Ephesian goddess, although teeming with fertility, was viewed by her devotees as a virgin and unbound to a male.[41]

Probably the rationale for this belief stemmed from a time when the

---

[37]W. Spiegelberg, "Eine Neue Legende über die Geburt des Horaz," *Zeitschrift für ägyptische Sprache und Altertumskunde* 53 (1917): 94–97.

[38]Plutarch *Moralia* 374F; for other views on female seed see 651C, 905B–C. Plutarch called upon his reader to embrace his own view that the seed of a woman "is not a power or an origin" (*Moralia* 374F). With Plato he opined that the female spiritual principle was the nurse and receptacle of that which was supplied by the male, and that the masculine philosophic, religious and even mathematical principle was always dominant over the feminine (Plutarch *Moralia* 372E–373B, 374, 378A–B). Like Diodorus of Sicily (1.80.3–4), he cited the Egyptian belief that the seed of a woman was merely hylic and nutritive in generation *(hylēn de kai trophen geneseō)* rather than being of itself a power or an origin *(dynamin oud' archen)*. Both the vocabulary and the debate begin to have Gnostic overtones. Compare this with the Naasenes' "placing the originative nature of the universe in causative seed" (Hippolytus *Refutation of Heresies* 5.1 [*Ante-Nicene Fathers* 5:50]). The Marcosian formula ran: "I am a vessel more precious than the female who formed you. If your mother is ignorant of her own descent, I know myself and am aware whence I am, and I call upon the incorruptible Sophia who is in the Father, and is the mother of your mother, who has no father, nor any male consort; but a female springing from a female formed you, while ignorant of her own mother, and imagining that she alone existed; but I call upon her mother" (Irenaeus *Against Heresies* 1.21.5 [*Ante-Nicene Fathers* 1.346]).

[39]W. M. Ramsay, *Pauline and Other Studies* (London: Hodder and Stoughton, 1906), pp. 125–59.

[40]For parthenogenic activity of goddesses, see Pausanias 7.17.4–5; B. H. Legge, *Forerunners and Rivals of Christianity* (Cambridge: At the University Press, 1915), pp. 40, 46; Ramsay, *Cities*, 1:9; compare with Irenaeus *Against Heresies* 1.28.227–28.

[41]Achilles Tatius 6.21 [Loeb Classical Library, p. 345]. For another cult associated with the Amazons, in which the name of the sexual partner of a mother goddess was revealed only in the mysteries, see Diodorus of Sicily 3.55.9.

masculine role in generation was not understood, and the Great Mother was considered the all-sufficient source of life and being. A male was apparently not thought necessary for the mighty Artemis, whose cult had been founded by the male-rejecting Amazons. This power was not confined to deity alone. Among the Lycian worshipers of Artemis, the generative role of the male was held to be unimportant. Descent was claimed only through the mother, and a man might even hold the rank of senator without knowing his own paternity.[42] The genealogy of the mother provided his rank, and she was the author of his existence.

In Gnostic cosmologies, female activity was often responsible for the creation of the material universe, and Eve was a potent force. She was said to possess the ability to procreate without male assistance: "Eve is the first virgin, who gave birth without a man. She is the one who played her own doctor."[43] Among the Powers and Archons, strange celestial beings who filled the Gnostic world, Eve found a place. She was identified both as a Power and as the daughter of a Power.[44] As such, she was said to have pre-existed Adam and gained a knowledge that she would later impart to him.[45] In one account, she was the hermaphrodite from whose side man was formed.[46]

---

[42]Herodotus 1.173-74; Herakleides Ponticus *Pol. 15* [*Fragmenta Historicorum Graecorum*, ed. Muller 2:217]; Nicholas of Damascus [*Frag. Hist. Gr.*, 3:461]; Plutarch *mul. virt.* 248D; Aristotle *Pol.* 2.6.4 (1269 b 24); Simon Pembroke, "Women in Charge: The Ancient Idea of Matriarchy," *Journal of the Wartburg and Courtauld Institutes* 1, no. 30 (1967), pp. 1-35. On many Lycian tombstones the name of the mother replaces that of the father, and sometimes there is the added notation, "Father unknown" (Ramsay, *Cities*, p. 66, inscription no. 21). See also G. Doublet, "Fragment d'un sénatus-consulte de Tabae en Carie," *Bulletin de correspondance Hellenique* 13 (1889): 504 and G. Cousin, "Les Inscriptions d'Oenoanda," *Bulletin de correspondance Hellenique* 16 (1892): 1-70. For an opposing view, see Simon Pembroke, "Last of the Matriarchs," *Journal of Economic and Social History of the Orient* 8, no. 3 (1965), pp. 217-47.

[43]*On the Origin of the World* 114.4-5, trans. Rose Horman Arthur, *The Wisdom Goddess: Feminine Motifs in Eight Nag Hammadi Documents* (Lanham, Md.: University Press of America, 1984), p. 131.

[44]*On the Origin of the World* (II, 5) 115.32, 116.26.

[45]*The Apocalypse of Adam* (v, 5) 64.12-13.

[46]"Now the begetting of the Instructor (the Serpent) came to pass in this way. When Sophia had cast forth a drop of light, it floated upon the water. Immediately the Man was manifest, being an androgyne. That drop took its first form as a feminine body. Afterwards, she (Eve) took her bodily form in the image of the Mother (Sophia) which has been revealed. She (Eve) was completed in twelve months. An androgyne (Eve) was born, whom the Greeks call 'Hermaphrodite.' But its mother (Sophia) in Hebrew called her (Eve) 'the Living-Eva,' that is,

In other accounts, Eve was involved in the creation activities of John 1:1-3 and became mother of everything in the world.[47] Valentinus (second century B.C.) called her "the great creative power from whom all living things originate."[48] In the tradition of the great mother-goddesses who preceded her, her maternity extended to both gods and men. Seduced by Yaldabaoth, she gave birth to Jave and Elohim—all three, names for the deity of the Old Testament.[49] Quite naturally, then, she was credited with the creation of Adam and the bestowal on him of the gift of life. "Sophia sent Zoe, her daughter, who is called 'Eve (of life),' as an instructor to raise up Adam, in whom there was no soul, so that those whom he would beget might become vessels of the light. [When] Eve saw her co-likeness cast down, she pitied him, and she said 'Adam, live! Rise up upon the earth!' Immediately her word became a deed. For when Adam rose up, immediately he opened his eyes. When he saw her, he said, 'You will be called "the mother of the living" because you are the one who gave me life.' "[50] The extant text of *On the Origin of the World,* from which some of this material is taken, dates back to the fourth century A.D. It demonstrates the presence of motifs that must have had an earlier stage of development. Irenaeus, a native of Asia Minor, appears to have known a similar text when he composed his treatise *Against Heresies* in A.D. 180.

It cannot be established for certain that the false teachers in the Pastorals possessed a full-blown system of Gnostic theology, though it is not impossible. Quispel is now of the opinion that Gnosticism arose in the second century B.C. at Alexandria as rebellious Jews circulated myths which stood in direct opposition to the biblical accounts. By the late first century, Cerinthus had brought a form of Gnosticism to Ephesus. He was steeped in Egyptian lore and named the chief deity Authen-

---

'the instructoress of Life.' And her (Eve's) son is the begotten one (Seth) who is the lord. Afterwards, the Authorities called him 'the Beast' in order to deceive their creatures. The interpreting of 'the Beast' is 'instructor' for they found that he (the Serpent) was wiser than all of them" (*On the Origin of the World* 113.21-114.4 [Arthur, p. 117]).

[47]Hippolytus *Refutation of Heresies* 16.6.12-13.

[48]Irenaeus *Against Heresies* 1.18.1. See also 1.2.2-3, 2.29.3.

[49]*The Apocryphon of John* (II, 1) 24:1-25.

[50]*On the Origin of the World* (II, 5) 115.31-116.8, translated in James M. Robinson, ed., *The Nag Hammadi Library* (San Francisco: Harper and Row, 1977), p. 172. For a similar account, see *The Hypostasis of the Archons* (II, 4) 89.11-16.

tia, an appellation also used very early by Satornilus and other Gnostics.[51] This name was based on the same root as *authenteō*, the verb
in 1 Timothy 2:12 that is customarily translated "to exercise authority."

In the Pastorals, there is certainly a complicated mythology with a
Jewish background and some highly controversial genealogies (1 Tim
1:7; Tit 1:10–14). The question of origins, who had issued from whom,
was a topic of heated debate (Tit 3:9). In a Jewish genealogy, Adam and
Eve would hold a place; and Eve as source of Adam could not fail to
be an inflammatory topic.

The theological system of the Ephesian opponents included direct
contradictions to the orthodox Scriptures and is termed "oppositions of
falsely called Gnosis" (1 Tim 6:20). Gnosticism was indeed a "religion of
rebellion." The phrase "not the way Moses said" runs as a recurring
theme through the *Apocryphon of John*.[52] The message of 2 Timothy
3:8–9 specifically connects the heretics to those who opposed Moses.
One Gnostic account tells how the evil celestial beings known as Archons conspired to trick Adam and Eve into believing that she had
actually issued from his side. The Genesis version of the story was
construed as a deliberate ruse to place Eve at a disadvantage.[53] This
rendering stands in the Gnostic tradition, for one hallmark of all true
Gnostics was their interpretation of the Old Testament in an antibiblical
sense.[54]

In the Pastorals, there are two direct commands to stop the false
teaching: one in 1 Timothy 1:3–4 and the other in Titus 1:14. Paul bade
Timothy to stop not only the heterodoxy but also the genealogical controversy and the preoccupation with myths. He told Titus that the opponents must be silenced and that he should rebuke them so sharply
that they would desist from their promulgation of Jewish myths (Tit 1:11,
13–14). Both commands denounce myths. The writer complains that

---

[51]Hippolytus *Refutation of Heresies* 7.1, 21, 23; 10.17; Epiphanius *Panarion* 38; Irenaeus
1.31.1. See also the note by Walter Scott, *Hermetica* (Oxford: Clarendon Press, 1925),
2:17ff.
[52]*The Apocryphon of John* (II, 1) 13.19–20, 22.22–23, 23.3, 29.6.
[53]"Let us bring a stupor upon him [Adam], and let us teach him in his sleep as though
she came into being from his rib so that the woman will serve and he will rule over her"
(*On the Origin of the World* (II, 5) 116.21–25 [Robinson, p. 173]).
[54]Jean Doresse, "Nouveaux appercus historiques sur les Gnostiques Coptes; Ophites et
Sethiens," *Bulletin de l'Institut d'Egypte* 31 (1948/49): 411.

some individuals are turning away from the truth and devoting themselves instead to myths apparently containing distortions of the truth (2 Tim 4:4). Moreover, 1 Timothy 4:1-7 not only represents these myths as part of the doctrine of demons but specifies that they were opposed to God and perpetrated by old women (v. 7). Younger widows were going about saying what they ought not to say, just as the opponents in Titus taught what they ought not to teach.[55] In view of the known involvement of women in the opposition (see 1 Tim 4:8; 5:11-15; 2 Tim 3:6-7). I suggest that 1 Timothy 2:12 prohibits false teaching and the propagation of a feminine genealogical myth in which woman was originator of man.

The passage, 1 Timothy 2:11-12, begins and ends with an appeal for women to learn from the Word of God. The phrase "silence and submission" was used in the Near East to indicate a readiness to do God's will.[56] Thus, in 1 Timothy 2:11, women were asked to learn with an attitude of receptivity and, at the end of verse 12, to be in harmony rather than on a collision course with the truth of the Word. If my theory is correct, verses 13 and 14 supply the reason for the prohibition: its nonconformity to the Genesis account. Verses 13 and 14 also refute a myth that directly contradicted a biblical account.

These verses emphasize the absolute deception of Eve and repudiate her disobedience to God's will. Gnostic lore pictured Eve as instructor of Adam and mediator of the knowledge, or *gnosis,* brought by the serpent. Among second-century heretics, the message of Eve was prized as a divine revelation. The tenet of second-century Montanist female leaders—that it was a great honor for Eve to be the first to taste of the tree of wise understanding and that female bishops and elders should be ordained "because of Eve"—demonstrates the strength of the tradition in Asia Minor quite apart from Gnosticism.[57] Legge finds evidence that the Adam and Eve stories already circulating in the area were adapted in one form by the Ophites and in another by the Manicheans.[58]

---

[55] 1 Tim 5:13, Tit 1:11. In each case, the teaching is being carried to private households, as in 2 Tim 3:6-7.

[56] James B. Pritchard, ed., *Ancient Near Eastern Texts Relating to the Old Testament* (Princeton: Princeton University Press, 1950), p. 379.

[57] Epiphanius *Panarion* 49.

[58] Legge, *Forerunners and Rivals of Christianity,* pp. 299-300.

The Roman satirist Juvenal, about A.D. 112, wrote a description that had no apparent ties to Gnosticism. He portrays in his sixth satire an aged Jewess who will for a price divulge the secrets of Jerusalem. She is the interpreter of Jewish law, "mediator of highest heaven" and "high priestess of the tree."[59] The tree must be that of knowledge, a knowledge conveyed to the world through the serpent and a woman. The theological viewpoint she represents has marked similarities both to the opponents of the Pastorals and to later Gnostics. Her claim of mediatorship may be related to Paul's insistence in 1 Timothy 2:8 on the one mediator between God and man. Phrygian and Gnostic cosmology alike postulated an enormous series of intermediaries.[60] Female figures often served as mediators of Gnostic truth: Norea, Mariamme, Philoumene, Mary of Bethany, Sophia, Sige and Eve. Of Helena it was said that her revelation passed from one feminine body to another.[61]

The Serpent and Gnostic Myths

The role of the serpent was pivotal in Ophitism. Both Hebrew and Gnostic writers created a play on the words for serpent, Eve and instructor. Eve became the instructor of Adam—among the Hebrews for ill, among the Gnostics to disabuse Adam of the deliberate deceptions that the malignant Archons had foisted upon him. Coached by the Archons, Adam viewed the malevolent and stupid Yaldabaoth as supreme ruler until he was enlightened at the advent of the beneficent serpent. Only then did he understand that his ultimate source lay in a supreme being far higher than Yaldabaoth and that to this superior deity his soul-particles must ultimately rise.[62]

In contrast to these Gnostic ideas 1 Timothy 2:14 insists that Adam was not deceived but that Eve who listened to the serpent was utterly deceived. In addition, 2 Corinthians 11:3 uses the very same terminology

---

[59]Juvenal *Satires* 6.540-47.

[60]Plutarch *Moralia* 415A-B.

[61]Irenaeus 1.23.2. For resentment of woman as preferred recipient of Gnosis, see *Pistis Sophia* 1.57; *Gospel of Mary* (Berlin Gnostic Codex 8502, *1*) 18.10-16, 10.1-3). Celsus wrote of "Marcellians who follow Marcellina, and Harpocratians who follow Salome, and others who follow Mariamme, and others who follow Martha" (Origen *Against Celsus* 5.62 [Ante-Nicene Fathers, 4:570]).

[62]*On the Origin of the World* (II, *5*) 103.11-21; Irenaeus 1.30.6-9; *Apocryphon of John* (II, *1*) 20.15—22.10.

of Eve, *exapatao* ("she was completely deceived") and mentions the *ophis,* the snake, as the agent of deception. This is part of Paul's warning about false apostles who bring another gospel and may lead the Corinthians astray as the serpent did Eve. Like the opponents of the Pastorals, the false apostles have a Jewish background (2 Cor 11:22). These false apostles are ministers of Satan, who can still transform himself into a messenger of Gnosis and light (2 Cor 11:13-15). This clearly refers to the Garden of Eden story, but it also warns the readers against receiving the still-seductive message.

Although the Pastorals speak repeatedly of myths, only one other Old Testament story besides that of Adam and Eve is mentioned. Serpents figure prominently in the second story also. Jannes and Jambres, the traditional names given to the Pharaoh's magicians, opposed the truth of Moses' message by their necromancy with snakes (Ex 7:11-12). They are likened to the opponents who are endangering the church (2 Tim 3:8-9).

This may suggest that the heresy of the Pastoral Epistles involved a veneration of Satan as serpent. The younger widows, presumably part of the opposition, have gone astray after Satan (1 Tim 5:15); these heretics are said to be caught in the devil's snare (2 Tim 2:26). There are doctrines of demons (1 Tim 4:1), and two of the heretics, Hymenaeus and Alexander, have been consigned to Satan for a course of instruction (1 Tim 1:20).

Like the Pastorals, Revelation tells of a blending of Jewish and heretical elements and speaks of "synagogues of Satan" at Smyrna and Philadelphia (Rev 2:9; 3:9). Pergamum, the chief cult center in Asia Minor for the serpent-god Asclepius, is designated as the location of Satan's seat (Rev 2:13). Jezebel, the false prophetess at Thyatira, teaches the "deep things of Satan" (Rev 2:13, 20, 24; note also two references to "that old serpent called the Devil," Rev 12:9; 20:2). These may be indications of an Ophitic type of theology, in which the snake *(ophis)* was worshiped as bringer of knowledge.

The church fathers, for what their testimony may be worth, identified these heretical Nicolaitans of the Apocalypse as the original Ophites. The apocryphal Acts of Phillip tells of the worship of Satan as Echidna, or viper, at Hierapolis. Filaster, writing about A.D. 380, held that Ophitism existed before the advent of Christ and was a precursor to other types of Gnosticism.[63]

Ophite Gnosticism, especially the Naasene variety, (from *naas,* Hebrew for "snake") appears to have arisen in western Asia Minor, where Ephesus was located. This area remained a stronghold of Ophitism until at least the fifth century. Large colonies of Jews had lived there and enjoyed royal favor. About 200 B.C., Antiochus the Great brought in 2,000 Jewish families from Babylonia and resettled them in Lydia and Phrygia. Phrygian Jews were so noted for their easy assimilation of alien culture and religion that Judaism came to call them "the Ten Tribes." Like the original ten tribes, they failed in large part to maintain their identity. One prominent Jewess, Julia Severa, served as high priestess in the imperial cult, and her case was not unique. The Talmud lamented, "The baths and wines of Phrygia separated the Ten Tribes from their brethren."[64]

Coins minted in Apameia, a Phrygian city that boasted a strong Jewish population, demonstrate Jewish influence on local religion, for on some coins people stand in a boxlike ark that bears the inscription "Noah." Outside stand two more people, who may represent elements of a non-Jewish flood story, such as that of Deucalion and Pyrrha. Other coins reveal snakes emerging from the sacred basket of the mystery religions. On the reverse side, serpents are intertwined in a mystic pattern. Yet other coins from Apameia show Artemis of Ephesus.[65] These coins, dating from the second century B.C. to the third century A.D., represent the diverse religious elements that existed side by side in Asia Minor.

To some scholars, the fusion of Phrygian Judaism and indigenous elements appears to have produced the religious phenomenon known as Ophitism. A basic ingredient of the Naasene cult, along with Jewish ele-

---

[63]Filaster *de Haer* .1.1.

[64]Ramsay, *Cities,* 2:674; Legge, *Forerunners and Rivals of Christianity,* pp. 32–33; Franz Cumont, *The Oriental Religions in Roman Paganism* (New York: Dover Publications, 1956), pp. 62–66; Alfred T. Kraabel, "Judaism in Asia Minor," (Th.D. Dissertation, Harvard Divinity School, 1968).

[65]For the Noah coins, see *British Museum Catalogue of the Coins of Phrygia,* plate 1: Apameia, and Sammlung v. Aulock, *Sylloge Nummorum Graecorum Deutschland* (Berlin, 1962): Phrygien, Heft. 9, nos. 3506, 3510, 3513, plate 114 [these coins date from A.D. 222–253 and bear the names of three different rulers]. For the coins with snakes, see Aulock, *Sylloge,* Heft. 9, nos. 3448–64, plate 112 [these coins date from 189 B.C.—133 B.C.]. For the coins with Artemis of Ephesus, see Aulock, *Sylloge,* Heft. 9, no. 3502, plate 114 [these coins date ca. A.D. 200].

ments and a veneration of the serpent, was participation in the Phrygian mysteries of the Great Mother.[66] The fourth-century B.C. playwright Menander complained that the priests of the Phrygian Mother went about with an old woman and sneaked into private houses.[67] The description in 2 Timothy 3:6-7 of the false teachers who sneak into private houses appears to be an echo of Menander and suggests an involvement with the Phrygian mysteries. Significantly, the same 2 Timothy passage speaks next of the Egyptian snake-magicians, Jannes and Jambres.

According to Hippolytus (ca. A.D. 200), the Naasene sect drew not only on the Phrygian mysteries but also on the Egyptian mysteries of Isis.[68] Ephesus, where Egyptian elements so profoundly influenced the religion, may have been one of the locations where this fusion took place.[69] Isis, a goddess who bore the uraeus serpent as her symbol, was equated with both the Phrygian deity and Artemis of Ephesus.[70] Isis was closely associated in Gnostic literature with Eve.[71] Even the Jewish tractate *Against Idolatry* especially forbade the representation of Isis as nursing goddess because it symbolized Eve as nurse of the whole world.[72]

There is considerable art-historic evidence of pre-Ophitic elements. Snake veneration was well established in Asia Minor, as it was throughout the Greco-Roman world, and of powerful female figures there is no dearth. Goddesses holding snakes are a commonplace of ancient Cretan religion, too, and Pausanias (A.D. 150) tells of an image of Artemis with two snakes, which was reminiscent of Crete.[73] Artifacts show a golden

---

[66]Hippolytus *Refutation of Heresies* 5.2-4, 15.

[67]Menander *The Charioteer*, fr. 202 (Koch). This fragment was apparently popular because it was familiar to at least two of the Church Fathers. Quoted by Clement of Alexander, *Advice to the Heathen* 7, and by Justin Martyr, *On the Sole Government of God* 5.

[68]Hippolytus *Refutation of Heresies* 5.2.

[69]For the pervasive influence of Egyptian religion on Ephesus, see Gunter Holbl, *Zeugnisse Aegyptischer Religionsvorstellungen für Ephesus* (Leiden: Brill, 1978).

[70]Apuleius *The Golden Ass* 2.11.5, 2.14.5; Macrobius *Saturn* 1.20.18; R. E. Witt, *Isis in the Graeco-Roman World* (Ithaca, N.Y.: Cornell University Press, 1971), pp. 149-50.

[71]Michel Tardieu, *Trois Mythes Gnostiques* (Paris: Etudes Augustiniennes, 1974), pp. 113-15. Arthur, *Wisdom Goddess,* pp. 157-64. "The assimilation of Isis material within an account of Eve is a remarkable instance of the interweaving of Egyptian and Jewish material" (Arthur, *Wisdom Goddess,* p. 116).

[72]*Abodah Zarah* (On Idolatry) 43a.

[73]This he saw at Damophon in Arcadia (Pausanias 8.37). In Lydian Meonia, near Ephesus, there was an Artemis with seven snakes (Jacques Bonnet, *Artemis d'Ephese et la Legende des Septs Dormants* [Paris: Geuthner, 1977], p. 33.

snake that was offered to Artemis of Ephesus before 500 B.C.[74] Amulets, with snakes and Hebrew lettering, indicate that in the following centuries superstitious folk with Jewish leanings attached a positive value to the serpent.[75]

In 1980, a coiled bronze snake was excavated at Ephesus from the same house as were busts of Livia and Tiberius, whose reign coincides with the life of Jesus.[76] The snake may be the serpent-god Asclepius or another god derived from him, Glycon.[77] Although the main shrine was at nearby Pergamum, identified in the book of Revelation as "the place where Satan dwells," the Asclepius cult was also very active at Ephesus.[78] In an area already influenced by Judaism and given to serpent veneration, Satan's snake manifestation as bringer of knowledge *(gnosis)* can scarcely have been ignored.

Conclusion

It is not possible to pinpoint the Ephesian position along the trajectory of nascent Ophitism. My theory does not necessarily postulate an elaborate Gnostic system of the type that had developed by the second century. Nevertheless, I maintain that in the apparent cradle of Ophitism there were already strong Ophitic tendencies at the time of the composition of the Pastorals, whether one adopts an early or a late dating. The presence of Christian female teachers, not necessarily orthodox ones, is attested very early in Asia Minor, both in and out of Scriptures.[79]

[74]Hogarth, *Archaic Artemesia*, pp. 115, 165, 236, 337, plate 7 no. 16, plate 27 no. 6. See also "Artemis, le Serpent et l'Abeille," in Bonnet, *Artemis*, pp. 33-35.

[75]E. R. Goodenough, *Jewish Symbols in the Greco-Roman Period*, Bollingen series (New York: Pantheon Books, 1965), 2:290ff., 3:958-60.

[76]Machteld J. Mellink, "Archaeology in Asia Minor," *American Journal of Archaeology* 86 (1982): 569. See also the report of H. Vetters in *Anzeiger der Akademie der Wissenschaften* 118 (1981): 137-60.

[77]The development of the cult of Glycon is the subject of Lucian's *The False Prophet*. See also M. Louis Robert, "Le Serpent Glycon d'Abonouteichus à Athenes et Artemis d'Ephese à Rome," *Comptes Rendus de l'Academie des Inscriptions et Belles Lettres* (July-October 1981), pp. 513-35.

[78]*Forschungen in Ephesos* 2:22, 30B. See also Oster, *Artemis*, p. 26 n. 19.

[79]Rev 2:20; Stevan L. Davies, *The Revolt of the Widows: The Social World of the Apocryphal Acts* (Carbondale, Ill.: Southern Illinois University Press, 1980), pp. 58, 62-66, 70-73, 96-99, 102-3, 106; Dennis MacDonald, *The Apostle and the Legend: The Battle for Paul in Story and Legend* (Philadelphia: Westminster, 1983), passim; W. M. Ramsay, *The Church in the Roman Empire* (reprint, Grand Rapids, Mich.: Baker, 1979), pp. 67-68, 161, 375-428, 438, 452-59.

If Paul was prohibiting women from providing instruction of a Gnostic nature, the emphasis of 1 Timothy 2:13-14 on Adam as first-created and undeceived is easily understood.

If this passage is a reaction to a proto-Gnostic type of teaching, verse 15 becomes more comprehensible. Childbearing and marriage were forbidden by certain Gnostic groups because they pulled the soul-atoms back into material bodies instead of liberating them to ascend to their ultimate source.[80] The Gnostic Phibionites, who cherished a "Gospel of Eve," engaged in ritual promiscuity that ended in coitus interruptus. Any woman found to be pregnant was forcibly aborted and the fetus consumed in a sacramental meal.[81] According to the Gospel of the Egyptians, Jesus came to do away with the works of women, that is, childbearing.[82] Only after women ceased from childbearing could the final consummation take place.[83] Women must become men in order to be saved, according to the Naasene Gospel of Thomas, while Zostrianos urges believers to "flee from the bondage of femininity and to choose for themselves the salvation of masculinity."[84]

The heretics of the Pastorals who forbid marriage (1 Tim 4:2) oppose the orthodox view, that women should marry and have children (1 Tim 5:14). But the writer of 1 Timothy asserts that women are acceptable to God within their childbearing function and need not change their sexual identity to find salvation. He extols the virtues of faith, love and holiness with self-control. What splendid maternal attitudes!

Such an interpretation of 1 Timothy 2:11-15 would recognize more fully the numerous statements in the Pastorals about false teaching and the need to resist it. It accounts for the mythological and genealogical

---

[80]Stephen Benko, "The Libertine Gnostic Sect of the Phibionites according to Epiphanius," *Vigiliae Christianae* 21 (1967): 107ff.

[81]Epiphanius *Panarion* 26.13.2-6.

[82]Clement of Alexandria *Miscellanies* 3.45, 63-64.

[83]Ibid. Compare with *On the Origin of the World* 109.21-25, as translated by Arthur (*Wisdom Goddess*, p. 130):

The first pleasure (Hedone) sprang up on the earth
The woman followed the earth
and marriage followed after the woman
Generation followed after marriage
Dissolution followed after generation.

[84]*Gospel of Thomas* (II, 2) Saying 114 (Robinson, p. 130); Zostrianos (VIII, 1) 131 (Robinson, p. 393).

concerns of the writer. There are other possible interpretations as well. Time and space limitations forbid discussing the persistent mingling of the motifs of sex and death in connection with Artemis of Ephesus and Isis, especially in ancient novels. *Authenteō,* with its connotations of murder and of "sexuality related to death," may imply a ritual action, for the mysteries contained both sex and death. Possibly there was a ritual subjection to female dominance in order to gain purification, as Hercules was subject to the Lydian Omphale.

These remain possibilities, but I have dealt here only with the motif that seems most congruent with the evidence of Scripture itself as well as with what is known of the religious systems of Asia Minor. My suggestion is submitted as a hypothesis, to be tested and examined, and to aid in scholarly discussion of this difficult passage. I do not claim to be right, except in my insistence that we must use all the tools at our disposal—classical texts, archaeological, numismatic, epigraphic and art-historic materials, as well as those more traditionally used by biblical scholars—if we are to understand this perplexing passage.

Catherine Clark Kroeger is a Ph.D. candidate, University of Minnesota, specializing in women in ancient religion, and cochair of the Women in tne Biblical World Section of the Society of Biblical Literature.

RESPONSE

Walter L. Liefeld

Catherine Kroeger's paper is the result of an intensive study conducted over a period of years. Her knowledge of classical literature is demonstrated throughout. Since her earlier article on *authentein,* "A Strange Greek Verb," only a few other studies have appeared on the subject. One of them, an article by George Knight III to which she refers briefly in a footnote, launches a serious challenge to her conclusions. In another article, she provides a strong critique of his own method and results. As I respond to this phase of Kroeger's continuing study, I do so with the hope that my comments will be useful in her further work.

It is important first of all to note Kroeger's "thesis," stated in her second paragraph, and to analyze the component parts.

1. The first part of the thesis is that the verb *didaskō* "prohibits the erroneous teaching." This is related to an earlier observation that in the Pastorals "both *didaskō* and *didaskalos* . . . generally refer to the *content* [emphasis mine] of the message." Naturally a teacher teaches content, but it is true that in the Pastorals there is a great emphasis on what is taught. Further, mention of the act of teaching in these epistles is, as Kroeger realizes, usually accompanied by a specific reference to the content of the teaching. But in contrast, neither of the Greek words for the content of teaching *(didaskalia, didachē)* is used in the verse under consideration. The two nouns occur a total of seventeen times in the Pastorals and could easily have been used here. Kroeger's task is to explain how one can maintain that the verb *didasko* "prohibits the erroneous teaching" when Paul, who could have said clearly, "I do not permit women to teach *error*," omitted any such reference to the content.

Then, too, the verb itself is usually used in connection with good, rather than with erroneous, teaching in the Pastorals. To propose that the verb refers in a special way to the content, and specifically to erroneous content, goes beyond the natural meaning of the text. Also, while the verb *teach* is used absolutely, without an object expressing content, it does have a subject, *woman,* which is not mentioned in Kroeger's initial thesis statement at all. In summary, the Greek reader of this text would naturally understand the emphasis of the first words to be "I do not permit a *woman* to teach," whereas Kroeger proposes to demonstrate that its emphasis is "I do not permit a woman to teach *error*."

2. The second part of the thesis is that the other verb, *authenteō,* "represents either a ritual act or a doctrinal tenet propounded by the heretical teachers." This does not seem to fit any of the meanings proposed for *authenteō* in her first paragraph: "begin," "be . . . responsible for," "rule," "dominate," "usurp power or rights," "claim ownership, sovereignty or authorship." Further, it is something of a twist to claim that *authenteō,* which is a verb, could "represent a doctrinal tenet," when "tenet" is a noun. As her argument proceeds, it becomes clear that what Kroeger is really proposing is that *authenteō* followed by the word for *man* in the genitive case means here to declare oneself the originator

of man. She sees this in a religious context, hence the "doctrinal tenet" part of her proposal. In addition she seems to assume that the *authenteō* phrase expresses the object of the teaching, so that what Paul is prohibiting is (or at least includes) the teaching that woman is the originator of man. However, since the verb *didaskō* and the verb *authenteō* are not connected, but on the contrary separated into two distinct acts by the word *oude* (which is commonly used in a "neither . . . nor" construction) such an understanding of the verse is difficult if not ruled out. If Kroeger's understanding of *authenteō* is correct, the most straightforward translation of the verse would be, "I do not permit a woman to teach *or* to declare herself the originator of man."

To support her two propositions, Kroeger proceeds to provide an immense amount of background information. Her knowledge of the field is vast, so while its impact may be weakened at the beginning by the wording of her proposals, the data themselves call for serious consideration.

After a fine brief survey of the religious environment of Ephesus and the importance of Artemis, Kroeger discusses *authentein*. She accepts Chantraine's etymology and provides a short survey of primary sources. Authors often fail to indicate the relative dates of material. Kroeger dates some, but not all, of her primary sources. Many of these are well after the New Testament period. We need to know how the entire word group (verb, noun and any related forms) developed the significance(s) it had in the time of the New Testament. After reading Kroeger's earlier work and then Knight's article, I dated the materials that they cited as closely as I could and plotted them on a chart in the attempt to establish a trajectory. This method helps one to visualize the trends and changes of direction in the meaning of a word. The *Thesaurus Linguae Graecae* of the University of California, Irvine, now provides a complete computer printout that should deliver us from selective partial treatment. An appropriate method would be to: (1) attempt to establish the meaning in each context; (2) plot these examples on a chronological chart; (3) note such factors as geography, type of literature, subject matter and relevance to the New Testament (e.g., use by the early fathers, such as Clement of Rome); (4) establish a trajectory of uses; (5) take special note of those that are most pertinent to the New Testament according to the factors in point 3 above; and (6) draw some tentative conclusions about its use in 1 Timothy 2:12.

Kroeger's work seems to demonstrate that *authentein* means more than merely "to exercise authority" and should not be used to prove that women cannot have positions of authority in the church. It is not necessary to draw on the sexual and violent overtones of the verb to see that in the New Testament period it conveyed ideas of initiating action, originating and domineering.

The other part of Kroeger's paper brings us to the kind of study for which she has become known—reconstruction of the socioreligious background. Biblical scholars must exercise great care in such matters and resist sweeping hypotheses. Kroeger proposes a theory that involves a projection backward from the fourth-century Nag Hammadi materials. Kroeger recognizes the problem and seeks to be cautious. Nevertheless, the vivid descriptions can easily captivate the nonspecialist who does not realize how tenuous their relationship to the church at Ephesus is. It is precarious, as Edwin Yamauchi and others have shown, to assume gnostic backgrounds for New Testament books. Although the phrase, "falsely called knowledge," in 1 Timothy 6:20 contains the Greek word *gnōsis,* this was the common word for knowledge. It would seem anachronistic to transliterate and capitalize it "Gnosis" as Kroeger does.

Kroeger presents a wide range of material relating to the pervasive presence of the serpent in ancient religion. Here again, caution is needed. The serpent motif was so common that we must not read too much into its appearance. Its presence in the Timothy passage is only an inference. Kroeger develops a network of phenomena without carefully explaining how closely these items truly are to each other and to the text in 1 Timothy. This calls to mind the *religionsgeschichtliche* (history of religion or comparative religion) studies of the first part of this century. Sweeping comparisons were made that sometimes overlooked gaps and anachronisms. Yet I do believe that Kroeger's references to literature on Eve are important enough to pursue further. Any exegete of this passage should carefully evaluate such data. This is especially so because of the reference in the Pastorals to "myths."

I have found this a difficult paper to evaluate. The range of material and the lack of footnotes in the version that I was given have made thorough study of the primary sources impossible. In addition, some ideas are presented almost in isolation, without logical connection or proof.

Kroeger has obviously done exhaustive research. Her materials are fascinating, but she herself concludes by modestly saying, "I do not claim to be right." That is somewhat unsettling, since many people would assume in the process of absorbing her research that it must lead to a particular understanding of the text. But her caveat here is appropriate and admirable. Whether or not her construction is correct, it reminds us that God's Word came to people in real-life situations and that the more we can identify with those situations, the better we should be able to understand that Word. Background truths, like scientific truths, require patient exploration and involve theories that must be carefully formulated and readily modified.

Walter L. Liefeld is professor of New Testament, Trinity Evangelical Divinity School, Deerfield, Illinois.

RESPONSE TO SCHOLER AND KROEGER

Nancy Wiles Holsey

In response, I would like to ask where these papers lead us in relationship to the issues that we have been addressing. Both Scholer and Kroeger have provided a historical context for 1 Timothy 2:9-15. In doing so, they either state or suggest that this text is an occasional document written to a particular situation and, as such, does not function authoritatively or normatively for the contemporary issue of whether or not women should have full access to ministry in the church.

My primary question now is whether and how this text *is* authoritative for the church today. If we say that this (or any) text is an occasional text written for a particular situation and thus is not absolute or normative, and that is *all* we say, can we not be charged with weakening biblical authority in practice, if not in our intention? Or, if we as scholars go to these texts to discover "the answer" about the role of women in ministry (even if we do so by reading that "answer" in relationship to the historical context of the text), are we not approaching the Scriptures in basically the same way as those who oppose women in ministry, as an "answer book" for contemporary issues? Doesn't Scripture, even 1 Timothy 2, offer us more than an "answer" about a contemporary issue? In short, how does this Scripture bring life into the community?

Having used historical-critical method and having seen the text in relation to its context (and surely both Kroeger and Scholer have given good gifts to this end), what now? It seems that the best we can say at this point is that this text does not deny women today a functional ministry in the church. As students of the New Testament who stand within the community of faith, we hope for more than a statement of what a text does *not* say. We want to hear with the church what this text *does* say.

In response to these questions about the authoritative function of an occasional text like 1 Timothy 2 for the present-day community of faith, I suggest a threefold model of interpretation.[85] I posit three stages of interpretation.

The first stage is that of "pre-understanding." This involves both the broad context of the tradition/community within which the *interpreter* stands, and the narrower context of the questions or the pre-understanding that the interpreter brings to the text. Scholer's statements on the cultural conditioning of the interpreter and on the reality of agenda other than the biblical teaching coincide with the stage of pre-understanding. The purpose of this colloquium sets a certain pre-understanding, for we admittedly come to the various texts with a specific, contemporary problem, namely, that of the role of women in the ministry of the church. We do so out of a particular (albeit diverse) community— that of American evangelicalism. Therefore, we *did* begin this colloqui-

---

[85]This model was developed out of my own efforts at articulating the dynamics of how biblical authority had functioned in local church Bible studies I had led. For the purposes of this paper, I have borrowed some of the terminology from David Tracy and his work with the material of Hans-Georg Gadamer in some unpublished manuscripts of Tracy's. I believe these manuscripts were the basis of the material in the book that Tracy has recently coauthored with Robert M. Grant, *A Short History of Biblical Interpretation*. There is, however, at least one significant change that I will propose in their terminology, and I will note that shift at the appropriate point.

um on the proper note, for we did address some of the aspects of our pre-understanding, our predisposition to the texts and to the issue of women in ministry.

The second stage in interpretation involves our attention to the text itself on its own terms. Here the historical-critical exercise is performed. To this second stage of interpretation, both Scholer and Kroeger contribute. In our present setting, it is essential that such historical-critical (as well as literary-critical, etc.) tools be used in allowing the text to claim our attention.

The third stage of interpretation is what Hans-Georg Gadamer calls the "game of conversation." This conversation occurs as some form of correlation between the pre-understanding of the situation and the claim to attention of the text. Here we bring to the text our pre-understanding—the questions about the role and experience of women in the ministry of the church—and allow the text to claim our attention. In this case, Kroeger uses classical studies. David Scholer uses a historical-critical exegesis. Then we engage in a conversation between the subject matter of our pre-understanding and the subject matter of the text.

This conversation, however, involves more than a discussion of subject matter. The role of women in ministry is more than subject matter. We all experience certain sociological and faith-critical tensions in relation to the issue of the role of women in the church.[86] Our communities are engaged in such tensions. We may not have adequately defined those tensions, but we still bring them to the study of Scripture. These tensions, not just a cognitive understanding of a subject matter, constitute our pre-understanding.

Similarly, the text reveals tensions within itself. That is, the goal of the second stage of interpretation is more than an explanation of the subject matter of a text. This stage of exegesis will, we hope, lead to more than a principle that is transcultural and absolute. Rather than seek to "get behind" the particular cultural situation to the "transcultural principle" of the text, we can allow this stage of exegesis to lead us *into* or perhaps *up to* the particular cultural situation. Then we can genuinely enter into the "game of conversation" with the tensions of that early

---

[86]James A. Sanders in *Canon and Community* (Philadelphia: Fortress Press, 1983) speaks of the "ambiguity of reality." It is this ambiguity of reality that is striving for the "integrity of reality" that approximates what I mean when I speak of "tension."

community of faith and of that written text. We are not to demand of the text that it resolve our tensions, nor can we demand that exegesis resolve the tensions in the text. But I do aim for the conversation between the dynamic tensions. In stripping away what is occasional or cultural in a text to arrive at the transcultural idea in the text, we often exile that very dynamic in the text that engages us in vigorous conversation. This very conversation arises out of and bears witness to a genuine respect for the authority of that text. The cultural aspects of the text are not extraneous but are at the heart of the matter. Hence, historical-critical method can lead us more closely to the tensions inherent in the text and the early community.

I suggest that we entered stage one, as we talked about the tensions that our present communities face in relationship to the issue at hand. Scholer and Kroeger have brought us into the second stage, though there is still more work to be done in helping us hear the tensions in the early community and in the text. But have we yet been propelled into the third significant stage, conversation with the text? I suggest three questions deriving from this interpretive model, which we might address.

1. *What are the tensions inherent in our present situation?* That is, what are the tensions involved in the present question about the role of women in the ministry of the church, as posed by the evangelical communities? It is not enough to say that there is disagreement. It is not enough, as Scholer indicates, to say that some of us understand particular passages of Scripture differently from others. The tensions involve many personal, theological and sociological issues. These include a crisis of faith that a woman experiences as she hears a call of God that is rejected by the very community that nurtured her to the point of hearing it. There is also a struggle with the theological importance of the dynamics of dominance and submission as they relate to human relationships and to the God/human relationship. Some men fear that "the women will take over." We need to hear and exegete the tensions of the contemporary situation.

2. *What are the tensions in 1 Timothy 2:9–15 and in that early community of faith?* If I read Scholer and Kroeger correctly, the tensions have to do with heretical teaching. Kroeger suggests that the subject matter of the text might be the prohibition specifically of women "pro-

viding instruction of Gnostic nature" and a corresponding emphasis "on Adam as first-created and undeceived" in his communication with the God of the Old Testament. Or perhaps the tension occasioned by the domination of men by women in the history, legend or religions of Ephesus plays a part in this text and community.

Scholer argues that this text expresses concern for the propriety of women, especially in the light of "Paul's concern for the church's social reputation within Greco-Roman society." To read this as an occasional text to a particular situation implies that specific tensions are at work in this text (and in that community). We must seriously focus our thinking about the nature of those tensions if we are to engage in conversation with this text as Scripture (and thus authoritative). At this point I wanted more from Scholer's paper.

3. *How do the tensions inherent in our pre-understanding correlate with the tensions in the text and in the early community of faith?* Tracy suggests three forms of correlation: confrontation, identity and similarity. Where and how do the tensions of our contemporary situation meet the tensions of the text? How do they meet the tensions of the early community of faith? Some will say that this passes beyond the confines of exegesis. Yet we must demand that our exegesis raise the tensions of the text (and the early community) in such a way that the conversation can occur.

At this point we must question whether the text even addresses the questions we bring to it. If the text does not prohibit or sanction the full ministry of women in the church today, do the tensions in the text deal with the tensions that we have brought in our pre-understanding? For instance, 1 Timothy 2:9-15 may be saying more to us about the tensions of how the church relates to heterodox teachers in its midst than it does about whether faithful women in churches may function in leadership positions. If we continue to read this text only as it relates (or does not relate) to women in ministry, we likely will not engage in the conversation that the text itself offers us. In effect, we kick this passage out of the canon (whether we are traditionalists or biblical feminists). If, on the other hand, we want to discuss the role of women in the ministry of the church, perhaps we need to lay this passage aside and come back to it when we can honestly engage in the conversation that the text itself opens for us.

So I ask Scholer and Kroeger these questions: Moving beyond what the text does not say (i.e., it does not give an absolute prohibition of women's full participation of ministry in the church), what *does* the text say? What are the tensions involved? Do the tensions in this text correlate with the tensions inherent in our contemporary situation regarding the role of women in the church? Finally, what *in the world* (i.e., in ou⁻ world) does this text mean?[87]

Nancy Wiles Holsey is adjunct instructor of Greek, Northern Baptist Theological Seminary, and adjunct faculty for homiletics, Bethany Theological Seminary, Lombard, Illinois.

---

[87]David M. Scholer's response to my appeal that the positive message of 1 Tim 2:9-15 be clearly identified: (a) The text *speaks* clearly and urgently about the importance of the church's sensitivity to the destructiveness of "false teachings" within the church. Here the "false teaching" questions the integrity of creation and draws from it implications inimical to the church's commitment to the goodness of God's creation. (b) The text *speaks more powerfully* to the tension between the church's critique of culture and its concern for cultural and social appropriation and respectability within a social context in which the church was clearly a minority, and initially almost an inconsequential, movement. How *does* the church relate to culture today? (c) The text *speaks most powerfully* to a concern for sexual fidelity, faithfulness and respect between and among men and women and to a concern for a rejection of material extravagance. In the first century A.D. in the Roman Empire, sexual fidelity/infidelity and material extravagance/modesty were seen primarily as responsibilities of women. For us in conversation with this text in the church today, we must understand that faithfulness to each other as men and women and faithfulness to God with reference to material possessions are necessary for the "adornment" and integrity of the gospel in our world. 1 Tim 2:9-15 says to the church today that such faithfulness between men and women and that the demands of the gospel must be expressed *over against culture* in order to speak attractively and persuasively with integrity *to culture.* Today we understand that both men and women share these demands together.

CHANGING THE CHURCH

V

11

STRATEGIES FOR CHANGE: BEING A CHRISTIAN CHANGE AGENT

Joan D. Flikkema

SOMETIMES WE PLAN great changes for other people and the church concerning the full use of women's gifts, but then we find that we have few opportunities to put our desired changes into effect. Christian change agents need to understand the process of change and specific strategies for change so that we will have opportunities to effect change. No magic way brings this about. Change involves dedication to a cause and constant, diligent effort. I will share a Christian approach to the process of change so that we can interact with individuals and social institutions in ways that center us in Christ and minimize frustration.

Sometimes we think that change occurs peacefully. We read or hear the end results of a long process to change something in a social institution such as the church. (A church is a social institution as well as a body of believers.) History has many examples of change in individuals and institutions by way of conflict. When Martin Luther nailed his theses on the church door in Wittenberg and began the Protestant Reformation, he had wrestled with himself and then began to wrestle with the Roman Catholic Church. Henry VIII of England wrested the Church of England from papal control in conflict. When the Reverend Paul Washington conducted the service at the Church of the Advocate (Episcopal) in Philadelphia in 1974 to ordain eleven women as priests, conflict followed. The conflicts continued until the new practices became generally accepted norms.

Even among individuals, change occurs by conflict and by personal confrontation. Change is embodied in persons. In 1978, the Synod (highest assembly of the Christian Reformed Church) was meeting and was about to consider the question of opening the church offices (ordained positions of deacon, minister, elder and evangelist) to women. One of the delegates, a minister from Maryland, attended our local church's worship service on Sunday morning. I talked with him on the lawn during the coffee hour after the service. Five years later, he remarked at a conference that our conversation was a turning point for him. Before our conversation, he had given low priority to women's ordination. After our conversation, he was convinced that women should be ordained and that it was urgent to do so.

The key to being a Christian change agent is in understanding how to apply creative problem-solving processes to a controversial issue to effect change. There are seven steps to this process: (1) developing vision, (2) defining belief, (3) stating the goal, (4) determining resources, (5) focusing action, (6) taking action and (7) evaluating progress.

Step 1: Developing Vision

In a poem entitled "Dreams," Langston Hughes says that a life without dreams is like a broken-winged bird that cannot fly or a barren field frozen with snow.

Martin Luther King is famous for his speech on August 28, 1963, at a civil rights demonstration in Washington, D.C.

I say to you today, my friends, that in spite of the difficulties and frustrations of the moment, I still have a dream. It is a dream deeply rooted in the American dream.

I have a dream that one day this nation will rise up and live out the true meaning of its creed: "We hold these truths to be self-evident: that all men are created equal."

I have a dream that one day on the red hills of Georgia the sons of former slaves and the sons of former slave owners will be able to sit down together at the table of brotherhood.

I have a dream that my four little children will one day live in a nation where they will not be judged by the color of their skin but the content of their character.

I have a dream today.

> I have a dream that one day every valley shall be exalted, every hill and mountain shall be made low, the rough places will be made plains, and the crooked places will be made straight, and the glory of the Lord shall be revealed, and all flesh shall see it together.
>
> This is our hope. This is the faith with which I return to the South. With this faith we will be able to hew out of the mountains of despair a stone of hope. With this faith we will be able to transform the jangling discords of our nation into a beautiful symphony of brotherhood. With this faith we will be able to work together, to pray together, to struggle together, to go to jail together, to stand up for freedom together, knowing that we will be free one day.

We must develop a mental picture of the change desired. We can close our eyes and envision as concretely as possible the results of the change that we hope to bring about. We need to see clearly in our minds what we are working for. For me, I can envision local churches with ordained women and men carrying out the tasks of the church life and participating in the decision-making process. I see both women and men using their talents as delegates to the assemblies of our church government.

We need a vision of the local church as one body with many members and with each member having opportunity to use his or her spiritual gifts (see 1 Cor 12). We can imagine a local church that begins its church year (or develops a long-range plan) by doing a needs assessment, analyzing the gifts of its members and then matching the gifts to the needs. In such a church, girls and boys would have role models of women and men using their gifts fully. Without official or unofficial restrictions, both women and men could develop and use their leadership talents and their nurturing talents.

Our sense of vision must always be rooted in Scripture. A program entitled *Discover Your Gifts* indicates that Scripture identifies fifteen gifts as follows: administration, creative ability, discernment, encouragement, evangelism, faith, giving, hospitality, intercession, leadership, mercy, prophecy, service, shepherding and teaching (Rom 12:7-8; 1 Cor 12:8-10, 28-30; Eph 4:11-13). Scripture provides a guide for understanding spiritual gifts and their uses:[1]

---

[1] *Discover Your Gifts* (Grand Rapids, Mich.: Christian Reformed Home Missions, 1983), pp. 28-29.

1. "*Christ gives* spiritual gifts to believers *through the Holy Spirit.*" (Ephesians 4:8, 11; 1 Corinthians 12:8-9, 11)

2. "Spiritual gifts are given *to each believer* without exception." (1 Corinthians 12:7, 1 Peter 4:10)

3. "Spiritual gifts are *gifts of God's grace.*" (Ephesians 4:7, Romans 12:6, 1 Peter 4:10b)

4. "The Spirit gives *many different gifts,* providing for rich diversity of ministry in the church." (1 Corinthians 12:8-10, 28; Romans 12:6)

5. "Spiritual gifts are meant to be *employed for the benefit of others.*" (1 Corinthians 12:7b, 25; Romans 12:6, Ephesians 4:11-12, 1 Peter 4:10)

6. "The gifted members of the church *are parts of the body of Christ* and therefore individually members of one another." (1 Corinthians 12:13, 14, 27; Romans 12:5)

7. "Gifts must always be *used in love.* Without love they are useless." (1 Corinthians 13:1-3)

Women have the same gifts as men:

Many gifted women are introduced to us in Scripture. The New Testament church had such outstanding women as Dorcas (Acts 9:36-39), who had the gift of mercy, and the four daughters of Philip (Acts 21:8-9), who had the gift of prophecy. Many women worked in gift-related ministries. In Romans 16, Phoebe engaged in a service ministry for the church of Cenchreae and in that connection ministered to Paul himself (vv. 1-2). Prisca stood alongside of her husband, Aquila, as a fellow worker with Paul (v. 3). Mary "worked hard" among you, said Paul. The verb he used to describe Mary's work is the very word used to describe ministerial labors in 1 Corinthians 15:10 and 1 Thessalonians 5:12.

Today, one need not be active in the church very long to find that the ministry of the body still depends upon the gifts God gives to women as well as men.

The important point is that all gifts are meant for ministry, whether they are possessed by men or women. There are ample opportunities for ministry for all members of Christ's body in our needy, hurting world.[2]

---

[2]Ibid., p. 11.

Step 2: Defining Belief

We should state exactly what we believe about gifts based on our study of Scripture. Our sense of vision may develop by completing the following statement: "We believe that . . ." For example, we might state, "We believe that both women and men who are qualified should be able to serve in all of the ordained offices of the church." Then we must support our statement of belief with facts and ideas from Scripture, creeds and doctrines, rules of church government, past decisions of church government at various levels, writings of church leaders and other authorities, personal experiences, experiences of churches with which we have ecclesiastical fellowship, and so forth. The process of defining and supporting our belief leads to a deeper sense of commitment while it enforces the vision. Our desire is to move from a dream toward a reality.

Step 3: Stating the Goal

At this point in the creative problem-solving process, we must decide exactly what we want to accomplish. We might complete the following sentence: "The current situation is . . ." then we can state the specific change desired by completing the following sentence: "We desire . . ."

Here is an example: The current situation is that qualified women are not ordained to service in church offices because of the rules of church government. We desire to change these rules to permit the ordination of qualified women. (Note: One main goal may emerge, or several related goals may emerge.)

Step 4: Determining Resources

Resources are persons, things and actions that we can draw on for aid or to take care of a need. The best way to determine our resources is to answer as specifically as possible questions such as the following (in relation to the goal): (a) What talents do we have? (b) Who are the people in our community who can assist us? In what ways? (c) Who are the experts beyond our community who can assist us? In what ways? (d) What materials are available to us? (e) What are the occasions (specific times) for us to take action? (f) Where are the places for us to take action? (g) What funds are available to us?

Step 5: Focusing Action

To focus our action, we need the IWW question. *In what ways* can we accomplish the goal? For example, In what ways can we accomplish a change in the rules of church government to permit the ordination of qualified women? In what ways can we have the local church move women into leadership positions? In what ways can we increase the number of women who are members of boards and committees in the denomination?

First, we must gather ideas for accomplishing the goal. We can brainstorm, think individually, think as a group, do research, consult strategy lists, consult experts. We should list anything that comes to mind, even if it sounds unreasonable as initially suggested.

Second, we must evaluate the possible ways to reach the goal. To each of the ideas listed, we apply evaluation questions such as the following: (a) Is this way appropriate for us? (b) Is this way appropriate for the specific situation (including other people involved)? (c) Do we have time for this way? (d) Do we have the necessary resources for this way? (e) Are we willing to take the risk involved in this way? It is often worthwhile to do this in the form of a chart (see table 1).

Evaluation Questions **Possible Ways to Meet Goals**	a. Is this way appropriate for us?	b. Is this way appropriate for the specific situation (other people involved)?	c. Do we have time for this way?	d. Do we have the resources for this way?	e. Are we willing to take the risk involved in this way?	f. Etc.
1. Proposing changes in the church government through the correct channels	✓	✓				
2. Contacting delegates to higher assemblies to share information and ideas	✓	✓		✓		
3. Giving appropriate printed materials to offices and leaders in the local church	✓	✓	✓	✓	✓	
4. Encouraging more lay participation of both women and men in worship services	✓	✓	✓	✓	✓	
5. Etc.						

Table 1. Chart for Evaluating Ways to Reach the Goal

Risk (evaluation question *e*) is the chance of injury, damage or loss. For change agents, it is the degree to which human relations are questioned and conflict is aroused because the proposed activity disturbs "harmony." In other words, the activity may upset the customary ways in which people relate to each other; human relations may be damaged in the process of change. Here are some specific ways to bring change on behalf of the full use of women's gifts in the institutional church, according to the level of risk.

Low Risk

1. Praying regularly for God's assistance and guidance in the process of change.

2. Studying Scripture to learn as much as possible about God's will in the area of the change desired.

3. Reading materials to keep informed about women's issues, especially in one's own denomination.

4. Learning about the structure and functioning of the denomination in order to know the most effective and efficient ways to bring about change.

5. Studying church business at all levels in the denomination.

6. Encouraging more lay participation of both women and men in worship services.

7. Encouraging the governing board of the local church to make full use of all members' gifts (both women and men); suggesting specific ways to do this.

8. Contributing financially to organizations that help expand women's roles in the local church, the denomination and the Christian community.

Moderate Risk

9. Sharing concerns, feelings and ideas about the roles of women and men in the denomination and the Christian community with other women and men.

10. Attending meetings (conferences, retreats, programs, etc.) that are helpful and supportive regarding women's issues.

11. Attending the congregational meetings in the local church. Exercising the privilege of voting. Encouraging women in the church to

attend the meetings and to vote. Putting effort into acquiring the privilege of voting for women if it does not exist.

12. Attending church business meetings as an observer at the local
church level and the denominational level. (Usually such meetings are
open to church members, unless confidential matters such as individual
difficulties or discipline are discussed.)

13. Requesting that the pastor prepare and give sermons on relevant
topics so that he or she studies the issues and makes use of opportunities to educate the congregation.

14. Raising questions at appropriate times and places so that other
church members can clearly see the problems.

15. Donating appropriate books to the church library; writing book
reviews for the church newsletter.

16. Suggesting to the local church that there be study groups (adult
education classes, Bible study groups, discussion groups, etc.) to learn
more about the full utilization of all members' gifts.

17. Using every possible opportunity to be supportive of women.
(This means to recommend them, to use constructive comments to
build their confidence and help bring out their talents, etc.)

18. Contacting the people involved in all levels of church business
(members of local church councils, members of higher assemblies, wom-
en and men who provide denominational services or serve on denominational boards and committees, etc.) to offer information, ideas and
opinions about relevant items on the agenda.

19. Communicating with people who write or speak concerning wom-
en's issues. Congratulating and giving support when they are positive;
offering constructive criticism when they are negative.

20. Encouraging qualified young women to undertake theological
studies to exercise leadership in the Christian community.

21. Encouraging seminary staff members to be sensitive to women's
issues in the training of seminary students.

22. Encouraging men and women to be friends, to be partners in
kingdom work, to share leadership roles, to share nurturing roles, to
volunteer to serve in new capacities.

High Risk
23. Helping to organize a discussion group, conference or retreat to

deal with topics related to women's issues in the church.

24. Assisting in forming and maintaining speakers' services concerning women's issues.

25. Requesting pastoral care and advice (from the minister and officers in the local church) to deal with the issues that are problems (e.g., men "lording it over" women, ignoring specific women's gifts, etc.). Using such opportunities to educate others.

26. Giving appropriate printed materials to the officers and leaders in the local church.

27. Encouraging the nomination of qualified women to fill various denominational positions (boards, committees, etc.). (Note: Most denominations have nominating committees to make recommendations for positions on boards and committees.)

28. Requesting (by proposal, overture, appeal, protest, etc.) the local church—and, ultimately, higher assemblies in the denomination—to study the unresolved aspects of the women's issue.

29. Doing research and sharing the results by writing and speaking concerning various aspects of the full use of women's gifts.

30. Using various consciousness-raising techniques to help other women and men become aware of some of the women's issues.

31. Noticing sexist remarks, actions and atmospheres; indicating that they are inappropriate, especially for Christians.

32. Noticing sexist language and imagery in the church service (liturgy, sermon, music, etc.) and church materials. Indicating that it is inappropriate for Christians to be so male oriented in word choice and imagery when half of the church's members are female. Pointing out that men and women are, first of all, human beings created in the image of God and that they have much more in common than they have differences.

33. Requesting the local church to respond to denominational actions and recommendations in areas that are directly or indirectly related to the full use of women's gifts, especially if the actions and recommendations are restrictive.

34. Deciding whether or not to give full financial support to all organizational aspects of the church. (Several women have chosen to give their "fair share" of the budget to nonorganizational causes such as benevolence, Christian education, special relief causes, seminary scho-

larships for women students, etc., so that the local church becomes aware of their deeply felt concerns.)

Third, we must select the best way or ways to reach the goal. It is usually wisest to select those on the chart with the most checks ("yes" answers to the evaluation questions) because this will probably be the most successful. Success affirms change agents. It gives them confidence in their activities and ideas. It encourages them to proceed further.

Fourth, we must plan to implement the chosen way or ways. We must answer the following questions clearly: (a) *What* are we going to do? (b) *Why* are we doing this? (c) *Who* is going to do this? (d) *When* are we doing this? (e) *Where* are we doing this? (f) *How* are we doing this? Successful change agents usually have a back-up plan in mind if the original plan falters during implementation. They may modify the original plan in progress, or they may devise a new plan to accomplish the goal.

Step 6: Taking Action

When we take action as Christian change agents, we must go about it in ways that are constructive for both ourselves and the others who are involved. I propose that we consider the work of Christian change agents a form of ministry. In this ministry, Christians develop a scriptural foundation for the process of change, a scriptural model for responding to a controversial issue, an understanding of forces that promote and that deter change, and a frame of reference for particular strategies.

First, a scriptural foundation for the process of change begins with a true concept of humility. Humility means to be humble before God so that he empowers us to do his work on earth. Christians are to be strong and bold and influential people who have a realistic approach to themselves, others and their ministry as change agents. Many people want to keep the peace at all costs, but Christians who minister as change agents must remember to be the salt of the earth and the light of the world (Mt 4:13–15). "A little leaven leavens the whole lump" (Gal 5:9). Christ, whose name we bear, was a change agent in his culture. He threw out the money changers in the temple, talked to the Samaritan woman, healed people on the Sabbath and challenged the views of the Pharisees. For Christ, power centered on being the least and doing services (e.g., washing feet) while he boldly proclaimed the good news. Christ's disciples became change agents when they responded to his command to go into all the world and preach the gospel. Paul and Peter are role models as change agents.

Second, a scriptural model for responding to a controversial issue is important. In spite of recent gains by women in Western culture, affirming women as whole persons is still not the norm. In spite of recent gains by women in some Protestant churches, affirming women as whole persons in the evangelical community is still not the norm. To affirm women as whole persons is countercultural in both society and church. It is a complete turnabout from tradition.

We have a model in Scripture to guide us when we depart from tradition. The early Christian church consisted of converted Jews, and they did not envision Gentiles becoming Christians. In Acts 10, we read that Peter fell into a trance and saw something like a sheet descend from heaven. In the sheet were animals, reptiles and birds. Peter refused the command to eat because he considered the items common or unclean, but the voice said to him that he must not call common what God had cleansed. Then servants of Cornelius, the Gentile centurion, came to Peter; and Peter returned with them to Cornelius's home. The Gentiles who heard the gospel from Peter believed and received the Holy Spirit. Other Christians heard about this and were amazed. In Acts 15, we learn that the council at Jerusalem reviewed the reports of converted Gentiles and accepted them, with a few comments about rules to be observed.

Many traditionalists want cut-and-dried proof from Scripture about women's ordination, but they cannot find it. Just as it was unclear to the early church that Gentiles were to be accepted, it is unclear today to many that women are to be accepted. Yet God is showing us time and time again that women are gifted in all areas of church work, just as he showed the early church that Gentiles were included. Just as the early church knew it was right to include Gentiles and went forward in faith, so we must encourage others to trust God and believe in the work of the Holy Spirit when we affirm women as whole persons in Christ.

Third, some forces deter and some forces promote change. The primary force that deters change is apathy. Many people simply do not care about a controversial issue and its implications; they do not want to be involved. They may think of the church as a haven of rest in a troubled world or in their own troubled lives. They do not view the church as a service station to get refueled "to fight the good fight," to be soldiers of the cross. Thomas Sill, professor of public relations at Western Michigan University, states that there is a continuum of the public's responses to a controversial issue in which 10 per cent are supportive; 80 per cent are indifferent, undecided or uninformed; and 10 per cent are hostile. Change agents should enlist the aid of the 10 per cent who are support-ive, win over some of the 80 per cent who are indifferent or undecided or uninformed, and antagonize as little as possible the 10 per cent who are hostile.

Even change agents can slip into apathy and become ineffective. The antidote is to keep a sound perspective on themselves and their work and to remember that social change is a long process and that progress is often made in small steps. An old Chinese proverb states that "a journey of a thousand miles begins with a single step."

The primary force to promote change is disrupted harmony, some-times known as disequilibrium and cognitive dissonance. In the present evangelical community, men and women have learned to work within the system of restrictions on the use of women's gifts; therefore, they resist change. For women and men to be full partners in service is a new and radical idea. Just as many slaves did not want freedom during the Civil War because they understood their masters and how to function within the system of slavery, many women and men today do not want freedom from official and unofficial restrictions in the church because it calls for major adjustments in lifestyle. It is human nature to change only when compelled to do so, or when there is something in the change for us. Change comes for individuals and social institutions through conflict. People who are upset will make changes to restore so-called harmony. People in conflict will adjust to restore a sense of balance and wholeness. To make changes on behalf of the full use of women's gifts in the church, therefore, it is necessary to disrupt the harmony of the current situation, educate people emotionally and intellectually through experiencing women in new roles, and provide solutions to the conflict that help in reaching the goal.

Politics are often involved in change. C. R. Rogers says, "The word 'politics' has to do with power or control in interpersonal relationships, and the extent to which persons strive to gain such power—or to re-linquish it. It has to do with the way decisions are made. Who makes them? Where is the locus, or center, of decision-making power? 'Politics' concerns the effects of such power-oriented actions on individuals or on systems."[3] Power plays emerge in situations of disrupted harmony if the persons involved conceive of power in a zero-sum fashion, name-ly, that power is limited in supply. This approach "assumes that if one has, say, 20 units of power and gives 12 of them away, he (or she) only has 8 units of power left. The more one shares power or gives it up to others, the less one has for himself (or herself). There is only so much power available, and one had better scramble for it and hoard it. This concept of power is based on a scarcity model."[4] The alternative view of power is to conceive of it as infinite or limitless, much like love. "It is limitless, and when it is shared it regenerates and expands. There is no need to hoard it because it only increases when it is given away."[5] Power, like ideas, remains fresh and alive when it is shared because it increases, moves around freely and changes to meet the situations that arise.

In a social institution, action to change must ultimately be person to person. When White persons make racist remarks, they often change if Blacks confront them and say, "Your remarks are racist. We feel of-fended. Let's work this out." When women and men in church make sexist remarks, they often change if women confront them and say, "Your remarks are sexist. As sisters in Christ, we feel offended. Let's work this out." Actual experiences change people. That is why it is so important to go beyond the existing restrictions in denominations and local churches and make full use of women's gifts in specific situations. Experiencing the full use of women's gifts will change minds and hearts. As in other social institutions, the church will adjust its policy to catch up with practices.

Fourth, Christian change agents need a frame of reference with which to go about their work. One important aspect of the frame of reference is advocacy. In society at large and in churches, much effective work is done by advocates for hunger victims, crime victims, disaster victims,

---

[3]C. R. Rogers, *A Way of Being* (Boston: Houghton Mifflin Co., 1980), p. 294.
[4]A. W. Schaef, *Women's Reality* (Minneapolis: Winston Press, 1981), p. 125.
[5]Ibid.

the handicapped and others. Men need to be advocates for women with gifts, and women need to be advocates for other women as well as the daughters and granddaughters of the church. This is an effective antidote for inappropriate desires in the change agent for personal recognition. What this really comes down to is the concept of intercession and intercessory prayer. According to Daniel Boerman,

> The importance of intercessory prayer may also be viewed from a broader perspective: the bond of love that it establishes is the bond that gives strength and unity to the entire people of God. Intercessory prayer enables the church to become the loving community of fellowship God intended it to be. Without it the church cannot be the church.
>
> The importance of intercessory prayer goes even beyond the perimeter of the church. As Christians we are the light of the world and the salt of the earth. The task of enlightening and preserving must have its basis in intercessory prayer. Paul urged Timothy to intercede for all people and especially for those in positions of authority. This teaching suggests that social and political conditions correspond somewhat to how well Christians are praying for that society and the people who influence it.
>
> One of the most dramatic examples of intercessory prayer is recorded in Exodus 32. . . . The result of Moses' intercession is that God repents of the evil he was about to do to his people and spares the nation of Israel.
>
> As Moses put his life on the line for the Israelites, so Christ offered up his life for the church. Christ is our priest and intercessor. We too are called to be priests and intercessors—to pray for others, a struggling church, and a needy world. If we fail to intercede, the grace and the love of God will be withheld from many who desperately need them.[6]

Another important aspect of the frame of reference is a Scripture-centered attitude. It is important to respect self and others, to have compassion, and to meet others where they are in their spiritual journeys. When I work as a change agent, I often select a theme from a chapter

---

[6]D. Boerman, "The Importance of Intercessory Prayer," *The Banner* (November 28, 1983) pp. 16–17.

or a particular verse to guide me. The famous chapter on love, 1 Corinthians 13, is excellent. Keeping in mind the fruit of the Spirit (Gal 4:22) is useful. Romans 8:28 ("We know that in everything God works for good with those who love him, who are called according to his purpose") and 1 Thessalonians 5:16-18 ("Rejoice always, pray constantly, give thanks in all circumstances; for this is the will of God in Christ Jesus for you") are also uplifting.

It is also important to understand anger. Anger is an appropriate response to the injustice against which the change agent struggles. Anger can be a destructive force when it comes from hatred and seeks to tear down, but anger can be a constructive force when it comes from indignation at unrighteousness and is transformed into energy needed to build a better community. "Be angry, but sin not" (Ps 4:4).

A third important aspect of the frame of reference is understanding that a Christian change agent has a creative ministry. According to Henri Nouwen, this creative ministry requires the perspectives of hope, creative receptivity and shared responsibility. Concerning hope, he points out that we work toward our wishes, always placing trust and hope in him who is the giver of all good. Therefore, we work in faith and truth, with no guarantees or conditions.

He who works for social change usually has very specific things in mind, as he must, but he can only remain a man of faith when he views every result he has achieved as a gift to him which he is asked to accept in freedom. Nobody can force the soul of a community. The only possibility open is to create conditions in which the community can freely develop and discover the ways that lead to redemption.

A man of hope can give all his energy, time, and abilities to the people he works for, but when he attaches himself to any specific result he might lose sight of his ultimate objective. Through his attitude of hope, the agent of social change does not fall into the temptation of concretism. He does not worry about the results of his work because he believes that God will fulfill his promises and that it is only a temptation to desire to know exactly how this will happen. . . .

Martin Luther King was able to exercise such a powerful spiritual leadership because, although he asked for freedom NOW, he had learned to be patient and wait until God's will fulfilled His promises.[7]

[7]H. J. M. Nouwen, *Creative Ministry* (Garden City, N.Y.: Doubleday & Co., 1971), pp. 81-82.

Concerning creative receptivity, Nouwen points out that we need to avoid falling into the temptation of power:

> By developing in himself and others the willingness to receive, the minister can prevent man from falling into the temptation of power. He who wants to bring about change has first of all to learn to be changed by those whom he wants to help. This, of course, is exceptionally difficult for those who are undergoing their first exposure to an area of distress. . . .
>
> No true social agent gives in to the temptation of power since he has discovered that his task is not a heavy burden of a brave sacrifice but an opportunity to see more and more of the face of Him whom he wants to meet.[8]

Concerning shared responsibility, he points out that we should not wait for a few great individuals to do significant things. We should set up communities (support groups) that are able to bring about change, especially through the delegation of tasks: "If Christian laymen, ministers, and priests really want to be agents of social change, the first thing they have to learn is how to share leadership. We are used to saying to people that they have responsibilities. To say that they also have the authority which goes with it, however, is something else. It is amazing to find that most priests are still working very much on their own and have not yet found the creative ways to mobilize the potential leadership in their parishes and share their responsibilities with others."[9] I like to think of this as each of us blooming where we are planted, and the blooming garden changes the landscape.

An additional important aspect of the frame of reference is to understand that there will be both pain and pleasure for the change agent. Jesus paid with his life. Stephen was stoned. Peter and Paul and others were put in jail. Early Christians were thrown to the lions. Rose, a quiet and thoughtful woman in a Western city, told me how the adult education leader in her local church, which does not ordain women, asked her to lead two sessions in favor of ordaining women. She replied that she would consider the request. Later she heard through the grapevine that money was donated to bring in two outside experts to oppose her.

---

[8] Ibid., pp. 83–84.
[9] Ibid., p. 85.

She asked that experts be found to represent her position. The money suddenly disappeared. An elder called to suggest that her attitude and actions were disruptive. Another elder, a member of the Christian school board where she taught, informed her that she was disturbing the peace and that there might be problems in renewing her teaching contract. She sobbed as she told me how she withdrew her agreement to speak. But there will be rewards. People who have suffered due to the restrictions on the use of gifts will come forward and thank the change agent for affirming them. The change agent will see young women and men in the church have new opportunities to use gifts. Change agents will experience their faith growing as they fulfill a firm commitment to justice.

Step 7: Evaluating Progress
To measure progress, we ask the following questions: (a) How much progress have we made in reaching our goal? (b) Which action ideas were successful? partially successful? unsuccessful? (c) Which resources were very useful? somewhat useful? not useful? (d) What new understandings have we gained?

Then, if necessary, the cycle can be repeated by reaffirming vision, reaffirming belief, reaffirming or altering goals, reassessing resources, refocusing action and re-evaluting progress.

Conclusion
Change agents on behalf of the full use of women's gifts in the church must work in the abstract. They must do and publish research and scholarly explanations of difficult Scripture passages, the meaning of church membership, the meaning of church office, the meaning of ordination and much more.

They must also work in the concrete. The Committee for Women in the Christian Reformed Church, an independent organization considered by many to be a model for change agents, is dedicated to the full use of women's gifts in the Christian Reformed Church. This includes the ordination of women. Since 1975, it has accomplished the following: publishing a bimonthly newsletter, a position paper and two study guides ("The Place of Women in the Bible" and "What Is Headship?"); holding regular educational meetings; offering an annual retreat for women; establishing chapters in various geographical areas, an independent scholarship program for women students at Calvin Theological Seminary and making progress toward an endowed scholarship program at Calvin Theological Seminary for women students; obtaining membership in the Barnabas Foundation (a Christian stewardship agency to help people with planned giving and estates); encouraging several Christian Reformed churches that have ordained women in spite of restrictions; developing proposals to the church's assemblies to further the process of change; funding a survey of members of the Christian Reformed Church to determine attitudes about the use of women's gifts; setting up a network project to have members contact delegates to church assemblies at crucial times; encouraging church leaders and pastors of local churches to openly advocate the full use of women's gifts and offering them speakers' services; assisting women who suffer because their local churches ignore their gifts; and offering women opportunities to acquire leadership skills.

The evangelical community has a problem with women. Each of us can choose to be part of the problem or part of the solution. Nouwen writes,

> For a Christian is only a Christian when he unceasingly asks critical questions of the society in which he lives and continuously stresses the necessity for conversion, not only of the individual but also of the world. A Christian is only a Christian when he refuses to allow himself or anyone else to settle into a comfortable rest. He remains dissatisfied with the *status quo.* And he believes that he has an essential role to play in the realization of the new world to come—even if he cannot say how that world will come about. A Christian is only a Christian when he keeps saying to everyone he meets that the good news of the Kingdom has to be proclaimed to the whole world and witnessed to all nations (Mt. 24:13). As long as a Christian lives he keeps searching for a new order without divisions between people, for a new structure that allows every man to shake hands with every other man, and a new life in which there will be lasting unity and peace. He will not allow his neighbor to stop moving, to lose courage, or to escape into small everyday pleasures to which he can cling. He is irritated by satisfaction and self-content in himself as well as in others since he knows, with an unshakable certainty, that something

great is coming of which he has already seen the first rays of life. He believes that this world not only passes but has to pass in order to let the new world be born. He believes that there will never be a moment in this life in which one can rest in the supposition that there is nothing left to do. But he will not despair when he does not see the result he wanted to see. For in the midst of all his work he keeps hearing the words of the One sitting on the throne: "I am making the whole of creation new" (Rev. 21:5).[10]

Joan D. Flikkema is executive secretary of the Committee for Women in the Christian Reformed Church and teaches English at Forest Hills Central Middle School in Grand Rapids, Michigan.

RESPONSE

Frances F. Hiebert

Change. We live in a time of constant flux. Change is occurring faster than it ever has in history. Ironically, however, we are often stymied in successfully bringing about planned change. Seminars and conferences are held, many books and articles written, interest groups organized, individuals and groups lobby, and, after all, the most important element seems to be time. "In the fullness of time," or "in due time," is how the Scripture often describes it. For the Christian, of course, this means that things happen according to the will of God.

The fact that things "come to pass" according to God's will, however, never releases us from the obligation to pray and work so that the will of God that already has been revealed will be done in our lives and in the church. The church has a long way to go before it lives up to what it already knows and, in the case of women in ministry, to what it once knew and has sometimes forgotten. Joan Flikkema states, quite correctly, that in the present evangelical community it seems a new and radical idea for women and men to be full partners in service. Although women

---

[10]Ibid., pp. 88–89.

clearly had active roles in ministry in the early church, through the centuries this has been forgotten in some times and places. Now, for women to have the freedom to exercise their gifts in all areas of church life, a radical change is necessary.

The issue of whether or not to accept this change is a controversial one in the evangelical church today. Much will depend on the strategies of those who desire the change and how they go about implementing them. As Flikkema points out, controversy is not new or necessarily bad in the life of the church. "Peace at any price" is not an acceptable alternative to the pain of change, if the people who want the change believe that they are doing the will of God. Christians should remember to "speak the truth in love," giving equal emphasis to "truth" and "love." Unfortunately, it seems that the more acrimonious the debate, the more inevitable is a backlash and the more time it will take to get the change accepted.

The steps for problem solving enumerated by Flikkema are practical and action oriented. Perhaps more attention is needed on what sometimes is called receptor orientiation. Somewhere in the beginning of the problem-solving process, we need to analyze and try to empathize with the group that is being asked to change. In the end, change usually occurs most successfully when these people are also involved in setting the goals and implementing them.

Cooperation in Change

Ward Hunt Goodenough, an anthropologist, has written a book titled *Cooperation in Change*. Although the main focus of the book is cultural awareness in facilitating change with people of developing areas, the theory has wider application. The title of the book indicates what he believes about the process of planned change. Successful change depends on agent-client cooperation.

All of us, writes Goodenough, are born with an ego-centered approach to the world. The first preoccupations of children have to do with gratifiying their own wants and learning to manipulate their surroundings to their own ends. Gradually they learn to limit their behavior because of the sanctions others have the power to invoke. They also begin to identify with others as persons like themselves whose needs should be respected as well as their own. This second motivation allows for the development of an "other" orientation and leads us to regard the wishes and feelings of others, even when we have the power to disregard them. It also, however, causes us sometimes to suffer the deprivation of our own needs and wishes. It costs something. In the process of socialization, it is important to make identification with others desirable and rewarding. If not, we tend to remain ego centered and concerned only to manipulate others to our own ends.

The conflict of interest inherent in the individual's "other" orientation is fundamental to the problem of cooperation between change agent and the group that is expected to change. This conflict, according to Goodenough, is often resolved in favor of whichever party holds the power advantage. But that kind of resolution is likely to be more apparent than real. The conflict usually continues, manifesting itself in more subtle ways. If cooperation is to occur, a considerable increase in mutual identification will be necessary. Goodenough believes that the change agent has the greater responsibility in this process The agent must recognize that she or he also is motivated by self-centered factors and must take responsibility to identify to a greater extent with the community to be changed than might normally be expected.

The needs and wants of both the planners and the receptor group should be regarded with equal respect. The temptation, however, is that, once convinced of the rightness of the program, those who desire change may resort to coercion if efforts at winning cooperation by other means prove ineffective. A sense of urgency sometimes causes well-meaning change agents to act with impatience that is unwise and self-defeating.

Goodenough states that resistance from the receptor group signals unresolved problems in the change situation. These may be inevitable by-products of the change process itself, or they may result from the agent's own conduct. Whatever the reason, coercion is unlikely to achieve anything more than a temporary solution.

In spite of its negative side, resistance conveys information to change agents that tells them that they are treading on sensitive ground. It shows up the sore spots. At these points, cooperation is in jeopardy. Achieving constructive change will depend a great deal on whether the agents understand the meaning of the resistance and on their attitudes toward it.

The following suggestions from Goodenough for successful agent-client cooperation seem relevant to the present discussion.

1. The agent should have a clear idea of the nature and properties of what is being changed, including customs, institutions, ideas and beliefs.

2. Stereotyping of the community to be changed should be avoided, for it is likely not only to increase resistance but also to hinder discovery of the realities involved.

3. It is important that experience and ideas be analyzed and communicated to others who are seeking to achieve the same goals in order to contribute to the knowledge and understanding that will make further change possible.[11]

In what ways can we apply these anthropological insights to the question of developing strategies for change that will allow for full equality and freedom for women within the evangelical church today? I believe we must understand the motivation and needs of those who are being asked to change. Who are they and why are they so resistant? I expect that a constellation of motivating factors is involved in the question of the subordination of women in the evangelical community. While the power issue may be one of these, it is too simple to say that this is the only motivation. On the other hand, faithfulness to Scripture is not likely to be the only motivation either. Various mixes of motivations are no doubt present among different groups in different places.

In general, we have two basic groups to consider—men who believe in a traditional role for women and the women who accept that role. The former obviously have something to lose by granting full equality to women. Perhaps by many different kinds of efforts, especially good modeling of equal working relationships between women and men, they may see that change would be more rewarding than they now believe. Men need to understand that a husband who supports the development and growth of his wife has much more to gain than to lose. He will be living with an interesting, alive and much more attractive woman than if he elects to try to keep her barefoot and pregnant. He will need to share the power of decision making and be willing to accept critique,

---

[11]Ward Hunt Goodenough, *Cooperation in Change* (New York: Russell Sage Foundation, 1963), pp. 35–45.

but he will also be relieved of the dehumanizing burden of playing God.

Women who embrace the traditional role should be helped to understand that change is meant to increase their options and not deny them any fulfillment in being women. In *The Second Stage*, Betty Friedan writes that feminists who disparage the family are woefully out of step with most women. Virtually all women today, she writes, share a basic core of commitment to the family and to their own equality within and beyond it, as long as the family and equality are not seen to be in conflict.[12]

Perhaps one other comment is in order with regard to understanding the people who are resistant to change in the traditional role for women. Letha Scanzoni notes that there has been in evangelical circles a revival of interest in the great chain of being and the chain of command. *Hierarchy* is a word to be preferred over *egalitarianism*. One of her conclusions about this state of affairs is that when change occurs very rapidly, there is often a yearning for the security of rigid structure.[13] This is perhaps one answer to the question raised at the beginning why planned change is sometimes so difficult when it seems that all kinds of rapid change are occurring spontaneously.

Confrontation, Development and Scripture

Although Flikkema recognizes that people change when there is something in it for them, I think more attention needs to be given to the thoughts and feelings of those who are being asked to change. I also wonder whether disruption of equilibrium in the sense of disturbing the peace will bring about more positive than negative results. Would it not be likely that more and stronger sanctions might be applied to those who are disturbing the peace, thus escalating the conflict?

Flikkema seems to favor a more confrontational approach rather than a developmental approach, although at one point she concedes the importance of the latter with a Chinese proverb. Both these methods are important and effective. My caution, taken from the Goodenough model, is that the backlash often seems to be in direct proportion to the intensity of the confrontation. I believe with Flikkema, however, that there are

---

[12]Quoted by John Leo in "New Frontier for Feminism," *Time* (October 12, 1981), p. 118.
[13]Letha Scanzoni, "The Great Chain of Being and the Chain of Command," *The Reformed Journal* (October 1976), pp. 14-18.

times when confrontation is desirable and effective.

My one other concern has to do with the place given to Scripture in the problem-solving approach proposed in the paper. An ideology based on experience cannot take precedence over biblical authority. Fleming Rutledge, in her article "In Search of an Authentic Biblical Feminism," is well worth hearing on the need for astute theological discourse based on Scripture rather than the experience-as-argument approach. She notes that those opposed to feminism are much more likely than some Christian feminists to build their arguments on biblical and theological foundations.[14]

According to Flikkema, the ideal, goal or vision defined in Step 1 is to be supported with facts and ideas from Scripture. This might be misunderstood as the equivalent of proof texting—a method that is in general disfavor among most scholars but in fact is often used by people on both sides of a controversial issue. As Marianne Meye Thompson has stated, what is needed instead of proof texting is a more complete theology of ministry. David Scholer's comment about the need for interpretive consistency also reflects a criticism of method that seeks justification on the basis of only two or three passages of Scripture. A more complete and consistent theology of ministry will provide the needed support for the full partnership of women with men in all aspects of the church's common life and service.

There is an ample and adequate basis for such a theology of ministry within Scripture itself. But to convert our evangelical constituency, I believe that we, the change agents, must identify with those whom we hope to change. We must show them that we begin with the authority of Scripture and that we do not only use it in bits and pieces. The other sources of support mentioned in the paper are valuable, but to most evangelicals they cannot be put on the same level with the Bible.

A great deal of exegetical, hermeneutical and theological work based on the ultimate authority of the Word of God is needed. It will be essential, however, to determine not only what application was meant for the text in its own time but also how its meaning can be applied with integrity to our situation today. What does it mean to live "in front of

[14]Fleming Rutledge, "In Search of an Authentic Biblical Feminism," in *Women and Men in Ministry,* ed. Roberta Hestenes (Pasadena: Fuller Theological Seminary, 1984).

the text"? This effort already has been begun by a number of good evangelical scholars. May their tribe increase and may the rest of us work hard at getting their material out into the churches!

I commend Joan Flikkema for her concrete suggestions about how to bring change in the evangelical church with regard to its perspectives on women. These suggestions are so numerous and so varied that everyone will surely find something for their own situation. I applaud her exhortation to diligence that she aptly quotes from Henri Nouwen. We can never rest until the whole world knows the whole good news. But, thank God, we need not rely on our own efforts alone. It has come to pass that God's Spirit is speaking through daughters as well as sons. The time is now.

Frances F. Hiebert, the former director for Women's Concerns, Fuller Theological Seminary, Pasadena, California, is now a student in Fuller's School of World Mission and a member of the Mennonite Brethren Board of Missions and Services.

RESPONSE

Timothy P. Weber

With the aid of this fine paper by Joan Flikkema, we concentrate our attention on the "so what" or, more precisely, the "how" of our topic. We have not come here merely as academics, arguing technical points because of some abnormal interest in ancient religious texts. Most of us have come as evangelists. We want to change people's minds and the way churches do things. Flikkema gives us some practical, down-to-earth suggestions for doing that. Her comments and list of seven steps to creative problem solving are helpful, sane and, what is even more amazing, might even work. Too many people want change but do not have the slightest notion about how to get it; her remarks should help to turn wishes into realities. In response to her paper, I would like to isolate a few issues and raise a few questions.

First, there is the issue of structure. Changes in the role of women in the churches cannot occur without altering rules, requirements and the ways that people "officially" related to each other. This requires us to know something about the formal and informal ways that things actually work in our churches and denominations. Changing minds is hard enough, but changing institutions is harder still. In some denominations, decisions affecting the role of women in church life are made in high places, far from rank-and-file believers or individual congregations. In other churches, such matters are decided at the congregational level. Understanding the polity of one's own group is essential for bringing about change. Furthermore, different traditions define terms differently. Ordination, office and authority do not mean the same to all Christians. Evangelical Baptists will have to address issues differently from evangelical Lutherans, Presbyterians or Episcopalians. What works in a Baptist church, for example, might not have a ghost of a chance in the Christian Reformed Church. Thus there is no single strategy for change; we must use different approaches in different settings.

Second, there is the issue of power. As Cheryl Forbes has shown in her recent book *The Religion of Power,* Christians are not immune to using coercive power to get what they want. As I hope we would all agree, we have no business justifying the use of such power on the grounds that we are correct. Such reasoning has produced Crusades and inquisitions. Change does involve the use of politics, and by definition politics means the use of power. To what extent ought we to use coercive power to defeat the users of coercive power? Many of us realize that if we are smart and know what we are doing, we can fight fire with fire and beat them at their own game. But what will we have won if we do? To what extent should the servants of Christ power their way into getting what they know to be right? Are there situations in which we should choose to lose, if winning means that we become like the people who stand in our way? That does not mean that we throw up our hands and do nothing, but it does mean that we make up our minds that we will not play the game by anybody's rules but Christ's.

Third, there is the issue of the "hidden agenda." Though the role of women in the church is usually debated in theological and exegetical terms, the argument frequently has little to do with the Bible or theology. Academic types may actually believe that everything is going to be determined by the parsing of Greek verbs or what we can discover about first-century Greek culture. But for most people, such matters are simply beside the point. More important to them are personal concerns such as self-image, sexuality and relationships. There are people on both sides of this question who will not change their minds no matter how cogent or persuasive the exegetical arguments because they personally have too much at stake in the outcome. There is a lot riding on this issue, including how husbands and wives relate to each other and how people view themselves as males and females. Thus, in many cases we can do everything that Flikkema suggests—develop a vision, define beliefs, state our goals, determine our resources—and it won't make a bit of difference. Somehow we have to get down to the hidden agenda, the personal and psychological side of things. There have been a few pioneering studies on psychological aspects in biblical exegesis on this topic, but much more work needs to be done.[15] Until we get people to face up to these kinds of issues, we may be wasting our time.

This hidden agenda forces us to consider the role of the local pastor in the change process. Pastors are often more strategic in changing things than professors. Many rank-and-file evangelicals do not especially trust professional academics, mainly because they cannot understand what they are talking about. Technical papers on *kephalē* or the first-century usage of *authentein* will not fire up most laypeople. If professors are unwilling or unable to boil their work down so that normal people can understand it, then pastors have to. An ounce of pastor may be worth more than a pound of professor. Change will most likely occur when pastors of local churches decide to stand up and tell their people that this is an important issue—then find ways to help people come to their own conclusions. Most people will not be willing to deal with their hidden agendas until their pastors help them discover what they are.

Fourth, there is the issue of tradition. In some contexts knowing something about the history of one's congregation or denomination can raise the issue and promote study like nothing else. There are many "traditional" evangelical groups that have a "liberated" history that people

---

[15]Richard D. Kahoe, "The Psychology and Theology of Sexism," *Journal of Psychology and Theology* 2 (Fall 1974): 284-90; Colleen Zabriskie, "A Psychological Analysis of Biblical Interpretations Pertaining to Women," *Journal of Psychology and Theology* 4 (Fall 1976): 304-12; Cedric B. Johnson, *The Psychology of Biblical Interpretation* (Grand Rapids, Mich.: Zondervan, 1983).

know nothing about. How surprised current supporters of the Moody Bible Institute would be to learn that, until the 1930s, women graduates were serving as ordained pastors, full-time evangelists and Bible teachers, all with the institute's knowledge and apparent blessing! What would some contemporary evangelical Baptists say if they knew that their grandparents had the opportunity regularly to hear women Baptist preachers? This kind of historical information does not settle anything, but it does force people to deal with the heart of the issue: How could our forebears, who believed in the Bible the same way we do, have done such a thing? Maybe there is another way to understand these texts. Historical awareness can raise biblical and theological issues with new urgency. Some denominations do not have that kind of history, but people cannot be sure until they look into it.

Likewise, knowing something about other Christian traditions can teach us all something new. We have spent most of our time here discussing a few Pauline texts. We have called Galatians 3:28 the Magna Charta for women's participation in the church. But there are other traditions—the holiness and pentecostal peoples, for example—that would stress Acts 2 over Galatians 3, and 1 Corinthians 12 over 1 Corinthians 11 and 14. From their perspective, such texts put the issue in its proper context: the work of the Spirit who builds the church by dispensing gifts to all God's people. This conference, it seems to me, could have used a little more emphasis on the work of the Holy Spirit. What place should spiritual gifts have in our discussion? What is the relationship between gifts for ministry and ecclesiastical office? To what extent should our reading of certain difficult New Testament texts be informed by what we see the Spirit actually doing in our churches today?

Fifth, there is the issue of deciding when enough is enough. Flikkema's paper did not deal with this dilemma, and most of us would rather not think about it. But what should people do when they have done everything they can, and nothing happens? What should we say to those called and gifted women whose ministries are being denied and thwarted? We shiver at the prospect of pitting our loyalty to God against our loyalty to our churches, but sometimes it comes down to that. How long should one wait when there are other options out there? No one can answer that question for someone else. I never know what to say to women at my seminary who believe that their own churches will never let them minister. But any discussion of strategies for the future must at least recognize that sooner or later many people will have to make hard decisions about staying or leaving. If the past can predict the future, I expect that people may hear God telling them to do different things.

Timothy P. Weber is associate professor of church history, Denver Seminary, and pastor of Heritage Baptist Church, Aurora, Colorado.

WHAT HAVE WE ACCOMPLISHED?
VI

12

HEARING THE CRY

Nicholas Wolterstorff

WHAT IS THE upshot of our papers and discussions at this excellent conference? Much of it was, of course, intellectually fascinating; and that, in my judgment, is something worthwhile in its own right. God did not make us to be just hewers of wood, wearers of clothes and eaters of bread. He also made us to find delight and fulfillment in knowledge. We experienced such delight in these days together. I was impressed, more than ever before, by the high quality of evangelical biblical scholarship. I was also impressed by the fact that this scholarship interacts with biblical scholarship in general; it is no longer "ghetto-ized" scholarship.

Nonetheless, we did not assemble for intellectual delight and fascination. What motivated this conference is the fact that a cry is being heard in the church. It is a cry of pain and suffering. It is a cry of women in the church that they are being treated unjustly. It is the cry that this new community, which is Christ's body, called to show forth his glory, including then the glory of his justice, is not doing that. That cry was articulated powerfully in the paper by Patricia Gundry.

Men must learn to hear that cry for justice. Invariably, when one group deprives another of just treatment, it excuses that treatment by insisting that close scutiny reveals that the oppressed group does not really deserve better treatment—that given its nature or its behavior, it is already being treated as well as it has a right to expect. One of the saddest of all the results of oppression is that, after a while, the oppressed group begins to internalize this low esteem that the oppressor has of it. It begins to adopt a low *self*-esteem. One sees this happening, for example, in South Africa where many of the Blacks, having internalized the Whites' opinion of them, believe that they are indeed inferior and ask why God cursed them by making them Black. We heard at this conference that when women in the church are made to feel less than fully human, they begin to wonder why God cursed them with femaleness. Women at conferences such as this wonder whether they are really adequate. They begin, so they tell us, in paranoid fashion to turn over various episodes to discern whether the men did not regard them as really "up to snuff" as scholars.

Now the impulse of men in this situation is to become analytic and criticize the *statements* that women make. "Less than fully human? Of course we don't believe that. We believe that you women are just as human as we are. It's unfair of you to accuse us of any such thing." I suggest that the precise formulation is of no importance; the feeling coming to expression *is* important. Women are expressing the low self-esteem that they have acquired by internalizing the low esteem that they perceive us men as having of them. They are expressing their doubts over their own self-worth. Consequently, rather than criticizing the particular manner in which the feeling gets expressed, we men have to answer this fundamental question: Do we or do we not think that women are equal partners with men in God's creation and kingdom—and, in particular, do we think that they are equally gifted? If we do think they are equal, we had better listen carefully to a description of the ways in which, in the past and yet today, we indicate otherwise.

But why is the cry coming forth now? We learned at this conference that the cry is not coming forth *just* now. Women in the church have been crying out for more than a century. The cry has now reached a crescendo. Why?

The Decline of Ascriptivism
It is regularly said that this is just the latest manifestation of an ideology, stemming from the Enlightenment, which says that everybody must be treated as equal and all differentiations rubbed out. The cause, supposedly, lies in the currency of certain *ideas*—academics, of course,

always like to attribute great power to ideas. Evangelical women, so it is said, are being duped by the ideology of secular feminism.

I think that this reading of the history is almost entirely mistaken. Of course, an ideology of secular feminism is abroad in the land. But Christian women were pleading for justice long before secular feminism was heard of. Rather than presuming that evangelical Christian women have swallowed the ideology of secular feminism, we should listen to what evangelical Christian feminists are actually saying. Women in evangelical churches have swallowed far less of the secular ideology of feminism than men have swallowed of the secular ideology of capitalism.

What has happened is that women who have enjoyed the benefits of universal education have read their Bibles and have heard there the message of God's justice and liberation. They have then looked at themselves and noticed that they have been graced with gifts of the Spirit; they have listened carefully and heard the call of God to use those gifts. Then they have discovered that the church refuses to let them use those gifts, usually without denying that they have them, and has refused to acknowledge that they heard a call from God. That has pained our women. Right there you have one of the major causes for the crescendo.

This cause, as I see it, interacts with another. In the modern West, we have participated in a long social process whereby what sociologists call ascriptivism has been radically diminished. In former times, the social roles that a person occupied were largely determined by factors over which the person had no control. One's position in society was determined, for example, by the status and occupation of one's father; by the religion, race and ethnic identity of one's parents; by one's sex; and so forth. In short, one's social roles were simply ascribed to one. To a remarkable degree, this has changed in the modern West, so the social roles we now occupy are determined much more by choice and talent than by ascription. Most of those who complain most loudly about the movement of Christian feminism would themselves be confined to spending their lives as indentured farmers and servants if this vast social process had not taken place.

As ascriptivism diminishes, its remnants prove more infuriating. In our century, two areas have been the focus of controversy: race and sex. Today almost everybody in American society says that people should not be forbidden from certain social roles or assigned to others just because of race, and many are saying that the same should be true for gender. Yet some in the church say that because certain persons are women, they should be kept out of offices of the church.

My suggestion, in short, is that what has led to the crescendo of voices calling for equal treatment of women in the church is not primarily an ideology, not primarily a cluster of ideas, but rather a social process in which we all participate. Failure to notice this makes our discussions socially disembodied. Even if the ideology of feminism disappeared entirely, the pressure would still be there.

We must ask ourselves, then, whether we approve of this diminishing of ascriptivism. We cannot, without hypocrisy, assume that it is good when it yields us benefits and bad when it causes us discomfort. Remember, too, that breaking down of the walls of ascriptivism has never occurred without struggle and controversy. We now take for granted the right of everyone to be educated; we forget the struggle for this right in the nineteenth century. In my opinion, the message of the Christian gospel gives powerful support to this lessening of ascriptivism. Furthermore, I think that, as a matter of history, the coming of the gospel into the world has contributed to the process.

Let me cast what I have been saying into a slightly different form. As ascriptivism diminished, people asked why such and such differences were relevant to the distribution of social benefits and deprivations. "Why is my being born of a commoner and your being born of a noble relevant to whether we will become educated?" At each point a question of justice was raised, for people are being treated unjustly when benefits and deprivations are distributed on the basis of differences that are not relevant. The question that women in the church are raising is a question of justice. There are, indeed, a good many more dimensions involved than this one of justice, but justice is basic. Women are not asking for handouts of charity from us men. They are asking that in the church—in the church, of all places—they receive their due. They are asking why gender is relevant for assigning tasks and roles and offices and responsibilities and opportunities in the church. The gifts of the Spirit are relevant. But why gender?

The answer they are given is that this is how God wants it. Immediately it is added that we are, of course, all spiritually equal; between men and women there is full spiritual equality. Nonetheless, God does not want women preachers and elders and deacons. I need not tell you how frustrating it is to women to hear this combination of granting full spiritual equality while insisting on ecclesiastical inequality. What we are dealing with here is again the fundamental question whether we will allow the gospel to be socially embodied. Over and over, the church, when confronted by social realities that are unjust but that it prefers not to change, retreats into spirituality. I notice it in the publicity that I receive from South Africa: the church, so it is said, must stick to spiritual matters. My own denomination, the Christian Reformed Church, has always, to its credit, resisted this spiritualizing. True spirituality, it has insisted, is spirituality embodied in life obedience. Yet now, when the issue of women arises, a chorus of voices insists that spiritual equality between men and women must remain purely spiritual; it must not be expressed in the concrete life of the church.

In earlier days, men in the church insisted that women were not equal. They were inferior—made inferior by God. At this conference, we have once again heard some of those embarrassing comments from the great theologians of the Christian church. But notice: If we do in fact believe that women are inferior, we also believe that there is a difference between men and women that is relevant to the unequal distribution of benefits and deprivations. Such a way of thinking at least makes sense. But nowadays we are in the strange position where those who insist that women must be kept out of the offices of the church insist that they are fully equal with men. I have heard some of these people give rousing speeches to the effect that the Spirit distributes its gifts equally while insisting, nonetheless, that no woman may use her gifts as a preacher. Where men in the church once justified the unequal position of women with the insulting claim that God had made them inferior, now they grant that there is no relevant difference between men and women but insist that God demands this inequality of treatment. They defend it, in short, by making God appear utterly arbitrary.

It becomes pivotal, then, that we look carefully at the Bible to see whether God does indeed say that he wants women kept out of church office. Before I turn to that, though, let me comment on one way in which the feminist case should not be argued. Some women appear to make their case by arguing for the abolition of all authority and all hierarchism. All of that, they say, is simply the reflection of male power.

I think that is profoundly mistaken. I do not see how there can be human society without authority—understood here as the right to ask obedience. Furthermore, the Bible, so far from repudiating all authority, sacralizes at least a good deal of it. Governmental authorities, it says, are ministers of God. As for hierarchism, God has inherent authority over us and parents have inherent authority over children. No diminishing of ascriptivism will change that. The point is not that authority and hierarchy are to be entirely eliminated but that gender is simply not relevant to the assignment of benefits and deprivations, neither within the church nor without. In particular, gender is not relevant to the assignment of positions of authority.

Impressions and Advice

I found the biblical studies at this conference very impressive. I judge them to represent a large step forward. Let me offer some overall impressions and some overall advice. First, it seems to have been established fairly securely that, whatever headship means in the New Testament, it does not mean *having authority over.* The Greek word for "head," *kephalē,* seems never to have had the metaphorical sense of "an authority." Our situation seems to be that, though the English word *head* is indeed the literal translation of the Greek word *kephalē,* the English word fits into a very different metaphor system from that of the Greek word. It is a metaphor system in which, indeed, an authority can be spoken of metaphorically as a head, whereas that was not true in Greek. I also judge it to have been pretty securely established at our conference that whatever *authentein* means in 1 Timothy, it almost certainly does not mean "having authority over."

Second, our discussion reminded me that those who oppose the opening of church offices to women should not be permitted to set the entire agenda of the biblical discussion. We must look at the full sweep of the biblical message, seeing its message of justice and liberation for women. It is important for us to keep before the church the memory of such liberating passages as Acts 2 and Galatians 3. Within this larger affirmative context we must deal with those few, those *very* few, negative-sounding passages in 1 Corinthians and 1 Timothy.

Third, I think I saw emerging at this conference a consensus as to how, in general, the relevant biblical passages are to be read. When we look at the overall sweep of the New Testament, we discern a message of the full equality of men and women in Christ and, thereby, in the church. The male/female distinction is not relevant to the sorting out of roles in the church. What is relevant is the gifts of the Spirit. Nonetheless, the church of the New Testament existed in a social situation that was intensely patriarchal. The message of the apostles was addressed to that society. It was not couched in completely general terms, equally relevant to all societies at all times. The message had social specificity—even though over and over we discern elements that leap out of the specificities of that situation and speak to us as well. In Ephesians, for example, Paul speaks the message of the gospel to a patriarchal situation and specifies how men and women in Christ must relate as husbands and wives in that situation. He nowhere says that families must always be patriarchal in character; he is simply speaking the gospel to families that in fact were so. He knew no others. In 1 Corinthians, Paul is concerned with practices that were, in that society, bringing shame and dishonor to the church: women wearing short hair was one, and women speaking in a certain way in a certain situation was another—though the way and situation are not clear to us since in fact Paul allowed women to pray and prophesy in public. Paul does not say that such practices must always be avoided because they will always bring shame to the church. He just says they must be avoided there. In 1 Timothy, Paul is again concerned about shame and dishonor, but also now about heresy in the church, perhaps especially the heresy of Gnosticism. He does not say that in all situations the way to cope with heresy is to silence the women. In the first chapter of Titus, for example, he talks differently.

Suppose that it is along these lines that we must understand these passages. We twentieth-century Christians must then ask one further question, the most important question of all for us. We must ask what is the word of the Lord *to us* in these passages. Let us not slide into the assumption that there is no word of the Lord to us in them. The fact that Paul was not speaking in socially disembodied fashion but was speaking the word of the Lord to a particular social situation (a social situation that differs profoundly from ours) does not mean that in what he says there is no word of the Lord to us. Though the word to us is not that we must reintroduce old-fashioned patriarchal families, surely the Lord nevertheless asks of us mutual submission. Though the word of the Lord to us is not that women must be silent in the church and must be kept out of all positions of authority, surely he asks of us that we not needlessly bring shame on the church. Though the word of the Lord to us is not that we must cope with heresy by silencing our women, he continues to ask that we oppose heresy.

Exactly how one discerns the word of the Lord to us in a biblical passage that is socially specific is a complex question. A rough-and-ready description of what is to be done, though, is that one tries to discern the *reasons* the biblical writer had for saying what he did, and to continue digging deeper into those reasons until one comes to something that applies to us as much as it did to the people the writer was addressing. Sometimes in doing this we will discover, to our surprise, that the concrete application of those deep reasons to our society will be just the opposite of what it was to that ancient society. In our day, keeping women silent brings shame on the church.

It has been characteristic of the evangelical churches—indeed, of the Christian church in general—to think of the biblical writers as delivering timeless truths unsullied by the particularities of the cosmology, the anthropology, the social outlook and so forth of the day. Likewise it has been characteristic of them to overlook the internal biblical structure of centrality and peripherality and to see everything in the Bible as on the same level. Finally, it has been characteristic to resist granting that in the history of the church we discern a deepening of insight into the implications of the biblical message. On all these points this conference has represented, to my mind, a most important breakthrough. We are moving toward a new, more adequate, more realistic hermeneutic—more realistic in the fundamental sense that it takes with full seriousness that mysterious reality that the word of the Lord comes to us as the word of eminently human beings.

We have asked how we can bring the evangelical churches to see that God's message for women is not one of restriction but of justice and freedom. One immensely important approach is to offer a new and better way of reading the relevant biblical passages—and then, of reading *all* of them. The conservatives have never managed to give a plausible reading of all the relevant passages. I think what we saw emerging here at this conference is a plausible way of reading all the passages together. Until the evangelical churches have such a new way of reading the passages, I am persuaded that they will continue to wonder whether perhaps after all the Lord of the church does not want women kept out of the offices of the church.

But this new way of reading is not enough by itself. In my experience, issues of justice do not seize the hearts of most people until they acquire human faces and human voices. We must allow women to express their cry of pain. We must allow them to function with equality wherever that is permitted so that people will see concretely what they are missing when they do not allow women to use the gifts that the Spirit has granted them.

But even that is not quite enough. My experience in struggling for the rights of the Palestinian people has taught me that Israelis often cannot hear the cry for justice coming from the Palestinians, even though faces and voices are right there before them. They cannot hear because they are seized with fear—that the cup of suffering of the Jewish people is not yet full, that over the horizon somewhere is yet another holocaust. The same applies to the issue of women in the church. The reason some cannot hear the cry of women and cannot see the edification that will result from allowing their gifts to be used is that they are seized by the fear that, if they granted the justice of the cry and the benefits of the gifts, their world would change in ways too frightening for them to contemplate. Accordingly, just as I, who speak for the rights of the Palestinians, must stand by the Jewish people in their fear, so you and I, who speak for the full equality of women with men in the family of Jesus Christ, must stand by our fellow Christians in their fear. We must be pastors to them. Only in that way will they be able to hear that in Christ and in the church of Christ there is neither male nor female but all are equal.

Nicholas Wolterstorff is professor of philosophy, Calvin College, Grand Rapids, Michigan.

13

UNDERSTANDING THE DIFFERENCES

J. I. PACKER

SOMETIMES ONE LEAVES academic gatherings feeling that one has learned nothing, but not so this time. The colloquium taught me two things about myself that I am sure I shall never forget. The first is that as an ingenuous confessor of the humanness and giftedness of godly women, I qualify in some quarters for the label of "Christian feminist." It would never occur to me to call myself that, for Christian humanist is my preferred self-description; but clearly I must brace myself to be tagged that way. Over the years, however, I have been called so many things that I would not call myself that one more will not make much difference.

Also, I learned from Joan Flikkema's insecurity index (the "white-knuckle calculus," as one might call it) that, inasmuch as the colloquium was "helpful and supportive regarding women's issues," attending it had involved me in "moderate risk." This thought left me feeling a tiny bit heroic, which is a pleasant feeling indeed, and one to cherish. Whether, however, this amounts to saying that I left the colloquium a changed man is something that I will leave my readers to work out for themselves.

Baggage Brought

Before I comment on what the colloquium achieved, I should say what baggage I brought with me to it. I arrived with a full-fledged evangelical faith of Augustinian-Reformed-inerrantist type. I brought also a conscious pastoral identity, for God called me to be a pastor before he called me to be either an academic or an author, and these later vocations specify, not cancel, what went before. Also, I came with the conviction that one purpose of systematic theology is to achieve what I call a "canonical interpretation" of Scripture. I mean by that a theological exegesis showing what each part of canonical Scripture means for us today; in other words, seeing what word to us from the Lord is breaking forth from what is rightly called "God's Word written" (Anglican Article 20); or, to use old-fashioned language, telling us how what we read in the Bible applies to us; or, to put it in modern terms, grasping what God is communicating to us, here and now, in and through the inspired text. Along with this conviction, I brought a firm resolve always to distinguish between possibilities and certainties in my biblical study and to be led, as far as possible, by certainties only.

Then, too, I brought to the colloquium an ecclesiology of a type that has been commoner in holiness and pentecostal circles than among the Anglican and Reformed people who are, so to speak, my home base. This ecclesiology affirms, first, that gifts are theologically prior to offices, in the sense that offices are for gifts rather than vice versa; second, that gifts from the Holy Spirit, gifts of utterance included, are given to women as they are to men; and, third, that all spiritual gifts should be put to use in the church for its building up (see Rom 12:6; Eph 4:8-16; 1 Pet 4:10-11). To be sure, not all gifts require a stated office for their exercise, and I judge that the best of most women's ministry, like the best of some men's, will be informal, domestic and noninstitutional rather than official and role regulated. (Thus, women's ministry seems to me a far larger subject than women's ordination to office, which, whether I am for it or against it, is a peripheral matter; and those for whom women's ministry means only allowing women to do all that men do officially seem to me not to know what they are talking about.) One way or another, however, gifts given must be used, or the Holy Spirit is quenched.

You may call this ecclesiology charismatic if you will (though I learned it from an Anglican ex-missionary, from Plymouth Brethren friends and from the New Testament, years before the charismatic movement started). You may, if you desire, point out that it fails to exhibit the characteristic preoccupation with continuity and authority of ministries, which, understandably in the face of Roman Catholic claims, has marked most Anglican and Reformed minds for four centuries (though the two concerns remain compatible, if you want to combine them). If you say these things, I shall not dispute with you, but I shall continue to think that my stress on the need to harness all gifts is vital truth for our time and should in particular be the starting point for all reflections on women's place in God's church.

Then I brought with me two further items. One is a varied and wide-ranging experience of working with gifted women fulfilling responsible roles in local church ministry, seminary teaching, Christian journalism and counseling, and student evangelism and pastoral care. Inevitably, I theologize against the background of that experience; one starts from where one is.

The final item I brought is a theology of the sexes that, standing on Karl Barth's shoulders, I see as inescapably implied by Genesis 2:18–23, namely, that only through cooperative friendship with members of the other sex does anyone ever plumb the mystery and meaning of his or her own sexual identity and that without this discovery one's personhood remains incomplete. Such friendship is compatible with celibacy (think of Jesus' recorded relationships with women); monogamous marriage, however, which appears in verses 24–25, is, in idea at least, its supreme form. From this theology it follows that sexual segregation in all its forms is intrinsically antihuman; that feminism itself becomes antihuman when it involves only women campaigning for the privilege of disregarding or upstaging men; and that the question to be asked is not so much whether women are human (Patricia Gundry's question) as whether any of us are human. When our relationships with the other sex are not open and respectful enough, our own humanness remains deficient, whether we are male or female.

Someone said in the colloquium that we are all individually skewed, ecclesiastically conditioned and theologically located (which, I suppose, means anchored and stuck). I have tried to come clean on these matters so that you will see where I come from in assessing the colloquium itself, about which I have three observations.

Three Observations

First, the colloquium suffered from the built-in awkwardness of a dou-ble-barreled agenda. On the one hand, we were begged to function as a task force, strategizing to help the many gifted and godly women who have been hurt by the restrictions and put-downs of pseudo-Christian legalism in the realm of church order. (I say pseudo-Christian because all legalism is in itself anti-Christian; I would add that legalism, by which I mean here anxious observance of the letter of the law in disregard of its spirit, always reduces life to role play, always becomes relationally repressive, and is as such intrinsically hurtful and antihuman.) On the other hand, we were summoned as an academic working party, to explore critically what should be said about male headship in 1 Corin-thians 11 and Ephesians 5; about the demand for women's silence and the prohibition of their teaching role in 1 Corinthians 14 and 1 Timothy 2; and about hierarchy, patriarchalism, leadership, equality and submis-sion in relations between the sexes in Christ. The combination of con-cerns may have generated urgency, but it also caused some unevenness and differences of focus in the material presented, as readers of this book will see. Academically, we needed to do more on the relation of the sexes together, and for lack of this the papers as a set may run some risk of being read as a theological counterpart to bra-burning. The col-loquium was, however, a much more serious venture than that, aiming not to fly kites, wave flags or make gestures, but to explore revealed truth in a fully responsible way, and the main academic papers do this impressively.

Second, while it would be inept euphoria to claim that all the exe-getical questions tackled have now been finally resolved, I think the New Testament papers in particular make it evident that the burden of proof regarding the exclusion of women from the office of teaching and ruling within the congregation now lies on those who maintain the exclusion rather than on those who challenge it. This is an important step forward in the in-house evangelical debate, one that makes renewed dialog with excluders (none of whom were present at the colloquium) a very de-sirable next step.

Third, while I am not keen on *hierarchy* and *patriarchy* as terms describing the man-woman relationship in Scripture, Genesis 2:18-23 (on woman as man's help in the order of creation) and Ephesians 5:21-

33 (on husbands and wives modeling Christ and the church in the dynamics of their marriage) continue to convince me that the man-woman relationship is intrinsically nonreversible. By this I mean that, other things being equal, a situation in which a female boss has a male secretary, or a marriage in which the woman (as we say) wears the trousers, will put more strain on the humanity of both parties than if it were the other way around. This is part of the reality of creation, a given fact that nothing will change. Certainly, redemption will not change it, for grace restores nature, not abolishes it. Therefore Clark Pinnock's proposal, that we should theologize reciprocity, spiritual equality, freedom for ministry, and mutual submission and respect between men and women—within this framework of nonreversibility and without aiming at any stage to abandon or transcend it (which would be showing disrespect to the created order)—has my support. In contrast, equality models that would let not just roles but also relational dynamics be reversed within the cooperative relationships of men and women do not have my support. It is important that the cause of not imposing on women restrictions that Scripture does not impose should not be confused with the quite different goals of minimizing the distinctness of the sexes as created and of diminishing the male's inalienable responsibilities in man-woman relationships as such.

An old friend of mine in England has founded an organization called the Campaign for the Feminine Woman, publishing a regular newsletter entitled *Vive la Difference*. How much notice England takes of him I do not know, but I should like to tell the world that on the questions of unisexuality and women as surrogate men, and in his pleas for men to be manly and women womanly, I go right along with him. Understanding and maintaining the God-created distinction and the God-appointed dynamics of men and women in their mutual relations seems to me far more important at the present time than removing inappropriate restrictions on women in the community and the church. An agenda for another colloquium? As Mr. Hardy sometimes (not always) said to Mr. Laurel, "Now that's a good idea."

J. I. Packer is professor of historical and systematic theology, Regent College, Vancouver, British Columbia.

14

TURNING REALITY INTO DREAMS

Jeannette F. Scholer

ONE ANALYTICAL TECHNIQUE useful to me is to identify pairs of opposing concepts or issues within a given topic. I first began to use this technique consciously after studying the system of phonetic analysis by linguists Morris Halle and Roman Jakobson. Within the context of this colloquium, however, I am aware that they were preceded long ago by the apostle Paul in the oft-quoted text "neither Jew nor Greek, slave nor free, male nor female." Establishing polarities may clarify mutually exclusive categories, or it may define or clarify issues or ideas and even help us discover that what appear to be opposing concepts may not be opposing after all.

In the colloquium, a number of such oppositions have emerged. I have chosen to comment on nine, most of which have recurred throughout our discussion.

The first is the question of experience versus the question of truth. It emerged with the opening paper, and we returned to it often. We have, on the one hand, the experience of the capabilities of women, their obvious gifts for ministry and, for many, the sense of God's call. On the other hand, we have what some perceive as the eternal truth that women are to follow, not lead, and that women are to be submissive to men in marriage and in the church and even in societal structures. Some see this as a simple question of whether one chooses to obey the truth or to bow to experience and thus either to reshape the truth or ignore it entirely.

For most of us, experience and truth are not mutually exclusive. Truth is often communicated through experience; in fact, God's truth has rarely been expressed apart from human experience. The ultimate revelation is the Incarnation. Story, as used by Patricia Gundry, has validity as truth. Acts 2 as a story of the outpouring of the Spirit on women and men and Galatians 3 as a theological statement both communicate the new order in Christ.

We have challenged what some believe to be the truth about the place of women. But 1 Corinthians 14 and 1 Timothy 2 are not the total statement of the truth. Read within the context of the whole of the New Testament, they do not eternally prohibit women from leadership in the church.

The second opposition that recurred frequently in our discussion is that of person versus status, or who we are as women versus what we as women can do in the church and society. Patricia Gundry focused the issue first, asking, "Are women fully human?" James Packer indicated that the issue is not limited to women but that men who are committed to male superiority are not fully human.

The belief that women are inferior is a real, although often unspoken, force in the church today. Some claim that it is possible to believe in the full personhood of a woman on the one hand, while limiting her function and status on the other. For me, and for most of us here, these terms are inextricably bound. As Gretchen Hull pointed out, "yes, but . . ." is really "no" and means that women are not fully redeemable. If women are fully human, Christ's death must be fully efficacious for them and, once redeemed, they cannot be limited in status and function in the church or society. As Richard Longenecker said, "How can we speak of a necessary subordination of status without also implying a necessary inferiority of person?"

The third opposition is that of feminism versus patriarchalism or, perhaps expressed better, egalitarianism versus hierarchism. No term in current vocabulary seems entirely satisfactory to most of us here. I have never liked the phrase "women's liberation" because I see *human* liberation as the true goal. Both "feminism" and "egalitarianism" have associations and even denotations with which we do not agree. What we long for is a restitution of the created order of mutuality in our humanity in all of life. The position of patriarchalism or hierarchism as presented in our discussions applied primarily to male headship in marriage and to some aspects of church governance, and it was not presented as a model for the whole of society. That fuzziness makes this position particularly difficult. Single persons must be accounted for, and all of us constantly move back and forth between our private lives, our lives in the church and our lives in the secular world.

A fourth opposition is the difference between prescriptions and descriptions. Within our context, this differentiation was applied primarily to texts in Scripture that deal with women. Yet prescriptions do not cover the totality of the situation in the church in New Testament times. We have clearly agreed that prescriptive and descriptive texts require our attention and interpretation and that prescriptions do not have inherent weight over descriptions.

A fifth opposition concerns our approach to and use of Scripture; I would characterize it as proof texting versus hermeneutical consistency. A proof-texting method extrapolates individual statements from the biblical record, not always with reference to context, and chooses to ignore texts that do not fit the expected conclusions, in the process of building a "biblical" case for a given point of view. In contrast, hermeneutical consistency requires taking account of all relevant texts in the biblical record and, while not seeking to harmonize by contortion of the texts, seeks to understand all texts as a basis for building a theological conclusion. Our consensus requires hermeneutical consistency—an approach that reckons with the entire biblical record.

The sixth opposition is Creation/Redemption versus the Fall. When the order of creation is appealed to as a basis for hierarchism, it is frequently a misreference to the effects of the Fall. We understand the creation narratives as foundational to understanding our humanity. Salvation must be understood as both a work of grace for individuals and a work of grace in the process of restoring the mutuality of Creation in human relationships.

The seventh opposition is in the meaning of the text in its historical setting and its meaning for us today. As those committed to a high view of Scripture, we cannot opt to take one over the other. For all of us, "both/and" is our concern. We must understand each text in its historical setting; we must also understand its meaning for us today. Nancy Holsey's call to make 1 Timothy 2 speak to us today is a dramatic statement of this; it provides the interesting exercise of imagination of a feminist preaching on 1 Timothy 2. But why not?

An eighth polarity is between the church's function as a critic of society and the church's concern to be sensitive and winsome to society. David Scholer identified this tension in what seems to be Paul's vascillation on the place of women in the churches that he established and nurtured. The gospel had a radical effect on the first-century understanding of the value and abilities of women. Paul encouraged their full participation with him in the work of the gospel. He was also acutely aware of the need for maintaining certain cultural mores so that the gospel would not be invalidated. This tension we sense within ourselves, as we see the need to critique hierarchism in our society and in the church and to critique forms of extreme feminism, both of which set up dehumanizing ranking or competition between men and women. We also want to make our message winsome, taking care not to scandalize those with whom we differ. Both hierarchism and feminism can produce the emptiness of competition; the gospel can bring us the fulfillment of complementarity. To bring others into that experience we need to be sensitive to behaviors that make it impossible for them to hear that message. By example as well as word we need to demonstrate our message in a winsome way.

For the ninth opposition, I borrow the terms of Timothy Weber: the Scripture solution versus the heart solution. The intensity of the discussion about the role of women among Christians suggests that more is at stake than our interpretation of Scripture. For all of us, there is more of an agenda than just "What does the Bible say?" We are far more culturally conditioned than we realize. We need to probe that conditioning as we read Scripture and to challenge other interpreters for that same self-awareness. If we are to be change agents in our society, we must find ways not only to change people's misconceptions of the biblical teaching (i.e., the Scripture solution) but also to motivate behavioral change (i.e., the heart solution).

This colloquium has been a heartening experience. To have a group of women and men in such balanced proportion address these issues has demonstrated our need for each other. Weber spoke of "turning wishes into reality," but I would like to borrow the expression of a friend of mine and reverse that statement. Within this conference we have experienced the miracle of turning reality into dreams—and that is what I believe grace is all about.

Jeannette F. Scholer is a homemaker, adjunct instructor in communication at Northern Baptist Theological Seminary and catalog editor for the Association of Chicago Theological Schools.